Town and Country Planning in the Scottish Borders, 1946–1996

Scotland's Land
Series editor: Dr Annie Tindley

Editorial Advisory Board
Dr Calum MacLeod, University of Edinburgh
Dr Malcolm Combe, University of Aberdeen
Dr Iain Robertson, University of the Highlands and Islands
Professor Terence Dooley, Maynooth University
Professor Ewen Cameron, University of Edinburgh
Dr John MacAskill, University of Edinburgh

This series presents the latest scholarly work to academic and public readers on Scotland's land issues. Predominantly focusing on the history of Scotland's economic, political, and social and cultural relationships to land, landscape, country houses and landed estates, it also brings in cutting-edge approaches to explore new methodologies and perspectives around this politically contentious but stimulating issue. As an interdisciplinary series, it will necessarily contain a wide range of approaches, including history, law, economics and economic history, philosophy, environment/landscape studies, and human/cultural geography. The aim of the series is to bring together and publish the best work on land issues across a wide range of disciplines for a diverse set of audiences.

Published titles

The Land Agent: 1700–1920
Annie Tindley, Lowri Ann Rees and Ciarán Reilly (eds)

Scotland's Foreshore: Public Rights, Private Rights and the Crown 1840–2017
John MacAskill

Land Reform in Scotland: History, Law and Policy
Malcom Combe, Jayne Glass and Annie Tindley (eds)

Land Reform in the British and Irish Isles since 1800
Shaun Evans, Tony Mc Carthy and Annie Tindley (eds)

Town and Country Planning in the Scottish Borders, 1946–1996: From Planning Backwater to the Centre of the Maelstrom
Douglas G. Hope

edinburghuniversitypress.com/series/slf

Town and Country Planning in the Scottish Borders, 1946–1996

From Planning Backwater to the Centre of the Maelstrom

Douglas G. Hope

EDINBURGH
University Press

Edinburgh University Press is one of the leading university presses in the UK. We publish academic books and journals in our selected subject areas across the humanities and social sciences, combining cutting-edge scholarship with high editorial and production values to produce academic works of lasting importance. For more information visit our website: edinburghuniversitypress.com

© Douglas G. Hope, 2023, 2025

Edinburgh University Press Ltd
13 Infirmary Street
Edinburgh EH1 1LT

First published in hardback by Edinburgh University Press 2023

Typeset in 10.5/13pt Sabon by
Cheshire Typesetting Ltd, Cuddington, Cheshire

A CIP record for this book is available from the British Library

ISBN 978 1 3995 0333 4 (hardback)
ISBN 978 1 3995 0334 1 (paperback)
ISBN 978 1 3995 0335 8 (webready PDF)
ISBN 978 1 3995 0336 5 (epub)

The right of Douglas G. Hope to be identified as author of this work has been asserted in accordance with the Copyright, Designs and Patents Act 1988 and the Copyright and Related Rights Regulations 2003 (SI No. 2498).

Contents

List of Figures and Tables	vi
Preface	vii
List of Abbreviations	x
Timeline	xiii
Map of the Scottish Borders	xvi
Introduction	1
1 Town and Country Planning Becomes Established	21
2 The First County Development Plans	45
3 Planning and Development Become Inexorably Linked	65
4 Planning in the Scottish Borders Broadens its Horizons	86
5 A Borders Region at Last!	113
6 Development Planning Takes Shape	142
7 The 1980s: Challenges and Achievements	174
8 The 1990s: A Time of Uncertainty	209
9 Preparing for the Twenty-first Century	231
Epilogue	258
Appendices	269
Bibliography	303
Index	307

Figures and Tables

FIGURES

5.1	The Borders Region	116
5.2	Department of Physical Planning, December 1975	128
6.1	Borders Region Structure Plan 1980: Key Diagram	147
6.2	Borders Region Structure Plan 1980: Settlement Hierarchy	149
6.3	Borders Regional Council 1980s Structure and Local Plans	153
6.4	Press coverage of Burnhead, Hawick Saga, 1975–1988	159
7.1	Planning and Development Department staff photograph, 1986	179
7.2	Sample press coverage from 1988	181
7.3	Electronics in the Scottish Borders	183
8.1	Department of Planning and Development, December 1993	214
8.2	Borders Region Structure Plan 1991: Key Diagram	219
9.1	Borders Regional Council 1990s Structure and Local Plans	233
9.2	Sustainable development publications	235

TABLES

3.1	Central Borders Study Projected Populations, 1966–1980	69
3.2	Projected and Actual Populations in the Central Borders in 1980/81	77
6.1	Borders Region Structure Plan 1980: Population Guidelines	150
8.1	Borders Region Structure Plan 1991: Settlement Hierarchy	220

Preface

The focus of this book is on the Scottish Borders and how the process and practice of town and country planning emerged from being a fringe activity of local government in the 1950s to become the driving force for change in the 1980s and 1990s. During the period 1946–1996, the subject of this book, this peripheral rural region was transformed from a quiet planning backwater, largely overlooked by central government, to become a beacon for rural regeneration, at the forefront of the development of rural development policy in Scotland.

The book provides a comprehensive appraisal of the changing role of town and country planning within a unique area of Scotland over a period of fifty years, examining continuity and change in policies and proposals for land use and development. It explores the relationship between planning and economic development in stimulating growth within a rural region of Scotland. It illustrates how town and country planning in the Scottish Borders developed from a simple land use control mechanism to a proactive, multi-disciplinary activity. The book is based on primary sources, including agenda, papers and minutes of the four original county planning authorities and the Borders Regional Council, official publications and the personal accounts of staff. It draws on the author's expert knowledge of town and country planning in Scotland at both central and local government level.

The book combines scholarly analysis with a practitioner's perspective on the journey that town and country planning has taken in the Scottish Borders over a period of fifty years from its origins in the 1940s. The book has been written not by an academic researcher but by someone who has fifty years' experience working in both central and local government in Scotland. With an honours degree in geography, a postgraduate diploma in town planning and five years town planning experience at Doncaster CBC, I joined the Scottish Development Department in 1969 to assist in the preparation of government guidance on the new structure and local plan system introduced by the Town and Country Planning (Scotland) Act 1969. With local government reorganisation looming, I left for Berwickshire County Council in 1973 and took up the post of Depute County Planning and Development Officer, where I was responsible for a number of rural planning studies. On the re-organisation of local government in 1975, I transferred to the Borders Regional Council as an Assistant Director of Planning and Development and rose to Depute Director of Planning and Development in 1987. During my twenty years at the Region, I was responsible, at varying times, for planning policy and research, structure and local planning, and development control. From 1989 to 1996, I was a member of the executive committee of the Scottish Society of Directors of Planning (SSDP) and its Chairman in 1994–1995. I was a Planning Advisor to the Convention of Scottish Local Authorities (COSLA) from 1989 to 1996 and a member of a number of working groups dealing with such matters as local planning, environmental policy, sustainable development and Agenda21, and forestry and Indicative Forestry Strategies. I took early retirement in 1996 and for the next twenty years was employed as an Inquiry Reporter with the Scottish Government's Directorate of Planning and Environmental Appeals (DPEA) dealing with a variety of planning appeals and local plan inquiries.

Writing this book could not have been accomplished without the help and assistance of a number of people. I could not have undertaken the necessary research of the records of the former county planning authorities without the help of the staff of Scottish Borders Council's Archives and Local History Centre at the Heritage Hub in Hawick. In this respect, special mention should be made of Paul Brough, Archive Manager, Kathy Hobkirk, Genealogy Registrar and Amy Thompson, Archive and Local History Assistant. I am also grateful to my former colleagues at Borders Regional Council, particularly Frank Bennett, John Gray and Alister McDonald, for their assistance with information on the Planning and Development Department and for their detailed comments on the draft manuscript. I should also like to thank Ian Aikman, Chief Planning and Housing Officer at Scottish Borders Council for allowing me to include illustrations from previous Borders Regional Council publications [Figures 5.1, 6.1, 6.2 and 8.2] and I am most grateful to Paul Welch for drafting the location map of the Scottish Borders. I must also thank Bill Chisholm, Borders District staff reporter for *The Scotsman* for thirty-six years from 1969, and Michael Gray, Chief Executive of printing and software manufacturer, McQueen, now Sykes Enterprises, in Galashiels, Chair of the Local Enterprise Company, Scottish Borders Enterprise in the 1990s, and present Chair of Energise Galashiels, for their personal contributions on their encounters with the planning system in the Scottish Borders.

It would be remiss of me not to thank Craig McLaren, Director of Scotland, Ireland and English Regions at the Royal Town Planning Institute, and Cliff Hague, Emeritus Professor of Planning and Spatial Development at Heriot-Watt University, Edinburgh and a Past President of the Royal Town Planning Institute, both of whom were supportive of my proposal for the book and provided me with constructive advice. Finally, I am enormously indebted to Annie Tindley, Professor of British and Irish Rural History at the University of Newcastle and Series Editor of 'Scotland's Land', who has cast her eye over various drafts of the manuscript and through her valuable comments has made a significant contribution to the quality of the finished text.

Abbreviations

1943 Act	Town and Country Planning (Interim Development) (Scotland) Act 1943
1947 Act	Town and Country Planning (Scotland) Act 1947
1972 Act	Town and Country Planning (Scotland) Act 1972
1973 Act	The Local Government (Scotland) Act 1973
AGLV	Area of Great Landscape Value
BCC	Berwickshire County Council
BDC	Berwickshire District Council
BGS	Broadleaved Woodland Grant Scheme
BRC	Borders Regional Council
BTS	Border Training Services Agency
CAP	Common Agriculture Policy
CCS	Countryside Commission for Scotland
COSLA	Convention of Scottish Local Authorities
DAFS	Department of Agriculture for Scotland
DHS	Department of Health for Scotland
DPEA	Directorate for Planning and Environmental Appeals
EAGGF	European Agricultural Guidance and Guarantee Fund
EBDA	Eastern Borders Development Agency
EC	European Community
EEC	European Economic Community [would become the European Community (EC) in 1993]
EIP	Structure Plan Examination in Public
E&LDC	Ettrick and Lauderdale District Council
ERDF	European Regional Development Fund
ESA	Environmentally Sensitive Area
ESF	European Social Fund
FEOGA	European Community Agricultural Guidance Fund
FFWAG	Farming, Forestry and Wildlife Advisory Group
FGS	Forestry Grant Scheme
FSB	Finance for Small Business Scheme
HIDB	Highlands & Islands Development Board
HMA	Housing Market Area

JPAC	Peebles, Roxburgh and Selkirk Joint Planning Advisory Committee
LDP	Local Development Plan
LPP	Local Place Plan
MSC	Manpower Services Commission
MoT	Ministry of Transport
NCCS	Nature Conservancy Council for Scotland
NNR	National Nature Reserve
NSA	National Scenic Area
NTS	National Trust for Scotland
PAG	Planning Advisory Group
PAN	Planning Advice Note [issued by SDD]
PCB	Printed Circuit Board
PCC	Peeblesshire County Council
PEP	Community Programme, Planning and Environmental Projects Scheme
RCC	Roxburgh County Council
RDC	Roxburgh District Council
RPU	Regional Planning Unit
RSPB	Royal Society for the Protection of Birds
RSS	Regional Spatial Strategy
RTPI	Royal Town Planning Institute
SBE	Scottish Borders Enterprise
SBTB	Scottish Borders Tourist Board
SCC	Selkirk County Council
SDA	Scottish Development Agency
SDD	Scottish Development Department
SDP	Strategic Development Plan
SE	Scottish Enterprise
SHD	Scottish Home Department
SHHD	Scottish Home and Health Department
SICRAS	Small Industries Council for the Rural Areas of Scotland
SIEC	Scottish Industrial Estates Corporation
SMR	Sites and Monuments Record
SNH	Scottish Natural Heritage
SoS	Secretary of State for Scotland
SSDP	Scottish Society of Directors of Planning
SSEB	South of Scotland Electricity Board
SSHA	Scottish Special Housing Association
SSSI	Site of Special Scientific Interest
SWT	Scottish Wildlife Trust

TDC	Tweeddale District Council
TIC	Tourist Information Centre
TPI	Town Planning Institute [became RTPI in 1959]
TPO	Tree Preservation Order
TRIP	Training for Rural Improvement Projects
TUCC	Transport Users Consultative Committee
WGS	Woodland Grant Scheme

Timeline

1909	The Housing, Town Planning, etc. Act 1909
1919	The Housing, Town Planning, etc. (Scotland) Act 1919
1932	The Town and Country Planning (Scotland) Act 1932
1935	The Restriction of Ribbon Development Act 1935
1946	New Towns Act 1946
1947	**Town and Country Planning (Scotland) Act 1947**
1948	Regional Survey & Plan for Central and South-East Scotland (Sir Frank Mears)
1949	National Parks and Access to the Countryside Act 1949
1953	**Historic Buildings and Ancient Monuments Act 1953**
1954	**Town and Country Planning (Scotland) Act 1954**
1955	Selkirk County Development Plan (approved April 1955)
1955	Peebles County Development Plan (approved December 1955)
1959	**Town and Country Planning (Scotland) Act 1959**
1960	**Caravan Sites and Control of Development Act 1960**
1965	Roxburgh County Development Plan (approved February 1965)
1965	County of Berwick Development Plan (approved February 1965)
1966	The Scottish Economy 1965–1970: a Plan for Expansion White Paper
1967	**Forestry Act 1967**
1967	**Civic Amenities Act 1967**
1967	**Countryside (Scotland) Act 1967**
1967	Roxburgh County Development Plan, 7th amendment (Kelso) 1967
1968	Quinquennial Review Selkirk County Development Plan (approved January 1968)
1968	The Central Borders: a plan for expansion
1969	**Town and Country Planning (Scotland) Act 1969**
1972	**Town and Country Planning (Scotland) Act 1972**
1973	**Local Government (Scotland) Act 1973**
1975	**Scottish Development Agency Act 1975**

1975 The Community Land Act 1975
1975 *Establishment of Borders Regional Council*
1975 The Borders Region, 1975
1976 Regional Report, Borders Regional Council
1980 Borders Region Structure Plan 1980
1980 **Local Government, Planning and Land Act 1980**
1981 **Town and Country Planning (Minerals) Act 1981**
1981 **Wildlife and Countryside Act 1981**
1981 Galashiels/Tweedbank Local Plan, adopted June 1981
1981 Eyemouth Local Plan, adopted October 1981
1981 Hawick Local Plan, adopted November 1981
1982 **Local Government and Planning (Scotland) Act 1982**
1982 Kelso Local Plan, adopted July 1982
1983 Selkirk Local Plan, adopted August 1983
1983 Peebles Local Plan, adopted December 1983
1984 Jedburgh Local Plan, adopted October 1984
1985 Ettrick & Lauderdale North Local Plan, adopted May 1985
1986 **Housing and Planning Act 1986**
1986 Tweeddale (Part) Local Plan, adopted December 1986
1986 Berwickshire (Part) Local Plan, adopted December 1986
1987 Ettrick Forest Local Plan, adopted May 1987
1988 **Housing (Scotland) Act 1988**
1989 Roxburgh (Part) Local Plan, adopted February 1989
1990 **Enterprise and New Towns (Scotland) Act 1990**
1991 **The Natural Heritage (Scotland) Act 1991**
1991 **Planning and Compensation Act 1991**
1993 Scottish Borders Region Structure Plan 'The Way Forward' 1993
1994 Berwickshire Local Plan, adopted November 1994
1994 **Local Government etc. (Scotland) Act 1994**
1995 Roxburgh Local Plan, adopted May 1993
1995 Ettrick & Lauderdale Local Plan, adopted July 1995
1996 Tweeddale Local Plan, adopted June 1996
1996 *Establishment of Scottish Borders Council*
1997 Town and Country Planning (Scotland) Act 1997
1997 **Planning (Listed Buildings and Conservation Areas) (Scotland) Act 1997**
1998 Scotland Act 1998
2002 Scottish Borders Structure Plan 2001–2011
2003 **Land Reform (Scotland) Act 2003**
2006 **Planning etc. (Scotland) Act 2006**

2008 Scottish Borders Local Plan 2008
2009 Consolidated Scottish Borders Structure Plan 2001–2018
2011 Scottish Borders Consolidated Local Plan
2013 Strategic Development Plan SESplan
2016 Scottish Borders Council Local Development Plan 2016

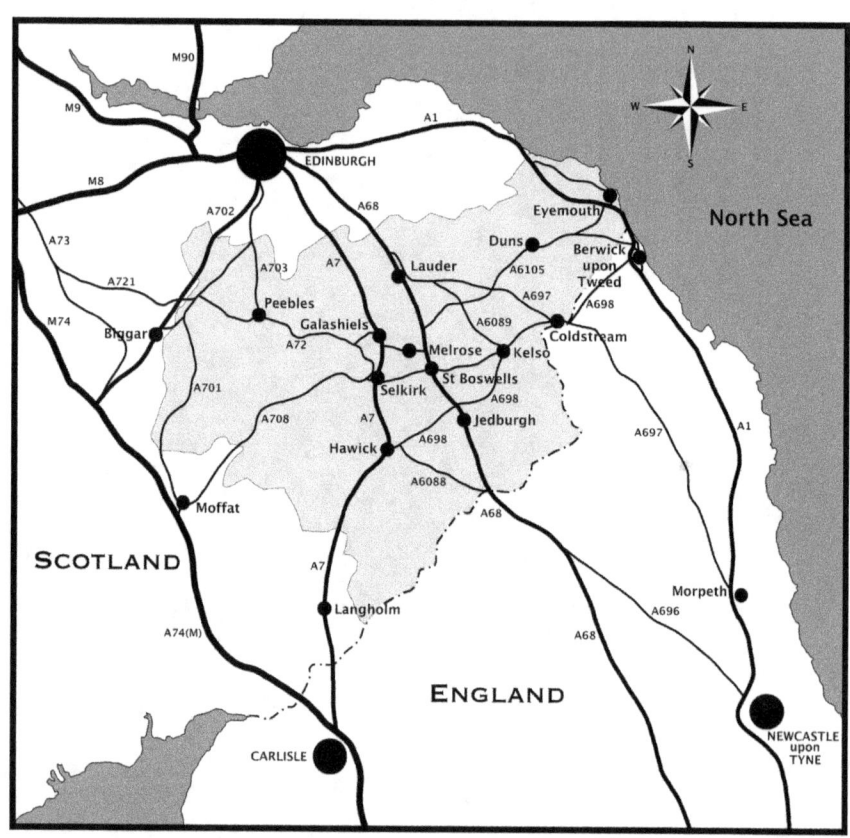

The Scottish Borders (tinted area)

Introduction

INTRODUCTION

THE SCOTTISH BORDERS STRETCHES from the environs of Edinburgh in the north to the English border to the south and from the rolling Tweedsmuir Hills in the west to the rocky North Sea coast in the east; an area of 1,820 square miles (4,714 square km). Through it, the River Tweed flows for 90 miles (145 km) from its headwaters near Tweedsmuir, through Peebles, Galashiels, Kelso and Coldstream to the sea at Berwick-upon-Tweed in neighbouring Northumberland. 'The Borders' is a long-established entity, epitomised in the Border Ballads and the writings of Sir Walter Scott, James Hogg (the Ettrick Shepherd) and John Buchan.

The Scottish Borders, as an administrative unit, was created when the Borders Regional Council (BRC) was established with the reorganisation of local government in Scotland in 1975. It is one of the most sparsely populated regions of Scotland, with an estimated population of 115,000 persons in 2020. The region comprises the historic counties of Peeblesshire, Selkirkshire, Roxburghshire and Berwickshire (and a small area of Midlothian), traditionally an area synonymous with woven cloth (tweed), high quality knitwear and agriculture. It is an area with a rich past as evidenced by its ruined towers, castles, abbeys and historic houses, and remembered in its common riding ceremonies.

The peaceful tranquillity of its landscape, however, gives little indication of the challenges faced by this area during the twentieth century as a result of the decline in its traditional industries and the loss of population (from a peak of 130,000 in 1881–1891 to less than 100,000 in 1971). Rural depopulation over a prolonged period of time resulted in a shortage of labour for traditional industries and the loss of young people led to an ageing population with its own demands on services and facilities. Furthermore, the region's population is dispersed throughout the area with no single town providing a focus for industry and commerce.

The largest towns of Hawick, Galashiels, Peebles, Selkirk, Jedburgh and Kelso have their own hinterlands, but the lack of a dominant centre and a history of strong, independent Border burghs has been a hindrance to the development of the region.

THE INFLUENCE OF THE LAND

The population of the Scottish Borders increased throughout the nineteenth century from a figure of less than 75,000 in 1801 to a peak of over 130,000 persons in 1881–1891.[1] The area was synonymous with the tweed and knitwear industries, spread across the main towns in the region. However, the economic and social welfare of the Scottish Borders is deeply tied to the use of the land. Approximately 85 per cent of the region's surface area is devoted to agricultural production. Arable farming predominates in the drier east of the region, in the lower Tweed Valley and around Kelso, whilst livestock rearing and finishing is more important in the middle Tweed Valley. In the upland areas of the south and west of the region, hill sheep farming predominates. In the *Land Utilisation Survey of Britain*, carried out in 1938, 22 per cent of the land in agricultural use in the Borders was arable land, 16 per cent was permanent pasture and 62 per cent was rough grazing. There were large contrasts across the region, however; in Berwickshire, 45 per cent of the land area was arable, compared to 8 per cent in Selkirkshire and 9 per cent in Peeblesshire. Only 30 per cent of the land area in Berwickshire was rough grazing compared with 80 per cent in Selkirkshire and Peeblesshire.[2]

The present rural landscape bears the imprint of the passion for 'improvement' that reached its climax in the late eighteenth century, sweeping away the medieval landholding system and subsistence farming. During the eighteenth century, dry-stane dykes and hedges began to define the landscape as land was enclosed. 'Improvement' took many forms – improved drainage, new and improved seed and stock, crop rotation and use of fertilisers, improved implements, new roads, new farmhouses and steadings. Creeping mechanisation was the key to subsequent development. The development of steam traction led to

---

[1] Population figures quoted here and in the following paragraphs are taken from the various Population Census Reports published between 1801 and 1931.

[2] Mears, F. C., *A Regional Survey and Plan for Central and South-East Scotland* (Central and South-East Scotland Regional Planning Advisory Committee: Edinburgh, 1948), pp. 28–29.

steam ploughing and to the travelling mill. Farm chimneys associated with the mid- to late nineteenth century steam engines survive in the arable farming area of the Merse.[3]

Much of the initial impulse for improvement came from the large landowners, such as the Earl of Marchmont, who introduced a variety of new techniques to his Polwarth holdings in Berwickshire. Neat estate villages, such as Swinton and Gavinton in Berwickshire, replaced earlier townships. The largest venture was the creation of Newcastleton in Liddesdale by the Duke of Buccleuch in 1793 as a weaving centre for displaced cottars.[4] The Duke of Buccleuch, together with the Duke of Roxburghe, had large landholdings in the Scottish Borders: Buccleuch Estates owned land in the Ettrick and Yarrow valleys, Teviotdale and Liddesdale; Roxburghe Estates owned land around Kelso, in the Cheviot Hills and in the Lammermuirs. Other landowners such as Lothian Estates held land around Jedburgh and Wemyss & March Estates held land in the Yarrow Valley and in Peeblesshire. At the beginning of the twentieth century, well over half of the total agricultural area in the Borders was covered by the large estates.[5]

Thus, both in the uplands and the Tweed Valley, the landlord-tenant relationship of the estate farm was the norm with a near-feudal social atmosphere, the tied cottage tying the farm labourer and estate worker to the landlord. The estates brought stability at a time of great change in agriculture, combining a variety of activities, ranging from the maintenance of the mansion, its gardens and policies, woodland and moorland management and the employment of tradesmen in agriculture-related activities, as well as its farm tenants and farm workers. In so doing, the estates helped stabilise the social fabric of the region by sustaining the rural school, village hall and kirk, and ameliorated the effects of the agricultural revolution on the rural population in both the lowlands and the upland valleys of the Scottish Borders.

The movement from the land became apparent in the nineteenth century as smallholdings were amalgamated into larger and more

---

[3] For a descriptive account of the agricultural changes in the eighteenth and nineteenth centuries see: Moffat, A., *The Borders* (Selkirk: Deerpark Press, 2002), Chapter 10, Day in, Day Out, pp. 291–322. See also Baldwin, J., 'Modern Times: 18th–20th Centuries', in D. Omand (ed.), *The Borders Book* (Edinburgh: Birlinn, 1995), pp. 94–95.

[4] White, J. B., *The Scottish Border and Northumberland* (London: Eyre Methuen, 1973), pp. 125–128.

[5] Mears, F. C., *A Regional Survey and Plan for Central and South-East Scotland*, p. 29.

efficient farm units. As the hitherto home-craft woollen industry began to centralise in the towns as mills were established, agricultural workers who were experienced weavers and spinners were attracted to the mill towns. However, it was the internal combustion engine that triggered revolutionary change with the replacement of the horse by the tractor between the two world wars, which led to a major reduction in manpower and exacerbated the movement of population away from the countryside.

The number of workers employed in agriculture in the Scottish Borders plummeted from 12,300 in 1871 to 7,000 in 1931. Nevertheless, the proportion of persons 'gainfully employed' (which included farmers as well as their employees) in agriculture in the Border counties in 1931 far exceeded the Scottish average of 10 per cent; in Berwickshire, 38 per cent of the total working population were employed in agriculture, in Roxburghshire, the proportion was 20 per cent, in Peeblesshire, 18 per cent but in Selkirkshire, the proportion was only 10 per cent. By contrast, the proportion of the total workforce employed in manufacturing (mainly textiles) was more than 50 per cent in Selkirkshire, the highest in Scotland, and 35 per cent in Roxburghshire.[6]

INDUSTRIAL DEVELOPMENT IN THE NINETEENTH CENTURY

The growth in population during the late eighteenth and nineteenth centuries was largely due to the expansion of the textile industry in the region, which began as a cottage-based, rural concern, producing woollen fabrics for local use, whilst the local linen industry with its bleachfields and lint mills was essentially domestic. Improvements to animal husbandry and farming methods around the middle of the eighteenth century led to the breeding of Cheviot sheep in the Borders, replacing the coarser Blackface variety and woollen manufacturing began to boom. Before wool is ready for manufacture, it must be washed and 'carded'; the fibres opened out and debris removed. It is then ready for spinning. Woven cloth is then 'waulked' or pre-shrunk before use. All these processes were originally cottage industries. Fulling or waulking was mechanised first: in the late Middle Ages there were three waulk mills in Galashiels. Then carding mills were added to these or built new at the end of the eighteenth century – Caerlee Mill at Damside,

---

[6] Based on figures from tables of Industries in the 1931 Census, Mears, F. C., *A Regional Survey and Plan for Central and South-East Scotland*, Appendix 3, pp. 172–173.

Innerleithen, built in 1788, was the first water-powered carding mill in the Borders, converted to steam power in 1858. Water powered spinning jennies or mules were added in around 1820. Built in 1835–1836 and doubled in size in 1850, Ettrick Mill in Selkirk was the largest multi-storey spinning mill in the Borders. The mules provided yarn for weaving in tweed mills or knitting in hosiery mills.[7]

Mills were located close to a source of water – the River Teviot in Hawick, the Gala Water in Galashiels and the River Ettrick in Selkirk. However, waterpower was not regular enough, so the expansion of power loom weaving came with steam engines that were made economical when the railway arrived. The construction of the Waverley Line between 1849 and 1862 helped the bringing in of coal from Midlothian for engines and boilers and also helped with the distribution of goods. Most spinners added weaving sheds or built new combined spinning and weaving mills in the period 1850–1890. Woollen cloth in the form of tartan received a massive boost when it was a key feature of the celebrations surrounding King George IV's visit to Edinburgh in 1822. Four years later, Sir Walter Scott commissioned the first pair of black and white 'shepherd-check' trousers, prompting other members of the gentry to follow suit. Soon, tartan-like fabrics were being produced in heather and granite colours for shooting and deer stalking. The accepted myth is that the word 'tweed' first entered the language through an administrative error. Sometime in the 1830s, on receiving goods reputedly from Dangerfield Mills, Hawick, a London clerk misread the word 'tweel' (the Scottish form of 'twill' for a piece of cloth), coining a new term that evoked visions of the River Tweed gently flowing through the rolling Borders countryside. By the mid-1870s there were more than 250 woollen mills in Scotland; the Borders contained over half of Scotland's spinning capacity and over 40 per cent of its powered weaving capacity and labour force.[8]

Galashiels was little more than a village at the end of the eighteenth century, constructed to house pilgrims destined for Melrose Abbey. However, the 1840s and 1850s saw the establishment of five large woollen spinning mills, and wars in Europe and the Civil War in North America increased demand for tweed; existing mills were extended to incorporate weaving sheds and new combined spinning and weaving

---

[7] For a general history of the growth of the textile industry in the Borders see Baldwin, J., 'Modern Times: 18th–20th Centuries', pp. 101–103.

[8] Adamson P. and Lamont-Brown, R., *The Victorian and Edwardian Borderland* (St Andrews: Alvie Publications, 1981), p. 11.

mills were constructed in the late-1860s and 1870s.⁹ By 1891, there were twenty-one mills in the town, dominating the townscape, and its population soared from 800 persons in 1801 to a peak of 14,650 persons in 1911.¹⁰ Selkirk expanded in the sixteenth and seventeenth centuries as a centre for shoemaking but emerged as an overflow for Galashiels in the eighteenth century and by 1869 there were seven mills employing over 1,000 people. Expansion continued in the later nineteenth century and by 1894 there were eleven mills along the riverside employing over 1,500 people. As a result, by 1891, the population of the town exceeded 7,000 persons, a tripling of the 1755 population of 1,900 persons.¹¹ Woollen mills were built in Innerleithen and Walkerburn by manufacturers from Galashiels and Selkirk. The first woollen mill in Peebles was opened a year after the railway arrived in 1856 and, in 1884, David Ballantyne & Sons opened March Street Mills using electricity for lighting and subsequently to drive machinery. The population of Peebles rose dramatically between 1851 and 1881; from less than 2,000 persons to 3,500 persons in thirty years.¹²

The products of these mills, marketed through merchants in London and Glasgow, were largely exported to North America and the prosperity of the mills was, therefore, very sensitive to international trading conditions. When the US Government imposed massive protective tariffs on imported woollen cloth in the 1890s, the effects were devastating; employment in textiles in Galashiels dropped by 25 per cent! To compensate for the loss of trade, greater attention was paid to Europe, particularly Germany. However, with the outbreak of the First World War, the developing trade with Europe disappeared overnight. Contracts for service cloth compensated for this loss, however, and the scarcity of male employment was met by employing women.

After the First World War, the Galashiels mills concentrated on manufacturing high-class men's cloth, a large part of which went for export. However, the 1920s saw the continuing decline in the export market and increasing competition for cheaper cloth, which could be supplied by other areas, principally Yorkshire. In the 1920s, many mill workers from Galashiels emigrated to New Zealand and Australia. The worldwide depression of the early 1930s exacerbated the situation and

---

⁹ Ibid., p. 63.

¹⁰ See 'The Textile Industry', in Galashiels History Committee, *Galashiels: A Modern History* (Galashiels: Ettrick & Lauderdale District Council, 1983).

¹¹ See Selkirk feature page on undiscoveredscotland.co.uk/selkirk.

¹² Brown, J. L. and Lawson, I. C., *History of Peebles: 1850–1990* (Edinburgh: Mainstream Publishing, 1990), pp. 25–27.

mills began to close. In its prosperous years before the First World War, 80 per cent of the industry depended on foreign trade but by the mid-1930s this had all virtually disappeared. Inability to change was also a factor in forcing the closure of mills, with a lack of investment in new machinery and out-dated working practices.

The hosiery industry began when Baillie John Hardie installed four knitting frames in Hawick in 1771. By the mid-1840s, more than 2,000 of Scotland's 2,605 knitting frames were located in the Borders: more than half of these in Hawick, producing well over one million pairs of stockings per year. In the mid-nineteenth century, manufacturers broadened their ranges to include items such as undershirts and drawers as well as stockings. As manufacturers expanded into larger mill complexes, sometimes converted woollen mills, the small-scale 'stocking-shops' went into decline. From the late nineteenth century, finer raw materials such as cashmere were increasingly imported for use and in the early part of the twentieth century the product focus changed from underwear to fully fashioned outer wear. Hawick concentrated on luxury knitwear, such as sweaters, shawls, cardigans, coats and 'twin-sets'; a concept developed in the 1930s by Otto Weisz, head designer for Pringle.[13] The population of Hawick increased fourfold between 1801 and 1861, from less than 3,000 to over 12,000, reaching a peak of 19,800 in 1891. The knitwear industry become the backbone of the economy, attracting immigrant workers from across Britain and Ireland with the establishment of manufacturers such as Pringle of Scotland, Barrie Knitwear, Innes Henderson, Lyle & Scott, Peter Scott and Robert Noble, with Blenkhorn Richardson and Wilson & Glenny making worsted cloth. Mills, such as Rodono Mill, Glebe Mill, Eastfield Mills, Wilton Mills, Annfield Mill and Victoria Mills, dominated the Hawick townscape.

Elsewhere, at Jedburgh, the opening of the branch railway in 1856 and the establishment of a number of woollen mills along the Jed Water resulted in the expansion of the town; by 1901 the population had risen to over 4,500 persons. Although some mills closed in the 1920s, Canongate Mill was redeveloped by North British Rayon (NBR) in 1928 and employed 800 people in the 1930s, with a worldwide reputation as makers of the finest artificial silk.[14] The arrival of the railway in Kelso in the 1860s led to development around the station at Maxwellheugh,

---

[13] Historic Scotland, *Hawick and its place among the Borders Mill Towns* (Edinburgh: Historic Scotland, 2009).
[14] SBA/1210/4, Roxburgh County Development Plan: Survey Report, May 1958, pp. 171–172.

across the River Tweed. The town grew as a centre for the rich surrounding agricultural area with related trades. Grain milling expanded and by the early twentieth century there were two grain mills in the town. There were a number of other agriculture-related trades, the principal being George Henderson Limited, which manufactured and repaired agricultural machinery.[15]

Essentially an agricultural county, Berwickshire was not totally devoid of industry. Paper mills were erected in Ayton and Edrom Parishes in the eighteenth century. A paper mill established at Broomhouse in Edrom Parish in 1786 was transferred three miles down the River Whiteadder to Chirnside Bridge in 1842 and expanded by Young, Trotter & Co, producing high quality paper in the 1930s (closed in 1969, it would be re-opened by the C. H. Dexter Corporation from Windsor Locks, Connecticut in 1972 to manufacture non-woven material for use in tea bags). At Cumledge, near Preston, a waulk mill dating from the fifteenth century was converted to a spinning mill in the 1850s and expanded by a Hawick weaver for the manufacture of blankets.[16] Earlston, on the Leader Water, possessed two mills at the end of the eighteenth century. Rhymer's Mill, originally a corn mill, was converted to a textile mill at the beginning of the nineteenth century to manufacture gingham. It closed in 1911 when the building was taken over by an agricultural engineer. Mid Mill manufactured blankets and tweed, employing over seventy workers in 1861. Greatly expanded in 1900 by Simpson & Fairburn, the mill weathered the global depression, tariff barriers and instability of the 1930s and, during the Second World War, was fully employed on service and utility clothing, employing more than 300 workers.[17]

RURAL DEPOPULATION IN THE SCOTTISH BORDERS

The generally accepted story of Scotland's population during the nineteenth century is one of natural increase, brought about by an excess of births over deaths, being outweighed by emigration to Australia, New Zealand and Canada. Internally, migrants flooded into the central belt, chiefly from the Highlands but also from Dumfries and

---

[15] SBA/1210/4, Roxburgh County Development Plan: Survey Report, May 1958, pp. 237–238.
[16] Omand, D. (ed.), *The Borders Book*, p. 102.
[17] See *Auld Earlston: The Textile Mills of Earlston* (Earlston Community Heritage Group, 2015).

Galloway and the Tweed Basin. During the period 1861–1911, the Tweed Basin lost 39,370 persons to the central belt (34 per cent of its mean population) whilst 14,710 people (13 per cent) were attracted to the region, a net loss of 24,660 people. The total loss of the four Border counties by net migration during this period was 61,414 people.[18] It was as a result of the dramatic changes in agriculture and the downturn in the fortunes of the textile industry that the population of the four counties declined from a peak of 130,000 in 1881–1891 to 110,000 in 1931. Whilst the population of the main towns, the burghs, remained relatively stable, the population of the landward areas declined by almost 50 per cent as a result of rural depopulation caused by the mechanisation of agriculture and the rationalisation of landholdings.

The population of Selkirkshire grew from a lowly figure of 4,000 in 1755 to 10,000 by 1851 before increasing rapidly to a peak of 27,300 in 1891. Thereafter, the population slowly declined to a figure of 22,600 in 1931. The population of the two burghs, Selkirk and Galashiels, was relatively stable between 1891 and 1931, the population of Galashiels reducing marginally from 14,650 to 13,500; whilst the population of Selkirk remained around the 7,000 mark. Consequently, in 1931, 20,500 (90 per cent) of the 22,600 population of Selkirkshire resided in the two burghs.

The population of Roxburghshire, a much more populace county with historic burghs such as Hawick, Jedburgh and Kelso, increased from 33,700 in 1801 to a peak of 54,100 in 1861. Thereafter, it remained fairly stable until 1891 but then declined to a figure of 45,788 by 1931. During the same period, the population of Hawick declined from a peak of 19,800 persons in 1891 to 17,000 by 1931, whilst the population of Jedburgh remained fairly stable around the 4,000 mark. The population of Kelso reached a peak of 4,800 in 1851 and thereafter declined to 3,500 persons by 1931, largely as a result of the loss of agricultural employment in its surrounding rural hinterland. In the fifty years between 1861 and 1911, the landward population of Roxburghshire declined by 10,000 persons: from 33,000 to 23,000 persons, and by a further 2,000 persons in the next twenty years.

Peeblesshire largely escaped the more serious consequences of rural depopulation exhibited in the rest of the Scottish Borders. The population of the county continued to rise until the First World War; from a

---

[18] Mears, F. C., *A Regional Survey and Plan for Central and South-East Scotland*, pp. 18–19.

figure of 8,700 in 1801 to 15,300 persons in 1911. At the same time, the population of Peebles rose from less than 2,000 persons to over 5,500 persons whilst the population of Innerleithen rose from about 1,000 persons to over 2,500 persons. Between 1911 and 1931 the population of the county changed little although the population of Peebles continued to increase, to a figure of 5,800 persons.

The population of Berwickshire, essentially an agricultural county, grew throughout the late eighteenth and early nineteenth centuries from roughly 24,000 in 1755 to a peak of 36,613 in 1861. However, during the latter part of the nineteenth century, large-scale imports of wheat from America and the increasing mechanisation of agriculture were instrumental in the emergence of depopulation in an area which had not shared in the Industrial Revolution. The population of the county slowly declined by 7,000 to 29,643 by 1911 with a decline of approximately 5,500 in the landward population. The burghs of Duns, Coldstream and Lauder suffered population decline in the latter half of the nineteenth century, being largely dependent on their surrounding agricultural hinterland. The population of Eyemouth, the chief white fish port on the coast between St Abbs and Amble in Northumberland, continued to grow until the town was struck by disaster in 1894 when 189 fishermen, half the male fishing population, were drowned in a freak storm.[19] It then declined from a population of 2,800 to less than 2,500 persons in 1911. Rural depopulation continued after the First World War as the population of the county fell by a further 3,000 persons to a figure of 26,600 in 1931.

The continued loss of population in the region, due to net out-migration over a long period of time, besides thinning out the population in the countryside and the small villages, also eroded the demographic stability of the region. The loss of, particularly, young people over several decades led to a gradual reduction in birth rates (from thirty-two per 1,000 population in 1871 to sixteen per 1,000 population in 1931) such that the birth rate barely exceeded the death rate in 1941, further exacerbating the problem of depopulation.

---

[19] Adamson P. and Lamont-Brown, R., *The Victorian and Edwardian Borderland*, p. 12; Omand, D. (ed.), *The Borders Book*, pp. 98–100. For a detailed account of the Eyemouth Disaster, see McIver, D., *An Old-time Fishing Town: Eyemouth* (Glasgow: John Menzies & Co. Ltd, 1906 [reprinted by Centenary Disaster Committee, 1981]).

THE FOCUS OF THE BOOK

Against this background, the book examines the changes and continuities in the practice of town and country planning in the Scottish Borders from its origins in the early twentieth century to the reorganisation of local government in Scotland in 1996. There is nothing in the Town and Country Planning Acts which explicitly states the purpose of 'Planning' but, as originally set out in the Town and Country Planning (Scotland) Act 1947, its broad objective is to regulate the development and use of land in the public interest through the preparation of development plans and the control of development by the granting of planning permission.[20] Although the principles of the planning system remained largely unchanged, the practice of 'Planning' changed fundamentally during the period 1946–1996. In the 1940s and 1950s, 'Planning' paid scant regard to rural areas. Agriculture and forestry operations were largely exempt from planning control. On development plans, most of the countryside, the landward area of county development plans, was uncoloured 'white land' where no development was proposed. Planners were 'town planners', the professional body was the 'Town Planning Institute'. Only in the 1960s did attention turn more to the countryside, with an increasing involvement in rural land use issues prompted by an increasing awareness of the need to stem rural depopulation, the rise in countryside recreation pressures and the growing concerns over the environmental impact of large-scale development in the countryside, including overhead power lines and afforestation.

Under the 1947 Act, the planning system rested on a uniform system of development plans containing proposals to be largely implemented by the public sector and land use zonings to regulate the private sector. From the 1960s onwards, the private sector took an increasing lead in deciding the scale and location of new development and in its implementation. Development plans became out-dated and, in an increasingly competitive economy, 'Planning' changed from a simple regulatory system to a more complex collaborative activity requiring the assistance of a range of public bodies and the private sector to implement development plans.

In addition, increasing financial control over local government impinged on the ability of planning authorities to undertake development and implement development plans. In 1947/48 local authorities

---

[20] Cullingworth, B. and Nadin, V., *Town and Country Planning in the UK* (London: Routledge, 1996, 13 edn), p. 2.

relied on central government grants for only 23 per cent of their revenue whereas in 1996/97 it was 83 per cent, with the influence of central government further reinforced by capital expenditure capping.[21] Increasingly, planning authorities had to rely on new sources of finance, through partnerships with other agencies, to implement planning policies, competing with other authorities for regional and European funds.

Intervention by central government in planning policy has increased during this period. Whilst under the 1947 Act development plans required to be approved by the Secretary of State, there was little guidance from central government on their policy content. With the advent of National Planning in the 1960s, central government (the Scottish Development Department [SDD]) became involved in regional policy through technical studies and working parties and, following the reorganisation of local government in 1975, National Planning Guidelines (NPG) and Planning Advice Notes (PAN) laid down firm and specific guidance and advice on policies which planning authorities must have regard to, otherwise they risked the Secretary of State making changes to structure and local plans or overturning development control decisions on appeal.[22]

In the 1950s, public participation in the preparation of development plans did not exist. The planning system was based on the principle that a planning application concerned only the applicant and the planning authority; consultations were minimal, largely restricted to statutory undertakers and selected statutory bodies. With the replacement of development plans prepared under the 1947 Act by structure and local plans, originally enacted by the Town and Country Planning (Scotland) Act 1969 and re-enacted in the Town and Country Planning (Scotland) Act 1972, public participation became a formal requirement of the development plan process. An increasing awareness of the need for more openness and public involvement in planning, combined with the growth of the conservation movement prompted by the Civic Amenities Act 1967, reinforced the desire for people to be involved in planning decisions that affected their communities.

---

[21] Burgess, T. and Travers, T., *Ten Billion Pound: Whitehall's Takeover of the Town Halls* (London: Grant McIntyre, 1980); and Chartered Institute of Public Finance and Accountancy, *Finance and General Statistics, 1996–1997* (Statistical Information Service, London, Chartered Institute of Public Finance and Accountancy, 1996).

[22] See Appendix 4 for a list of Government Circulars, National Planning Guidelines and Planning Advice Notes.

INTRODUCTION

Whilst town and country planning is predominantly about land use, social and economic influences cannot be ignored. The social origins of town planning lie in the concerns for public health in the late nineteenth century and the intervention of the planning system in the use of land has an economic dimension. Planning is also a political function; the planning powers vested in local government by central government legislation are subject to government guidance. Thus, planning powers can only be exercised to the extent permitted by the political framework operating at the time.[23] The purpose of 'Planning' has, therefore, developed over the decades from one of simply regulating the use of land in order to ensure that the post-war reconstruction of Britain would be in the best interests of national prosperity to a goal of ensuring sustainable economic development and a better quality of life in the face of climate change. As a consequence, there has been a dramatic change in planning practice in the region, from a simple, uniform system of land use control to a dynamic, proactive, multi-disciplined collaboration encompassing not only spatial planning but also economic development and promotion, project design and implementation, urban conservation, rural heritage and countryside management, and environmental planning.

THE SCOPE OF THE BOOK

The book is an objective case study of a unique area of Scotland, a rural region sandwiched between the central industrial belt of Scotland and the urban areas of northeast and northwest England, set within the context of the evolution of the planning system in Scotland and the UK as a whole. Chapter One explores the origins of town and country planning in the UK and details the government's post-war proposals for the regeneration of the Borders Region.[24] Chapter Two examines how thefour county councils in the region put town and country planning into practice during the 1950s. The early 1960s was a period of great social, economic and political change and 'Planning' in its widest sense took centre stage both nationally and regionally, with the publication of the Central Borders Plan.[25] Chapter Three reviews the government's

---

[23] For a discussion of the objectives of 'Planning' see Collar, N. A., *Planning* (Edinburgh: W. Green/Sweet & Maxwell, 1994), pp. 12–16.

[24] Mears, F. C., *A Regional Survey and Plan for Central and South-East Scotland* (Edinburgh: South-East Scotland Regional Planning Advisory Committee, 1948).

[25] Scottish Office, *The Scottish Economy 1965–1970: A Plan for Expansion*, Cmnd. 2864 (Edinburgh: HMSO, 1966). Scottish Development Department, *The*

proposals for the Borders and details how planning and development became inexorably linked as industrial development, promotion and marketing became an integral part of town and country planning in the region. Modernity came to the Borders in various guises and Chapter Four explores how, influenced by the social, economic and political changes taking place nationally, town and country planning in the Borders broadened its horizons. Planning adopted a more positive role in urban development with a greater emphasis on conservation, and increasing attention was placed on the future of the smaller settlements in the landward areas of the Borders as focal points for services and facilities in order to stem rural depopulation. Rural issues came to the fore with the increasing impact of changing farming practices on the landscape and the growing pressure for countryside recreation.

With the perceived failure of the 'old style' county development plans to respond to the increasing pace of development, the development plan system was transformed in 1969 with the introduction of structure and local plans.[26] The reorganisation of local government in Scotland in 1975 established a two-tier structure of regional and district councils with the Borders Regional Council responsible for all planning functions. Chapter Five describes how the four county councils prepared for local government reorganisation and how the new regional council set about the task of administering planning in the new region with the production of a Regional Report, an 'Action Plan for Development' and a new development control system. Over the next ten years the regional council would prepare a structure plan and twelve local plans to guide future development. Chapter Six discusses the process whereby these plans were prepared and examines the key policies and proposals set out in the first structure and local plans for the Scottish Borders. The 1980s was a period of economic volatility, during which time the Borders Region lost its Assisted Area Status and thus access to European Community (EC) funds. Nevertheless, much was achieved in resolving issues identified in the approved structure plan and implementing its policies and proposals. The regional council's role in economic development expanded and partnerships with a range of organisations was key to securing investment and implementing proposals. Chapter Seven

Central Borders: A Plan for Expansion: Vol. 1, Plan and Physical Study (Edinburgh: HMSO, 1968); Scottish Development Department, *The Central Borders: A Plan for Expansion: Vol. 2, Economic and Geographical Report* (Edinburgh: HMSO, 1968).

[26] Ministry of Housing and Local Government, Ministry of Transport, Scottish Development Department, *The Future of Development Plans: Report of the Planning Advisory Group* (London: HMSO, 1965).

details the challenges and the achievements of the planning authority during the 1980s.

The 1990s was a period of uncertainty, with a downturn in the economy and a number of significant organisational and operational changes amongst Scotland's principal agencies. The 1990s also saw an increasing involvement of central government, the SDD, in the provision of planning policy and guidance on a range of matters. Chapter Eight details how the regional council dealt with these challenges and, against an uncertain future, produced a new structure plan, *The Scottish Borders 2001: The Way Forward*, signalling new directions for planning in the Borders Region. Environmental issues came to the fore at the dawn of the 1990s with the publication of the White Paper 'This Common Inheritance', and attention was drawn towards promoting environmentally sound and sustainable development. With the reorganisation of local government looming in 1996, Chapter Nine examines the role of the Planning and Development Department in preparing for the new challenges of the twenty-first century. The final chapter, the Epilogue, draws together the changes and continuities in the practice of town and country planning in the Scottish Borders during the period 1946–1996 and looks forward to the impact of the significant changes to the planning system resulting from the reorganisation of local government in Scotland in 1996, the establishment of the Scottish Parliament in 1999 and the subsequent changes made to the town and country planning system in Scotland.

A number of recurring themes have emerged through this study of town and country planning in the Scottish Borders. Firstly, the increasing complexity of the planning process. During the period under consideration, the development of 'planning' in both central and local government mushroomed to encompass economic development, urban renewal, recreation planning and environmental management, impinging on people in a myriad of ways with increasing regulation and bureaucracy. This has been accompanied by an increasing diversity in the planning profession, from the town-planning assistant in the surveyor's or architect's department to large multi-disciplinary planning departments.

Secondly, the increasing involvement of the public both in development control decision-making and the formulation of planning policy. From being the sole concern of professionals in the 1950s, planning became a matter of the widest public importance and interest. The planning legislation of 1947 proceeded on the basis that a planning application concerned only the applicant and the planning authority. Over the years, concessions were made in the face of growing pressure for increased publicity and in 1981 it became the duty of applicants to notify neighbours of proposals for planning permission. The involvement of the public in the structure and local plan process became a requirement of the 1969 Planning Act. Community councils were introduced in 1975 to improve communication between communities and public authorities, including local authorities. Planning in the Scottish Borders also gained the increasing attention of the press.

Thirdly, the growth in proactive planning. Through the course of the fifty years 1946–1996, planning in the Scottish Borders became a much more enabling process, whether it be through the preparation of structure and local plans, village plans, the provision of industrial sites and buildings, the implementation of urban renewal projects and environmental improvement schemes, or the provision and management of countryside recreation facilities. However, positive planning was hindered by the inability to assemble land quickly in order to implement planning proposals; the acquisition of land through compulsory purchase where there was an unwilling seller was a cumbersome procedure. In addition, increasing constraints on local authority capital spending meant that enabling development depended very much on partnerships between the regional council and a range of agencies and between the public and private sector.

Fourthly, the increasing attention given to rural issues and rural development. Rural depopulation attracted little attention until the late 1960s. Rural planning concentrated on coping with the impact of the increase in countryside recreation and the effects of the mechanisation of agriculture on the landscape. Government rural policy was fragmented and it would be the 1980s before the potential impact of changes in agriculture on the rural economy and the social fabric of rural communities was fully recognised. As the emphasis of EC and government policy switched from supporting production to encouraging diversification and less intensive farming, rural development took centre stage in the Borders, with comparisons made with the success of the Highlands and Islands Development Board (HIDB).

Fifthly, the growing awareness of the impact of development on the environment. This manifested itself in the late 1960s with the growing interest in conservation, town centre rehabilitation and environmental improvement schemes. In the countryside, there was increasing concern at the loss of deciduous woodland and hedgerow trees. The creation of Scottish Natural Heritage (SNH) integrated nature conservation with landscape conservation and access to the countryside, with the purpose of improving the management of the natural heritage. Although afforestation was outwith planning control, growing concerns over the scale and nature of commercial forestry in the 1980s resulted in the increasing involvement of planning authorities in forest design and the preparation of Indicative Forestry Strategies. In response to a growing awareness in the 1990s of the threat to the environment from inappropriate development and what we now call 'climate change', the regional council committed itself to the principles of sustainable development and the production of a renewable energy strategy for the Borders.

HISTORIOGRAPHY

Use has been made of a number of texts on the modern history of the Scottish Borders, principal amongst them *The Borders Book*, edited by Donald Omand and published by Birlinn in 1995, and *The Victorian & Edwardian Borderland* by Peter Adamson and R. Lamont-Brown, published by Alvie Publications in 1981. There are also a number of histories of the main towns of the Borders that have proved useful. Mears *Regional Survey and Plan for Central and South-East Scotland*, published in 1948, has provided much of the information about the Scottish Borders at the commencement of statutory planning in the region. There are a number of texts on the evolution of Scotland's towns and urban Scotland.[27] A paper, 'Planning and Development in Scotland', by F. R. Stevenson in the *Town Planning Review*, published in 1955, looks back at how Scotland has developed since Roman times to show that town planning did not commence with the Town Planning Act of 1909.[28] Stevenson reminds us that many burghs in Scotland exhibit the results of 'Planning', not least the New Town of Edinburgh.

There are a number of titles that touch on the history of town and country planning in a general way. Lewis Keeble's *Principles and Practice of Town and Country Planning* published in 1951 became the standard textbook for planning under the Town and Country Planning Acts.[29] This was followed by Barry Cullingworth and Vincent Nadin's *Town and Country Planning in the UK*, first published in 1964.[30]

---

[27] Adams, I., *The Making of Urban Scotland* (London: Croom Helm, 1978) and Dennison, P., *The Evolution of Scotland's Towns* (Edinburgh: Edinburgh University Press, 2017).

[28] Stevenson, F. R., Planning and Development in Scotland, *The Town Planning Review*, Vol. 26, No. 1 (Apr. 1955), pp. 5–18.

[29] Keeble, L. B., *Principles and Practice of Town and Country Planning* (London: Estates Gazette, 1951).

[30] Cullingworth, B. and Nadin, V., *Town and Country Planning in the UK* (London: Routledge, 1996, 13th edn).

William Ashworth's *The Genesis of Modern British Town Planning*, published in 1954, charts the emergence of the planning movement in response to the industrialisation of Britain and Gordon Cherry's *The Evolution of British Town Planning* in 1974, which was written to mark the Diamond Jubilee of the Royal Town Planning Institute (RTPI), describes its subsequent evolution and the development of the statutory planning process.[31] Cliff Hague's *The Development of Planning Thought*, published in 1984, provides a more critical perspective of the development of planning. It spotlights the economic, political and ideological dimensions of planning in the UK.[32]

In 1997, Professor H. W. E. Davies of the University of Reading's Department of Land Management and Development presented a paper under the title 'Fifty years of planning achievements – the evolution of the planning system since 1947' at the National Planning Conference and Exhibition 1997 of the Royal Town Planning Institute in Edinburgh on 12 June 1997. A revised and extended version of that paper was published in *Town Planning Review* in April 1998.[33] This paper has proved most useful in examining how planning practice in the UK changed during the period under consideration; from a uniform, comprehensive system to one that is more diverse in its aims and methods. Use has also been made of journal articles published in a variety of journals during the period under consideration to provide further insight into the evolution of planning, particularly in Scotland, during the period 1946–1996.

There is a relatively small, practitioner-focussed literature on the practice of town and country planning in Scotland: *Scottish Planning Law and Procedure* by Eric Young and Jeremy Rowan-Robinson, published in 1985, was considered the Scottish Planning 'Bible' for many years.[34] A more recent publication, *Scottish Planning Law* by Ray McMaster, Alan Prior and John Watchman, first published in 1994 and revised in 2013, provides a comprehensive guide to town

---

[31] Ashworth, W., *The Genesis of Modern British Town Planning: A Study in Economic and Social History of the Nineteenth and Twentieth Centuries* (London: Routledge & Kegan Paul, 1954); Cherry, G. E., *The Evolution of British Town Planning* (Leighton Buzzard: Leonard Hill Books, 1974).

[32] Hague, C., *The Development of Planning Thought* (London: Hutchinson, 1984).

[33] Davies, H. W. E., 'Continuity and Change: The evolution of the British planning system, 1947–1997', *The Town Planning Review*, Vol. 69, No. 2 (Apr. 1998), pp. 135–152.

[34] Young, E. & Rowan-Robinson, J., *Scottish Planning Law and Procedure* (Glasgow: William Hodge & Company Ltd, 1985).

and country planning in Scotland.[35] However, the only book that goes some way to explaining the changing role of planning in local government since 1947 is the autobiographical book by Frank Tindall entitled *Memoirs and Confessions of a County Planning Officer*, published in 1998.[36]

INFORMATION SOURCES

Extensive use has been made of the records of the four original planning authorities, Berwickshire, Peebles, Roxburgh and Selkirk County Councils, from the establishment of the first county planning committees in the early 1940s to the reorganisation of local government in 1975. Thereafter, use has been made of the records of Borders Regional Council from May 1975 to May 1996, when the Regional Council was merged with its four constituent District Councils; Tweeddale, Ettrick and Lauderdale, Roxburgh and Berwickshire, to form the all-purpose Scottish Borders Council (see Appendix 2). Use has also been made of the extensive library of Borders Regional Council publications originating during the period 1975–1996, including structure and local plans prepared under the 1972 Act, planning policy guidance, technical reports and studies, annual reports and promotional material (see Appendix 3). A trawl has also been made of the local press, particularly the *Scotsman* and *The Southern Reporter*, to obtain a further viewpoint on the practice of town and country planning in the Borders. I have also been able to call upon my own personal perspective gained from more than fifty years of working in planning and the views of former colleagues, who have also provided further insight into the operation of town and country planning in the Scottish Borders.

CONCLUSION

This book is unique in that it deals, comprehensively, with continuity and change in the evolution of town and country planning in a distinct area of Scotland, the Scottish Borders. There is no such comparable study of how the practice of town and country planning has evolved at the local authority level. It is hoped that this book will appeal not only

---

[35] McMaster, R., Prior, A. and Watchman, J., *Scottish Planning Law* (London: Bloomsbury Professional, 2013).
[36] Tindall, F., *Memoirs and Confessions of a County Planning Officer* (Ford, Midlothian: The Pantile Press, 1998).

to scholars and researchers of town and country planning but will also have an audience beyond planners to those with an interest in human geography, the environment, modern studies, politics, the economy and social sciences. Those who have an interest in the history of the Scottish Borders will also find this book informative and illuminating.

1

Town and Country Planning Becomes Established

INTRODUCTION

CHAPTER ONE EXPLORES THE origins of town and country planning in the UK and describes how planning was put into practice in the Scottish Borders in the 1940s and 1950s. Planning committees were established in the 1940s and were advised by the county clerk assisted by the county surveyor or county architect supported by technical staff. In the 1950s, most staff in Scottish county planning departments was unqualified in planning, or architects who might have taken an additional course in 'Town Planning'. Sir Frank Mears was responsible for Scotland's first Town Planning course, introduced at the Edinburgh College of Art in 1932. Architecture students successfully completing the one-year course were awarded the Diploma in Town Planning and exempt from the final examinations of the Town Planning Institute (TPI). It would be 1948 before a separate School of Town Planning was established at the College of Art, awarding diplomas in town planning similar to the schools of town planning in the universities of Liverpool, London, Manchester and Durham.[1]

There were only eighteen qualified town planners working in Scotland at this time, most of whom were in the Department of Health for Scotland (DHS).[2] Local government had been slow to appoint 'Planners' to head their new Planning Departments; instead, entrusting the task to their road surveyors or architect's departments. John Somerville (Jack) Baillie, appointed County Planning Officer of Midlothian County

---

[1] Lawrie, S. J., *The Edinburgh College of Art (1904–1969): A Study in Institutional History*, unpublished thesis submitted for degree of M.Phil., Edinburgh College of Art (Heriot-Watt University), Department of Humanities, 1996, p. 95 & pp. 101–105.

[2] Tindall, F., *Memoirs and Confessions of a County Planning Officer*, pp. 5–6.

Council in 1948 and Frank Tindall, appointed County Planning Officer of neighbouring East Lothian County Council in 1950, would be two of the first fully qualified county planning officers in Scotland. John C. Hall, and subsequently his son John B. Hall, trading as J & J Hall, Architects of Galashiels, would act as county planning officer for Selkirk County Council (SCC) providing planning advice to the county clerk. Peebles County Council (PCC) would be advised by Jack Baillie and Assistant County Planning Officer, Charles Ross (Charlie) Mackenzie, of Midlothian County Planning Department. In Roxburghshire the county architect provided advice to the county clerk, and in Berwickshire the county surveyor was appointed county planning officer. It would be the late 1960s before Roxburgh and Berwickshire County Councils appointed qualified county planning officers.

The lack of qualified planning staff restricted the four counties in their ability to produce the required development plan under the 1947 Act within the three-year timescale set down by the DHS. The county development plans for Selkirkshire and Peeblesshire were submitted to the Secretary of State for Scotland (SoS) in 1953 but it would be December 1960 before the Berwickshire County Development Plan was submitted and December 1961 before the Roxburgh County Development Plan arrived in St Andrew's House in Edinburgh. As Gordon Cherry remarks: 'In Scotland, chronic shortages of staff delayed the submission of plans longer than in England, and there was little progress until into the sixties in some Border and Highland counties. The planning system became centred round "development control"'.[3]

Membership of the four county councils, although including representatives from the constituent burghs, was largely dominated by the landward members, and these members tended to come from the landed gentry, retired military, farming or the professions rather than the working population; they tended to be elderly and there were no women members. Thus, elected members were not representative of the wider population but this seems to have been largely accepted by the majority of the electorate. Indeed, many members were regularly re-elected unopposed. This relationship between elected representative and electorate is reminiscent of the feudal relationship between landowners and tenants (of course many constituents were tenants of large hereditary landowners) and reflected the strong Borders tradition and sense of identity. Politics had little role to play in local government decision making in the Border counties, unlike many of the Central Belt

---

[3] Cherry, G. E., *The Evolution of British Town Planning*, p. 153.

local authorities, for the vast majority of members stood as independent councillors, strongly tied to their local area and electorate rather than any national organisation.

The membership of the respective county planning committees reflected the membership of the councils as a whole, with major landowners occupying positions of authority. For instance, in July 1950, Berwickshire County Council's Planning and Property & Works Committee comprised six landowners, two ministers and a retired sea captain. Major Askew, from Ladykirk, who would become convener of Berwickshire County Council (BCC) and the first convener of the Borders Regional Council, was the chairman. Not unsurprisingly, these committees were largely 'conservative' in their approach to development. Few planning applications were refused, the respective councils preferring negotiation and compromise. Development plans showed little ambition and planning was largely a reactive process.

ORIGINS OF TOWN AND COUNTRY PLANNING

The origins of town and country planning in Britain lay in the dramatic changes in nineteenth-century society caused by the Industrial Revolution with an influx of people from the countryside into the towns. Houses and factories were constructed cheek by jowl; there was no control over standards of construction and little and no regard for proper ventilation and sanitation. Model villages built by industrial philanthropists, such as New Lanark, the brainchild of David Dale and his son-in-law Robert Owen, showed how workers could be housed in healthy surroundings. The Garden City movement, formed in 1899, promoted well-laid out towns with extensive open spaces and houses with gardens.[4] In Scotland, the Public Health (Scotland) Act 1897 gave local authorities powers to secure proper standards of drainage and sewage and regulate the width of streets, space between houses and size of rooms. However, these powers did not deal with more general land-use problems, such as the proximity of housing to heavy industry.[5]

Until the passing of The Housing, Town Planning, etc. Act 1909, which applied to England, Wales and Scotland, local authorities did not

---

[4] Hardy, D., *From Garden Cities to New Towns* (London: Spon Press, 1991).

[5] Cullingworth, B. and Nadin, V., *Town and Country Planning in the UK*, pp. 14–15; Cherry, G. E., *The Evolution of British Town Planning*, pp. 6–23. For a brief summary of the way in which planning legislation has evolved over the years in Scotland, see Young, E. and Rowan-Robinson, J., *Scottish Planning Law and Procedure*.

possess any right or power to control or regulate the development of the towns and districts under their jurisdiction. The 1909 Act was the first enactment in Great Britain to deal with the subject of town planning. Section 54 of the 1909 Act empowered local authorities to make 'town planning schemes ... with the object of securing proper sanitary conditions, amenity and convenience in connection with the laying out and use of land'. Here was the opportunity to control not merely the construction of individual buildings but of building development as a whole. Thus, residential districts could be safeguarded against the undesirable intrusion of industrial buildings and industrial areas could be set apart for the purpose of industrial development only.[6]

Under the 1909 Act, local authorities could make town planning schemes for defined areas which were in the course of development, or which appeared likely to be used for building purposes. By 1919, only thirteen schemes had been submitted in England and Wales and none in Scotland.[7] The Housing, Town Planning, etc. (Scotland) Act 1919 introduced compulsory town planning schemes for every burgh in Scotland with a population of 20,000 or more. These burgh councils were required to produce town planning schemes by 1 January 1926 but there was still no requirement to prepare a plan for the whole town. The 1919 Act also introduced Interim Development Control for the period between the passing of a resolution to prepare a scheme and the scheme becoming effective, which could be several years. However, the largest burgh in the Scottish Borders, Hawick, had a population of only 16,900 and so this Act had no effect in the Scottish Borders. The Town and Country Planning (Scotland) Act 1932 extended the scope for planning action by enabling all local authorities to make planning schemes for almost any land. However, planning schemes were very inflexible and the prospect of having to pay heavy compensation to those who sustained financial loss in consequence of such a scheme deterred many authorities from making planning schemes. No action was taken in the Scottish Borders under this Act.[8]

In the 1930s, major land use problems began to emerge; urban sprawl and ribbon development attracting most attention. The Restriction of Ribbon Development Act 1935 was designed to prevent the sprawl of

---

[6] Cullingworth, B. and Nadin, V., *Town and Country Planning in the UK*, pp. 15–16; Cherry, G. E., *The Evolution of British Town Planning*, pp. 63–67.

[7] Cherry, G. E., 'The Housing, Town Planning, etc., Act, 1919', *The Planner*, vol. 60 (1974), p. 681.

[8] Cullingworth, B. and Nadin, V., *Town and Country Planning in the UK*, pp. 16–17; Cherry, G. E., *The Evolution of British Town Planning*, pp. 82–87.

towns and cities across the countryside but the 1930s was characterised by the construction of ribbons of bungalows and semi-detached houses along the main arteries into and out of towns and cities. A series of Royal Commissions set up during the Second World War looked into specific problems related to urban development and the control of development in anticipation of the need to rebuild the country after hostilities had ceased. The Scott Report (1941) called for local planning to become compulsory. The Uthwatt Report (1942) recommended that all land should be brought within Interim Development Control to prevent development prejudicial to post-war reconstruction plans. The Barlow Report (1940) recommended the decentralisation of industry away from the congested areas and a reasonable balance of population throughout the country. Barlow mainly focussed on Britain's industrial areas, but his report does record the Ministry of Agriculture's concerns about the loss of farm workers to the urban areas. His focus in Scotland was on 'Mid Scotland', the Central Belt.[9]

In Scotland, Patrick Geddes (1854–1932), biologist, sociologist, geographer, philanthropist and pioneering town planner, who is often referred to as 'The Father of Town Planning', advocated a regional approach to town planning that took account of the complex relationships between humans and their environment, based on a detailed regional survey of a region's hydrology, geology, flora, fauna and natural topography as well as its social and economic opportunities.[10] This approach bore fruit after the Second World War when Sir Patrick Abercrombie (1879–1957), Professor of Town Planning at University College, London, who had prepared the Greater London Plan (the Abercrombie Plan) in 1944, and Sir Robert Matthew (1906–1975), Chief Architect and Planning Officer with the DHS, which had the responsibility for planning at national level, led the team that prepared the Clyde Valley Regional Plan in 1946, which proposed the New Towns of East Kilbride and Cumbernauld. Sir Frank Mears (1880–1953), architect and planning consultant and Patrick Geddes' son-in-law, led another team that prepared the *Regional Survey and Plan for Central and South-East Scotland*, published in 1948, which included the Scottish Borders.[11]

---

[9] Cullingworth, B. and Nadin, V., *Town and Country Planning in the UK*, pp. 17–20.

[10] Cherry, G. E., *The Evolution of British Town Planning*, pp. 52–53; see also Pepler, G. L., '"Geddes" Contribution to Town Planning', *Town Planning Review*, vol. 26, no. 1 (April 1955), pp. 19–24.

[11] Mears, F. C., *A Regional Survey and Plan for Central and South-East Scotland* (Edinburgh: Central and South-East Scotland Regional Planning Advisory Committee, 1948).

REGIONAL PLAN FOR CENTRAL AND SOUTH-EAST SCOTLAND 1948

The *Regional Plan for Central and South-East Scotland* was one of three major regional plans for Scotland's post-war reconstruction, together with Patrick Abercrombie's Clyde Valley Regional Plan and the Tay Valley Plan by Robert Lyle and Gordon Payne published in 1950. The *Regional Plan for Central and South-East Scotland* was prepared for the Central and South-East Scotland Regional Planning Committee, at the instigation of the SoS, Tom Johnston MP. The Committee was formally constituted on 2 November 1943 with representatives from eleven county councils and six burgh councils.[12] Notwithstanding wartime difficulties, an interim report was produced by March 1945 and a draft final report in July 1946. The final report was published in April 1948.

The report included a number of recommendations that would influence the future development of south-east Scotland; a new Forth road crossing and by-pass for Edinburgh and a New Town in the coalfield area of Fife (at Glenrothes to house miners at the new Rothes Colliery). The report provided a comprehensive assessment of the geography, history, population, economy and land use of the Tweed Basin. It confirmed the scale of depopulation in Berwickshire and Roxburghshire during the period 1871–1931 (there was no census in 1941), during which time the population of Berwickshire decreased from 36,382 to 26,518; and that of Roxburghshire from 48,241 to 45,729. There was a drift from the country to the town throughout the Borders, from the landward areas to the burghs. Statistics for the younger age groups showed substantial falls throughout the area, and the proportion of the population over fifty-five years of age had nearly doubled since 1871, the proportion of children under five had halved and the number of births was exceeded by the number of deaths in 1931; the population was reducing as a result of both natural decrease and emigration. The immediate concern was the shortage of labour in the tweed industry and in agriculture.

The report also drew attention to the emphasis on north-to-south road communications through the Tweed Basin, which tended to starve the region rather than serve it, and an improvement in east-to-west communications was postulated with an improved road linking

---

[12] Mears, F. C., *A Regional Survey and Plan for Central and South-East Scotland*, pp. v–vi.

Berwick-upon-Tweed with Peebles and Lanarkshire. The route outlined utilised existing roads from Berwick-upon-Tweed south of the River Tweed to Coldstream then Kelso and St Boswells. From St Boswells a new road was proposed south of Melrose and Galashiels to cross the River Tweed just below its confluence with the River Ettrick, before continuing to Fairnilee and Caddonfoot to join the A72. By-passes to Walkerburn and Innerleithen were proposed on the A72. In Peebles, the proposed route passed to the north of the High Street cutting through existing property in the Old Town before following the A72 to Blyth Bridge and then westwards to Biggar and Lanark.

Mears recommended that Newtown St Boswells/St Boswells (rather than Galashiels) be developed as an administrative hub for the Central Borders with housing, offices, hospital, agricultural college and student accommodation and that it should become the headquarters for a planning and development organisation for the whole Tweed Basin. It was envisaged that Newtown St Boswells would be at the centre of an urban constellation comprising Hawick, Jedburgh, Kelso, Galashiels and Selkirk with a population of 50,000 persons. No new land for industrial development was proposed at Newtown St Boswells (it was proposed that this should be concentrated in the existing burghs) but the munitions factory at Charlesfield, near St Boswells, was identified as a site for an assembly plant to build the thousands of prefabricated houses that would be required for new housing development following the end of the Second World War. Charlesfield was an incendiary bomb factory during the Second World War, built around 1942 by ICI, with its own railway halt. At its peak, the factory employed 1,300 people and produced over one million bombs a month. Production ceased in 1945 and, thereafter, a small part of the site was used by the Royal Navy to store small arms and guns. Although the council had the opportunity to purchase the majority of the site for development, no action was taken, and the majority of the site returned to agriculture.

The report recommended the establishment of an informal joint committee for the Tweed Basin to co-ordinate action, to include representatives of Midlothian County Council, Berwick-upon-Tweed Borough Council and the northern district councils of Northumberland in addition to the four Border counties. Little action was taken on the part of either central government or the local authorities on this recommendation. Central government's attention was more focussed on the Central Belt and Fife. Any cross-border co-operation on planning and development would have to wait until the establishment of the Eastern Borders Development Association (EBDA) in 1966.

The Mears Report would pave the way for the preparation of the first county development plans by Berwickshire, Peebles, Roxburgh and Selkirk County Councils. However, the subsequent county development plans paid little attention to the Mears report, which did not take due account of the historic pattern of development and local politics (the 'independence' of the Border burghs). There would be little enthusiasm for the development of Newtown St Boswells as the hub of the region and it would be 1975 before Newtown St Boswells was established as the headquarters of the Borders Regional Council, the organisation responsible for planning and development in the region as a whole. East-to-west road communications would remain an issue in seeking to unify the eastern and western extremities of the region with the centre.

TOWN AND COUNTRY PLANNING EMERGES IN THE SCOTTISH BORDERS

The Town and Country Planning (Interim Development) (Scotland) Act 1943 extended the control of development beyond those areas that were the subject of a planning scheme to cover the whole of a local authority's area. As a consequence, planning committees were set up by each of the four counties in the Scottish Borders. Their first task was to establish systems for dealing with applications submitted under the Interim Development Control powers conferred by the 1943 Act and initiate surveys of their area: of the use of land, the use and condition of buildings, the provision of services such as water and drainage, gas and electricity, school provision and bus routes.

Peebles County Council pre-empted the enactment of the 1943 Act by appointing its first Town Planning Committee in December 1940.[13] However, this committee undertook little business until September 1942 when consideration was given to the carrying out of a survey of the area in connection with the post-war planning of the county. Frank Mears, who would produce the *Regional Plan for Central and South-East Scotland* and who was undertaking a survey of Peebles for the burgh council in connection with its post-war housing scheme, was approached and agreed to undertake a survey of the county.[14]

---

[13] Scottish Borders Archive, P/CD/1/8, Meeting of Peeblesshire County Council, 12 December 1940.

[14] SBA, P/CD/1/9, Meeting of Peeblesshire Town Planning Committee, 15 September 1942.

Frank Mears commenced work on the survey of the county in January 1943 but, although surveys of Peebles, Innerleithen, Walkerburn and other villages had been carried out, considerable dissatisfaction was expressed by the Town Planning Committee in early 1944 at the lack of progress on any definite proposals for the county. Perhaps Frank Mears was concentrating on his regional plan for central and southeast Scotland. A great deal of time was taken up updating the OS base maps and a lack of transport had inhibited survey work. In April 1944, B. Mottram, the architect carrying out the survey work, was provided with a 7hp Austin car and the Regional Petroleum Officer was approached to sanction a supply of petrol.[15] However, it would be another year before preliminary proposals were set out for postwar housing in Peebles and Innerleithen. A report on housing in the landward area to sustain farming after the end of the war identified the requirement for 446 houses to meet the needs of agricultural workers and an ageing population.[16] It would be May 1946 before Frank Mears produced his report and draft plan for Peeblesshire for consultation with Peebles and Innerleithen burgh councils. However, following the enactment of the Town and Country Planning (Scotland) Act 1947, which included the requirement to prepare development plans, it was decided to start afresh and Jack Baillie, the newly appointed County Planning Officer of neighbouring Midlothian County Council, took over responsibility for producing the county development plan. Frank Mears's plan, on which doubts had been expressed about a number of proposals for Peebles and Innerleithen, was ditched.[17]

The County Surveyor, A. Anderson, was appointed Planning Officer for the county in February 1944 and made responsible for advising on the determination of applications under the 1943 Act. There was a rash of applications in Peeblesshire for the erection of prefabricated houses in Peebles and Innerleithen by the respective burgh councils to tackle the acute housing shortage resulting from six years of inaction during the war years. As the number of planning applications increased, thoughts turned to staffing and the council reluctantly decided in November 1948 to enter into an arrangement with Midlothian County Council whereby the staff of that council's planning department would take over the

[15] SBA, P/CD/1/10, Meeting of Peeblesshire Town Planning Committee, 14 April 1944.
[16] SBA, P/CD/1/10, Meeting of Peeblesshire Town Planning Committee, 29 May 1945.
[17] SBA, P/CD/1/12, Meeting of Peeblesshire Town Planning Committee, 16/17 August 1948.

responsibility of advising on planning applications. Accordingly, Jack Baillie also took over responsibility for advising the county clerk on planning applications.[18]

Selkirk County Council's Town and Country Planning Committee met for the first time on 28 October 1943 but it was at the second meeting on 18 January 1944 that it appointed its first chairman and conducted its first business.[19] There was pressure from Selkirk Town Council for it to have the powers and duties under the 1943 Act to make planning schemes and determine applications for Interim Development Certificates within the burgh but the SoS rebuffed this idea as being 'contrary to the spirit of the time'.[20] SCC agreed to employ John C. Hall, architect of Galashiels, to advise the county clerk on applications for Interim Development Certificates. Only six applications were received in 1944, submitted by Selkirk and Galashiels town councils for the erection of temporary housing on various sites. Proposals for local authority housing at Forest Gardens/Balmoral in Galashiels and Philiphaugh in Selkirk to accommodate incoming workers were granted approval in the 1940s.[21] A survey of the whole county commenced in 1944. The Edinburgh Architectural Association had undertaken a preliminary survey of Galashiels Burgh in 1943 for the DHS and the burgh surveyors of Galashiels and Selkirk were asked to undertake a comprehensive survey of their respective burghs and John C. Hall undertook the survey of the landward area.[22]

Roxburgh County Council's Planning Advisory Committee first met on 2 February 1944. The county architect provided planning advice to the county clerk. The new Planning Advisory Committee was soon approving major housing developments in Jedburgh and Hawick proposed by the respective burgh councils to provide much-needed rented housing; at Headrig in Jedburgh and at Silverbuthall in Hawick where forty-eight acres of land at Burnfoot was identified for

---

[18] SBA, P/CD/1/12, Meetings of Peeblesshire Town Planning Committee, 5 November 1948 & 4 February 1949.

[19] SBA, S/CD/1/16, Meetings of Selkirkshire Town and Country Planning Committee, 28 October 1943 & 18 January 1944.

[20] SBA, S/CD/1/16, Meeting of Selkirkshire Town and Country Planning Committee, 28 April 1944.

[21] SBA, S/CD/1/17, Meetings of Selkirkshire Town and Country Planning Committee, 25 August 1944 & 14 March 1945.

[22] SBA, S/CD/1/16, Meeting of Selkirkshire Town and Country Planning Committee, 3 May 1945.

post-war housing.[23] John A. W. Grant, Architect and Chartered Town Planner, with offices in Rutland Square, Edinburgh was engaged to undertake a survey of the county and prepare a planning scheme.[24]

Berwickshire County Council established its Town and Country Planning Committee in June 1944 to deal with the first applications for Interim Development Certificates under the 1943 Act. T. D. Anderson, from the council's Roads Department was appointed Planning Officer. He had no qualifications in town and country planning and only a typist to assist him. Minor applications were dealt with by the county clerk, in consultation with the planning officer. T. D. Anderson was also charged with undertaking a survey of the county, apart from Eyemouth Burgh where the burgh surveyor was asked to undertake this task.[25] The DHS, concerned at the lack of progress on the survey of the county, met the council in March 1946 and suggested that additional staff be appointed to undertake this work and recommended the appointment of two planning assistants and a draughtsman. However, the council considered that the size of the county did not warrant such a large department and was content with its planning officer and typist in support. Over the next year, the DHS made further attempts to persuade the council to enlarge its staff but, with only an average of five applications for Interim Development Certificates a month, the council was not persuaded.[26]

IMPLEMENTING THE TOWN AND COUNTRY PLANNING (SCOTLAND) ACT 1947

The recommendations contained in the Barlow, Scott and Uthwatt reports produced during the Second World War indicated that a complete overhaul of the planning system was required to allow reconstruction after the war. The 1947 Act sought to give effect to the recommendations contained in these reports. It heralded a new era and introduced a universal requirement to obtain planning consent for development. It was the foundation of the modern town and country planning system. According to Sir Desmond Heap, expert on planning law and author

---

[23] SBA, R/CD/1/76, Meeting of Roxburghshire Planning Advisory Committee, 23 March 1944.

[24] SBA, R/CD/1/76, Meeting of Roxburghshire Planning Advisory Committee, 2 February 1944.

[25] SBA, B/CD/1/125, Meeting of Berwickshire Town and Country Planning Committee, 12 June 1944.

[26] SBA, B/CD/1/125, Meeting of Berwickshire Town and Country Planning Committee, 11 March 1946.

of the seminal book *An Outline of Planning Law*, originally published in 1949: 'It is impossible to exaggerate the importance of July 1, 1948, for the 1947 Act contained some of the most drastic and far-reaching provisions ever enacted affecting the ownership of land (which term includes buildings), and the ability of an owner to develop and use his land as he thinks fit.'[27]

The Act gave wide ranging planning powers to the four county councils in the Scottish Borders: as well as the power to approve or refuse development proposals, they must prepare development plans; they could also carry out redevelopment themselves and they could use compulsory purchase powers to buy land and make it available for development by developers. The Act also extended the provisions relating to amenity: to the preservation of trees and woodlands, buildings of special architectural and historic interest and the control of outdoor advertisements.[28]

The Act also took away the right to financial compensation for a refusal of planning permission and provided for the acquisition by the local authority of a proportion of the betterment value arising from an approval of planning permission. Thus, if an agricultural field was approved for housing, the developer would pay the agricultural value to the owner and the added development value would be paid to the government, who would share it with the planning authority. The capital accrued would be invested in new roads, infrastructure, parks and other amenities. However, this section of the Act was never fulfilled; landowners were not prepared to sell land at existing value and the Labour government did not enforce the compulsory purchase powers in the Act. On its election in 1951, the Conservative government repealed this section of the Act and so all increases in land value as a result of the grant of planning permission went straight to the landowner or developer, less a small element of capital gains tax.[29]

During the 1950s there was a progressive failure to achieve the high expectations of planning. In the early 1950s unemployment remained low as the traditional industries of coal mining, shipbuilding and textiles experienced a post-war boom. As a consequence, the government failed to act on the Barlow Report's recommendations for the re-distribution of industry and population. The economic boom slowed down in the

---

[27] Heap, D., *An Outline of Planning Law* (London: Sweet & Maxwell, 1963 [4th edn]), p. 12.
[28] Cherry, G. E., *The Evolution of British Town Planning*, pp. 144–145.
[29] Cherry, G. E., *The Evolution of British Town Planning*, p. 153.

second half of the 1950s and the basic economic structures of the regions, with their inherent imbalance and dependence on 'problem' industries, remained. In Scotland, the focus was on New Towns, with the designation of Cumbernauld New Town in 1955 and town developments under the Housing and Town Development (Scotland) Act 1957, which enabled overspill agreements between Glasgow and local authorities such as Grangemouth, Hamilton and Haddington. Little attention was paid, at government level, to the plight of peripheral rural areas such as the Scottish Borders.

Consideration was given in 1947 to the establishment of a joint planning advisory committee for the counties of Berwickshire, Roxburghshire and Selkirkshire to jointly appoint a consultant to prepare a comprehensive plan for future development in the Central Borders, as suggested in Sir Frank Mears's *Regional Plan for Central and South-East Scotland*. It was considered at the time that Peeblesshire was more closely related to Edinburgh and the Lothians than to the Central Borders. Architect F. W. B. Charles, a partner in Sir Frank Mears & Partners, who had taken the lead in the *Central and South-East Scotland* study, was approached to act as Planning Consultant to the Joint Committee for Roxburghshire, Selkirkshire and Berwickshire.[30] However, after producing a paper setting out his proposals (and costs), it was decided, in view of the progress that was being made on preparatory surveys in Roxburghshire and Selkirkshire, not to proceed with such an appointment and the four councils proceeded to prepare individual development plans in accordance with the 1947 Act.[31]

Thus, in the Scottish Borders, the planning system was centred round the preparation of development plans and 'development control'. There were a number of recurring themes: the difficulties of staffing, the time taken to prepare the county development plans; and the administration of development control.

Staffing

Whilst PCC utilised the services of Midlothian County Council's planning department, staffing was a major issue for Selkirk, Roxburgh and Berwickshire County Councils. In Selkirkshire, John C. Hall was

---

[30] SBA, R/CD/1/76, Meeting of Roxburghshire Planning Advisory Committee, 22 July 1947.

[31] SBA, R/CD/1/76, Meeting of Roxburghshire Planning Advisory Committee, 27 October 1948.

given authority to employ additional staff to carry out the statutory duties required by the 1947 Act and two draughtsmen were appointed in December 1948; a young George Ovens from Selkirk and Harold Hudson from Edinburgh, primarily to assist with the preparation of the county's development plan.[32] On completion of the development plan in 1953, Harold Hudson sought pastures new and left for Midlothian County Council and George Ovens moved to Roxburgh County Council (RCC), to be replaced by Duncan Laing.[33] Throughout the 1950s there was only one dedicated member of staff, Duncan Laing, to support John C. Hall, the County Planning Officer, in providing advice on planning applications, which amounted to some 180 per annum. When Duncan Laing left for West Lothian in September 1957 and his position could not be filled, John C. Hall was given authority to utilise other staff within his practice on planning work.[34] Consequently, two people who would become well-known Border characters would emerge onto the Borders planning scene; Frank Entwistle, an architectural technician within John C. Hall's practice, who took over responsibility for development plan matters, and John Gray, who had been taken on as an apprentice draughtsman in December 1956 and would administer the development control function. Frank Entwistle's involvement in planning in Selkirkshire would continue until the reorganisation of local government in 1975, after which he would establish his own architectural practice. John Gray would become an established figure in planning in the Borders and would subsequently pursue a career with the Borders Regional Council (BRC) after 1975, eventually becoming a prime mover in the economic development of the region.

In Roxburghshire, George Ovens, poached from SCC was appointed Town Planning Draughtsman (with a car allowance for an 8hp car!) in May 1953 to work on the development plan.[35] (He would be promoted to Assistant Planning Officer with an increased car allowance for a 10hp car in May 1954.) He would rise to become Depute County Planning Officer by 1968 and would be appointed Depute Director of Planning and Development with BRC in 1975. In November 1953, a

---

[32] SBA, S/CD/1/21, Meeting of Selkirkshire Town and Country Planning Committee, 24 September 1948.

[33] SBA, S/CD/1/24, Meetings of Selkirkshire Planning Committee, 24 January 1952 & 7 May 1953.

[34] SBA, S/CD/1/29, Meeting of Selkirkshire Planning Committee, 15 October 1957.

[35] SBA, R/CD/1/72, Meeting of Roxburghshire Property & Works Committee, 5 May 1953.

planning assistant, Peter McGregor, was appointed to provide further assistance with development control matters.[36] Peter McGregor left for Kirkcudbright County Council in December 1957 and it would be two years before a replacement was found, which placed a great deal of work on the shoulders of George Ovens, who was also involved in the preparation of the development plan, until it was decided to fill the vacancy with an apprentice in the architects department on condition that he attend the part-time planning course at Edinburgh College of Art. Robert Turner was seconded to the planning department as planning assistant in April 1960.[37]

In Berwickshire, the council decided to merge the Planning Department with the Property & Works Department, which dealt with applications for building warrants, in 1949 and T. D. Anderson took up the post of head of the new department. Two members of staff were transferred from the council's Public Health Department to assist with the additional workload, but all planning matters remained the responsibility of T. D. Anderson alone.[38] In October 1950, having merged the committees, the council decided to split the Planning and Property & Works Department and T. D. Anderson was appointed Head of the Planning Department, with sole responsibility for dealing with the day-to-day activities of development control.

Preparation of county development plans

In Peeblesshire, following the appointment in 1948 of Jack Baillie, the County Planning Officer of Midlothian County Council, as County Planning Officer for Peeblesshire, surveys were carried out of Peebles and Innerleithen but it would be September 1952 before a draft development plan was produced for consultation with the Peebles and Innerleithen burgh councils.[39] There was considerable discussion on the road proposals for Peebles and the route for a town centre relief road, a by-pass for Innerleithen on the A72 and by-passes for West Linton and Carlops on

---

[36] SBA, R/CD/1/72, Meeting of Roxburghshire Property & Works Committee, 24 November 1953.

[37] SBA, R/CD/1/77, Meeting of Roxburghshire Planning Committee, 12 April 1960.

[38] SBA, B/CD/1/125, Meeting of Berwickshire Planning and Property & Works Committee, 21 March 1947.

[39] SBA, P/CD/1/16, Meeting of Peeblesshire Town Planning Committee, 5 September 1952.

the A702. The development plan was submitted to the SoS in June 1953 but not without objections to the road proposals in Peebles.

In Selkirkshire, there was rapid progress on the survey of Galashiels and Selkirk and the villages in the county and a draft development plan was produced for discussion with Galashiels and Selkirk Town Councils by October 1950.[40] Trunk road proposals were a significant issue, particularly in relation to the A7 through Galashiels, and it would be March 1953 before the County Development Plan was submitted to the SoS.

In Roxburghshire, progress on the preparatory survey of the county by the appointed consultant John A. W. Grant was slow; much time was spent on updating the out-dated 1:2500 scale OS Maps for the burghs (1921 editions for Hawick, Jedburgh and Kelso). There was little prospect of a development plan being prepared within the three years stipulated by the 1947 Act. As a consequence, the DHS voiced its concerns in a report on the future administration of planning in Roxburghshire, which suggested that the council should employ its own planning staff but the council was not persuaded.[41] It was December 1949 before an interim survey report was produced by John Grant.[42] With increasing dissatisfaction at the lack of progress on the development plan, it would be January 1953 before the council finally decided to employ staff in-house and gave authority to the County Architect to appoint an additional draughtsman to assist with the development plan.[43] At the same time, the council decided to dispense with the services of John A. W. Grant and the County Architect (Alastair M. Milne) was appointed County Architect and Planning Officer in March 1953.[44] Work on the development plan continued throughout the 1950s and it was 1957 before proposals maps for the burghs were finalised. Further delays would ensue, partly due to staffing shortages but also due to the time taken up by consultation with the respective burgh councils and it would be the end of 1960 before proposals maps for Hawick, Jedburgh, Kelso, Melrose and St Boswells/Newtown St Boswells were agreed. The Development Plan was submitted to the

[40] SBA, S/CD/1/23, Meeting of Selkirkshire Planning Committee, 4 October 1950.
[41] SBA, R/CD/1/76, Meeting of Roxburghshire Planning Advisory Committee, 30 June 1949.
[42] SBA, R/CD/1/76, Meeting of Roxburghshire Planning Advisory Committee, 8 December 1949.
[43] SBA, R/CD/1/72, Meeting of Roxburghshire Property & Works Committee, 27 January 1953.
[44] SBA, R/CD/1/72, Meeting of Roxburghshire Property & Works Committee, 17 March 1953.

SoS in December 1961 but not without continuing objections from Kelso and Melrose town councils.[45]

In Berwickshire, with little progress on a survey of the area, the DHS sought to persuade the council to appoint additional staff to undertake the preparation of the development plan but it would be July 1949 before two planning assistants were appointed and set to work on a survey of Eyemouth and Duns burghs.[46] Again, one of their first tasks was to bring the out-dated Ordnance Survey (OS) maps up-to-date, a major challenge for many planning departments at this time. In Berwickshire, the most recent edition of the 1:2500 OS maps was produced in 1908. In December 1949, after further pressure from the DHS, the council decided to appoint a consultant to prepare the development plan and, after interviewing three candidates, the council appointed architect/planner F. W. B. Charles, who had worked for Sir Frank Mears, and he quickly set to work.[47] Unfortunately for the two planning assistants, appointed by the council in July 1949, they were not required by the planning consultant who had his own team and they were duly given notice to quit in February 1950, after only nine months in the job.[48]

F. W. B. Charles produced progress reports at regular intervals throughout 1950 and 1951 on his survey of the area and draft plans for the burghs in the county; Eyemouth, Duns, Coldstream and Lauder, as well as Earlston and Chirnside.[49] However, he took increasing exception to changes to his proposals, which were agreed between the Planning and Property & Works Committee and the burgh councils, and in September 1953 he tended his resignation.[50] Subsequent approaches to J. & J. Hall, Architects of Galashiels, and to Frank Tindall, County Planning Officer of East Lothian Council, to undertake the preparation of the development plan proved fruitless and it would be January 1957 before

---

[45] SBA, R/CD/1/77, Meeting of Roxburghshire Planning Committee, 22 January 1962.

[46] SBA, B/CD/1/126, Meeting of Berwickshire Planning and Property & Works Committee, 14 July 1949.

[47] SBA, B/CD/1/126, Meeting of Berwickshire Planning and Property & Works Committee, 6 December 1949.

[48] SBA, B/CD/1/126, Meeting of Berwickshire Planning and Property & Works Committee, 8 February 1950.

[49] SBA, B/CD/1/126. There are regular, almost monthly, reports attached to the Minutes of Meetings of the Berwickshire Planning and Property & Works Committee from September 1949 to September 1951.

[50] SBA, B/CD/1/127, Meeting of Berwickshire Planning and Property & Works Committee, 14 September 1953 (see also letter of resignation dated 5 September 1953 attached as Appendix I).

Jack Baillie, County Planning Officer at Midlothian County Council (who was also overseeing planning responsibilities in Peeblesshire) agreed to take over the preparation of the development plan.[51] Harold Hudson, who had previously worked for J. & J. Hall on the development plan for Selkirkshire but was now employed by Midlothian County Council, would undertake the work. It would be December 1959 before a draft development plan was approved and December 1960 before the development plan was submitted to the SoS.[52]

Development control

During the 1950s, the number of planning applications received in the four counties gradually rose from a modest 500 per annum to 1,000 per annum by 1960. The planning legislation of 1947 was based on the principle that a planning application concerned only the applicant and the planning authority. There was, therefore, little involvement of the general public. Consultations were minimal; burgh surveyors would be consulted on applications in the burghs. Outwith the burghs, consultations would be restricted to the county surveyor and statutory undertakers, such as water and drainage authorities. Although applications required to be recorded in a register of planning applications, and were therefore a matter of public knowledge, there was no obligation to give any public notice or notify neighbours. The respective registers of applications amply illustrate the speed within which decisions were taken. These show that decisions took only a few days or weeks (the DHS expected applications to be decided within fourteen days!).[53]

There were a number of common issues throughout the four border counties. The vast majority of planning applications submitted in the Borders in the post-war period related to housing development by the local housing authorities, the burgh councils and the county councils, supported by the Scottish Special Housing Association (SSHA), which was established in 1937 to provide good quality social housing.[54]

---

[51] SBA, B/CD/1/128, Meeting of Berwickshire Planning and Property & Works Committee, 30 January 1957.

[52] SBA, B/CD/1/129, Meeting of Berwickshire Planning and Property & Works Committee, 16 December 1959 & B/CD/9: County of Berwick Development Plan 1958–1960.

[53] SBA, S/CD/9/1; B/CD/12/1; P/CD/30/1.

[54] The SSHA was abolished in 1989 as a result of the Conservative government's privatisation of housing and replacement by Scottish Homes. The 75,000 homes owned by SSHA in 1989 were transferred to housing associations and co-operatives

TOWN AND COUNTRY PLANNING BECOMES ESTABLISHED 39

At the end of the war, most attention was directed at the large towns and cities where slums remained a major problem and through enemy action nearly half a million houses had been destroyed or made uninhabitable. In many towns and cities, temporary accommodation was provided by prefabricated houses and, although they were only ever intended as a temporary measure, many outlived their life expectancy. The top priority for the post-war government was the provision of new council housing and 75 per cent of the houses constructed nationwide between 1946 and 1957 were local authority owned.[55]

In the Scottish Borders, new rented housing and the replacement of existing dwellings deemed to be below the tolerable standard and previously erected temporary housing (prefabs) was mainly focussed on Hawick and Galashiels. Overspill agreements were negotiated between both burgh councils and Glasgow Corporation to attract additional workers to meet the needs, particularly for female workers, of the traditional tweed and knitwear industries. In 1946, Hawick Town Council acquired Burnfoot Farm and between 1946 and 1960 almost 1,000 local authority houses were constructed at Burnfoot, where the SSHA also constructed over 200 dwellings. A primary school and small parade of shops was opened in 1952.[56] From 1952, both the SSHA and Galashiels Town Council constructed a substantial number of houses at Gala Policies (Forest Gardens/Balmoral), which had been earmarked for housing by the DHS in 1944, and at Wester Langlee.[57] New primary schools were provided at Balmoral (opened 1955) and Wester Langlee (opened 1958).[58] In Jedburgh, a large rented housing development was undertaken at Doom Hill to provide accommodation for workers in the expanding North British Rayon factory.[59]

Housing was also a significant issue within Peeblesshire. In Peebles, Peebles Burgh Council acquired twenty-six acres of land for housing at

between 1990 and 2005. See SDD Review of the Scottish Special Housing Association, National Audit Office, London: HMSO, 1986, Appendix 1, p. 16.

[55] University of the West of England, *The History of Council Housing* (Bristol: UWE, 2008).

[56] Roxburghshire County Development Plan: Survey Report, May 1958, pp. 222–225.

[57] SBA, S/CD/1/24, Meeting of Selkirkshire Planning Committee, 3 April 1952; see also, Register of planning applications, S/CD/9/1, Nos. 467, 654 & 945.

[58] SBA, S/CD/1/29, Meetings of Selkirkshire Planning Committee, 18 July 1956 & 14 November 1956.

[59] Roxburghshire County Development Plan: Survey Report, May 1958, pp. 182–183.

Kingsmeadows in 1946 with a capacity of some 200 houses.[60] It would be 1952, however, before a housing layout, including a new secondary school, was approved and construction commenced.[61] Planning permission was granted in 1950 to Innerleithen Burgh Council for the development of seventeen acres of land at The Pirn for some 150 houses with a site set aside for a new secondary school.[62] Over the next twenty years, this site would provide local authority and SSHA housing to serve the needs of the textile industry in Innerleithen.[63] In Berwickshire, housing development was concentrated in the four burghs, particularly Eyemouth and Duns. Over three-quarters of the 1,000 dwellinghouses constructed in Berwickshire in the fifteen years 1945–1960 were rented houses built by the four burgh councils or the SSHA.[64]

There was little private housing development in the Borders in the post-war years, largely due to the severe shortage of materials and a restrictive borrowing policy. The private houses constructed during this period were mainly single houses built by local contractors. Only Peebles saw any substantial private housing development, concentrated south of the River Tweed at Frankscroft, Kingsmuir and Kingsmeadows; a reflection of its growing attraction as a retirement location and as a commuter settlement. The growth in car ownership and leisure activity during the 1950s had perhaps the greatest impact on the Scottish Borders.

An issue that would dominate planning in Peeblesshire for many years to come would raise its head; the proliferation of holiday huts, mainly erected and occupied by residents from Edinburgh and the Lothians on small areas of 'surplus' agricultural land and woodland strips. A report in 1949 describes the variety of structures (bus bodies, trams, caravans and huts) scattered throughout the county, including hut encampments at Peebles, Eddleston, West Linton and Carlops.[65] Subsequent reports describe the proliferation of individual structures

---

[60] SBA, P/CD/1/11, Meeting of Peeblesshire Town Planning Committee, 29 July 1946.

[61] SBA, P/CD/1/15, Meeting of Peeblesshire Town Planning Committee, 1 February 1952.

[62] SBA, P/CD/1/14, Meeting of Peeblesshire Town Planning Committee, 6 October 1950.

[63] SBA, P/CD/1/22, Meeting of Peeblesshire Town Planning Committee, 5 September 1958.

[64] Housing and Industry in Berwickshire Report, Berwickshire County Planning Department, 1974, p. 10.

[65] SBA, P/CD/1/13, Meeting of Peeblesshire Town Planning Committee, 2 December 1949.

at various locations along the A703 between Peebles and the county boundary at Leadburn and along the A702. However, reflecting the council's general attitude to intervention, enforcement action was only pursued on rare occasions. A joint Planning and Landward Health & Housing Sub-Committee was formed to tackle the issue in 1951 and a report in 1952 recommended that individual structures in the countryside should be discouraged and bus bodies and so on replaced by caravans or huts concentrated on specific sites, such as Hattonknowe near Eddleston, subject to the installation of a water supply and sanitary facilities.[66] It would be 1956 before the situation at Hattonknowe was formalised with the granting of planning permission for twenty units with planning permission for individual huts limited to five years to ensure that they were properly maintained.[67] A plan for the Glebe in Eddleston was agreed in 1959, based on a mix of caravans and huts, which should be painted green or brown with a fenced area on which toilet facilities would be provided.[68] A similar plan was prepared for the Soonhope site in Peebles.[69] Planning permission was also granted in 1959 for an additional hut site at Burnside Farm, Eddleston.[70]

The year 1950 saw the first reports on the illegal siting of buses, caravans and other structures in the Berwickshire countryside for use as holiday accommodation. A report on the Oxton area, north of Lauder, itemises twelve structures such as 'Engineless single deck bus, on wheels'; 'Three roomed wooden hut'; 'Railway carriage without wheels'; 'Double-deck bus on wheels'; 'Tramcar'; and 'Two-wheel trailer' located in fields and small enclosures close to the A68. The majority were owned by residents from Edinburgh, Dalkeith and mining villages in Midlothian.[71] Similar structures could be found at Hume, north of Kelso and scattered throughout the Lammermuir Hills. The illegal siting of railway carriages, shacks and other structures in various

---

[66] SBA, P/CD/1/15, Meeting of Peeblesshire Town Planning Committee, 4 April 1952.

[67] SBA, P/CD/1/19, Meeting of Peeblesshire Town Planning Committee, 3 February 1956.

[68] SBA, P/CD/1/23, Meeting of Peeblesshire Town Planning Committee, 19 May 1959.

[69] SBA, P/CD/1/23, Meeting of Peeblesshire Town Planning Committee, 5 June 1959.

[70] SBA, P/CD/1/23, Meeting of Peeblesshire Town Planning Committee, 4 September 1959.

[71] SBA, B/CD/1/126, Meeting of Berwickshire Planning and Property & Works Committee, 26 September 1950; Appendix I.

parts of the county prompted the county council to establish a Camping and Caravans Sub-Committee in 1953 with the aim of taking enforcement action to remove the illegal encampments and encourage bona fide mobile caravan sites in suitable locations.[72] However, these structures would continue to exist, with minimal maintenance and in a state of increasing decay, for a number of years until finally succumbing in the mid-1960s. In the late-1950s, as caravanning became a favourite form of holidaymaking, the first rumblings were heard about visitor pressure along the Berwickshire coast; at Coldingham Sands unauthorised car parking and the erection of increasing numbers of holiday huts caused erosion of the sand dunes.[73]

To meet the growing post-war demand for visitor accommodation in Peebles, Venlaw House was converted into a hotel in 1949 and both the Minden (Park) Hotel and the Langside Hotel were expanded in 1951.[74] Planning applications were submitted for tourism related proposals on the A7, including a proposed motel and petrol filling station (PFS) at Groundistone Heights between Hawick and Selkirk, a café and caravan site south of Teviothead and a similar proposal at Buckholm Corner north of Galashiels.[75] None came to fruition. The growth in leisure motoring was accompanied by the proliferation of illuminated and non-illuminated signs at PFSs, hotels and public houses, which increased rapidly as such businesses sought to attract the growing number of car-borne travellers. There was a plethora of applications for advertisements such as the ubiquitous 'John Player' and 'Senior Service' shop signs and illuminated Shell-Mex and Esso signs at garages. A proposal in 1957 to replace nine-feet-high red lettering stating 'WHIM HOTEL', painted on the hotel's roof, by six-feet-high neon tubing reading 'HOTEL' was an extreme example and refused consent. An appeal to the SoS was summarily dismissed.[76]

A number of advanced signs appeared for major hotels such as the Peebles Hydro. A sign at Newtown St Boswells at the junction of the

[72] SBA, B/CD/1/127, Meeting of Berwickshire Planning and Property & Works Committee, 8 April 1953.

[73] SBA, B/CD/1/128, Meeting of Berwickshire Planning and Property & Works Committee, 11 September 1957.

[74] SBA, P/CD/1/12, Meetings of Peeblesshire Town Planning Committee, 5 November 1948 & 7 December 1951.

[75] SBA, R/CD/1/77, Meeting of Roxburghshire Planning Committee, 27 September 1960.

[76] SBA, P/CD/1/21, Meetings of Peeblesshire Town Planning Committee, 3 May 1957 & 3 January 1958.

A68 and A6091 stating 'Peebles Hydro 25 miles' was one such example, which would cause continuing debate about its merits and its effect on visual amenity. It would remain in situ for almost thirty years. Another advertising the Marine Hotel in North Berwick, sited on the A68 at Earlston, would gain less sympathy with the Planning Committee, presumably because the hotel referred to was located outwith the Borders.[77] However, large signs for the Langside Hotel, north of Peebles, the Tweed Valley Hotel in Walkerburn, and the Black Barony Hotel and Horse Shoe Tearoom in Eddleston, were approved after some deliberation.[78] In a bid to control the proliferation of signs in the countryside, all four county councils designated the landward area of their respective counties as Areas of Special Control for Advertisements in the 1950s.[79] Nevertheless, unauthorised signs for PFSs, countryside cafés and hotels proliferated. Enforcement of the advertisement regulations was a cumbersome process and staffing shortages meant the control of advertisements would continue to be a significant issue throughout the 1950s and 1960s.

CONCLUSIONS

The county development plans for Selkirkshire and Peeblesshire were submitted to the SoS in 1953 but it would be December 1960 before the Berwickshire County Development Plan was submitted and December 1961 before the Roxburgh County Development Plan arrived in St Andrew's House in Edinburgh. In the Scottish Borders, reliance was put on the appointment of consultants, or in the case of Peeblesshire and Berwickshire, the use of qualified planners from the neighbouring authority, to produce the first development plans. In common with most authorities across Scotland, the first development plans took far longer than was intended and thus provided little guidance for development during the 1950s.

Staffing was a major issue in the 1950s. There were few qualified planners and the administration of development control in the Border counties, as in most other rural areas, was largely undertaken by other professionals and/or untrained technical staff. The difficulty of attracting

---

[77] SBA, R/CD/1/76, Meeting of Roxburghshire Planning Advisory Committee, 3 February 1949.

[78] SBA, P/CD/1/21, Meetings of Peeblesshire Town Planning Committee, 4 October 1957 & 1 May 1959.

[79] SBA, R/CD/1/76, Meeting of Roxburghshire Planning Committee, 21 March 1956.

suitable candidates would be a recurring problem until the mid-1960s when the profile of town and country planning in the Borders increased as the government's attention turned to the plight of rural areas such as the Scottish Borders.

In relation to development control, the main issues revolved around the replacement of sub-standard housing in the main towns and the provision of housing for incoming workers to support the traditional textile industry. Major housing developments commenced in Galashiels and Hawick with overspill agreements with Glasgow Corporation. Housing was also required to replace unfit housing in the countryside and provide for an ageing agricultural population in order to arrest the drift of population from the country to the town.

Demands on the planning system increased as a result of the growth in car ownership and leisure time. In Peeblesshire, the proliferation of holiday huts and other structures across the county tested the Town Planning Committee. The illegal siting of buses, caravans and other vehicles for holiday accommodation was also an issue in Berwickshire. The demand for camping and caravan sites in rural locations grew. With the increase in car ownership, there was an increasing demand for PFSs on the edges of towns and villages and in the countryside. Across the Scottish Borders, the proliferation of both illuminated and non-illuminated signs on commercial premises in towns posed problems, as did the growing number of advanced signs in the countryside advertising hotels and tearooms.

Throughout the 1950s, planning was largely a reactive process, with minimal interference from the council's planning committees in the control of development. It would be the early1960s, a period of great social, economic and political change, before planning came to the fore in guiding the direction of development in the Scottish Borders.

2

The First County Development Plans

INTRODUCTION

UNDER THE 1947 ACT it was the duty of every planning authority to carry out a survey of their area and, within three years of 1 July 1948, the date the Act came into force, prepare a development plan based on the survey and submit it for the approval of the SoS. Planning authorities were also under an obligation to review their development plans at five-yearly intervals and could put forward amendments for approval by the SoS at any time. The Midlothian County Development Plan, which included the Gala Water valley north of Bowland incorporating the villages of Stow, Fountainhall and Heriot, an area that would be included in the Borders Region in 1975, was submitted to the SoS in 1952, the first to be produced in Scotland, and approved in May 1955.[1] The Selkirk County Development Plan was approved by the SoS in April 1955 and the Peeblesshire County Development Plan in December 1955 but it would be February 1965 before the county development plans for Berwickshire and Roxburghshire received his approval.[2] Other than the Quinquennial Review of the Selkirk County Development Plan, approved in January 1968, which excluded Galashiels Burgh, there would be no other attempts to review the approved development plans; they would be modified as required by formal amendment to enable major developments not in accordance with the approved development plan to take place.

---

[1] SBA/1210/37/3, Midlothian County Development Plan, written statement (in 3 volumes), July 1956.
[2] SBA/1210/3, Selkirk County Development Plan, April 1955; SBA/1210/3, Peebles County Development Plan, December 1955; SBA/1210/4, Roxburgh County Development Plan, February 1965; and SBA/1210/5, Berwick County Development Plan, February 1965.

The 1947 Act stipulated that the development plan should indicate the manner in which the authority proposed that land in their area should be used and the stages by which any development should be carried out. Development plans had to include a survey report, a written statement summarising the authority's proposals, and a basic map defining the sites of proposed roads, public buildings and so on and allocating or 'zoning' areas of land for particular uses such as residential development, industry and open space. Regulations stipulated a wide range of details, from the contents of the survey report to the number and type of accompanying plans and the colours to be used to depict the different land uses.[3] Survey reports, based on an extensive survey of the local authority's area, were expected to be very comprehensive and cover such subjects as physical background (geology, relief, drainage, soils and climate), natural resources (mineral deposits, water and water power, inland fishing, scenic resources), population, agriculture and forestry, industry and employment, communications, public utility services, community facilities and housing. The reports of survey, in providing a comprehensive and detailed account of the principal physical and economic characteristics of the area, the size, composition and distribution of population, and the transport system, constitute a valuable source of information on the Scottish Borders during the first part of the twentieth century. Perhaps, the most onerous task was the updating of the OS base maps for the area, which in some cases were twenty or thirty years out of date. As has been described in Chapter One, the task of preparing the survey was the unenviable task of the first consultants employed by the county councils in the Scottish Borders and it is no surprise that up-dating the OS base maps and undertaking the survey of each county took several years.

As an example, the Roxburgh County Development Plan: Survey Report was more than 300 pages in length.[4] Half the report gave a detailed overview of the county as a whole, the other half related to the main towns; Hawick, Jedburgh, Kelso and Melrose. The report analysed the distribution and density of population, population change since 1801, age and gender structure and a population forecast for the future. It analysed agriculture by farming type, livestock, crops, markets, mechanisation, farm units and employment, and examined the structure of existing industry and its problems. Employment was analysed by

---

[3] Town and Country Planning (Development Plans) (Scotland) Regulations 1948 and Circular 40.

[4] SBA/1210/4, Roxburgh County Development Plan: Survey Report, May 1958.

age and sex and by travel to work areas. The communications section described the road network and its traffic use and included a detailed analysis of road accidents and black spots. An extensive account of community facilities listed all the trades and shops in the county, schools, medical and hospital facilities, playing fields, village greens and open spaces, cemeteries and allotments, camping and caravan sites, indoor recreational, cultural and entertainment facilities, ancient monuments and other visitor attractions. On housing, the number of houses in each settlement was categorised as being: (1) fit in all respects; (2) capable of being rendered fit economically; and (3) unfit, and the number of persons on the house waiting list was itemised. The regulations required a separate survey for each of the burghs and the survey report includes a chapter on Jedburgh, Hawick, Kelso and Melrose, and the two largest villages, Newcastleton and St Boswells/Newtown St Boswells. These separate chapters covered similar subjects: population, industry and employment, communications, public utility services, community facilities and housing. The burgh chapters included a use, age and condition survey of all the buildings in each settlement, which enabled areas of obsolete buildings to be identified for possible comprehensive redevelopment.

By comparison with the survey report, written statements were relatively brief, the Roxburgh County Development Plan: Written Statement amounting to fifty pages. A Proposals Map and a Programme Map, differentiating between proposals to be implemented within five years and those projected for the succeeding fifteen years, were required to accompany the written statement. Such maps were required of the whole county at a scale of one inch to the mile (1:63,360) with town maps at six inches to the mile (1:10,560) for the larger settlements. In the Roxburgh County Development Plan, this amounted to fourteen maps in all, two for the county and twelve town maps. Plans, printed on linen, had to be hand-coloured with special coloured inks by renowned paint supplier, Winsor and Newton; residential zones were coloured red-brown 3.1 and industry, purple 1.2. Hand-colouring was time-consuming but a necessary task for the ubiquitous draughtsman that every department possessed. As an expression of the views of the planning authority, the written statements and Proposals Maps provide an insight into the council's attitude towards development in the 1950s.

Although public consultation was limited by today's standards, the process required consultation with government departments, bodies such as the Agricultural Executive, Nature Conservancy Council and Royal Commission for Ancient and Historic Monuments in Scotland,

and with the bus and rail authorities and trade organisations, and of course the burgh councils. Particular difficulties could arise between the ambitions of the burgh councils and the county councils resulting in time-consuming dialogue.

THE MAIN THEMES OF THE DEVELOPMENT PLANS

There were a number of common themes running through the four county development plans produced by the Border counties: the maintenance of a stable population, the provision of housing for incoming workers for the textile industry, the replacement of unfit housing, industrial development and camping and caravanning. However, road proposals influenced by the growing dominance of the motor car took precedence over proposals for housing and industry. Scant attention was paid to the countryside. On Proposals Maps, most of the countryside, the landward area of county development plans, was uncoloured 'white land' where no development was proposed or envisaged.

Roads and transportation

Trunk road proposals were a significant issue in all the county development plans. The Ministry of Transport (MoT), which was responsible for trunk roads in Scotland at the time, proposed an A7 by-pass for Selkirk prior to the Second World War and, following the publication of the *Regional Plan for Central and South-East Scotland* in 1948, consulted both RCC and SCC on a new trunk road linking the A68 and the A7 between Newtown St Boswells and Galashiels involving a by-pass of Melrose and a new bridge over the River Tweed at Galafoot. Whilst SCC and Selkirk Town Council welcomed a by-pass for Selkirk, both SCC and Galashiels Town Council had concerns over the impact on Galashiels of the proposed new trunk road link between the A68 and the A7. Both the county council and the town council favoured an A7 by-pass to the west of Galashiels involving a new road from the A7 south of Galashiels, via Hollybush and Mossilee to cross the Gala Water and railway line at Wood Street and a re-connect with the A7 to the north of Galashiels at Torwoodlee. The MoT did not favour this expensive solution and also pointed out that such a route would not serve the traffic arriving at Galafoot along the new link road from the A68. Much to the consternation of the county council and the town council, the MoT proposed a new road through the centre of Galashiels along Bank Street, requiring a portion of Bank Street Gardens, an important green area, and thence to the rear of High Street and Island Street, to connect with Wood Street and cross the Gala Water to Torwoodlee. Meetings between the county council, the MoT and the DHS ensued throughout 1950 and 1951. The view of the MoT prevailed, however, and the county development plan submitted to the SoS in March 1953 included a new road through the centre of Galashiels.[5]

A large number of other road improvement schemes were proposed to bring trunk roads up to a standard to cope with the ever-increasing traffic volumes. Responsibility for trunk roads in Scotland was transferred from the MoT to the Scottish Office in 1956 and became the responsibility of the Scottish Home Department (SHD). Development plans incorporated proposals by the SHD's Road Division for improvements to the A1, A68, A7 and A702. The whole length of the A1 in Berwickshire was identified for improvement through realignment, principally at Lamberton near the border with England, at Reston, Grantshouse and Cockburnspath. A by-pass for Ayton was proposed beyond the twenty-year period of the development plan. On the A68, improvements were proposed between the English border at Carter Bar and Jedburgh, at Newtown St Boswells, where a by-pass was proposed east of the village alongside the railway line, which was still in operation, with a new Leaderfoot Bridge over the River Tweed to replace the narrow historic existing bridge. By-passes were proposed for Earlston and Lauder with the realignment of the A68 between Earlston and Lauder. Other improvements were proposed at the Carfraemill junction with the A697 and on Soutra Hill, near the border with Midlothian. The realignment of the A7 was proposed at various locations, south of Hawick, between Hawick and Selkirk and north of Galashiels. In Hawick, the A7 passed along the High Street and the development plan proposed the widening of the A7 at the western end of the town centre, at Sandbed/Tower Knowe, combined with improvements to the junction with the Newcastleton Road (B6399), requiring the demolition of Tower Mill and a number of adjoining properties. In Peeblesshire, by-passes were proposed at Carlops, West Linton and Dolphinton on the A702, the trunk road linking Edinburgh with the A74 south to Carlisle.

BCC was of the view that the A697 route between Newcastle and Edinburgh via Morpeth, Coldstream and Greenlaw, which joined the A68 at Carfraemill, north of Lauder, would be likely to become a more important road, nationally, as road transport grew. It campaigned for

[5] SBA/1210/2, Selkirk County Development Plan, April 1955.

the road to be designated a trunk road and pressed for a by-pass to Coldstream. Various routes for a by-pass were examined, together with Northumberland County Council, but little agreement was reached; indeed, Northumberland County Council was concerned that trunking the A697 might impact on proposed improvements to the A1 in Northumberland. BCC favoured a by-pass to the west of Coldstream involving a new bridge over the Tweed. However, following a formal objection from Northumberland County Council and meetings with the MoT and the SHD's Roads Division, the council decided to retain reference to the need for a by-pass in the development plan but not to define the route. Reference to the possible trunking of the A697 was removed from the approved development plan.

Proposed improvements to east–west routes included the realignment of the A6105 at various locations between Berwick-upon-Tweed and Earlston on the A68. In Duns, a by-pass to the north and east of the town centre was proposed linking Newtown Street and Bridgend. Improvements were also proposed to the A698 at various locations between Coldstream and Kelso, between Kelso and the junction of the A698 with the A68 at Bonjedward, and between Bonjedward and the A7 at Hawick. Far-reaching roads proposals were made for Kelso in the submitted Roxburgh County Development Plan, including a new road from the A698 east of the town centre to the south of the abbey to the Tweed Bridge, the widening of Kelso's historic Tweed Bridge and a new road through Springwood Park to connect with the A698 west of Maxwellheugh. In addition, the plan also included the widening of various town centre streets to allow the easier passage of traffic through the town centre. This involved the demolition of a considerable number of residential and commercial properties. As elsewhere in the Borders, accommodating the projected increase in traffic took precedence over maintaining the character of the region's historic towns. In Melrose, in addition to the new A68–A7 link road, which by-passed the town to the south, a new road was proposed around the town centre to take traffic out of Melrose Square. Other related improvements included the widening of the B6360 through Gattonside and the widening of the B6361 through Newstead 'affecting several properties, which are generally in poor condition'. In the early 1960s, nothing stood in the way of road improvements. Not surprisingly, objections to these proposals were received from Kelso and Melrose town councils and, following a public inquiry in November 1962, the development plan approved in February 1965 was subject to certain modifications, including the removal of the proposed improvements to the A698 through Kelso and the proposals for new roads through Melrose. A working party was recommended for Kelso to consider the town's future growth potential and the future road pattern.

Emphasising the priority given to an improved east–west link between the Central Borders and the west of Scotland, by-passes were proposed for Innerleithen and Walkerburn on the A72 between Galashiels and Peebles, and west of Peebles at Skirling. There was considerable debate over road proposals within Peebles itself. Proposals, inherited from the Mears Plan, included a new road to the east of the town centre passing through the East Station Goods Yard to connect the A703 with the A72 and a new road round the north side of the town centre from the north end of Northgate to the A72 at the east end of the Old Town, incorporating the widening of the Old Town westwards involving the demolition of property. The Railway Executive expressed concerns about the designation of a 60-ft wide corridor for a new road through the goods yard at the East Station. Although Peebles West Station, south of the Tweed, closed to passengers in 1950, the Peebles West Goods Depot continued in use, connected by a seven arch skew bridge over the Tweed to Peebles East Station, until August 1959. Peebles East Station would not close until February 1963. Following a number of meetings, the road proposal was amended to a 20-ft wide one-way road along the town side of the East Station Goods Yard with the possibility of a two-way road beyond the twenty-year period of the plan.

Following the receipt of a number of public objections, the proposed new road around the north side of the town centre between the north end of Northgate and the east end of the Old Town was deleted from the plan, as was the possibility of a two-way road through the East Station Goods Yard beyond the twenty-year period of the plan. However, the widening of the Old Town, requiring demolition of some forty properties (houses and shops) on the north side, was retained, as was the proposed one-way road from the north end of Northgate to the A72 Edinburgh Road through the station yard. Thus, the A72 east–west route would continue to pass along the High Street and over the Cuddy Bridge and then along Old Town. Recognising the growing attraction of Peebles to Edinburgh residents, a number of improvements were proposed between Peebles and Leadburn on the A703 connecting Peebles with Edinburgh, and a by-pass was proposed at Romanno Bridge on the A701, which connected Moffat with Edinburgh.

Maintaining a stable population

The first county development plans were rather conservative in their approach to tackling the long-term decline in population. The Selkirk County Development Plan was based on maintaining a stable population in the landward area with small increases in Galashiels and Selkirk; with a target 1973 county population of 22,253 compared with a 1951 population of 21,724.[6] The Roxburgh County Development Plan was prepared on the basis of no overall change in population between 1951 and 1982 (a 1982 target population of 45,500 compared with a 1951 population of 45,557).[7] It was based on maintaining the landward population at around 18,000 persons with the population of the burghs largely unchanged; Hawick (16,400), Jedburgh (5,000), Kelso (4,100) and Melrose (2,100). The impact of the loss of population on rural services was recognised in the development plan; for instance, some twenty primary schools had been closed in the landward area between 1945 and 1955.[8] However, there were few positive proposals for the landward area; only a vague policy of encouraging a diversity of employment and the maintenance and improvement of facilities and amenities in the villages. In Peeblesshire, it was expected that the county population would change very little in the short term from its 1953 level of 14,600 persons; a population increase of approximately 1,000 people over the twenty-year period 1953–1973 was proposed. It was anticipated that the landward population would remain stable.[9] In Berwickshire, the population of the county had been declining steadily from a peak of 36,613 in 1861, largely as a result of changes in agricultural practices. Nevertheless, the county development plan was, optimistically, based on the assumption that the government population estimate for 1957 of 23,700 persons could be maintained.[10] It was anticipated that the landward population would continue to decline but that an increase in the population of Duns, Eyemouth, Coldstream, Earlston and Chirnside could be achieved to compensate for this loss, if new industries could be attracted to these towns.

---

[6] SBA/1210/2, Selkirk County Development Plan, April 1955.
[7] SBA/1210/4, Roxburgh County Development Plan, approved 1965 (4 volumes).
[8] SBA/1210/4, Roxburgh County Development Plan: Report of Survey, 1958, pp. 127–129.
[9] SBA/1210/3, Peebles County Development Plan, December 1955 (3 volumes).
[10] SBA/1210/5, Berwick County Development Plan, February 1965.

Housing provision

In relation to housing provision, development plans were very much focussed on the redevelopment of sub-standard housing areas, the replacement of temporary prefabricated housing and allocating sites for the provision of local authority rented housing for incoming workers in the main towns. In Galashiels, a number of obsolete housing areas were identified for redevelopment for housing; Church Square and the Croft Street area. The Ash Street/Mill Street/Wheatlands Road area, occupied by temporary prefab housing, was allocated for industry, as was the King Street/Queen Street area. In Roxburghshire, there were almost 500 temporary houses in Hawick, Jedburgh and Kelso identified for redevelopment. In Hawick, several areas of sub-standard housing close to the town centre were identified for redevelopment: Allars Crescent, Dickson Street, Princess Street, Garfield Street, Langlands Place and Lothian Street. Areas of prefabricated houses at Bankend in Jedburgh and Spylaw Road, Maxwellheugh in Kelso were identified for industrial development. In the landward area, it was estimated that about 366 general needs houses were required, in part to replace 150 obsolete farm cottages and 125 temporary houses.

Greenfield sites for local authority rented housing were identified in Galashiels; at Balmoral and Wester Langlee (with a new primary school at each location). In Selkirk, local authority housing was concentrated at Bannerfield. In Hawick, major allocations were made for local authority housing at Silverbuthall and Burnfoot. Large areas of land for local authority housing were allocated at Howdenburn in Jedburgh and at Abbotseat and Maxwellheugh in Kelso. In Peebles, land at Kingsmeadows and Edderston Road was allocated for local authority housing. In Innerleithen, it was considered that the site of the former Pirn House and grounds would accommodate all the burgh's rented housing needs, including a new school. In Berwickshire, provision was made for sites for local authority housing in the largest settlements; Eyemouth, Duns, Coldstream, Lauder, Earlston and Chirnside.

In the 1950s, with full employment, more people bought their own home and ran a car. In the expectation that there would be an increasing demand for private housing as the economy rebounded after the end of economic restrictions, including rationing, which only fully ended in 1954 (petrol rationing ended in 1950), the county development plans allocated substantial areas of land for private housing. In Galashiels, sites for private housing were allocated at the Ladhope Estate and along the A7 Abbotsford Road at Binniemyre, Sunningdale and Brunswickhill.

In Hawick, a number of sites for private housing were allocated, principally at Heronhill and Wilton Hill/Wilton Dene. Land was allocated for private housing at Blair Avenue, Jedburgh and between Shedden Park and Edenside Road and at Springwood Bank in Maxwellheugh, Kelso. In Peebles, private housing was concentrated south of the river, at Kingsmuir, Frankscroft and Kingsmeadows. In Innerleithen, land below Caerlee Hill at St Ronan's Terrace was allocated for private housing. In Berwickshire, land was allocated for private housing in Eyemouth, Duns, Coldstream and Lauder. A novel idea in the Berwick County Development Plan was a major proposal for housing in the grounds of Foulden House at the small village of Foulden, where a residential development of some 150 houses with an estimated population of 450 persons, would form a new village. Foulden, only one mile from the Scottish border and close to Berwick-upon-Tweed, was considered to have potential for private development. Nothing would come of this novel idea although, in due course, some private housing would eventually be built in Foulden. Elsewhere, it was not envisaged that there would be a demand for housing in the landward area. Only houses for agricultural and forestry workers were allowed outwith villages.

Industrial development

The county development plans depended largely on the retention of existing industrial sites for the expansion of existing firms. In Galashiels, only one small area at Wheatlands, occupied by temporary prefab housing, and an area of sub-standard housing in the King Street/Queen Street area, both sites situated within primarily industrial areas, were allocated for new industry. A similar situation applied in Hawick, where only one new area, the Wellington Road/Wellington Place area was designated for industry, requiring the demolition of 280 unfit houses. In Selkirk, with an expansive industrial area along the valley of the Ettrick River, a greenfield site was allocated for industrial expansion at the north end of the riverside area. The development plan also proposed a new access to the A7 to improve access to this area. Jedburgh presented a special problem after the collapse of the North British Rayon Factory in 1956 with the loss of 500 workers. Many now travelled out of the town, mainly to Hawick. New industries were required, therefore, to fill the vacuum created by the loss of the rayon factory and a large site at Hartrigge was allocated for industry to accommodate the expansion of L. S. Starrett, an American company manufacturing precision instruments, which opened its factory in Jedburgh in 1958. In Kelso, the only site allocated was an area of sixty temporary houses at Spylaw Road, Maxwellheugh, to be removed and the site developed for industry.

In Peebles, the Peebles County Development Plan made extensive industrial allocations; twenty-two acres of land at South Parks and six acres on Rosetta Road for development in the longer term. In Innerleithen, land on Traquair Road between the railway line, which was still operational in 1955, and the proposed A72 by-pass was identified for industrial use and an area north of the railway line, west of Traquair Road, was allocated for other business uses. In Berwickshire, a large area of land at Acredale Farm, Eyemouth was allocated for industry and sites also identified in Duns, Coldstream, Lauder, Earlston and Chirnside. A new deep-water entrance to Eyemouth harbour was proposed together with improved harbour facilities for the fishing industry.

The countryside

Post-war government policy was based on the principle that a prosperous agriculture was strategically necessary and would also provide the best means of preserving the countryside. Nevertheless, in both Roxburgh and Berwick county development plans, concerns were expressed at the loss of hedgerow trees as a result of agricultural activity, mainly related to arable farming, and policies set out to encourage the replanting of hedgerow trees and shelterbelts, with grant assistance. Development plan policy also supported continued afforestation and re-afforestation. Although large areas were covered in commercial forestry, the Forestry Commission was encouraged to consider further areas for afforestation. It was considered that forestry could play an important part in maintaining the rural population and in encouraging ancillary industries (attitudes to forestry practice would change).

In county development plans, most of the landward areas (those areas outwith the burghs) were uncoloured 'white land' where no development was proposed, mineral working being the main exception. In the Border counties mineral working was an important activity and the county development plans reflected this. In Peeblesshire, mineral working had been a substantial industry in the county since the 1930s and there were a number of sand and gravel workings and quarries spread throughout the county, some with planning permission for further extensions to workings. There were large mineral working allocations in the north of the county at Shiplaw and Nether Falla (for sand and gravel working). Roadstone quarries were located at Edston, west of Peebles, near Horsburgh Castle and at Milkieston, near Eddleston.

A large area (1,200 acres) east of Carlops adjoining the county boundary with Midlothian was allocated for open cast coal working. In Roxburghshire, major sites were allocated in the landward area for stone quarrying at Dunion Hill, near Jedburgh and for sand and gravel working near Eckford. There were fourteen small quarries and mineral workings distributed around Berwickshire.

In Scotland, though a Scottish Committee, the Ramsay Committee, recommended the establishment of five national parks in 1945, no national parks were designated under the National Parks and Access to the Countryside Act 1949 (the St Mary's Loch area of the Scottish Borders was one of three areas on the reserve list). However, the designation 'Area of Great Landscape Value' (AGLV) was established in the 1947 Act. Within AGLVs, the primary objective was conservation and enhancement of landscape quality and the individual character of the area. Government policy at the time was centred on protecting areas of mountains and moorland, established lowland estates and river valleys, as well as specific beauty spots, from inappropriate development but there was little guidance on the selection of areas for designation or the policy implications of designation. The whole of Peeblesshire and substantial parts of Berwickshire, Roxburghshire and Selkirkshire were designated AGLV in the various county development plans, amounting to 60 per cent of the four counties. The designation of AGLVs was, largely, symbolic and inherently negative, restricting development in the countryside, and it was not until the Countryside (Scotland) Act 1967 that positive measures were set out for countryside planning

The Peebles County Development Plan recognised the existence of holiday hut sites in the county. Such holiday camps, as they were called, were located at Carlops (West Mains), West Linton (Tarfhaugh), Eddleston (Hattonknowe and The Glebe) and Peebles (Soonhope). Hutting originated between the two world wars when landowners made land available on lease to ex-servicemen and families from deprived inner-city areas to erect temporary dwellings, primarily to enjoy the benefits of the countryside and fresh air at weekends and during the summer holidays. The hutted developments in Peeblesshire originated in the 1930s and were considerably expanded after the Second World War. The structures varied from wooden huts to touring caravans and included old railway carriages, trams and buses. There were little or no facilities; no running water and no water closets. They were meant to be used for limited periods only, but were gradually used for longer periods, some eventually becoming permanent residential accommodation. The development plan recognised their existence as a valuable recreational facility for those inhabitants of Edinburgh and surrounding towns who lived in congested urban surroundings. Individual huts were also scattered throughout the northern part of the county, on small areas of land not fit for agricultural use, sometimes in woodland. The development plan indicated that the county council was prepared to allow huts of good standard to be erected outwith the designated sites, in small numbers, on sites which would not be injurious to amenity or create a nuisance from a public health point of view. The Berwickshire County Development Plan took an opposing view and discouraged the sporadic siting of weekend and holiday huts and caravans throughout the landward area but supported the creation of holiday camps in addition to the existing caravan sites at Eyemouth and Coldingham. Little was said in the Selkirk and Roxburgh county development plans about caravan site policy for the landward area, presumably because this was not an issue. However, specific allocations were made in the Roxburgh County Development Plan for a caravan and campsite at Melrose and Jedburgh, both burghs being recognised as tourist centres.

UPDATING THE DEVELOPMENT PLANS

Planning authorities were under an obligation to review their development plans at five-yearly intervals but could put forward amendments for approval by the SoS at any time. In addition, under Article Eight of the Town and Country Planning (General Development) (Scotland) Order 1948, a planning authority could, subject to the approval of the SoS, grant planning permission for development not in accord with the development plan. In Peeblesshire, thoughts turned to a review of the development plan, approved in December 1955, in 1962, prompted by the closure of the railway line through Peebles and the renewed prospects of a town centre by-pass. In addition, the growing demand for houses in Peebles for both retirement and for the increasing number of commuters to Edinburgh required further land for housing to be identified.[11] However, additional allocations for housing were pursued through formal amendments to the development plan; town council and SSHA housing continued at Kingsmeadows Gardens, south of the Tweed. Private housing was concentrated at Edderston Road and Gallowhill. The East Station Yard was allocated for an eastern town centre by-pass, car parking and bus station; the March Street marshalling yard for industry; and the West Station Yard for residential and

---

[11] P/CD/1/26, Meeting of Peeblesshire Town Planning Committee, 26 July 1962.

commercial use, including a hotel. It was decided not to pursue a formal revision of the development plan in 1966.[12]

Following the publication of the Central Borders Study in 1968, which recommended a population increase of 800 persons in Peebles by 1980 (from 5,500), Peebles Burgh Council commissioned a 'Growth Plan' for Peebles.[13] This report, based on a population increase of 1,500 persons, proposed substantial allocations of land for housing and industry and made radical proposals for the central area; through traffic would be removed from the High Street by the construction of a new northern relief road from the north end of Northgate to the Old Town, involving the demolition of a considerable number of properties. The report recommended the designation of the High Street/Old Town area as a conservation area and identified areas for redevelopment; Damdale Mills and Cuddyside for housing, and an area to the north of the High Street for car parking (possibly multi-storey). In response, the county council asked Jack Ballie, the County Planning Officer, to examine the potential for growth in Peebles and in March 1969, he produced an 'Urban Structure Plan' along the lines recommended by the Planning Advisory Group (PAG) in 1965.[14] This plan set out future areas for growth with major expansion for both housing and industry to the north of the town, opposite Rosetta House, and the redevelopment of the Cuddyside area north of High Street, which proved to be a very contentious issue. No action would be taken on either of these plans for the future growth of Peebles.

In Innerleithen, SSHA housing continued at the Pirn.[15] Planning permission was granted for private housing on twenty acres of land at St Ronan's Terrace in 1965 and at Leithen Valley Nurseries in 1970.[16] In response to the growing pressure for development at West Linton, which was becoming increasingly attractive to Edinburgh commuters, private housing development was approved at Bogsbank Road in 1968

---

[12] P/CD/1/30, Meeting of Peeblesshire Town Planning Committee, 17 June 1966.
[13] SBA/1210/36/4, Royal Burgh of Peebles Growth Plan, 1969.
[14] SBA/1210/36/6, Royal Burgh of Peebles Proposed Urban Structure Plan, 1969; see also *The Future of Development Plans*, Report of the Planning Advisory Group, London, HMSO, 1965, Figure 1.
[15] P/CD/1/28, Meetings of Peeblesshire Town Planning Committee, 5 February 1965 & P/CD/1/33, Meetings of Peeblesshire Town Planning Committee, 6 March 1970.
[16] P/CD/1/28, Meetings of Peeblesshire Town Planning Committee, 5 March 1965 & P/CD/1/33, Meetings of Peeblesshire Town Planning Committee, 6 February 1970.

and Linton Bank Drive in 1970.[17] A large-scale housing development at 'The Hiddles' was granted planning permission in principle in 1972, subject to the preservation of the line of the proposed West Linton by-pass.[18] Although this development would never come to fruition, it prompted the formation of the West Linton Residents Association, which would play a pivotal role over the next twenty years in articulating the views of the local community against the expansion of the village.[19] At Eddleston, Prestoplan commenced the development of an eight-acre site at Bellfield in 1973 but any further extension of the village to the north was resisted.[20] Housing would be a major issue for the new BRC with pressure for more development at West Linton and Eddleston.

Staffing difficulties curtailed any work on the revision of the Roxburgh County Development Plan and changes to the development plan, approved in February 1965, including additional allocations of land for housing and industry, were achieved through formal amendments. The development plan would be the subject of some twenty-four such amendments submitted to the SoS between 1965 and 1972.[21] In Hawick, for instance, a large area at Burnfoot was allocated, by way of amendment to the development plan, for industrial development in February 1966, and land at Overhall was allocated for housing development in November 1966.[22] Additional land for housing was identified at Crumhaughhill and Havelock Nurseries by way of amendments to the development plan, approved in April 1968.[23] A large area of land (fifty acres) was allocated at Stirches for some 600 houses, primarily SSHA housing, through an amendment approved in February 1971.[24] In Jedburgh, additional land was allocated for industry at

---

[17] P/CD/1/32, Meetings of Peeblesshire Town Planning Committee, 5 January 1968 & 1 November 1968, and P/CD/1/33, Meetings of Peeblesshire Town Planning Committee, 5 December 1969.

[18] P/CD/1/36, Meetings of Peeblesshire Town Planning Committee, 11 August 1972.

[19] P/CD/1/36, Meetings of Peeblesshire Town Planning Committee, 27 April 1973.

[20] P/CD/1/37, Meetings of Peeblesshire Town Planning Committee, 7 December 1973.

[21] SBA/1210/7, Roxburgh County Development Plan Amendments.

[22] Amendments 4 & 6 to the Roxburgh County Development Plan, SBA/1210/7/7, 17 February 1966 & 23 November 1966.

[23] Amendments 10 & 11 to the Roxburgh County Development Plan, SBA/1210/7/7, 30 April 1968.

[24] Amendment 16 to the Roxburgh County Development Plan, SBA/1210/7/7, 26 February 1971.

Hartrigge/Oxnam Road in 1971, to be occupied in due course by Mainetti, manufacturers of coat hangers.[25] In Kelso, land was allocated for industry at Pinnaclehill, to be subsequently developed as a major industrial area.

In Berwickshire, housing provision was dominated by the local housing authorities. Almost 1,100 of the 1,400 houses completed during the period 1945–1966 were built by the four burgh councils and the county council, over 700 of which were in the six main settlements, Eyemouth, Duns, Coldstream, Lauder, Earlston and Chirnside. Private housing development was slow to develop with few substantial housing developments other than small-scale infill housing in the towns and villages, and single houses in the countryside.[26] Amendments to the county development plan, approved in February 1965, allocated a substantial area of land for local authority and private housing, respectively, at Deanhead and Barefoots in Eyemouth and for industrial development at Acredale. Land for industry was also allocated in Duns, at the former Station Yard, and in Coldstream.

In Selkirkshire, the quinquennial review of the development plan, approved in April 1955, commenced in 1958. By 1960, draft proposals for Galashiels and Selkirk had been prepared and were circulated for consultation with the respective burgh councils but it was October 1964 before the quinquennial review was eventually submitted to the SoS. Notwithstanding the aim of the approved development plan to maintain a stable population in the landward area with small increases in Galashiels and Selkirk, the population of the county continued to fall to a figure of 21,052 in 1961 compared with a 1951 population of 21,724. Accordingly, the objective of the quinquennial review was:

> To bring to a halt, in the first instance, the continual and steady depopulation of the County and then by introduction and provision of facilities to encourage new industries to develop within the Burghs, and the existing industries to modernise and expand, in order to raise the population to a reasonable and realistic figure necessary to create a thriving industrial and commercial community within a balanced environment providing adequate housing and a full range of social, commercial and recreational facilities and at the same instance to protect the amenity and character of the area from despoilment.

---

[25] Amendment 18 to the Roxburgh County Development Plan, SBA/1210/7/7, 26 February 1971.

[26] SBA/1210/34/7, report entitled 'Housing and Industry', County Planning and Development Department, January 1974, Table 4, p.10.

Trunk road improvements remained significant proposals in the quinquennial review, including the proposed Selkirk by-pass, and improvements to the A7 between the Roxburghshire county boundary and Selkirk, and between Selkirk and Galashiels to connect with the A68 link road (the A6091) at Galafoot. In relation to the A7 through Galashiels, the county council continued to press for a by-pass to the west of the town, but the Scottish Office would not agree to the inclusion of such a by-pass in the quinquennial review and the route for the A7 through Galashiels remained unchanged from that proposed in the approved development plan. Elsewhere, the disused railway line through Clovenfords was identified as the preferred route for the realignment of the A72 as opposed to the by-pass to the south of the village proposed in the approved development plan.

In Galashiels, additional sites were identified for local authority housing at Mossilee and Hollybush to the south-west of Gala Policies, and at Langlee Policies (Wester Langlee). Land at Gala Policies was identified for a new secondary school and for public open space, to replace Victoria Park, which was allocated for housing. Land for private housing was identified at various sites; principally at Buckholm Corner. Land at Netherdale was identified for a new Technical College. In the town centre, the area between Channel Street and Overhaugh Street, previously identified for car parking, was allocated for redevelopment for commercial/residential uses. Stirling Street was identified as the location for a new car park and bus station (instead of the Station Yard). In Selkirk, sites were identified for local authority housing and private housing. In the town centre, the area of obsolete housing bounded by Market Place, Tower Street, Back Row and Kirk Wynd was identified for redevelopment for housing.

The quinquennial review was approved by the SoS on 26 January 1968.[27] However, in approving the quinquennial review, the SoS excluded Galashiels Burgh. The reasoning behind this is explained in his approval letter, as follows:

> In view of the proposals for the expansion of the Burgh of Galashiels and the Central Borders contained in the Government White Paper 'The Scottish Economy 1965–1970' and as study of the subject is currently being carried out for the Secretary of State for Scotland, the Quinquennial Review of the proposals for the Burgh of Galashiels as contained in the Development Plan 1955 has been postponed.

[27] SBA/1210/8, Selkirk County Development Plan Quinquennial Review, January 1968.

The White Paper on the Scottish Economy, published in 1966, and the subsequent report, *The Central Borders; A Plan for Expansion*, published in 1968, which had been prepared in draft at the time the SoS approved the quinquennial review, presented significant changes to the government's attitude to development in the Scottish Borders and particularly in the Central Borders.[28] The Central Borders Plan proposed a significant increase in the population of Galashiels (by over 5,000 persons to a figure of 17,500 by 1980).[29] Consequently, the SoS determined that proposals for the Burgh of Galashiels would be the subject of review through the establishment of a Galashiels Technical Working Party of local authority and SDD officials.[30]

Accordingly, development in Galashiels throughout the 1960s and early 1970s proceeded through formal amendments to the approved development plan. Through such amendments, large land allocations for housing were made in Galashiels at Gala Policies and Wester Langlee, north of the Melrose Road, which would be the major area for expansion of the town.[31] Development at Wester Langlee comprised housing by both the burgh council and SSHA, with associated facilities such as a church, shops, public house and community centre. A new secondary school (Galashiels Academy) was constructed within Gala Policies and playing fields at Netherdale were developed for the new technical college (the College of Textiles, now part of Heriot-Watt University). In the town centre, a new bus station was established in Stirling Street in 1967, removing buses from the Market Square and preparing the way for its pedestrianisation. Planning permission was granted in 1968 for the redevelopment of the area bounded by Channel Street, Overhaugh Street and the Market Square for retail units.[32] In Selkirk, the redevelopment for local authority housing of the area to the south of the town centre,

---

[28] Scottish Development Department, *The Central Borders: A Plan for Expansion: Vol. 1, Plan and Physical Study*, HMSO: Edinburgh, 1968; Scottish Development Department, *The Central Borders: A Plan for Expansion: Vol. 2, Economic and Geographical Report*, HMSO: Edinburgh, 1968.

[29] Scottish Development Department, *The Central Borders: A Plan for Expansion: Vol. 1, Plan and Physical Study*, p. 7.

[30] Scottish Development Department, *Galashiels: Second Report by the Galashiels Technical Working Party*, January 1973.

[31] See Amendments 2 (Netherdale), December 1963; Amendments 3 & 4 (Gala Academy), June 1964; Amendments 10 (Wester Langlee), July 1968; and Amendment 11 (Gala Policies), September 1968.

[32] Galashiels History Committee, *Galashiels: A Modern History*, pp. 36–37.

bounded by Market Place, Kirk Wynd, Back Row and Tower Street, was accomplished in four phases between 1966 and 1975.[33]

Private housebuilding in the Scottish Borders was limited, provided by a small number of local building firms; for instance, James Clyde (Builders) in Peebles, J. S. Crawford and Murray & Burrell in the Central Borders. Colvin-Smith, a housebuilder from Newcastle, who commenced house construction in Clovenfords in the late 1960s was perhaps the first housebuilder from outwith the Borders. Substantial areas of land were allocated for private housing through amendments to the approved county development plans in anticipation of an increased interest in private housing development. This was particularly evident in the Central Borders where planning permissions were granted for private housing in Galashiels and nearby settlements, such as Melrose, Gattonside and Bowden, many to one particular house-building firm, J. S. Crawford, which would subsequently become a major player in private housebuilding, with housing sites throughout the Borders, including Hawick, Jedburgh and Kelso. However, the vast majority of these sites remained undeveloped, or only partially developed, for many years, indeed well into the 1980s.

CONCLUSIONS

There are a number of common themes running through the four county development plans, principally, the need to resist rural depopulation. The optimistic assumption of the development plans was that any loss of population in the landward areas would be offset by growth in the burghs scattered throughout the Scottish Borders. However, this would be largely dependent on the fate of the region's traditional industries, textiles and agriculture. Large allocations of land for rented housing were made in order to accommodate the incoming workers it was hoped would be attracted to the region. Comprehensive redevelopment was seen as the answer to the legacy of obsolete and unfit housing in Hawick and Galashiels. In the event, the population of the region declined by over 10,000 people between 1951 and 1971; from 110,000 to less than 99,000 persons. However, the position in the burghs was one of relative stability with some growth in Galashiels, Kelso, Peebles and Eyemouth during

---

[33] S/CD/1/35, Meetings of Selkirkshire Town and Country Planning Committee, 6 December 1961; also S/CD/9/1, Selkirkshire Register of Applications, refs. 2563, approved 22 July 1966.

the 1960s. Nevertheless, this growth was insufficient to compensate for the continuous net out-migration suffered by the region as a whole.

Perhaps the most striking feature of the development plans was the emphasis on major road proposals for the trunk roads through the Borders, the A1, A68, A7 and A702, involving by-passes for almost every town and village along these routes. Major improvements were also proposed for the principal road network linking the main towns and for the centres of Galashiels, Hawick, Kelso and Peebles, involving road widening that required the demolition of properties. In the countryside, the burgeoning of countryside leisure and recreation with increasing leisure time and the growth in car ownership was reflected in proposals for camping/caravan sites in addition to the holiday hut sites in Peeblesshire and Berwickshire.

The county development plans, updated by formal amendments and augmented by non-statutory studies and reports would provide the framework for development decisions until the reorganisation of local government in 1975 and the introduction of the new development plan system of structure and local plans. As time went by, the county development plans would become increasingly out-dated and a source of conflict, but it would be December 1980 before these development plans were replaced by the Borders Region's first structure plan and 1981 before the first local plans, for Galashiels/Tweedbank, Eyemouth and Hawick, were adopted.

3

Planning and Development Become Inexorably Linked

INTRODUCTION

CHAPTER THREE EXAMINES THE growing influence of central government, the Scottish Office, on town and country planning in the Scottish Borders in the 1960s through the issue of the White Paper on the Scottish Economy, the decision to proceed with the Tweedbank Development and the revival of the regional approach to planning with the commissioning of the Central Borders Study. It discusses the local planning authorities' response to the Scottish Office's initiatives and describes how planning and development became closely intertwined in a bid to stem the long-term depopulation of the region.

Following the introduction by the Labour government of the 1947 Planning Act along with a raft of other pioneering legislation such as the New Towns Act 1946 and the National Parks and Access to the Countryside Act 1949, there followed a period of consolidation in terms of planning legislation with the election of the Conservative government in 1951. During the 1950s, the planning system became centred around development control. Development plans were little more than land use maps and, as the pace of change increased in the early 1960s, they become increasingly out of date and of diminishing value in determining the future direction of growth and development.

The early 1960s was a period of great social, cultural, economic and political change; the 'Swinging Sixties'.[1] The legacies of the Second World War, unrepaired and unfit housing and temporary prefabs, were replaced by burgeoning local authority housing schemes. New styles of architecture, using concrete and steel, became common. The established industries of shipbuilding, iron and steel, coal mining and the textile

---

[1] Sandbrook, D., *White Heat: A History of Britain in the Swinging Sixties* (London: Little Brown, 2006).

industry were in irreversible decline. In Scotland, the SHD, which had responsibility for the promotion of Scottish industry and the DHS, which had the responsibility for planning, were replaced by the Scottish Home and Health Department (SHHD) and the Scottish Development Department (SDD), which henceforth had the combined responsibility for planning and economic development. Most contemporary commentators attribute this decision of the Conservative government to the publication of the inquiry into the Scottish economy by the Scottish Council (Development and Industry) in 1961, which urged the creation of a new government department to combine the Scottish Secretary's statutory responsibilities for planning and the promotion of industry.[2] The white paper *Central Scotland: A Programme for Development and Growth*, published in November 1963, set out a positive programme for both physical and economic development in selected growth areas within the Central Belt.[3]

With the election of the Labour government in 1964, 'planning', in its widest sense, again took centre stage as an alternative to the 'stop-go' pattern of economic performance during the 1950s. The Labour government's ambitious *National Plan*, launched in August 1965, sought a higher rate of growth in the domestic economy to reduce the country's reliance on imports and solve Britain's balance of payments problem.[4] In Scotland, the plan aimed to create a significant increase in employment opportunities to reduce emigration from Scotland and proposed the creation of at least 130,000 jobs to offset those lost in older industries and stem depopulation. A housing programme of up to 5,000 houses per year, in support of industrial growth, would be provided by the SSHA, in addition to those built by the New Towns Corporations. Local authorities would also be encouraged to provide a wide range of housing to promote increased labour mobility. A major programme of motorway building and trunk road improvement was proposed, including improvements to the trunk roads through the Borders.

The White Paper, *The Scottish Economy 1965 to 1970: A Plan for Expansion*, published in January 1966, set out in more detail the government's plans for the expansion of the Scottish economy. The bulk

[2] Levitt, I., 'The Origins of the Scottish Development Department, 1943–62', *Scottish Affairs*, No. 14, Winter 1966, pp. 42–63.
[3] Scottish Development Department, *Central Scotland: A Programme for Development and Growth*, Cmnd. 2188 (Edinburgh: HMSO, 1963).
[4] Department of Economic Affairs (DEA), *The National Plan*, Cmnd. 2764 (London: HMSO, 1965).

of the effort would be concentrated in the Central Belt where four-fifths of the population and the bulk of manufacturing industry were located. Substantial development was proposed in North Ayrshire, Lanarkshire and Falkirk/Grangemouth and in the emerging New Towns of Cumbernauld, Livingston and Irvine. Elsewhere, development would be concentrated, north of the Central Belt, in the Perth–Dundee area, the Aberdeen area, the Beauly/Cromarty Firth area, Wick/Thurso and Fort William (this White Paper preceded the discovery of oil in the North Sea in 1969/1970). South of the Central Belt, the potential for development in Dumfries would be examined.

In relation to the Borders, the White Paper suggested that, in order to generate demographic and industrial recovery, some 25,000 people should be attracted to the 'Western Area' by 1980 at the latest; the catchment area of Galashiels, which included the whole of Selkirkshire and Peeblesshire and the western half of Roxburghshire. In the 'Eastern Area' – Berwickshire, the Kelso area of Roxburghshire and north Northumberland – the Development Commission would be tasked with stimulating new growth to arrest depopulation. New industrial enterprises should be attracted to the 'Eastern Area', in association with a local authority housing programme to meet the needs of new industry. Berwick-upon-Tweed was the natural focal point for this area and the Development Commission would establish a programme of development and assistance, including advance factories, at Berwick-upon-Tweed and other locations.[5]

The White Paper went on to say that the injection of 25,000 people into the 'Western Area', an area with limited resources, called for a novel co-ordinated programme and a planning consultant would be appointed to identify the main possible lines of development. In the meantime, in order to make an immediate start with housing development, provision was to be made in the Scottish housing programme for the construction of 1,000 houses east of Galashiels, south of the Tweed, to be completed by 1970. This development was very much seen as an extension to Galashiels rather than a separate entity. In relation to industrial development, the diversification of industry, with a male-employing slant due to the dominance of female employment in the textile industry, was the primary objective. Accordingly, potential industrial sites in Galashiels, Hawick, Selkirk and Jedburgh would be developed with the aid of a programme of advance factories.

[5] SBA/1210/6, Scottish Office, *The Scottish Economy 1965–1970: A Plan for Expansion*, Cmnd. 2864 (Edinburgh: HMSO, 1966), pp. 57–58.

Immediately following the publication of the White Paper, Professors Percy Johnson-Marshall and James Nathan Wolfe of Edinburgh University were appointed to carry out the study of the 'Western Area'. Their report *The Central Borders: A Plan for Expansion*, in two volumes, commonly referred to as 'The Central Borders Plan', was published in 1968.[6]

THE CENTRAL BORDERS: A PLAN FOR EXPANSION 1968

The authors of the report considered that the Central Borders represented a unique challenge to Scotland, to Borderers and to 'Planners'. They drew attention to the fact that, although the area was one of the most attractive parts of Britain, its appearance concealed a situation of population imbalance and decline. The principal concern was depopulation as a result of the increasing efficiency and falling manpower requirements of agriculture, and of an industry dominated by textile firms with an acute shortage of labour. The report states that further depopulation would seriously affect existing industries and force the closure of factories, which would accelerate the process of depopulation. The remit of the study was to prepare a plan for development in the Central Borders up to 1980, based on an increase in population of approximately 25,000 people (on an existing population of approximately 74,000 people), including the already committed development of 1,000 houses (4,400 population) on land east of Galashiels, a development that would in future be referred to as the Tweedbank Development.

The study proposed that the target population of about 100,000 by 1980 would be accommodated within a formal pattern of settlements, including Hawick, Galashiels, Selkirk, Peebles and Jedburgh, closely linked by good road communications. The proposed population increases in the main settlements are shown in Table 3.1.

The first phase of development (up to 1976) would see housing on existing allocated sites, and at Tweedbank, with new sites in Galashiels (at Wester Langlee, Kingsknowes and Mossilee), Hawick (Burnfoot), Selkirk (Sentry Knowe) and Newtown St Boswells, sufficient to accommodate a population of 16,467 persons. In phase two, residential

---

[6] SBA/1210/9, Scottish Development Department, *The Central Borders: A Plan for Expansion: Vol. 1, Plan and Physical Study* (Edinburgh: HMSO, 1968); Scottish Development Department, *The Central Borders: A Plan for Expansion: Vol. 2, Economic and Geographical Report* (Edinburgh: HMSO, 1968).

Table 3.1 Central Borders Study Projected Populations, 1966–1980

Settlement	1966 pop. [actual]	1980 pop. [projected]	Net increase
Hawick	16,206	17,900	1,694 (10.5%)
Galashiels	12,260	17,512	5,252 (42.8%)
Selkirk	5,634	6,625	991 (17.6%)
Peebles	5,548	6,348	800 (14.4%)
Jedburgh	3,645	5,045	1,400 (39.9%)
Innerleithen & Walkerburn	3,162	3,407	245 (7.7%)
Melrose	2,642	2,642	nil (nil)
Newtown St Boswells	2,060	12,185	10,125 (500%)
Earlston	1,200	1,450	250 (20.8%)
Tweedbank	nil	4,400	4,400
Rural areas	21,330	21,330	nil
Total (approx.)	73,687	98,844	25,157 (34.1%)

development would continue at Newtown St Boswells with additional sites at Galashiels (Mossilee/Hollybush) and Hawick (Stirches and Lynwood), sufficient to accommodate an additional population of 8,590 persons.

Hawick and Galashiels would continue as the largest settlements but the latter, with an extensive population catchment in support, would become the main shopping/commercial centre. The largest single population expansion would be in the Newtown St Boswells area, where a new town of 10,000 people was proposed. Jedburgh, Selkirk and Peebles would remain centres of employment with Peebles expanded as a conference centre. No growth in population was proposed for Melrose, which would develop as a cultural centre. The Tweed Valley near Innerleithen would become a major recreational area.

Industrial development would be concentrated on areas allocated for industry in the approved county development plans, but two new sites were identified for industry; an area of twenty-five acres at Burnfoot in Hawick and an area of sixty acres to the east of Charlesfield, near St Boswells. The site of the former munitions factory at Charlesfield had been identified in the *Regional Plan for Central and South-East Scotland* as a site for an assembly plant to build the thousands of prefabricated houses that were expected to be required for new housing development following the end of the Second World War. Although the council had the opportunity to purchase the site for development, no action was taken and the majority of the site returned to agriculture after the war. The Royal Navy Armaments Depot (RNAD) occupied a small part of the site and employed some 175 male workers until the early 1960s. The potential use of Charlesfield for industry would be a constant source of debate.[7]

Newtown St Boswells was identified for major expansion because substantial growth within the existing burghs was inhibited by physical limitations; Hawick, Galashiels, Selkirk and Jedburgh were essentially valley towns with relatively steep valley sides where the cost of building was prohibitive. In contrast, Newtown St Boswells possessed suitable level sites for housing and industrial development, there was good road access to the national road network and to the other centres of population, and it was on the railway line in 1968. Public utility services could be provided economically.

In relation to the road network, the study recommended that the proposed A68–A7 link road (A6091) to the south of Melrose and the new Tweedbank Development, including a new bridge over the Tweed at Galafoot, should be constructed as soon as possible. Major trunk road improvements should be concentrated on the A68 and the A7 south of Hawick. Improvements should also be made to the A698 between Hawick and the A68, to the A699 between St Boswells and Kelso, to the A72 between Galashiels and Peebles and to the A703 between Peebles and Edinburgh. The A7 north of Hawick should be treated mainly as a tourist route with commercial traffic from Carlisle using the A698 and A68 from Hawick to Edinburgh. The report recommended that the previous proposal for improvements to the A7 through Hawick should not be pursued and the widening of Cuddy Bridge and the Old Town in Peebles should be resisted.

Other recommendations included a new District General Hospital on a site between Galashiels and Melrose close to the A68–A7 link road to replace the out-dated Peel Hospital, a Second World War service hospital for military casualties, taken over by the NHS in 1948 for civilian use.[8] It would be January 1969 before there was the first indication of the prospect of a new District General Hospital in the Central Borders, when the SDD requested the views of RCC on the use of a site at Huntlyburn, Melrose, situated immediately south of the railway line (still in use).[9] The subsequent purchase of this site would be the subject of a compulsory purchase order because of an unwilling landowner and

---

[7] SBA, R/CD/1/76, Meeting of Roxburghshire Planning Advisory Committee, 8 April 1947.

[8] For a summary of the recommendations, see SBA/1210/9, Scottish Development Department, *The Central Borders: A Plan for Expansion: Vol. 1, Plan and Physical Study*, pp. 7–8.

[9] R/CD/1/78, Meetings of Roxburghshire Planning Committee, 20 January 1969.

it would be after local government reorganisation in 1975 before any progress was made on this proposal.

CLOSURE OF THE WAVERLEY ROUTE

The North British Railway line, the Waverley Route, from Edinburgh to Hawick was opened in 1849, with the remainder to Carlisle opened in 1862, and nicknamed the Waverley Route after the popular Waverley Novels written by Sir Walter Scott. Throughout its lifetime, the Waverley Route only achieved moderate commercial success.[10] Returns from the line's intermediate stations were meagre, particularly south of Hawick. Its severe gradients required double-heading (the use of two engines) along some stretches, which were difficult to maintain in winter. Journey times between Edinburgh and London were appreciably slower than its competitors, the West Coast and East Coast lines. The line depended very much on cross-border passengers and traffic generated by the textile industries of Galashiels, Selkirk and Hawick. As road transport began to expand in the 1930s, passenger numbers dropped and passenger services on the branch lines stopped: passenger services to Lauder ceased in 1932; to Jedburgh in 1948; Duns and Selkirk in 1951; Hexham in 1956 and Peebles in 1962. After railway nationalisation in 1948, the need for two lines between Edinburgh and Carlisle was inevitably questioned.[11] The Caledonian Railway's main line from Edinburgh provided a faster connection and could be operated as a branch off the West Coast line between Carlisle and Glasgow. In March 1963, the British Railways Board published the Beeching report, *The Reshaping of British Railways*.[12] This showed that the section between Carlisle and Hawick fell into the lowest category of un-remunerative line, with a weekly patronage of less than 5,000 passengers. The Hawick–Edinburgh stretch fared little better, with between 5,000 and 10,000 passengers a week. The election of Labour in October 1964 did not stop the programme of Beeching closures, despite the party's manifesto commitment to halt major closures.

The proposal for the closure of the entire Waverley line and its twenty-four stations was issued by Barbara Castle, the Minister of Transport,

---

[10] Thomas, J. and A. J. S. Paterson, *Scotland: the Lowlands and the Borders, A Regional History of the Railways of Great Britain* (Newton Abbot: David & Charles, 1984).

[11] Mullay, Alexander J., *Rails Across the Border* (Stroud: Tempus, 1990), p. 81.

[12] Beeching, R., *The Reshaping of British Railways* (London: HMSO, 1963).

on 17 August 1966, closure to take place on 2 January 1967 if no objections were received. However, 500 objections were lodged with the Transport Users Consultative Committee (TUCC) within the allotted six-week period and a public hearing was held in Hawick on 16 and 17 November 1966.[13] The TUCC's report was submitted to Barbara Castle in December 1966 but it was April 1968 before Richard Marsh, the new Minister of Transport, decided that retention of the line could not be justified.[14] The report showed that passenger numbers between Hawick and Edinburgh had dipped by 30 per cent between 1964 and 1967, while car ownership in Hawick had more than doubled even though the local population had decreased by 10 per cent.[15] A separate study carried out in 1966 showed that, whilst some fifty women commuted to Hawick from Newcastleton daily by car or public transport (bus), less than twenty passengers per day boarded the train in Newcastleton.[16] In reply, those on the side of retention, which included David Steel, elected Member of Parliament at a by-election in 1965, argued that closure of the line at a time when government policy was to encourage industry to move to the Borders area would send the wrong message and asked the Minister not to reach a final decision until publication of the report *The Central Borders: A Plan for Expansion*. This was delivered to Willie Ross, the Secretary of State for Scotland, who opposed closure, on 19 April 1968 and, whilst concluding that the economic well-being of the region depended on good transport links with Edinburgh, it was nevertheless ambivalent on the need for the Waverley Route and its recommendations concerned improvements to road transport rather than rail. Consequently, the official decision to close the line was announced to the House of Commons on 15 July 1968. A petition against the closure with almost 12,000 signatures, organised by Madge Elliot, a Hawick housewife, supported by David Steel, was to no avail. The line closed on 6 January 1969.[17] Freight services between Edinburgh and Hawick continued until 25 April 1969. The closure was particularly felt in Hawick and Newcastleton. However, at the time, economics was stacked against the retention of the line.

[13] Spaven, D., *Waverley Route: The Battle for the Borders Railway* (Edinburgh: Argyll, 2012), pp. 50–52.
[14] Ibid., p. 55.
[15] Ibid., p. 59.
[16] SBA/1210/38/13, Newcastleton (Castleton Parish) Rural Planning Study, Edinburgh College of Art, 1966.
[17] Cattle, Alan G., 'Waverley Route Finale', *Railway World*, Vol. 30, No. 347, p. 169.

Track lifting was complete by late 1972. The whole of the route through Galashiels would be subsequently utilised as a walkway, with the station yard developed for industry, health centre and car parking. RCC would purchase the track bed between Galashiels and St Boswells, the whole length of the line within the burgh of Hawick and Newcastleton Station Yard.[18] Subsequently, that part of the route between Tweedbank and the A68 would be utilised for the Melrose by-pass. The viaduct over the Teviot in Hawick was dismantled in September 1975 and the route of the railway line would be used for a new road bridge and road (Mart Street) and the station yard developed for leisure use.[19]

It is difficult to assess the real impact of the loss of the Waverley line on the efforts to stem depopulation and revitalise the economy of the region. The additional bus services laid on by Eastern Scottish as a condition of closure were more frequent than the train service but the journey time from Edinburgh to Carlisle was 50 per cent longer. The residents of Hawick and particularly Newcastleton felt cut off from the rest of the region. Whilst there continued to be anger and regret at the loss of the railway, which meant that there was no railway station in the Borders, there was a general acceptance of the situation with future planning in the 1970s and 1980s concentrated on improving the road system within the region and the road links north and south. Economic development would thrive during this period. It would be almost thirty years before the pressure group, the Campaign for Borders Rail, was founded (1999) to advance the project to re-open the section between Edinburgh and Galashiels/Tweedbank.

THE TWEEDBANK DEVELOPMENT

In pursuance of the White Paper, *The Scottish Economy 1965 to 1970: A Plan for Expansion*, the SoS invited RCC in 1966 to amend the development plan to enable the development of 1,000 houses and industry on land south of the Tweed between Galashiels and Darnick.[20] Following a public inquiry in June 1967 into objections to the proposed amendment by the principal owners of the land, the Hamilton family of Lowood, and others, the Seventh Amendment to the County Development Plan, which

---

[18] R/CD/1/79, Meetings of Roxburghshire Planning Committee, 27 November 1970.
[19] Amendment 23 to Roxburgh County Development Plan, SBA/1210//7/7, approved May 1973.
[20] SBA/1210/6, Scottish Office, *The Scottish Economy 1965–1970: A Plan for Expansion*, Cmnd. 2864 (Edinburgh: HMSO, 1966), pp. 45–47 & pp. 57–58.

provided for the zoning of 147 acres of land for residential development, 45 acres for industry and 105 acres for special landscape treatment, was approved by the Secretary of State in April 1968.[21] However, progress was delayed as a result of the necessity for the compulsory purchase of the Lowood Estate and a number of legal challenges to the compulsory purchase order. As a result, ownership of the whole site (292.8 acres) was not transferred to RCC until September 1972.[22]

The Tweedbank Working Party, comprising representatives from RCC, SSHA, Scottish Industrial Estates Corporation (SIEC) and other organisations, was established in January 1968. In June 1969, the SSHA produced the first outline plan for the development but, because of the delays in acquisition of the land, it would be September 1972 before a master plan for the scheme was agreed by RCC.[23] The principal features of the scheme were:

1. 1,000 houses, the bulk to be provided by SSHA with an area reserved for approximately 200 private or co-ownership houses;
2. Approximately 30 acres for industry, which would accommodate some 500,000 square feet of floorspace and generate 700–750 jobs;
3. The A68–A7 link (the A6091) running along the south side of the development, initially 24 ft wide with provision for dualling if necessary, with two roundabouts to give access to Tweedbank;
4. A main distributor road through the development, 24 ft wide linking the two roundabouts on the A6091;
5. A two stream primary school accommodating approximately 240 pupils located in the centre of the housing area;
6. The local centre next to the primary school with provision for a library, community centre, shops, church hall, public house, car parking and other community facilities as may be required;
7. A public park, school playing field, boating lake and bowling green located near the local centre. Playing fields catering for football, rugby, hockey, athletics, tennis and other sports, located to the west of the industrial area;
8. Several large areas of tree planting, including an area alongside the A6091.

---

[21] SBA/1210/7/3, Report on objections into proposed Seventh Amendments to Roxburgh County Development Plan, 13 November 1967; SBA/1210/7/4, Report of decision on proposed Seventh Amendments to Roxburgh County Development Plan, 4 April 1968.

[22] R/CD/1/79, Meetings of Roxburghshire Planning Committee, Appendix to meeting dated 9 October 1972, pp. 282–292.

[23] SBA/1210/33/6, Report by SSHA for Tweedbank Working Party, June 1969.

A preliminary programme for the development envisaged work starting on the distributor road in March 1973 and the commencement of the first phase of houses in October 1973. It was optimistically suggested that the whole project would be completed by September 1977![24] However, phase IA of the housing by SSHA (103 houses) did not commence until 1974, quickly followed by phase IB (131 houses). Planning permission was granted for phases II and III in early 1975 and the purchase of the Lowood Estate was finally settled at a cost of £203,000.[25] Jeremy Ballantyne from Walkerburn opened the first factory on the industrial estate in September 1974. The construction of Tweedbank Lake (publicised as the second lake in Scotland after the Lake of Menteith but now known as Gunknowe Loch) commenced in 1975 together with the establishment of a walkway along the now disused railway line between Tweedbank and Galashiels town centre.

REACTION TO THE CENTRAL BORDERS PLAN

The remit of the Central Borders Plan was to prepare a plan for development in the Galashiels catchment area based on an increase in population up to 1980 of approximately 25,000 people (on an existing population of approximately 74,000), including the already committed development of 1,000 houses at Tweedbank. Elsewhere in the Central Borders, a 'new town' of some 10,000 people was proposed at Newtown St Boswells. The new 'village' at Tweedbank, with an estimated population of 4,400 persons, would be larger than a number of border burghs and would provide land for new industry to diversify the economy of the region. This development was welcomed by RCC although SCC saw it very much as a challenge to its plans for the expansion of Galashiels as the main centre of commerce in the Central Borders. However, as Tweedbank developed, even though it was located within Roxburghshire, it became more and more accepted as being part of Galashiels.

Excluding land allocated for housing in existing county development plans, which could accommodate an additional 5,000 people, housing land for only an additional 1,700 people (out of the total of 20,000) was identified in the Central Borders Plan for Hawick, Selkirk and Jedburgh. Not surprisingly, these town councils were not happy. There was also a strong body of opinion in Selkirk and Roxburgh County Councils

---

[24] R/CD/1/79, Meetings of Roxburghshire Planning Committee, 2 February 1973.
[25] R/CD/1/80, Meetings of Roxburghshire Planning Committee, 27 February 1975 & 24 April 1975.

against the proposed expansion of Newtown St Boswells. SCC wanted to see more development in Galashiels and Selkirk, and RCC favoured a more modest increase of 3,000 persons at Newtown St Boswells with an enlarged share for Hawick and Jedburgh.[26]

In response to the proposals in the Central Borders Plan, therefore, Roxburgh and Selkirk County Councils pursued plans for substantial growth in Hawick and Galashiels, respectively. RCC drew up its own proposals for the distribution of population and housing land amongst the communities in Roxburghshire.[27] The county council decided that efforts should be concentrated on expanding Hawick and Jedburgh and agreed 1980 target population figures for Hawick and Jedburgh of 23,000 (an additional 5,000 persons) and 6,000 (an additional 1,000 persons) respectively. Additional industrial land would also be identified in Hawick and Jedburgh. The Hawick Technical Working Party was established in 1967 to establish the capacity for additional housing to accommodate an additional 5,000 persons and reported in 1973 with proposals for some 140 acres of housing land on ten sites to accommodate 1,200 houses.[28]

In accordance with the SoS's decision on the quinquennial review of the Selkirk County Development Plan, the Galashiels Technical Working Party was established in March 1970 to assess the prospects of development and growth in the burgh to enable completion of the Galashiels component of the quinquennial review. The working party examined alternative routes for the A7 trunk road through Galashiels and the potential for the development of some twelve housing sites to accommodate the projected 5,000 population increase. The final report of the working party was published in 1973. Although it was hoped that the report would provide the basis for the comprehensive updating of the Galashiels Town Map in the county development plan, the impending reorganisation of local government meant that the future development of Galashiels was left in the balance as efforts were concentrated on implementing the proposals for Tweedbank.

However, as a result of severe delays in the acquisition of the Lowood Estate, the Tweedbank Development did not commence until 1974. Elsewhere, notwithstanding the strong efforts of the local authorities to

[26] R/CD/1/78, Meetings of Roxburghshire Planning Committee, 29 July 1968 & 17 September 1968.
[27] R/CD/1/78, Meetings of Roxburghshire Planning Committee, 24 October 1968 & 25 November 1968, including Report by County Planning Officer on consultations with town councils, pp. 226-246.
[28] SBA/1210/33/12, Hawick Technical Working Party report, 1973 (2 volumes).

Table 3.2 Projected and Actual Populations in the Central Borders in 1980/81

Settlement	1966 pop. [actual]	1980 pop. [projected]	1981 pop. [actual]
Hawick	16,206	17,900	16,697
Galashiels	12,260	17,512	13,314
Selkirk	5,634	6,625	5,829
Peebles	5,548	6,348	6,708
Jedburgh	3,645	5,045	4,168
Newtown St Boswells	2,060	12,185	2,203
Tweedbank	nil	4,400	1,000

attract industry to the area, aided by the SIEC (and subsequently, the Scottish Development Agency [SDA]), the very ambitious population targets in the Central Borders Plan proved difficult to attain. As shown in the table above, although the population of Hawick increased slightly during the period 1966–1980, it fell well short of the projected 17,900 persons in the Central Borders Plan and far below RCC's ambitious target of 23,000 persons. Whilst the population of Galashiels increased by over 1,000 persons during the period 1966–1980, it fell well short of the projected 17,512 persons. Only in Peebles did the increase in population exceed that projected in the Central Borders Plan, largely as a result of the provision of housing for commuters and the retired, rather than as a result of industrial development. Whilst the primary objective of the Central Borders Plan – a population of about 100,000 in the Central Borders by 1980 – was not achieved, nevertheless, the Central Borders Plan did concentrate the minds of the local authorities in the Borders and spur them on to adopt a more proactive approach to development in an effort to diversify the economy and stem depopulation.

ECONOMIC DEVELOPMENT

During the 1960s and 1970s fundamental changes took place in the woollen textile industry as a result of a shortage of labour, increasing competition, changes in fashion and lack of capital. The growth of knitwear as outerwear, which benefited Hawick, became serious competition to the woven sector. Nevertheless, the Galashiels mills continued to prosper and the shortage of labour was met by the transport of workers by bus into Galashiels from as far afield as Duns and Dalkeith. Some firms established out-working or branch factories elsewhere in the Borders, in Kelso and Eyemouth. In Selkirk, some ten or more weaving and spinning mills occupied the valley floor. Bernat Klein, a

Serbian textile designer who had established himself in the Scottish Borders in the 1950s and created designs for such couture houses as Coco Chanel, Dior, Pierre Cardin and Saint Laurent, obtained planning permission in 1970 for a design studio at High Sunderland, near Selkirk, designed by architect Peter Womersley, who had designed the Gala Fairydean Football Club stand and the RCC headquarters in Newtown St Boswells.[29]

In 1966, the Scottish Borders was included in the Development Area designation, which was expanded considerably and covered most of Scotland, within which special benefits were available from central government to firms moving into the region, or expanding or modernising an existing operation. In selecting areas for designation, consideration was given, not only to unemployment but also population change, migration and the objectives of regional policy, which benefited such areas as the Scottish Borders. The incentives introduced in 1966 included grants for new machinery and plant, loans, interest relief, the provision of factories for rent or sale, training assistance, tax allowances and help for transferred workers. However, the incentives were only attractive when compared with the ineligible areas, the south-east of England and the Midlands, and the Scottish Borders was surrounded by Development Areas. Indeed, the north-east of England and Lanarkshire, to the west, were Special Development Areas where greater incentives were available.

Development Area designation coincided with the publication of the government's White Paper, *The Scottish Economy 1965 to 1970: A Plan for Expansion*. As a result of the proposals for the 'Western Borders' in the White Paper and the subsequent Central Borders Plan, the county councils of Peebles, Roxburgh and Selkirk decided the time was right to co-ordinate their efforts and established the Peebles, Roxburgh and Selkirk Joint Planning Advisory Committee (JPAC) in December 1967; its purpose to advise individual councils on the up-dating of their county development plans and the steps to be taken to implement proposals for industrial development.[30] Although ostensibly established to advise on planning matters as well as economic development, the promotion of industry became the main concern of the JPAC. BCC, with Berwick-upon-Tweed Corporation, Northumberland County Council and Kelso Town Council, established the Eastern Borders Development

---

[29] S/CD/1/43, Meetings of Selkirkshire Town and Country Planning Committee, 9 September 1970 (application ref. no. 3338).

[30] R/CD/37/1, Peebles, Roxburgh & Selkirk Joint Planning Advisory Committee, 20 December 1967.

Association (EBDA) in June 1966 to promote economic development in the eastern Borders.[31] Despite the competition from adjoining areas, with the aid of the SIEC and the Development Commission, there was considerable success over the ensuing ten years in attracting industry to the region and creating jobs.

Comparisons have been made between central government's attitude to tackling the problems in the Scottish Borders (and Dumfries and Galloway) with that adopted in the Highlands and Islands where much more favourable economic incentives became available as a result of the establishment of the Highlands and Islands Development Board (HIDB). The HIDB was established by the Labour government under the Highlands and Islands Development (Scotland) Act 1965 to 'improve the social and economic future of the Highlands and allow the area to play a wider role in the UK economy'.[32] It was given the powers to acquire land as needed. It was chaired by Professor Robert Grieve, one of Scotland's leading post-war planners. Willie Ross, the Secretary of State for Scotland at the time stated 'Land is the basic natural resource of the Highlands and any plan for social and economic development would be meaningless if proper use of land were not part of it. Land and who owns it, is at the forefront of the "Highland problem" and an organisation with the power to acquire land is needed.'

As in the Scottish Borders, retaining population and increasing job opportunities were seen as the key issues in the Highlands and Islands. In a similar way to the Scottish Borders, forestry, tourism and manufacturing industry were seen as the main hopes for a secure future. The HIDB had considerable advantages over the Scottish Borders, with a capital grant of £150,000 per annum in 1966 and the powers to acquire land, undertake projects such as advance factories, provide advice and financial assistance to businesses. Although the local authorities' efforts in the Scottish Borders were supported by the government through the SIEC and the Development Commission (the SDA after 1975), they lacked the same powers to acquire land and this would prove a stumbling block to the development of industry in the region. Unfavourable comparisons would be constantly made between the incentives for attracting industry to the Highlands and Islands and those pertaining to that part of Scotland south of the Central Belt.

In the Scottish Borders, although the dependence of the textile industry on female labour was the catalyst for efforts to attract male-employing

---

[31] SBA/1210/37/6, Eastern Borders Development Association, 1966–1977.
[32] See Highlands and Islands Development (Scotland) Act 1965, HMSO.

industries, many of the industries attracted were drawn by the skills of the female workers employed in the textile industry. Special mention should be made of the electronics industry, with its roots in the Ferranti plant established in Edinburgh in 1943 to manufacture gyroscopic gun sights, which took full advantage of the skills of the female work force in the Borders. In 1961, Robert Currie, a process engraver in the printing industry, and Kenneth Mill, a businessman trained in electronics, joined forces to establish the Borders first electronics company manufacturing Printed Circuit Boards (PCBs) in a modest building on the High Street in Galashiels. In 1962, Currie & Mill moved to Abbotsford Mill in Huddersfield Street but their partnership only lasted two years. Currie bought out Kenneth Mill in 1964 and Exacta Circuits was born. Kenneth Mill started his own company, BEPI Electronics, at Galabank Mill on Wilderhaugh. Whilst Currie subsequently left Exacta to progress his career in the United States, Exacta continued to expand and in 1971 moved to Selkirk to occupy the first British factory custom designed for the manufacture of PCBs. Meanwhile, BEPI expanded its works at Wilderhaugh in Galashiels, eventually demolishing Galabank Mill and occupying a purpose-built factory on the site of the mill, the adjoining public baths and playing field. Over the succeeding years, BEPI and Exacta would spawn a range of electronics companies.[33]

It was November 1968 before the JPAC appointed a development officer, Alistair Bilton, who would spearhead the promotion of industrial development over the next six years through advertisement campaigns in the national and regional newspapers to attract new industries, particularly male-employing industries, to the region and attract key workers. However, the co-ordination of the marketing and promotion effort was not without its problems. Some difficulties were encountered with the burgh councils who undertook their own initiatives and, as a result of the perceived need for confidentiality, did not always liaise with the JPAC's development officer on business enquiries. Nevertheless, the JPAC had considerable success in attracting new industries to the region. With the help of the SIEC, advance factories of 10,000 sq ft and smaller nursery factories of 2,500 sq ft were constructed in Galashiels, Jedburgh and Selkirk. By June 1970, firms such as Sprague Electrics was established in Galashiels; L. S. Starrett in Jedburgh undertook a large-scale expansion in 1972 and Mainetti would establish a 60,000 sq ft factory manufacturing coat hangers. In the textile sector, the Edinburgh Woollen Mill established its factory/outlet in Jedburgh in 1970, Thule

---

[33] BRC/PD/4, *Electronics in the Scottish Borders,* Scottish Borders Council, 1988.

Knitwear was established in Jedburgh in 1971 and West of Scotland Home Industries moved into Langhaugh Mill in Galashiels. Several other small textile firms were also attracted to the area, 'poaching' workers from existing firms.[34]

In Selkirk, a number of mills expanded during the late 1960s and early 1970s: Yarrow Spinners erected a new worsted spinning factory and Gardiners erected a new tweed mill; Laidlaw & Fairgreave extended Riverside Mill and John Claridge (Forest Mill) expanded into a purpose-built factory adjacent to Linglie Mill. The station yard was acquired by the town council for industrial development in 1971 and nursery factories erected on the site and on Dunsdale Road. Two major developments established the North Riverside Area in Selkirk as a major employment area – Exacta Circuits built their new factory in 1971 and moved operations from Galashiels, and RP Adam (Arpal) opened a new production unit in 1973 and moved operations from Galashiels, manufacturing a range of cleaning products, with major export agreements with the United Arab Emirates, based in Dubai.[35]

The 1960s heralded a more proactive approach to planning and development in Peeblesshire. A sub-committee of the Town Planning Committee was formed in 1963 to consider the provision of factories in an effort to stem depopulation; there was low unemployment and local textile manufacturers were importing labour from Midlothian. An overspill agreement was made with Glasgow Corporation, which was going through a period of massive slum clearance, and efforts began to attract male-employing industries to complement the textile sector.[36] Peebles Town Council purchased the former March Street marshalling yard for industrial development in 1964; photographic finishing company, Litsters, moved into a purpose built factory there in 1969.[37] Fidelitone of Chicago, manufacturing styluses (record players were still the main source of recorded music), followed in 1970.[38] In 1970, the county

---

[34] R/CD/37/1, Peebles, Roxburgh & Selkirk Joint Planning Advisory Committee, Quarterly Reports of Development Officer.

[35] R/CD/37/1, Peebles, Roxburgh & Selkirk Joint Planning Advisory Committee, 26 September 1973.

[36] P/CD/1/27, Meetings of Peeblesshire Town Planning Committee, 26 June 1963.

[37] P/CD/1/27, Meetings of Peeblesshire Town Planning Committee, 7 February 1964 & P/CD/1/32, Meetings of Peeblesshire Town Planning Committee, 6 December 1968.

[38] P/CD/1/33, Meetings of Peeblesshire Town Planning Committee, 6 February 1970.

council purchased six acres at South Parks for industrial development.[39] At Glenrath in the Manor Valley, John Campbell obtained planning permission for his first poultry rearing houses in 1967.[40] Glenrath Farms Ltd would expand over the following decades to become one of the largest employers in Peeblesshire and grow into one of the UK's leading egg production and marketing companies, producing over a million eggs per day.

In the eastern Borders, EBDA appointed John Reid as Development Officer in September 1966. Over the next ten years, EBDA oversaw the provision of advance factories in Berwick-upon-Tweed, Kelso and Eyemouth funded by the Development Commission and nursery factories provided by the local authorities in Eyemouth, Duns and Coldstream.[41] In Kelso, land for industry was allocated at Pinnaclehill in September 1968.[42] The first 10,000 sq ft advance factory provided by the Development Commission was occupied by the Galashiels firm, BEPI Electronics, employing fifty-eight people, and a town council factory of similar size was occupied by Lyle and Scott, knitwear manufacturers in Hawick. In 1970, a second 10,000 sq ft factory was occupied by Kenneth Forbes Plastics, which expanded rapidly with orders from the burgeoning North Sea Oil industry, and Neve Electronics (audio equipment) was established in a third Development Commission factory.

In Berwick-upon-Tweed, by the end of 1969, Pringle of Scotland employed some 300 people (eighty of which were male employees) in their 75,000 sq ft premises on the Tweedside Industrial estate, the largest employer in Berwick-upon-Tweed. Other firms, such as Jus-Rol, established by a baker from Coldstream, and Readymix Concrete were also attracted to the estate. The first nursery factories were erected in Eyemouth and Duns in 1967, the SIEC constructed the first advance factory at Coldingham Road, Eyemouth in 1968.[43] The county council purchased ten acres of land at Cheeklaw, adjacent to Duns Station Yard, and four acres of land at Greenlaw Station for industrial development. By 1974, advance factories in Eyemouth were occupied by Tweed Valley Foods, which processed frozen fish and soft fruit, and Cattermarine, which repaired and serviced boats. ELBA Growers, an agricultural

[39] P/CD/1/34, Meetings of Peeblesshire Town Planning Committee, 26 June 1970.
[40] P/CD/1/31, Meetings of Peeblesshire Town Planning Committee, 2 June 1967.
[41] For a detailed account of the establishment and activities of EBDA, see SBA/1210/37/5[SBA/551] & SBA/1210/37/6[D/5].
[42] See Amendment 13, Kelso (Pinnaclehill) to Roxburgh County Development Plan, SBA/1210//7/7, approved 4 September 1968.
[43] D/5/1-5, EBDA Records, 1968/69 Annual Report.

co-operative of farmers from East Lothian and Berwickshire, would subsequently construct a processing plant and cold store at the Coldingham Road site, initially concentrating on pea processing. J. M. Marshall, fish processers, would occupy a 5,000 sq ft factory built by Eyemouth Town Council. In Duns, nursery units constructed by Duns Town Council were occupied by HOMAC Foods, which processed shellfish, and Celtic Homes (later Clanwood Components) who manufactured the first timber framed houses in the area.[44]

In 1969, the Chirnside Paper Mill, operated by Y. Trotter & Sons, was closed with the loss of fifty-five jobs. As a result of sterling efforts by the County Planning and Development Officer, the C. H. Dexter Corporation from Windsor Locks, Connecticut was attracted to the site and in 1972 established a base for its European operation manufacturing non-woven material for use in tea bags, coffee filters, cigarette filters and later, medical equipment. By the end of 1974, the firm employed more than 200 workers, over 60 per cent of whom resided in Chirnside. Its establishment coincided with the rapid growth in demand for tea bags and led to the expansion of Chirnside village, although workers travelled to the factory from the whole of East Berwickshire.[45]

A survey of major manufacturing and construction firms, employing twenty or more workers, carried out in 1973 jointly by the development officers of the JPAC and EBDA, confirmed that in the previous six years nearly fifty new firms had established themselves in the Scottish Borders employing some 2,900 people; six of these firms were in electronics employing around 1,000 people but eleven were new textile firms employing 860 persons, six were in food processing and five in engineering. Together, as well as widening employment opportunities, these fifty firms had diversified the structure of manufacturing industry in the Scottish Borders. Nevertheless, in 1973 almost half of the 139 manufacturing and construction firms employing twenty or more workers were in the textile industry, employing 65 per cent of the workforce of 14,000 people.[46]

By the early 1970s, there was virtual full employment in the region and a shortage of housing, which restricted the region's ability to attract further investment in industry, particularly male-employing industries.

---

[44] D/5/1-5, EBDA Records, 1974 Annual Report.
[45] SBA/1210/34/8, report entitled 'Chirnside Village', County Planning and Development Department, May 1974, p. 3.
[46] *The Borders Region 1975,* Borders Regional Planning Unit, March 1975, Figure 13 on p. 8.

The housing and industry survey carried out by the development officers of the JPAC and EBDA in 1974 concluded that if the Scottish Borders was to expand, a considerable boost would be needed to the level of house completions achieved over the previous ten years, especially in the private sector; a challenge for the new planning and housing authorities.[47]

CONCLUSIONS

A regional approach to planning, which had lain dormant since the heady days of the immediate post-war period, was revived in the 1960s with the publication in Scotland in 1963 of the White Paper *Central Scotland: A Programme for Development and Growth*, which presented a positive programme for both physical and economic development in selected growth areas within the Central Belt.[48] This was followed by the Lothian Regional Survey and Plan in 1966 and the Grangemouth/Falkirk Regional Survey and Plan in 1968. The Central Borders Plan of 1968 was ambitious and was generally criticised as being too altruistic and not grounded in the reality of the Scottish Borders ethos, which reflected a more conservative approach to change (the 'It's aye been' attitude). The plan represented a marked departure from the existing pattern of development, which was not acceptable to local politicians. Whilst, in one sense, the plan failed, it nevertheless, galvanised the local authorities in the Borders to adopt a more proactive approach to planning and development. With the active encouragement of the SDD, the growth potential of the main towns in the Borders, Hawick and Galashiels, was examined by technical working parties, utilising the latest analysis techniques. The resulting plans would lay down markers for the future long-term development of these towns.

Until the mid-1960s, the attention of central government (the Scottish Office) was very much focussed on the Central Belt of Scotland and the rejuvenation of its run-down industrial areas. In the Central Belt, new towns were designated at Livingston (1962) and Irvine (1964) to attract new industries to West Lothian and Ayrshire respectively. The challenges being increasingly faced by areas such as the Scottish Borders were largely overlooked or poorly understood. However, with the

---

[47] See Survey of Housing and Industry by JPAC and EBDA Development Officers, 1974.

[48] Scottish Development Department, *Central Scotland: A Programme for Development and Growth*, Cmnd. 2188 (Edinburgh: HMSO, 1963).

publication of the White Paper, *The Scottish Economy 1965 to 1970: A Plan for Expansion*, the plight of peripheral rural areas such as the Scottish Borders came to the attention of central government. At the same time, the Highlands and Islands Development (Scotland) Act 1965 established the HIDB with the objective of improving economic and social conditions in that region. Unfortunately, a similar approach was not adopted in the Scottish Borders and this would be a recurring issue for the region, which would not be resolved until more than fifty years later with the establishment of South of Scotland Enterprise.

Nevertheless, with the establishment of the JPAC and EBDA, planning and development in the Borders would be inexorably linked for the next thirty years. As a result of marketing and promotion, and the success of the factory building programme, the range of businesses attracted to the region expanded, built on the primary industries of the area, textiles, agriculture and fishing, and helped to diversify the economy and stem depopulation. Notwithstanding these efforts to attract industry and incoming workers to the Scottish Borders, assisted by the SIEC and the Development Commission, the overall population of the region continued to decline in the 1960s, albeit at a slower rate than in the 1950s. Between 1961 and 1971, overall population decline was 3.5 per cent (3,690 persons) to a figure of 98,477 persons. However, mid-year population estimates from the General Register Office of Scotland for the first years of the 1970s suggested that out-migration had been reversed and small net migration gains had been achieved in 1971–1972 and 1972–1973. The mid-year population estimate for 1974, of 99,105 persons, indicated that the population of the Borders had increased for the first time in over 100 years, a testament to the efforts of the local authorities to attract industry and incoming workers to the region.

4

Planning in the Scottish Borders Broadens its Horizons

INTRODUCTION

MODERNITY CAME TO THE Borders in various guises: milk bars and tearooms, supermarkets, illuminated advertisements, pedestrian crossings and roundabouts. Architects and builders experimented with new forms of design and construction; new housing schemes, inspired by the innovative New Town designs, sprang up in Galashiels and Hawick. At Church Square, in Galashiels, a scheme designed by architect Peter Womersley for Galashiels Town Council was considered by the Saltire Society to be the best designed housing scheme in Scotland in 1963. Peter Womersley also won awards for his 'brutal' concrete design for the Gala Fairydean Football Club stand and for the Bernat Klein Studio, located at High Sunderland, near Selkirk.

The rate of development, as measured by the number of planning applications received across the four counties, fluctuated during the 1960s before increasing from about 1,000 per annum in 1967 to over 1,300 in 1974.[1] The vast majority of applications related to residential development, principally rented housing by the various town councils, supported by the SSHA, and an increasing number of private housing developments. Applications for PFSs and related signage in town and country reflected the growing car usage for leisure, as well as travel to work. The 'swinging sixties' also brought with it such diverse proposals as discotheques and youth clubs, bingo halls and a plethora of chewing gum machines outside corner shops in Galashiels and Hawick. The number of applications refused was relatively low; for instance, in 1972, only 7 per cent of the 540 applications received

---

[1] For the registers of applications received and decisions made across the four counties, see S/CD/9/1-3, R/CD/39-1-3, B/CD/12/1-4 & P/CD/30/1-2.

by RCC were refused, reflecting the practice of seeking to achieve a compromise rather than a refusal.

There was a more positive attitude towards urban development with the establishment of technical working parties in Jedburgh, Melrose, Kelso, Hawick and Galashiels. However, most development proceeded by way of amendments to the increasingly out-dated county development plans. Through such formal amendments, land was allocated in all the main towns for both industry and housing in an effort to stem depopulation. Non-statutory plans were prepared for the redevelopment of town centres in Hawick, Jedburgh, Kelso, Melrose, Eyemouth and Duns. However, apart from Jedburgh, where housing redevelopment and rehabilitation was undertaken and the North British Rayon factory was demolished and replaced by a large car park in association with the realignment of the A68, the redevelopment plans for the other towns were either shelved or significantly reduced, reflecting the change in attitude away from the wholesale redevelopment of run-down areas towards conservation and rehabilitation.

The conservation movement grew in the mid-1960s originally in response to the threat of over-population and the resultant over-use of resources, pollution and damage to wildlife; 'eco-doom' literature began to appear, such as Gordon Rattray Taylor's *The Doomsday Book*.[2] Land use planning and transport issues gained prominence in the press with large-scale protests and campaigns against overhead pylons, motorways and the third London airport. Awareness of the environment caught the public's attention and, whilst there was strong support for modernisation, there was growing concern over the threats to the urban environment from the use of the car, from unsympathetic new buildings and the loss of green space. In Scotland, the Scottish Civic Trust was founded in 1967 to provide 'leadership and focus in the protection, enhancement and development of Scotland's built environment'. With the enactment of the Civic Amenities Act 1967, some twenty-seven conservation areas were established across the Scottish Borders, as 'areas of special architectural or historic interest, the character or appearance of which it is desirable to preserve or enhance'. Many of these conservation areas were located in villages but the centres of all the main towns, except Galashiels and Selkirk, were designated as conservation areas. Indeed, there was no conservation area in Selkirkshire prior to 1975.

In the countryside, in addition to the ecological threat from modern farming methods, with the use of chemical fertilisers and pesticides,

---

[2] Taylor, Rattray G., *The Doomsday Book* (London: Thames & Hudson, 1970).

there was the loss of wildflower meadows, hedges and hedgerow trees, the impact of power lines, new roads and reservoirs, and the growing pressure for recreation in the countryside. The perceived threats to the environment are admirably described in Tony Aldous's book *Battle for the Environment*, published in 1972.[3] Ian Nairn drew attention to the urban sprawl, which threatened to engulf the countryside, particularly in the southern half of Britain.[4] In *Tomorrow's Landscape*, Sylvia Crowe looked at the impact of changing farming practices on the landscape, the monoculture of much of the forestry planting and the pressures caused by increasing leisure and recreation on the fragile uplands and the coast.[5] Perhaps the most influential views on the challenge of the leisure explosion were those expressed by Michael Dower, the son of John Dower, the architect of the National Parks and Access to the Countryside Act, in his study entitled *The Fourth Wave: The Challenge of Leisure*. He concluded that the demand from increasing leisure and recreation could be as damaging to the environment as the industrialisation of towns and urban sprawl.[6]

Only the provisions relating to nature conservation in the National Parks and Access to the Countryside Act 1949 applied to Scotland. The care of the countryside was largely in the hands of landowners, voluntary organisations and the local authorities. Increasing leisure time and an increasing desire to access the countryside in the 1960s, and the potential conflict between development and the preservation of natural beauty, led to the demand for more positive action on the part of government. The Countryside Act 1968 replaced the National Parks Commission with the Countryside Commission in England and Wales whilst, in Scotland, the Countryside (Scotland) Act 1967 established the Countryside Commission for Scotland (CCS) in 1968 with the remit 'to make provision for the better enjoyment of the Scottish Countryside and for the improvement of recreational and other facilities . . .'[7]

The CCS led the arguments on the creation of a park system for Scotland and, although the Commission failed to persuade the government of the time of the need for national parks, four regional parks and thirty-two country parks would be established across Scotland.

---

[3] Aldous, T., *Battle for the Environment* (Glasgow: William Collins, 1972).

[4] Nairn, I., *Outrage* (London: Architectural Press, 1955).

[5] Crowe, S., *Tomorrow's Landscape* (London: Architectural Press, 1956).

[6] Dower, J., *Fourth Wave: The Challenge of Leisure* (London: Civic Trust, 1965).

[7] See Countryside (Scotland) Act 1967 (Ch. 86) (London: HMSO).

There would be no such designations in the Scottish Borders.[8] However, most of the Borders was designated 'countryside' under the Countryside (Scotland) Act 1967, where 75 per cent grants were available for the provision of leisure and recreation facilities. All four county councils took advantage of these new grants to carry out countryside projects and provide car park/picnic sites on tourist routes through the region and at key locations such as viewpoints.

STAFFING

In less than ten years, planning in the Scottish Borders was transformed from simply a mechanism for controlling land use to a much more complex process; planning became a more diverse discipline. Until the 1960s most qualified planners were architects who had taken an additional planning qualification such as the Diploma in Town Planning awarded by the School of Town Planning at the Edinburgh College of Art. It would be 1963 before Professor Percy Johnson-Marshall set up the Planning Research Unit at Edinburgh University and 1967 before the Department of Urban Design and Regional Planning at Edinburgh University provided full-time degrees in town and regional planning.[9] Consequently, from the mid-1960s onwards, graduates with degrees in subjects such as sociology, economics and geography were adding a planning qualification to their CVs and taking positions in planning departments. The strengthening of planning as a profession was reflected in the creation of separate planning departments where previously planning had been combined with the roads engineering, surveying or architect's department. There were fundamental changes in the way town and country planning was administered by the county councils in the Scottish Borders, apart from Peeblesshire where, until local government reorganisation in 1975, Charles Mackenzie, Assistant County Planning Officer with Midlothian County Council, continued to provide planning advice to the Town Planning Committee.

In Roxburghshire, Alistair Milne, the County Architect and Planning Officer left for Kirkcudbright County Council in December 1961 and Alistair Sturrock, Kincardine County Architect and Planning Officer,

---

[8] Countryside Commission for Scotland, *A Park System for Scotland* (CCS: Perth, 1974).

[9] Johnson-Marshall, Percy Edwin Alan, *Oxford Dictionary of National Biography*, Ref: 109716.

was appointed and took his place in March 1962.[10] It would be March 1963 before any additional staff, in the form of a planning technician, was appointed to assist George Ovens with the planning responsibilities.[11] With the establishment of technical working parties for Jedburgh in 1962 and Melrose in 1964, the County Architect and Planning Officer requested additional staff arguing that, with the present staff complement, it was impossible to undertake the work being generated by the establishment of working parties in addition to daily development control matters.[12] It would be the summer of 1966 before the position was filled, with the appointment of Jim Thompson. Alistair Sturrock died, suddenly, in March 1967 and forthwith the architects and planning departments were separated. Frank Constable, a qualified planner from Stirling County was appointed County Planning Officer and immediately undertook a review of the department and obtained authority to augment its staff.[13] Three qualified members of staff were duly appointed: David Cottee, Julian Farrell and Ross Henderson, to tackle the increasing workload occasioned by the decision to develop Tweedbank and the establishment of the Kelso and Hawick Working Parties. They would be subsequently joined by Alan Whyte.

In Selkirkshire, John C. Hall tendered his resignation as County Architect and Planning Officer in April 1961 on health grounds and his son John B. Hall took over.[14] Frank Entwistle acted as Assistant County Planning Officer, responsible for the quinquennial review of the development plan and development plan amendments, and John Gray provided advice on planning applications. This arrangement continued until September 1966, when complaints were made to the Royal Institute of British Architects and the Town Planning Institute (TPI) regarding John B. Hall holding the position of County Architect and Planning Officer whilst also submitting planning applications as J & J Hall, Architects (it was contended that there was a conflict of interest).[15] As a result, the council agreed in March 1967 that John B. Hall's position as County Planning Officer should cease and that the firm of J & J Hall

[10] R/CD/1/72, Meetings of Roxburghshire Property & Works Committee, 28 December 1961.
[11] R/CD/1/77, Meetings of Roxburghshire Planning Committee, 25 March 1963.
[12] R/CD/1/77, Meetings of Roxburghshire Planning Committee, 27 September 1965.
[13] R/CD/1/78, Meetings of Roxburghshire Planning Committee, 27 November 1967.
[14] S/CD/1/33, Meetings of Selkirkshire Planning Committee, 18 April 1961.
[15] S/CD/1/39, Meetings of Selkirkshire Planning Committee, 13 September 1966.

should henceforth be employed on a consultancy basis in connection with development plan work only, whilst the processing of planning applications would become the responsibility of the County Clerk's department. To undertake this work, it was agreed that a member of J & J Hall's staff would be transferred to the council's employment; John Gray was appointed as Planning Assistant and his office moved to Thorniedean House on the Melrose Road. John Gray would become the council's de facto County Planning Officer.[16] Thereafter, advice to the council's Planning Committee, in relation to the development plan and related studies, would be provided by Frank Entwistle, and John Gray would administer the day-to-day development control function.

In Berwickshire, following the submission of the development plan to the Secretary of State in December 1960, the contract with Midlothian County Council for the services of J. S. Bailie, Midlothian County Council's Planning Officer was terminated.[17] Somewhat reluctantly, the council agreed that the council's County Planning Officer, T. D. Anderson, would need additional assistance to carry out the increasing day-to-day tasks of development control. However, there was little response to successive advertisements for additional planning staff and T. D. Anderson continued alone; it would be February 1965 before an assistant planning officer was appointed.[18] After thirty-six years' service with the council, twenty years as County Planning Officer, T. D. Anderson retired in July 1966 and Basil Knowles, a qualified town planner, arrived from Shropshire County Council, in September 1966.[19] He was given the title of County Planning and Development Officer in recognition of the more positive approach to planning being adopted by the county council. The Planning and Property & Works Committee was split, and a new Planning and Development Committee formed.[20] On the appointment of Basil Knowles, the planning assistant, who had been appointed in February 1965 to assist T. D. Anderson with the growing number of planning applications, resigned his position and it would be June 1967 before a replacement, Robert Johnston, was found. As the department's role

[16] S/CD/1/39, Meetings of Selkirkshire Planning Committee, 15 March 1967.
[17] B/CD/1/129, Meetings of Berwickshire Planning and Property & Works Committee, 25 July 1960.
[18] B/CD/1/131, Meetings of Berwickshire Planning and Property & Works Committee, 6 January 1965.
[19] B/CD/1/131, Meetings of Berwickshire Planning and Property & Works Committee, 28 September 1966.
[20] B/CD/1/132, Meetings of Berwickshire Planning and Development Committee, 28 June 1967.

expanded, David P. Douglas, a qualified town planner, was appointed Depute County Planning and Development Officer in June 1969 to assist Basil Knowles on planning policy and economic development matters. Alistair Lorimer replaced Robert Johnston as planning assistant in October 1969 and the staff of the burgeoning department was expanded further by the appointment of a draughtsman (John Corbett).[21] Basil Knowles unexpectedly died in February 1973 and David Douglas was elevated to the post of County Planning and Development Officer.[22] He would continue the work of Basil Knowles in promoting the economic development of Berwickshire in a bid to stem depopulation in the county. As a consequence of his elevation, the post of Depute was advertised and the author joined Berwickshire County Council in September 1973.[23]

This chapter examines how the involvement of planners in the Borders broadened from simply being a regulatory activity through development planning and development control with a more positive approach to urban development, a greater interest in urban conservation, the future of the smaller settlements, rural development and countryside issues.

TECHNICAL WORKING PARTIES

The Jedburgh Technical Working Party, comprising officials from both RCC and Jedburgh Town Council, was formed in 1962, prompted by the closure of the North British Rayon factory. The working party report, published in 1964, recommended major changes within the town centre, including a re-alignment of the A68 and redevelopment of the vacant North British Rayon site to form a hotel, tourist visitor centre and car parking.[24] Obsolete housing areas to the rear of Castlegate and Market Place were identified for redevelopment and/or rehabilitation. Sites at Bankend North (a prefab site) and Bongate were identified for industrial development and land at Hartrigge was earmarked for the expansion of toolmakers, L. S. Starrett, which had been established in 1958.[25] It would be 1972 before work commenced on the realignment

---

[21] B/CD/1/133, Meetings of Berwickshire Planning and Development Committee, 1 October 1969.
[22] B/CD/1/135, Meetings of Berwickshire Planning and Development Committee, 21 March 1973.
[23] B/CD/1/136, Meetings of Berwickshire Planning and Development Committee, 3 October 1973 & 6 February 1974.
[24] SBA/1210/33/1, Report of Technical Working Party, Burgh of Jedburgh, 1964.
[25] SBA/1210/33/8, Town Extension, Jedburgh by Jedburgh Technical Working Party, February 1970.

of the A68 and the redevelopment of the North British Rayon site for the provision of a national tourist visitor centre and major car park. A combined redevelopment and rehabilitation scheme for residential and commercial properties in the Castlegate/Market Square area was approved in 1974.[26]

The Melrose Technical Working Party was formed in 1964 in response to the growing volume of traffic passing through the town and its increasing attraction as a tourist centre. The working party report of 1966 recommended a relief road system around the historic town centre to protect the environment of this conservation town and proposed that the central area (High Street, Market Square and Abbey Street) be pedestrianised.[27] According to a quote by George Ovens in *The Scotsman* dated 8 February 1966: 'The first stage of the plan for the central area, including the distributor road, could be completed in five or six years and the whole central area development in twelve. It was impossible at present to estimate the total cost.'[28]

However, an amendment to the development plan, submitted in October 1969, for the proposed town centre relief road and comprehensive development of the town centre generated a considerable number of objections and was eventually withdrawn in February 1975.[29] These proposals were never implemented.

The future development of Kelso was not considered as part of the Central Borders Plan, it being located within the 'Eastern Area' identified in the White Paper *The Scottish Economy 1965 to 1970: A Plan for Expansion*. Kelso was seen as a growth point in the eastern part of the Borders and the Kelso Technical Working Party was established in February 1965. Comprised of officials from RCC and Kelso Town Council, the working party reported in 1968 and recommended major proposals for roads, housing and industrial sites based on a target 1985 population of 8,000 persons (compared with a 1961 population of 4,100).[30] Following an extended period of consultation and public meetings, the proposals were finalised in February 1972. An amendment to the development plan, Amendment 19, based on these proposals

[26] R/CD/1/80, Meetings of Roxburghshire Planning Committee, 29 August 1974.
[27] SBA/1210/33/3, Melrose Technical Working Party Report, 1966.
[28] See 'Traffic Segregation Plan for Melrose', *The Scotsman*, Tuesday, 8 February 1966, p. 6.
[29] See Amendment 15 (Melrose CDA) to Roxburgh County Development Plan, SBA/1210//7/7, submitted 23 October 1969.
[30] SBA/1210/33/4, Burgh of Kelso Working Party Report, 1968.

was not approved until May 1975.[31] In the intervening period, planning permissions were granted which would enable the population of Kelso to expand to 6,000 persons.[32] Amendment 19 allocated several sites for additional private housing, including a large area of twenty acres at the Broomlands Estate, east of the B6461, for development in the longer term. An additional sixteen acres of land at Pinnaclehill was allocated for industrial development. A proposed distributor road around the north and east of the town utilised existing roads with a new bridge crossing the River Tweed leading to a new road along the former railway line through Maxwellheugh to link with the Jedburgh Road (A698). Road proposals for the town centre were amended in response to the public consultation. The widening of Bowmont Street and Roxburgh Street, which would have required extensive demolition, was not pursued but a town centre relief road was proposed round the north side of the town centre. The comprehensive re-development of the Horsemarket/Woodmarket/Cross Street area, proposed by the technical working party, was aborted and a property improvement and facelift scheme adopted.[33]

Following the publication of the Central Borders Plan, technical working parties were set up for Hawick and Galashiels in 1967 and 1970 respectively. These were much more comprehensive affairs comprising planning and transport officials from the SDD, a range of county council and burgh council representatives providing a wealth of knowledge and representatives of other agencies such as the East of Scotland Water Board and the Tweed River Purification Board. The Interim Report of the Hawick Working Party, published in February 1970, established that there was capacity in Hawick for an additional 4,900 persons on top of the 1966 population of 16,206 and a large area of land (fifty acres) was allocated at Stirches for some 600 houses through an amendment to the county development plan, approved in February 1971.[34] The final report of the working party, published in 1973, identified an additional ninety acres of housing land on nine sites capable of accommodating 600 houses for development up to 1982 and a further sixty acres on four sites that could accommodate a further

---

[31] See Amendment 19 to Roxburgh County Development Plan, SBA/1210//7/7, approved 30 May 1975.

[32] R/CD/1/79 & 80, Meetings of Roxburghshire Planning Committee, 1969–1974.

[33] See Amendment 20, Kelso CDA (Woodmarket/Horsemarket) to Roxburgh County Development Plan, SBA/1210//7/7.

[34] See Amendment 16 to the Roxburgh County Development Plan, SBA/1210/7/7, 26 February 1971.

400 houses for development in the period 1982–1992; a total of some 1,600 houses.[35] A major new industrial site was proposed on land close to the A7 at Burnhead.[36] In the town centre, the working party proposed the re-routing of the A7 along Commercial Road as opposed to the proposed improvements to the High Street/Drumlanrig Bridge/Sandbed in the development plan, which involved the wholesale demolition of property. It was also proposed that the area of Hawick centred on the Sandbed, Tower Knowe and High Street should be designated a conservation area and alternative plans were drawn up for the rehabilitation of the Howegate/Drumlanrig Square area.

The Galashiels Technical Working Party was established in 1970. Its primary concern was the examination of the potential for urban and industrial growth against the background of the Central Borders Plan, which proposed an increase in population of 5,000 persons by 1980. The working party utilised the latest analytical techniques, including the novel Threshold Analysis pioneered by the Planning Research Unit at Edinburgh University.[37] Five alternative directions for growth were examined and, following two years of investigation of the potential for development, the report recommended a major expansion of the town at Mossilee, comprising some 1,000 dwellings. No further land would be required for industry. However, in order to achieve the target of an additional 5,000 population, additional housing sites at Gala Policies and Easter Langlee were proposed with additional industrial land at Hollybush or Easter Langlee. Three possibilities were examined for the re-alignment of the trunk road through Galashiels, but the working party concluded that there was no case to divert from the development plan route. The final report of the working party was published in January 1973.[38] Although it was hoped that the report would provide the basis for a comprehensive updating of the Galashiels Town Map in the county development plan, the impending reorganisation of local government meant that the future development of Galashiels would require to be assessed by the new Borders Regional Council (BRC).

Following on from the decision of RCC in September 1968 that only an additional 3,000 persons should be accommodated in Newtown St Boswells rather than the 10,000 persons recommended in the Central

[35] SBA/1210/33/12, Hawick Technical Working Party report, 1973 (2 volumes).
[36] SBA/1210/33/12, Hawick Technical Working Party report, 1973 (2 volumes).
[37] Edinburgh University Planning Research Unit, *Threshold Analysis Manual* (Edinburgh: HMSO, 1973).
[38] Selkirk County Council, *Second Report of the Galashiels Technical Working Party*, January 1973.

Borders Plan, the St Boswells/Newtown St Boswells Working Party examined alternative strategies for the housing required to accommodate this growth. The St Boswells Planning Report of January 1971 examined alternative routes for the A68 by-passing both St Boswells and Newtown St Boswells and alternative options for the distribution of housing to accommodate 3,000 persons, with a long-term potential of accommodating 10,000 persons.[39] St Boswells village was largely unaffected by the proposals put forward, the vast majority of the projected development being located between St Boswells and Newtown St Boswells or to the north and west of Newtown St Boswells. However, no decision was made on these draft proposals and the question of the scale of development to be accommodated in St Boswells/Newtown St Boswells remained unresolved.

In January 1969, the Ministry of Defence offered the council its landholding at neighbouring Charlesfield comprising a three-storey building of 21,000 sq ft formerly used as a hostel and dining block and a single-storey building of 4,000 sq ft.[40] Part of the former armaments depot was used by West Cumberland Farmers for grain storage but the largest share of the site had reverted to Charlesfield Farm and was now in use as a pig farm. The county council decided to take no action on the proposed purchase. When the owner of Charlesfield Farm offered the land to the council in August 1973 the council again decided not to proceed with a purchase.[41] The future development of Charlesfield as an industrial/service site would proceed in a piecemeal fashion thereafter and would be a constant thorn-in-the-flesh of the new regional planning authority after May 1975.

A report on Housing and Industry in Berwickshire, published in 1974, proposed an extensive local authority housing programme in the burghs of Eyemouth, Duns and Coldstream to house incoming workers and the development of further land for industry.[42] In Eyemouth, twenty-five acres of land at Deanhead was identified for local authority housing (200 houses) and a ten-acre site at Gillsland was granted planning permission for private housing, in addition to an extension to the existing Barefoots site. Some twenty acres of additional land was purchased for industry at Acredale and a study of Eyemouth Harbour proposed

[39] SBA/1210/33/7, St Boswells Planning Report, Roxburghshire County Council, September 1969.
[40] R/CD/1/78, Meetings of Roxburghshire Planning Committee, 20 January 1969.
[41] R/CD/1/80, Meetings of Roxburghshire Planning Committee, 2 May 1974.
[42] SBA/1210/34/7, report entitled 'Housing and Industry', County Planning and Development Department, January 1974.

alterations to the harbour entrance and major housing development at Gunsgreen.[43] In Duns, service constraints limited any large-scale local authority or private housing development but the former station yard was acquired for industrial development.[44] In Coldstream, any further housing development was limited to the extension of the present areas of housing at Priory Hill and Lennel Mount. Elsewhere, local authority houses were built in Lauder, Earlston and Chirnside (for workers at the C. H. Dexter's factory).[45] A report on population change in 1973–1974 showed that the population of Berwickshire had increased for the first time in over 100 years (by 313 persons); a major achievement which the council considered was a result of its efforts to diversify the economy of the county through the development of industrial estates in Eyemouth, Duns and Coldstream and the attraction of industry and incoming workers.[46]

CONSERVATION OF THE BUILT ENVIRONMENT

The Civic Amenities Act 1967 empowered local authorities to designate conservation areas and opened the door to conservation grants for building conservation. It also enabled planning authorities to take more control over building development through the restriction of permitted development rights. Planning permission was required for the demolition or alteration of any building within a conservation area and the permission of the planning authority was required for the felling, lopping, topping etc. of any tree.[47] However, conservation area designation was not simply a means of controlling development, it was also a means of encouraging a range of positive actions through grant-aid for the face-lifting of properties, paving and landscaping, the undergrounding of electricity and telephone cables and the removal of street lighting columns.

Encouraged by the SDD and the publication of booklets such as *New Life for Old Buildings* and *New Life for Historic Areas*, jointly produced by the Department of the Environment, SDD and the Welsh Office in 1971 and 1972, respectively, three of the four counties in the Borders embarked on designating conservation areas, preparing environmental

---

[43] Eyemouth Harbour Feasibility Study, P.A. Management Consultants, 1974.
[44] SBA/1210/34/7, report entitled 'Housing and Industry', pp. 22–27.
[45] SBA/1210/34/7, report entitled 'Housing and Industry', pp. 12–17.
[46] B/CD/1/136 Meetings of Berwickshire Planning and Development Committee, 19 March 1975.
[47] Civic Amenities Act 1967 (Ch. 69) (London: HMSO).

improvement and face-lift schemes and the undergrounding of overhead cables, with grants from the government and the South of Scotland Electricity Board (SSEB).[48]

In the period leading up to local government reorganisation in 1975, some twenty-seven conservation areas were designated in the region, stretching from Carlops and Skirling in the west to St Abbs and Coldingham in the east. Carlops and Skirling were Peeblesshire's first conservation areas, designated in 1968, followed by Peebles in 1970 and West Linton in 1973.[49] The undergrounding of electricity lines commenced in 1974, with a proposed scheme for Carlops.[50] A wide range of properties in the county were listed as buildings of special architectural or historic interest; perhaps the most notable being the cast-iron urinal at Walkerburn. Peebles Civic Society would be formed in 1973 in response to the proposed demolition of the whole of 'Bank House' at the end of the High Street in order to widen the Cuddy Bridge.[51] This building was highly regarded because of its association with John Buchan. In the event, a compromise would be reached resulting in only the partial demolition of the property, the majority of which remains to this day. The Civic Society would play a significant role in co-ordinating public opinion on the development of Peebles over the next fifty years.

In Roxburghshire, Bowden Conservation Area was the first to be designated, in July 1969, followed by St Boswells Conservation Area in March 1970 and conservation areas for Ancrum, Denholm, Midlem, Kirk Yetholm and Town Yetholm in January 1971.[52] The area of Hawick centred on the Sandbed, Tower Knowe and High Street was designated a conservation area in 1972. As well as controlling minor developments and encouraging building improvements, sometimes with grants, the designation of conservation areas prompted action on the undergrounding of overhead electricity lines and the removal of poles. Bowden village was the first to benefit from such action, in 1974.

---

[48] Department of the Environment, Scottish Development Department & Welsh Office, *New Life for Old Buildings* (London: HMSO, 1971); Department of the Environment, Scottish Development Department & Welsh Office, *New Life for Historic Areas* (London: HMSO, 1972).

[49] P/CD/1/33, Meetings of Peeblesshire Town Planning Committee, 4 September 1969.

[50] P/CD/1/37, Meetings of Peeblesshire Town Planning Committee, 4 January 1974.

[51] P/CD/1/37, Meetings of Peeblesshire Town Planning Committee, 29 June 1973.

[52] R/CD/1/78-79, Meetings of Roxburghshire Planning Committee, 28 July 1969 & 25 September 1970.

The first of a proposed programme of village reports was prepared for Bowden in March 1969.[53] The report provided a visual assessment of the landscape setting of the village and its character, and suggested improvements such as the removal of overhead electricity and telephone wires, the rehabilitation of derelict buildings, the infilling of gap sites and proposed tree planting and landscape improvements. However, perhaps reflecting the difficulties of putting plans into practice, the foreword to the report warned: 'Nothing in this booklet commits the County Council to any action. It will enable members and the public at large to see the problem as a whole so that, whatever action has to be taken, the reasoning can be understood in the whole context'. The second village report, for Gattonside, was produced in December 1971.[54] This followed a similar format to the Bowden Report with an environmental and visual appraisal of the village. It went further, however, and analysed the potential for growth in the village, including the rationalisation of the road system, prompted by the removal of restrictions to development through the construction of a sewage works and improvements to the water supply. The proposals in the report were approved for consultation with the local community but were never implemented.

In Berwickshire, Eyemouth, Dryburgh, Swinton and Greenlaw were the county's first designated conservation areas.[55] By 1973, eight towns and villages had been designated as conservation areas; Eyemouth, Dryburgh, Swinton, Greenlaw, Duns, Coldingham, Cockburnspath, Foulden and St Abbs, and conservation areas for Lauder and Coldstream were under consideration. Proposals for the redevelopment of Eyemouth town centre produced in 1970 by A. T. McIndoe, an Edinburgh planning consultant, which involved the wholesale demolition of run-down properties in Chapel Street/George Street/Queen Street were re-assessed in the light of the conservation area designation and the growing preference for rehabilitation.[56] It would be after the reorganisation of local government in 1975 before an alternative strategy for the renewal of the town centre would be produced. In Duns, the town hall was unfortunately

---

[53] SBA/1210/33/5, Bowden Village Study Report, Roxburghshire County Planning Department, March 1969.
[54] SBA/1210/33/9, Future Development of Gattonside, Roxburghshire County Planning Department, December 1971.
[55] B/CD/1/133, Meetings of Berwickshire Planning and Development Committee, 26 March 1969.
[56] B/CD/1/134 Meetings of Berwickshire Planning and Development Committee, 7 October 1970.

demolished in 1965 and a plan for the redevelopment of the town centre was proposed in 1968 but little progress was made. It would be 1975 before any positive proposals were approved for the future of Duns town centre, based on the limited demolition of property, with the emphasis on rehabilitation and environmental improvements.[57] A report on conservation areas in Berwickshire in June 1973 proposed face-lift schemes, a co-ordinated approach to street furniture design, the undergrounding of electricity lines and a strict control over advertisements.[58] The undergrounding of electricity lines was pursued in Ayton, Duns and Lauder.[59] Tree Planting Year in 1973 prompted proposals for tree planting on village greens, playing fields and other incidental open space in towns and villages throughout the county. A Tree Planting Incentive Scheme (with 25 per cent grants) encouraged hedgerow planting and tree planting along roadside verges.[60]

RURAL DEVELOPMENT

In his analysis of the influences on the demand for planning in the early twentieth century, Cherry identifies housing and social problems, industrialisation and the spectre of urban growth as the main factors. The 'rural problem' – rural depopulation, poor rural housing conditions and low wages – attracted little attention.[61] The principal aim of planning in the post-war period was to keep agricultural land in agricultural use and preserve the open countryside for those who live there. However, during the late 1950s there were mounting concerns over the impact on the countryside of urban expansion, the effects of increasing mechanisation in agriculture on rural landscapes with the loss of hedgerows and hedgerow trees, and the growing pressure for recreation in the countryside.

In the Scottish Borders, countryside policy was dominated by the requirement to strictly control new building to that which was essential for the purposes of agriculture and forestry in order that the landscape

[57] B/CD/1/136 Meetings of Berwickshire Planning and Development Committee, 5 February 1975.

[58] SBA/1210/34/13, Conservation Area Policy, Berwickshire County Planning and Development Department, June 1973.

[59] B/CD/1/134, Meetings of Berwickshire Planning and Development Committee, 3 July 1973.

[60] B/CD/1/134, Meetings of Berwickshire Planning and Development Committee, 3 October 1973.

[61] Cherry, G.E., *The Evolution of British Town Planning*, pp. 6–32.

and character of the countryside remained unspoilt. In relation to other land uses, mineral working within the region was mainly confined to the abstraction of sand and gravel with a small number of hard rock quarries for road building. Policy on mineral working was based on any new workings being returned, on completion, to agricultural use with all buildings and equipment removed. The expansion of mineral working, generated by the growth in the housing market, was the most contentious planning issue in the landward part of Peeblesshire during the 1960s. Many of the existing planning permissions dated from the 1950s when planning applications were approved for the resumption of sand and gravel working at Shiphorns Farm, Nether Falla and Cowieslinn quarries, all situated north of Eddleston.[62] In 1953, the county council resumed the working of Edston Quarry, west of Peebles for the working of Greywacke for road construction.[63] Throughout the 1950s, applications would be received for major expansion of the workings north of Eddleston and at Carlops and West Linton to serve the burgeoning road and housebuilding industry in Edinburgh and Midlothian. These planning permissions lacked any restoration conditions, and the opportunity was taken where possible, when granting extensions to these existing workings, to add conditions requiring full restoration to agricultural use. In 1965, over 400 acres of land at Darnhall, north of Eddleston, were granted planning permission for sand and gravel working over a thirty-year period, subject to such conditions.[64] Other quarries at Nether Falla, north of Eddleston, and Tarfhaugh (West Linton) were expanded subject to full restoration.

There were a number of reservoirs in the headwaters of the Tweed and its tributaries. The Alemoor reservoir, north-west of Hawick, dating from the 1960s, was the largest scheme serving the region. The Baddinsgill (1930) and West Water (1969) reservoirs in the Pentlands, and the Talla (1905) and Fruid (1968) reservoirs in the Tweedsmuir Hills served Edinburgh and the Lothians. The Megget Reservoir above St Mary's Loch, with a surface area extending to over 260 ha (640 acres), was first considered in 1963 and approved in 1974; it would be the

---

[62] P/CD/1/15, Meeting of Peeblesshire Town Planning Committee, 11 January 1952; SBA, P/CD/1/16, Meeting of Peeblesshire Town Planning Committee, 3 April 1953; SBA, P/CD/1/18, Meeting of Peeblesshire Town Planning Committee, 1 October 1954.

[63] P/CD/1/16, Meeting of Peeblesshire Town Planning Committee, 9 January 1953.

[64] P/CD/1/28, Meetings of Peeblesshire Town Planning Committee, 5 March 1965.

subject of a wide-ranging environmental assessment of its impact on the land use and landscape character of the area and its potential use for recreational purposes.[65] Construction would commence in 1976 and it would be officially opened in 1983.

Perhaps the largest construction project in the countryside, located in neighbouring East Lothian just beyond the county boundary, was the proposed nuclear power station at Torness, which was the subject of a public inquiry in Dunbar in July 1974. The route of the two proposed 400kv power lines that were required to link with the existing 275kv line from Edinburgh to Newcastle that passed through Berwickshire via Soutra Hill and Coldstream would be the subject of lengthy negotiations between the SSEB and East Lothian and Berwickshire county councils (and subsequently, Lothian and Borders regional councils). The preferred route for one of the lines was through Berwickshire along the route of an existing 132kv line between Dunbar and Eccles, near Coldstream.[66] Consent for the power station was granted by the Secretary of State in March 1975 and formal consultation on the proposed 400kv transmission lines commenced; an issue that would be taken up by BRC and Lothian Regional Council after May 1975.

The growing awareness of rural depopulation in the Borders led both Roxburgh and Berwickshire county planning departments to undertake comprehensive surveys of the smaller settlements in their areas. Roxburgh's *Landward Community Development Strategy* was published in 1972.[67] Based on a wide-ranging analysis of the characteristics of each village within four settlement groupings centred on Kelso, Jedburgh, Hawick and Melrose respectively, a strategy for development in the landward area was proposed based on a hierarchy of settlements. Newtown St Boswells was identified as capable of considerable expansion and Ancrum, Denholm, Gattonside, St Boswells and Town Yetholm were identified as capable of accommodating moderate expansion. Moderate expansion was considered desirable but unlikely in Bonchester Bridge, Lilliesleaf, Morebattle and Newcastleton. However, this document was never formally approved but remained on the table for future consideration by the new regional planning authority after 1975.

---

[65] Cairns, W. J. and Partners, *Megget Valley Reservoir: Environmental Report Summary* (Edinburgh: Lothian Regional Council, 1977).

[66] See *Proposed Torness Power Station: Overhead Transmission Lines*, Berwickshire County Council, April 1974.

[67] SBA/1210/33/11, Roxburgh Landward Development Strategy, 1972.

The *Draft Rural Policy for Berwickshire* published in March 1972 aimed at stemming the decline in population in the landward areas of the county.[68] To utilise to the best advantage the limited economic resources available and exploit the potential of the county, it identified a number of settlement groupings based on 'growth points' where the main housing and employment opportunities should be concentrated and where a range of facilities could be supported: Eyemouth, Duns and Coldstream within the county and Dunbar, Berwick-upon-Tweed, Kelso and Galashiels outwith the county. The report proposed that detailed plans be prepared for each settlement grouping to identify opportunities for development. This report went out to consultation with a wide range of organisations but was never formally adopted as council policy.

In Selkirkshire, the Yarrow and Ettrick valleys were the subject of a detailed settlement study in 1974.[69] Covering an area of 153 square miles, the study area had a population of 1,120 in 1931 reducing to 608 in 1971. This area had suffered from severe rural depopulation as a result of the loss of employment in agriculture, partly due to afforestation. Sheep farming was the backbone of these valleys, with a sheep population in excess of 100,000; over 70 per cent of the land area was rough grazing. Forestry planting by the Forestry Commission dated from the 1930s and 1940s but planting by private forestry groups in the late 1960s and early 1970s had increased woodland cover so that, by 1973, the combined Forestry Commission and private woodlands amounted to 5,900 ha (14,578 acres) with a further 1,800 ha (4,448 acres) in reserve, in total roughly 19 per cent of the study area. Recently, the integration of forestry and farming had been pursued in the Upper Ettrick valley where two farms, measuring over 4,600 acres in total, had been utilised for forestry planting (2,800 acres) and the creation of a single sheep farm of 1,800 acres.

Almost 60 per cent of the fifty-two farms in the study area were tenanted from four landowners: Buccleuch Estates, Philiphaugh Estates, Wemyss and March Estate, and the Duke of Sutherland. The estates, therefore, exerted a strong influence upon the rural life and economy of the valleys. Farms were normally between 1,000 and 3,000 acres in size, rearing mostly hill sheep but a number with a herd of suckler cows. Hill sheep farming had undergone minimal change over the

---

[68] SBA/1210/34/5, a Rural Policy for Berwickshire, County Planning and Development Department, March 1972.

[69] SBA/1210/35/6, The Yarrow & Ettrick Valleys: a settlement study, Selkirk County Council, March 1975.

past forty years, but the agricultural labour requirements had fallen sharply. Nevertheless, 60 per cent of the working population remained in agriculture employment. In 1971, less than 180 people (29 per cent of the 608 people in the Ettrick and Yarrow valleys) lived in the five villages of Yarrowford, Yarrow, Yarrowfeus, Ettrickbridge End and Ettrick. The original function of the villages of serving an agricultural hinterland had been reduced and the range of facilities and services had diminished. Other emerging issues were the increasing attraction of the villages, particularly Ettrickbridge End, to local commuters to nearby Galashiels and Selkirk and the growth in demand for second and holiday homes. This demand could be seen as a positive and a negative influence; as a means of rescuing empty property that might otherwise fall into disrepair, but at the same time leading to inflated house prices thus edging the local population out of the housing market and exacerbating depopulation. The report, produced in March 1975, set out policies and proposals for the five villages in order to retain and attract population: for the improvement of water and drainage provision, the retention and attraction of business opportunities such as craft and tourist-related industries, the opportunities for infill housing, and the provision of facilities and innovative public transport, such as the 'post-bus'. The report would form the basis for future planning in this relatively remote area and would lead to a relaxation of housing in the countryside policy.

A report on agriculture in Berwickshire, published in July 1974, examined the pattern of agriculture in the county and how the local authority could assist this major employer of the county (20 per cent of the employed population compared with 3 per cent in Scotland as a whole).[70] It showed that the number of farm units had almost halved since 1951 (from 700 to 360 farms); the average farm size had more than doubled from 200 acres in 1951 to 462 acres in 1971, compared with a Scottish average of 376 acres. The acreage under barley and wheat had doubled and intensive pig and poultry farming had expanded. The report pointed out that, with the increased mechanisation of agriculture, the need was for more skilled workers. The report showed that 87 per cent of agricultural workers lived on the farm in tied houses, but younger workers preferred living in settlements so local authority housing was required for farm workers in the smaller settlements. The report also showed that there were a considerable number of vacant and semi-derelict farm buildings and cottages in the countryside, which

---

[70] SBA/1210/34/9, Agriculture in Berwickshire, County Planning and Development Department, July 1974.

could be brought back into use. Future planning policy would respond to these changing circumstances and housing in the countryside policy would become much more flexible.

THE COUNTRYSIDE

The designation 'Area of Great Landscape Value' (AGLV) was established in the 1947 Act. Within AGLVs, the primary objective was the conservation and enhancement of landscape quality and the individual character of the area. That part of Midlothian County that would become part of the Borders Region, the whole of Peeblesshire and substantial parts of Berwickshire and Roxburghshire were designated AGLV. In Selkirkshire, the AGLV designation was limited to two small areas centred on the Three Brethren hill and Bowhill Estate and the St Mary's Loch area. However, no systematic evaluation of the landscape was undertaken as a basis for designation and the approach of the four Border county planning authorities to development in AGLVs varied considerably. In general terms, there was a strong presumption against development within designated areas, except where it was plainly necessary in connection with existing development or was consistent with the purposes of AGLV designation in providing appropriate recreation facilities. In cases where development was permissible, a high standard of architectural layout and design was considered essential. In response to increasing leisure and recreation pressure on the countryside, SDD Circular 2/1962 was produced by the Scottish Office to provide more guidance on the considerations to be borne in mind in defining AGLVs in development plans and on the preparation of tourist development proposals.[71] This circular placed the onus on local planning authorities not only to 'safeguard the most outstanding beauty spots' but also to encourage the provision of visitor facilities.

In Peeblesshire, a Report on Tourist Development Proposals and Areas of Great Landscape Value was published in 1967, which maintained the area designated as AGLV but also identified the valleys of the Tweed and its tributaries as specific Areas of Tourist Attraction. The report made proposals for caravan and camping sites, car parks, picnic sites and other tourist-related facilities.[72] Existing caravan sites, such

---

[71] Scottish Development Department Circular 2/1962: Development Plans, A Areas of Great Landscape Value, and B Tourist Development Proposals, SDD, 1962.

[72] SBA/1210/36/8, Peeblesshire Tourist Development Proposals and AGLVs, December 1966 & April 1967 (approved June 1968).

as Crossburn caravan site in Peebles, expanded in the 1960s, reflecting the growth in holidaying and car touring.[73] In 1969, the county council purchased Rosetta House and grounds, on the outskirts of Peebles, with a view to its development as a caravan and camping park with sites for 100 touring caravans, tents, toilets, café/restaurant and shop.[74] At West Linton, following an appeal to the Secretary of State in 1968, the former community centre on the north-west side of the A702 was converted into the Pantiles Hotel, with an adjoining caravan site.[75] The replacement of holiday huts on the hut sites at Carlops, West Linton, Eddleston and Peebles continued with planning permissions granted for replacement structures of a similar size, design and materials. Considerable effort was put into the Hattonknowe site at Eddleston with the production of an overall plan for the continued use of the site with the renovation of huts, the provision of proper sewage facilities, and tree planting and landscaping. However, it would take many years of negotiation with the farmer/landowner and occupiers to achieve any success. Enforcement remained an issue.[76] Milk bars, tearooms and cafés became established at a number of rural locations on the main roads through Peeblesshire during the 1960s. Peter Maxwell-Stuart opened up Traquair House to the public and obtained planning permission for a shop and tearoom in 1965, marking the start of the commercialisation of this premier historic house in Peeblesshire.[77] In 1970, the Bakehouse Tearoom in West Linton was established in the former Children's Mission House as a popular destination for coffee and cake.[78] In Eddleston, the Horseshoe Tearoom was converted into a restaurant and public bar.[79]

[73] P/CD/1/27, Meetings of Peeblesshire Town Planning Committee, 7 June 1963 & 5 June 1964.

[74] P/CD/1/32, Meetings of Peeblesshire Town Planning Committee, 2 May 1969.

[75] P/CD/1/32, Meetings of Peeblesshire Town Planning Committee, 5 September 1968.

[76] The first reports on Hattonknowe Hut site date from the early 1950s, when concerns were raised regarding the unsatisfactory sanitary conditions, see P/CD/1/18, Meetings of Peeblesshire Town Planning Committee, 3 December 1954. Complaints continued throughout the 1950s and 1960s and it would be 1968 before a plan was agreed for the future of the Hut site, see P/CD/1/32, Meetings of Peeblesshire Town Planning Committee, 7 June 1968.

[77] P/CD/1/26, Meetings of Peeblesshire Town Planning Committee, 1 February 1963.

[78] P/CD/1/33, Meetings of Peeblesshire Town Planning Committee, 3 October 1969.

[79] P/CD/1/31, Meetings of Peeblesshire Town Planning Committee, 13 October 1967.

In approving the Berwickshire County Development Plan in 1960, the SoS deleted the proposed AGLV designation and requested that the council consider more specific areas for designation.[80] A local consultant, T. D. Thomson, was engaged to review the landscape designation and, in March 1966, the council approved a report on Areas of Great Landscape Value and Tourist Development, which contained a number of more specific AGLV designations; the Lammermuir Hills, Lauderdale, the Berwickshire coast and the Tweed valley around Scott's View, near Bemersyde. These proposals were submitted as a formal amendment to the development plan and were approved by the SoS in January 1968.[81] The Berwickshire coast, where there was an increasing pressure for caravan and camping sites with demands to increase site capacity in Eyemouth and Coldingham, was a particular area of concern.[82] At Coldingham Sands, the erosion of the sand dunes as a result of its increasing use by caravanners and the proliferation of bathing huts, prompted the investigation of anti-erosion methods similar to those employed in East Lothian (where Frank Tindall, the County Planning Officer, was a pioneer of dune stabilisation at Gullane). However, the beach was in private ownership and any action was thus hindered.[83]

In Roxburghshire, a wide-ranging report on Areas of Great Landscape Value and Tourism Development was prepared in February 1965, which identified a number of areas suitable for AGLV designation: the Scottish side of the Cheviot Hills, the Carter Bar area, Hermitage Valley, Eildon Hills, along the Tweed at Kelso and the Jed Water valley south of Jedburgh.[84] The tourism development proposals were very much related to car and bus touring. A range of tourist facilities was recommended, including a new hotel and national tourist information centre at Jedburgh (on the site of the former North British Rayon Factory), outdoor centres in the Cheviots and the Bowmont Valley, short-term

---

[80] SBA/1210/5, Berwick County Development Plan, February 1965.

[81] SBA/1210/34/1, County of Berwick, Report on AGLVs and Tourist Development, March 1966.

[82] B/CD/1/130, Meetings of Berwickshire Planning and Development Committee, 9 October 1962.

[83] Various reports were considered by Berwickshire's Planning Committee from 1957 onwards before any specific action was taken in the early 1970s; see Meetings of Berwickshire Planning and Development Committee, 11 September 1957, 13 October 1964, 11 December 1967 & October 1973.

[84] SBA/1210/33/2, Report on AGLVs and Tourist Development, Roxburgh County Planning Department, February 1965.

parking and national signage at the English border at Carter Bar, touring caravan sites in Hawick and Kelso, a number of lay-by/picnic sites at viewpoints and at the start of important footpaths, and the signposting of rights of way. Amendment No. 3 to the development plan, approved by the SoS in April 1966, confirmed the recommendations of the Area of Great Landscape Value and Tourism Development Report.[85]

In pursuance of the tourism development proposals, planning permission was granted in September 1966 for a caravan site for sixty caravans at Hornshole, on the A698 just east of Hawick.[86] In 1969, the SoS sustained an appeal against the refusal of planning permission for a motel, restaurant, caravan site and petrol filling station at Lilliardsedge on the A68 north of Jedburgh; planning permission was refused mainly because the council considered that Jedburgh was the preferred location for such development.[87] This development by Lothian Estates would become a recognisable feature and valued tourism facility and would be continuously updated and expanded. A large caravan site at Springwood Park, Kelso, established in 1962 was extended in 1972 and, again, in 1974.[88]

In Selkirkshire, it would be 1974 before a Report on Areas of Great Landscape Value and Tourist Development was produced with an enlarged AGLV covering the Tweedsmuir Hills/St Mary's Loch area.[89] Proposals were agreed in 1970 with Wemyss & March Estates for the development of St Mary's Loch as a major recreational attraction.[90] Access to the shore of the loch was improved with informal picnic areas, the council provided toilets at St Mary's Loch in 1970 and improvements were undertaken to the Glen Café on the shore of the loch.[91]

More action on the provision of leisure and recreation facilities would be taken by the four planning authorities following the enactment of the Countryside (Scotland) Act 1967, which designated large areas of

[85] SBA/1210/7, Roxburgh County Development Plan Amendments.
[86] R/CD/1/77, Meetings of Roxburghshire Planning Committee, 29 September 1966.
[87] R/CD/1/78, Meetings of Roxburghshire Planning Committee, 10 April 1969.
[88] R/CD/1/77, Meetings of Roxburghshire Planning Committee, 22 January 1962, and R/CD/1/79, Meetings of Roxburghshire Planning Committee, 12 November 1972 & 2 May 1974.
[89] SBA/1210/35/5, Areas of Great Landscape Value and Tourist Development, County of Selkirk, 1974.
[90] S/CD/1/43, Meetings of Selkirkshire Town and Country Planning Committee, 3 December 1970.
[91] S/CD/9/2, Selkirk County Council, Planning applications and decisions, No. 3142, approved 19/9/69 & No. 4019, approved 20/11/72.

the Borders as 'countryside' where 75 per cent grants were available from the CCS for the provision of leisure and recreation facilities. The whole of Peeblesshire and Berwickshire, the whole of Roxburghshire excluding the burgh of Hawick, and the whole of Selkirkshire excluding the burgh of Galashiels, was designated as 'countryside'. However, the local authorities' ability to take full advantage of the substantial grants available was hindered by cutbacks in local authority expenditure and the effect of inflation on capital costs.

In Peeblesshire, a sub-committee of the Town Planning Committee, the Tourist Development Sub-committee co-ordinated the provision of picnic sites in the Meldon Hills (including toilets), at Cademuir Hill, Manor Sware and in the Leithen Valley. With the Forestry Commission, Glentress Forest was promoted as an area with potential for major recreational development. In 1973, a Joint Planning Advisory Committee was established for the Pentland Hills, which stretched into Peeblesshire (it would become a regional park in 1986).[92]

In Berwickshire, the Countryside (Scotland) Act 1967 opened the door for countryside projects such as conservation measures at Coldingham Bay and the provision of car park/picnic sites on the main tourist routes through the county. Cove Harbour, which had been falling into disrepair for a number of years, was purchased from Dunglass & Angus Estates in 1971 with grant assistance from the CCS and plans approved to repair the access road and pier, remove the overhanging cliff and convert the fishermen's stores into toilets and a shelter.[93] In February 1972, the council agreed to purchase Coldingham Sands in order to control the increasing visitor pressure on the bay and a management plan was agreed, resulting in the removal of a number of unsightly and ill-positioned holiday huts, dune stabilisation, the prohibition of vehicular access to the beach and the provision of limited formal car parking above the beach.[94]

In Roxburghshire, one of the first developments under the Countryside (Scotland) Act 1967 was the provision, in 1970, of a car park/picnic site with toilets on the A7 at Teviothead, at a cost of £5,500.[95] In March

[92] P/CD/1/36, Meetings of Peeblesshire Town Planning Committee, 2 March 1973.
[93] B/CD/1/134, Meetings of Berwickshire Planning and Development Committee, 6 July 1971.
[94] SBA/1210/34/10, Coldingham Bay Recreation Management Study, Berwickshire County Planning and Development Department, August 1974.
[95] R/CD/1/79, Meetings of Roxburghshire Planning Committee, 27 November 1970.

1972, the county council established a Countryside Committee, chaired by the chairman of the Planning Committee.[96] Over the next two years, this committee, comprising representatives from a range of countryside, recreational, country sports and tourism organisations as well as officers from the county council, provided advice on matters such as the provision of picnic sites in the Bowmont Valley and in Craik Forest (combined with forest trails), mapping rights of way, the promotion of farm trails, environmental improvements and amenity tree planting, the identification and preservation of wildlife sites, the promotion of outdoor education and the expansion of the outdoor centre at Towford.

CONCLUSIONS

There were fundamental changes in the way town and country planning was administered in the Scottish Borders in the 1960s when it was transformed from simply a mechanism for controlling land use to a more proactive process. The strengthening of planning as a profession was reflected in the creation of separate planning departments where previously planning had been combined with the roads engineering, surveying or architect's department.

In addition to an active involvement in the promotion of industrial development, town and country planning in the Scottish Borders adopted a more positive role in urban development with the establishment of technical working parties to assess the potential for growth of the main towns in the region. The Hawick and Galashiels Working Parties provided the opportunity for close co-operation between county and burgh council departments and illustrated the increasing interest of central government, the SDD, in regional and local studies. Having said that, the working party reports make it clear that the views expressed, and the recommendations made, by the various officials of the local authorities and SDD are their own professional opinions and cannot be regarded as committing their authorities or the SoS to direct action (and capital expenditure).[97] In the meantime, development in the main towns proceeded by way of amendments to the increasingly out-dated county development plans. Land was allocated in all the main towns for both

---

[96] R/CD/1/121, Roxburghshire Countryside Committee Minutes, March 1972–March 1974.
[97] Selkirk County Council, *Second Report of the Galashiels Technical Working Party*, p. 5.

industry and housing in an effort to stem depopulation.[98] To complement the promotion of economic development and the provision of industrial sites, the local housing authorities and the SSHA provided substantial numbers of rented housing to meet the needs of the existing population and accommodate incoming workers. Nevertheless, the overall population of the Borders continued to decline in the 1960s, albeit at a slower rate than in the 1950s. It would be the early 1970s before there were the first indications that the efforts of the local authorities had been successful in reversing the long-term trend of out-migration from the region.

Non-statutory town centre redevelopment plans were prepared for Hawick, Jedburgh, Kelso, Melrose, Eyemouth and Duns but few proposals were implemented. As the 1960s progressed there was a significant shift in attitude in favour of the rehabilitation of town centres rather than redevelopment; consequently, redevelopment proposals for a number of town centres in the Borders were re-assessed in favour of improving existing property, face-lift schemes and the pedestrianisation of shopping streets. The Civic Amenities Act 1967 signalled a fundamental change in attitude to the future of the historic centres of towns and villages across the Borders. Twenty-seven conservation areas, stretching from Carlops and Skirling in the west to St Abbs and Coldingham in the east, were designated in the region. This Act enabled more control over building development and led to the implementation of schemes for the enhancement of selected conservation areas with the undergrounding of electricity and telephone lines and tree planting schemes. Civic and amenity societies sprang up across the region, reflecting the growing public concern for local amenity and the environment.

In the 1950s, planning paid scant regard to rural areas. A growing awareness of rural depopulation in the 1960s led both Roxburgh and Berwickshire County Councils to produce strategies for development in the villages spread throughout their landward areas as a focus for employment and social, cultural and educational facilities and services in order to stem rural depopulation. SCC examined the problems of the remote Ettrick and Yarrow Valleys where increased afforestation and the resultant loss of agricultural employment threatened the viability of the upland farming communities.

There was also mounting concern over the effects of the increased mechanisation of agriculture on rural landscapes and the growing pressure for recreation in the countryside. Over 60 per cent of the Borders

---

[98] Scottish Border Local Authorities Joint Committee, *The Borders Region 1975*, Regional Planning Unit, Newtown St Boswells, 1975, p. 2.

region was designated as an AGLV in county development plans. However, this designation was largely symbolic and restricted development in the countryside. A more positive attitude was adopted with the production of reports on Tourist Development Proposals and AGLVs in the mid-1960s, but it was not until the Countryside (Scotland) Act 1967 that more positive action was taken to provide leisure and recreational facilities across the Borders. Thoughts would also be given to the preparation of management plans for particularly sensitive areas, such as St Mary's Loch in Selkirkshire and Coldingham Sands in Berwickshire. Tree Planting Year 1973 would see a co-ordinated effort throughout the region to add to the depleted deciduous woodlands and hedgerow trees.

During the 1960s, therefore, there was a much more positive attitude to urban development with the establishment of technical working parties to assess the potential for growth in the region, and action in relation to the conservation of the urban and rural environment and the provision of tourism and leisure facilities. A range of policy reports were produced by the out-going county planning departments, covering such matters as conservation, tourism and recreation, caravanning and the control of housing in the countryside. It would be for the new regional council to re-assess the policies and proposals in all these documents and set out the future strategy for land use and development in the Scottish Borders countryside.

5

A Borders Region at Last!

INTRODUCTION

PRIOR TO 1975, LOCAL government in Scotland represented a distinctly Scottish set of institutions. The roots of Scottish local government can be traced back to the royal burghs of the Middle Ages and was one of the items guaranteed in the Treaty of Union in 1707. Prior to 1929, Scottish local government consisted primarily of royal burghs, which were typically small towns or villages that organised trade and basic services within communities, and county councils established in 1889.[1] As the functions of local government expanded, notably during the nineteenth century, the demand for a more systematic structure of local government developed. This resulted in the complex structure of 430 local authorities established in 1929, which consisted of thirty-three county councils and four counties of cities (Edinburgh, Glasgow, Dundee and Aberdeen), twenty-one large burghs, generally those with a population of 20,000 people or more, 176 small burghs and 196 landward district councils.[2] In 1975, there were fifty-seven Scottish local planning authorities, comprising thirty-one counties (two of them joint), twenty-four large burghs and two small burghs, with planning powers under the 1947 Act, ranging in size and character from the City of Glasgow, with over one million people, to the County of Sutherland, with 13,500 people scattered over 2,000 square miles.[3] In the four Border counties of Berwickshire, Peeblesshire, Roxburghshire and Selkirkshire, there were twelve small burghs: Coldstream, Duns, Eyemouth and Lauder

---

[1] Atkinson, M., 'The Organization of Local Government in Scotland', *Political Science Review*, Vol. 18, No. 1 (March 1903), pp. 59–87.

[2] McConnell, A., *Scottish Local Government* (Edinburgh: Edinburgh University Press, 2004), p. 47.

[3] Report of the Planning Advisory Group, *The Future of Development Plans* (London: HMSO, 1965), p. 55.

in Berwickshire; Innerleithen and Peebles in Peeblesshire, Hawick, Jedburgh, Kelso and Melrose in Roxburghshire; and Galashiels and Selkirk in Selkirkshire. Planning powers were held solely by the four county councils.

By the mid-1960s, the generally held view was that there was a need to reform local government in Scotland. The multiplicity of local authorities, many of them serving small areas and small populations were inefficient. As population had migrated to the towns and cities as a result of the Industrial Revolution and these towns and cities had expanded into the surrounding countryside, boundary anomalies caused friction between neighbouring authorities. Also, given the emerging culture of regional, economic and strategic planning in the 1960s, pressure developed behind the concept of larger, regional local authorities that could improve service provision.[4] The Wheatley Commission was appointed by the Labour government under Harold Wilson in February 1966 to review local administration in Scotland and reported, following extensive consultation, in September 1969. Lord Wheatley was a former Lord Advocate and Member of Parliament for Edinburgh East. The Commission comprised eight other notable members of the political and business community, including Henry Ballantyne, Chairman of Ballantyne's Knitwear and a former provost of Innerleithen in the Scottish Borders.[5]

The Commission recommended a two-tier structure for local government in Scotland and also suggested that local areas should be given a voice through the creation of non-statutory community councils. The Commission divided Scotland into seven regions, subdivided into thirty-seven districts. A South-East Region comprised the counties of Peeblesshire, Roxburghshire, Selkirkshire, Berwickshire, East Lothian, Edinburgh, Midlothian, West Lothian and most of Fife. The Conservative government returned to power in June 1970 and it would be February 1971 before a White Paper on the reform of local government in Scotland was produced. In response to the comments received on the Wheatley Commission Report, the government accepted the formation of the Western Isles, Orkney and Shetland Islands Councils separate from the Highland Council but rejected the idea of separate

---

[4] Wannop, Urlan A., *The Regional Imperative: Regional Planning and Governance in Britain, Europe and the United States* (London: Regional Studies Association, 1995), pp. 9–14.

[5] Royal Commission, *Report of the Royal Commission on Local Government in Scotland 1966–1969*, Cmnd. 4150 (Edinburgh: HMSO, 1969).

regions for Fife and the Scottish Borders. However, during the passage of the bill through parliament, the campaign for Fife and the Scottish Borders to become separate regions was successful and the reduced south-east region was renamed the Forth Region (subsequently changed to the Lothian Region).[6]

The Borders Region comprised the counties of Peeblesshire, Roxburghshire, Selkirkshire and Berwickshire, and the Gala Water part of Midlothian County, which included Heriot, Fountainhall and Stow. A proposal to remove Liddesdale, including Newcastleton, from Roxburghshire and include it in the new Dumfries and Galloway Region was not pursued. The bill received royal assent on 25 October 1973 with a system of nine regional councils, fifty-three district councils and three all-purpose island councils, and the Local Government (Scotland) Act 1973 gave statutory effect to the Borders Regional Council (BRC) and its constituent District Councils of Berwickshire, Ettrick and Lauderdale, Roxburgh and Tweeddale on 16 May 1975 (see Figure 5.1).[7]

Berwickshire District was somewhat smaller than the old county area, having lost Earlston and Lauderdale to Ettrick and Lauderdale District; Ettrick and Lauderdale District comprised the whole of Selkirkshire plus the Gala Water valley, previously in Midlothian County, Earlston and Lauderdale, and the Melrose/St Boswells area previously in Roxburghshire; Roxburgh District comprised Roxburghshire without the Melrose/St Boswells area; Tweeddale District covered the same area as the previous Peeblesshire County. This resulted in a re-distribution of the 1971 census population as follows:[8]

Old Counties		New Districts	
Berwickshire	20,779	Berwickshire	16,980
Roxburghshire	41,959	Roxburgh	35,400
Selkirkshire	20,868	Ettrick & Lauderdale	32,421
Midlothian (part)	1,195		
Peeblesshire	<u>13,676</u>	Tweeddale	<u>13,676</u>
	<u>98,477</u>		<u>98,477</u>

---

[6] See Local Government (Scotland) Act 1973 (Cmnd. 65) (London: HMSO, 1973).

[7] For information about the new Regional Council and the four new District Councils in the Scottish Borders, a guide was published jointly by the five authorities entitled *The New Local Government: Who's Who in the Borders?*

[8] See inside cover of *The Borders Region 1975*, published by the Scottish Border Local Authorities Joint Committee and produced by the Regional Planning Unit, March 1975.

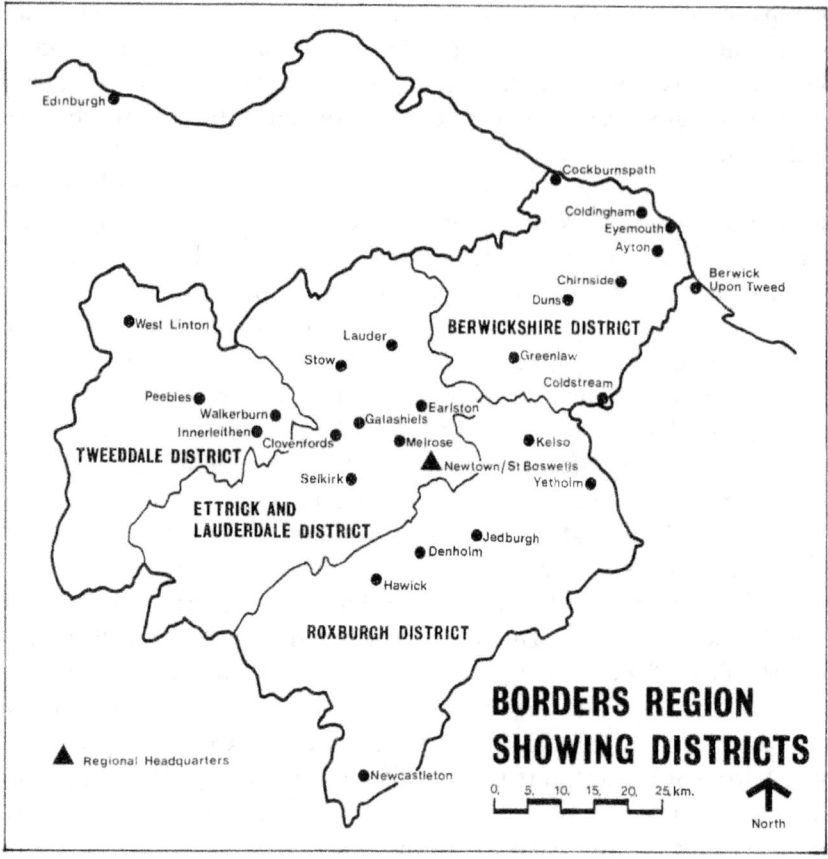

Figure 5.1 The Borders Region

The new regional councils were responsible for the major strategic functions that required large resources, such as police, fire, education, social work, water and drainage and roads, whilst the district councils were responsible for the more localised functions of housing, environmental health, refuse collection, road cleansing, parks and burial grounds. The 1973 Act allowed for the possibility of the concurrent exercise of some functions, such as museums and art galleries, tourism and countryside, and industrial development but this soon led to problems with the duplication of effort and resources, inefficiency, public confusion and lack of accountability. Following the review of working relationships within the new local authorities by the Stodart Committee in 1981, which recommended that the concurrence of functions should be abolished, the Local Government and

Planning (Scotland) Act 1982 ended virtually all concurrent functions in Scottish local government.[9] In the Scottish Borders, museums and art galleries, parks and recreation became the sole responsibility of the district councils and tourism and countryside and industrial development became the sole responsibility of the regional council. Stodart considered that whilst most functions could be allocated to one or other tier of authority without serious difficulties, planning could not be treated in this way.[10]

The Wheatley Commission also recommended that community councils should be established to improve communication between local communities and local authorities and other public bodies. Consequently, community councils were introduced in 1975 by the 1973 Act and the new district councils were required to prepare a scheme for the establishment of community councils in their area. Some sixty-seven such community councils would be established in the Scottish Borders; they would be designated as statutory consultees for the purpose of development plan preparation thus providing local communities with the opportunity of influencing development and changes in land use in their area.

As regards the planning function, from the early 1960s, development plans prepared under the 1947 Act had been subject to increasing criticism. Because of the great amount of detail they contained, plans tended to be inflexible and, although planning authorities were under an obligation to review development plans at five-yearly intervals, this rarely happened. Amendments required the approval of the SoS and these required the same time-consuming procedure whether they were for major developments or detailed proposals. Consequently, it proved difficult to keep plans up-to-date and forward-looking. It was argued that they were little more than land use plans and they often paid little attention to economic realities and investment priorities. The PAG, set up jointly by the Ministry of Housing and Local Government in England & Wales and the SDD, reported in 1965 on the *Future of Development Plans* and recommended a new system of structure plans and local plans: structure plans would provide a regional policy framework for accommodating new development, deal with strategic matters and provide a

---

[9] Stodart, J.A., *Report of the Committee of Inquiry into Local Government in Scotland*, Cmnd. 8115 (Edinburgh: HMSO, 1981).

[10] Cmnd. 8115, para. 49. See also Keating, M., 'The Stodart Committee and Planning in Scotland', *The Planner*, Vol. 68, p. 22.

context for local plans; local plans would apply the regional guidance and set out detailed land use policies and proposals.[11]

At the same time, the Skeffington Committee Report of 1969, *People and Planning* prompted a new interest in openness and public involvement in planning.[12] The groundbreaking Skeffington Report proposed that the new development plans should be the subject of full public scrutiny and debate. The report marks an important moment in the evolution of British town planning, bringing about the recognition of the different sectors of society (now called 'stakeholders') affected by expert-prepared development plans. The report emphasises that public participation would not mean that planners or elected representatives would become entirely deferential to the public, elected officials must make the final decisions, but the public should share in the formulation of policies and proposals and not be faced, simply, with a fait accompli. Although there were no specific recommendations, the report sets out techniques for enhancing participation and publicity and paved the way for the 1972 Act, which required planning authorities to afford the public an opportunity to put forward their views on structure and local plans before planning authorities had become firmly committed to particular policies and proposals.

Mention should also be made of Scotland's Planning Exchange, established in 1972 by the Centre for Environmental Studies and the Scottish Office, 'to seek closer relationships between researchers and policy makers, developers, voluntary bodies and the public, help local councillors to familiarise themselves with the planning process, and assist public participation'.[13] Opened in Glasgow in April 1973, it organised conferences, seminars and inter-disciplinary study groups on subjects relevant to local authorities. In the early years its work was very much concentrated on the west of Scotland but gradually its activities broadened across the whole spectrum of planning and across the whole of Scotland, strongly supported by planning authorities. After 1975, the Planning Exchange was particularly active in training and educating elected members (councillors) as well as keeping planning staff up to

---

[11] PAG Report, *The Future of Development Plans*, pp. 9–10.

[12] *People and Planning: Report of the Committee on Public Participation in Planning (the Skeffington Committee Report)* (London: HMSO, 1969). For an evaluation of the evolution of public participation in planning, see Damer, S. and C. Hague, 'Participation in Planning: A Review', *The Town Planning Review*, Vol. 42, No. 3 (July 1971), pp. 217–232.

[13] Burton, T., 'Scotland's Planning Exchange – The First Seven Years', *Local Government Studies*, Vol. 5, Issue 5 (1979), pp. 7–19.

date on new topics of interest but also in the exchange of information between authorities through forums.

The legislation on the new type of development plan was contained within the Town and Country Planning (Scotland) Act 1969 and re-enacted in the 1972 Act, but only came into force with the enactment of the 1973 Act on 16 May 1975. In the new system, town and country planning powers were split in most areas of Scotland, somewhat uneasily, between the regional councils and the district councils. Regional councils were responsible for strategic planning; this required the production of a Regional Report within one year of the reorganisation of local government setting out the main issues affecting life in the region, and the subsequent preparation of structure plans, which would 'provide a strategic policy framework for the development and control of the physical environment in the interests of the community'. District councils were responsible for the preparation of local plans, the determination of planning applications (development control), enforcement of planning, the protection of listed buildings, designation of conservation areas and tree preservation orders. The Highlands, Dumfries and Galloway and Borders regions were designated general planning authorities because of their low population density and were, hence, responsible for all planning functions. The four district councils in the Borders Region possessed no planning powers, which irked more than one district council chief executive.

PREPARING FOR REGIONALISATION

The new BRC comprising twenty-three elected members – eight from the new Ettrick and Lauderdale District, eight from Roxburgh District, four from Berwickshire District and three from Tweeddale District – was elected on 15 May 1974 and replaced the existing county councils and burgh councils on 16 May 1975. Only two of the twenty-three members were female. The majority were of the landowning or professional classes; most were retired with only a handful in full-time employment. Thirteen members stood as Independents, seven as Conservative candidates and three as Liberal. Only one of the twenty-three constituencies was contested by a Labour candidate so it is little surprise that there were no Labour members of the regional council. In fact, there would be no Labour members during the whole lifetime of the regional council. Two of the twenty-three members were elected unopposed in 1974 and this number rose to ten in 1978 (nine in 1982), perhaps an indication that the general populace was content with the achievements of the council or a reflection of the conservatism/paternalism prevalent at the time.

There would be little change in the constituency of the regional council until 1986 when the number of members increased to twenty-four, and the political distribution was as follows: fourteen Independent, six Conservative, two SDP/Liberal and two SNP. It has to be said that during the 1970s and 1980s, many of the Independent members were either Conservative or Liberal party members but were of the view that national politics did not play a part in local government. Four of the twenty-four members were female in 1986; two farmer's wives, a mill owner's wife and a businesswoman.[14]

Major John M. Askew, Convener of BCC was elected Convener of BRC, a post he would hold until 1982. Victor Parle, who had been Chairman of BCC's Planning and Development Committee, was elected Chairman of the Planning and Development Committee. David P. Douglas, BCC's County Planning and Development Officer was appointed Director of Physical Planning (subsequently changed to Physical Planning and Development and then simply Planning and Development). Kenneth Clark, appointed Chief Executive of the regional council, had been Depute County Clerk at BCC before taking up an appointment as County Clerk in Ross and Cromarty from where he moved back to the Borders. Some surprise was expressed at the dominance of Berwickshire personalities in the new organisation when both RCC and SCC had more members and had more influence. It would seem that the Berwickshire members were seen as a neutral influence between the two 'opposing forces' based in Newtown St Boswells and Selkirk.

RCC's offices at Newtown St Boswells were the obvious choice for the location of the headquarters of BRC. These modern offices were the only ones with sufficient capacity to accommodate the main departments of the new regional authority; administration, finance, roads, planning, education and social work (the water and drainage department would be located in Melrose). The original offices, comprising the council chamber and accommodation for the county clerk and his staff, dated from 1932 when the offices were relocated from Jedburgh. Major expansion took place in 1967–1968 with the construction of the three-storey square concrete building designed by Peter Womersley to

---

[14] For detailed information on the election results, see Bochel, J. M. and D. T. Denver, *Local Government Elections: Results and Statistics* (Edinburgh: Scottish Academic Press, 1974) and succeeding elections.

accommodate growing staff numbers. BRC's Department of Physical Planning would occupy the first floor of the 'new' building.

Anticipating the reorganisation of local government, the existing local authorities in the Borders established the Scottish Border Local Authorities Joint Committee (SBLAJC) in January 1972 with membership from the five county councils (including Midlothian County Council) and the twelve town councils.[15] In June 1972, a working group of planning officers from the four counties in the region, chaired by Frank Constable, County Planning Officer of Roxburghshire, suggested the formation of a Regional Planning Unit (RPU) to prepare a report on the Borders Region as a basis for a future regional strategy for the planning and development of the region.[16] Paul Gregory, a Planner in SDD, was appointed Regional Planning Co-ordinator in June 1973 and the RPU was established with a complement of five staff.

A report by P. A. Management Consultants, appointed to advise on the organisation of the new authority, recommended that the Planning Committee in the new regional authority be responsible for all planning activities, industrial promotion and development, the promotion of tourism and countryside activities under the Countryside (Scotland) Act 1967, and that a Director of Physical Planning be appointed to be responsible for planning and building control, industrial promotion and development, tourism promotion and countryside activities.[17] An analysis of existing staff in May 1973 showed that there were twenty-nine staff employed in planning and development in the four existing county authorities; nine in Berwickshire, eleven in Roxburghshire, one in Selkirkshire and two in Peeblesshire (employed from Midlothian) in addition to the six in the RPU. A report by the Planning Officers Working Group recommended that the new regional planning department should have a staff of forty people. However, this recommendation was not accepted by the SBLAJC and in March 1974, a staffing structure with a complement of thirty-three was approved, comprising:[18]

---

[15] SBA/R/CD/1/119, Scottish Border Local Authorities Joint Committee, 13 January 1972.

[16] SBA/R/CD/1/119, Scottish Border Local Authorities Joint Committee, 1 June 1972.

[17] SBA/R/CD/1/119, Scottish Border Local Authorities Joint Committee, 6 December 1973.

[18] SBA/R/CD/1/120, Scottish Border Local Authorities Joint Committee, 7 March 1974.

Director	1
Depute Director	1
Assistant Directors	3
Development Officers	2
Regional Tourist Officer	1
Senior Planning Assistants	2
Planning Assistants	11
Tourism Assistant	1
Technicians	5
Administration	6
Total	33

Meanwhile, the RPU produced an Interim Report entitled *A Profile of the Borders* in June 1974 and a final report *The Borders Region 1975* in April 1975.[19]

THE BORDERS REGION 1975

The report confirmed that the enumerated population for the Borders Region in 1971 was 98,477 persons, 10,000 less than the 1951 population, and that there had been a steady population decline since the peak of 128,000 persons in 1881–1991, with the majority of the loss from the landward areas. The population of the burghs had remained fairly stable with growth in recent years in Eyemouth, Galashiels, Kelso and Peebles. A high proportion of the population was over retirement age (20.4 per cent compared with a Scottish average of 15.3 per cent). The old age structure of the Borders population meant that, in recent years, deaths had exceeded births resulting in the natural decrease of the population. This, combined with a loss of population due to outward migration to other parts of Scotland and the UK, meant that population decline had been inevitable. The consequences of a further ageing of the population and further out-migration would be serious for the future of the Scottish Borders.[20]

The report pointed out that, in spite of the efforts of the local authorities since the White Paper on the Scottish Economy in 1966 and the Central Borders Plan of 1968, the Borders' economy continued to be narrowly based on agriculture and textiles and vulnerable to economic recession. The report confirmed many of the views expressed in the

---

[19] SBA/1210/10/2, *A Profile of the Borders 1974*, Interim Report of the Regional Planning Unit, June 1974; SBA/1210/10/3 *The Borders Region, 1975*, Regional Planning Unit, March 1975.

[20] SBA/1210/10/3, *The Borders Region, 1975*, p. 2.

development plans and non-statutory reports prepared by the existing county councils, that the high proportion of jobs in the more volatile sectors of the economy, particularly textiles, and the absence of a reasonable pool of jobs in the public services, distribution and other parts of the service sector, undermined the employment stability of the region. Both agriculture and textiles had a disproportionate number of older workers and high numbers of women workers were employed in textiles.[21] In relation to textile employment, some 1,400 jobs had been lost in the hosiery sector between 1966 and 1973 and almost 1,500 jobs had been lost in the woollens sector over the same period.[22] However, during the same period, nearly fifty new manufacturing firms had established themselves in the region, employing 2,900 people in 1973.[23] The report concluded that the regional economy needed to be more broadly based if young persons were to be retained and that the provision of houses by SSHA for essential incoming workers was vital if the economy was to diversify and grow.[24]

In terms of housing, although the population had declined over the past twenty years, the number of households had increased as a result of a reducing household size. Of the 39,000 dwellings in the region, almost 9 per cent were classified as vacant, with the bulk of these in the landward areas, for instance, agricultural tied cottages. There were almost 3,000 dwellings in the region below the tolerable standard, over 60 per cent of which were in Hawick and Galashiels. The Borders lagged behind other areas of Scotland in terms of the proportion of owner-occupied housing with a much larger proportion of private rented, including tied, housing. There was a shortage of reasonably priced, modern, terraced and semi-detached houses, which Borderers with incomes lower than average could afford. House completions were on an upward trend, however, largely as a result of an expanding local authority and SSHA building programme. Only 26 per cent of completions were in the private sector in 1974.[25]

In relation to transport, although there was no railway station in the Borders, there was a comprehensive network of good roads and major improvements had been carried out in the past two years to the A1, A68 and A7, the north to south through-roads. East–west links were less

---

[21] SBA/1210/10/3, *The Borders Region, 1975*, p. 5.
[22] SBA/1210/10/3, *The Borders Region, 1975*, p. 7 (para. 27).
[23] SBA/1210/10/3, *The Borders Region, 1975*, p. 7 (para. 30).
[24] SBA/1210/10/3, *The Borders Region, 1975*, p. 9 (para. 38).
[25] SBA/1210/10/3, *The Borders Region, 1975*, p. 10.

clearly defined. Many buses on rural routes carried few passengers and 160 miles of routes only survived because of subsidies. The Post Office provided six Postbus services, but passenger levels were low. The wide distribution of settlements and rural population and the convenience of the car were undermining the public transport service.[26]

In relation to rural land uses, the area in agricultural use had declined by 8 per cent (30,000 hectares) over the past ten years (largely to forestry). In 1974, 11 per cent (4,856 persons) of the economically active population was involved in agriculture, compared to 3 per cent in Scotland as a whole. A similar number of jobs were dependent on agriculture, off the farm. However, the number of workers was declining, and the age structure of the labour force suggested that more workers would retire in the near future and agriculture would need to recruit new younger labour. The report also warned that agriculture was susceptible to world markets and decisions taken in London and Brussels had a large influence on this important sector of the Borders economy.[27]

Some 14 per cent of the Borders Region was planted with forest trees, exclusively softwoods for commercial production, or acquired for planting in 1974. The area had increased four-fold since the end of the Second World War. At the same time, the area of hardwoods had halved. Most of the area afforested was in Tweeddale and Roxburgh Districts but rough grazing on the Border hills amounted to over 200,000 hectares and, although 12 per cent of this area was above tree planting level, the remaining area was potentially available for forestry planting. In response to growing concerns over large-scale commercial afforestation in the uplands, new procedures had been introduced by the government in October 1974 requiring regional planning authorities to be consulted on future schemes. The report suggested that the new planning authority should draw up a regional strategy for forestry and local guidelines for areas sensitive to forestry on amenity and landscape grounds.[28]

As regards tourism and recreation, it was well known that most visitors to Scotland travelled straight through the Borders to Edinburgh and the Highlands without stopping. Only 2 per cent of the bed-nights spent in Scotland in 1973 were in the Scottish Borders. Of the 70,000 inquiries at the region's nine tourist information centres in 1974, 75 per cent were at the Jedburgh and Berwick-upon-Tweed Tourist Information Centres (TICs), on the main routes through the Borders. The Borders Tourist

---

[26] SBA/1210/10/3, *The Borders Region, 1975*, p. 15.
[27] SBA/1210/10/3, *The Borders Region, 1975*, pp. 23–26.
[28] SBA/1210/10/3, *The Borders Region, 1975*, pp. 28–31.

Association, formed in 1971, employed a full-time Tourist Officer to promote the region and co-ordinate the TICs. However, less than one per cent of Scottish Tourist Board grants for projects had come to the Borders Region. Nevertheless, some notable tourist developments had taken place, such as the Museum of Border Life created by Jedburgh Town Council, the Scottish Museum of Woollen Textiles at Henry Ballantyne's mill in Walkerburn and the proposed visitor centre alongside Melrose Abbey being provided by the National Trust for Scotland (NTS).[29]

In the countryside, over £110,000 had been given in grants by the CCS under the Countryside (Scotland) Act 1967 for recreational facilities such as car parks, picnic sites and toilets, and footpath waymarking and maintenance. However, although areas such as St Mary's Loch and Glentress Forest, near Peebles, were magnets for visitors, no formal country parks had been established that could attract finance for countryside facilities. The region's reservoirs, such as Talla and the proposed Megget reservoir, had potential for recreational development. The twenty-mile coastline was another attraction where visitor pressure was concentrated on a number of access points, such as Coldingham Bay, St Abbs and Cove. An overall strategy for the coastal zone was a priority to balance the pressure for additional facilities, such as caravan sites, with the conservation of vulnerable habitats.[30]

In looking to the future, the report points out that the existing development plans, updated by amendments, allocated land for housing with a capacity to accommodate some 18,000 people. However, little had been done to incorporate the proposals put forward by the Central Borders Plan in 1968, which had been considered too radical a departure from the historic pattern of development. Where additional housing land had been allocated, it was within or adjacent to burghs. There had been no development at Newtown St Boswells.[31] The report emphasised 'Any future plan for the region which does not take account of the political, social and economic momentum of the Borders' burghs could founder in a similar way'.[32]

The financial resources of the region were constrained by the relative narrow base of the regional economy. The rateable value of the region was lower than that of Scotland but did not reflect the substantial capital

---

[29] SBA/1210/10/3, *The Borders Region, 1975*, pp. 32–33.
[30] SBA/1210/10/3, *The Borders Region, 1975*, p. 33.
[31] SBA/1210/10/3, *The Borders Region, 1975*, p. 52 (paras 203–207).
[32] SBA/1210/10/3, *The Borders Region, 1975*, p. 54 (paras 214–215).

wealth in agriculture and forestry, which was not rated. In relation to local authority expenditure, this could only be increased if rateable value increased as a result of new development and redevelopment or through an increase in government grants. The experience of the past showed that grants associated with Development Area Status were not sufficient to ensure the revitalisation of the economy. Alternative measures were required. However, membership of the European Economic Community (EEC) in 1973 opened the door for additional grant aid under the European Community's Agricultural Guidance Fund (FEOGA) and the Regional Development Fund. Three projects in the Borders had already benefited from FEOGA grants, including the construction of a vegetable processing factory at Eyemouth. The Borders Region, with low income per head, a history of net outward migration and depopulation, and an imbalanced employment structure, had a strong claim for the allocation of regional development funds.

Population forecasts produced by the Scottish Office for planning purposes forecast a population for the Borders Region of 99,000 by 1991 (compared to a 1971 population of 98,477). However, if outward migration continued at the level experienced in the period 1961–1971, combined with natural decrease (an excess of deaths over births), the population of the region would drop to 96,000 by 1991. If net outward migration could be extinguished, then natural growth (an excess of births over deaths) would commence in 1981 and the population of the region could exceed 103,000 by 1991. If the success of the previous five years of attracting development to the region could be continued, with the creation of an estimated 200 new jobs per annum, the population of the region might reach 110,000 by 1991.[33] In the event, the population of the region reached 99,800 by 1981 and 103,000 by 1991 although the region still suffered from natural decrease (an excess of deaths over births). The population growth during the period 1971–1991 was entirely due to the inward migration of people as a result of the regional council's policy of industrial promotion and development and the attraction of the region as a retirement location.

THE DEPARTMENT OF PHYSICAL PLANNING COMMENCES WORK

Following the decision to appoint David P. Douglas as Director of the new department, Frank Constable, County Planning Officer in

[33] SBA/1210/10/3, *The Borders Region, 1975*, p. 37 (paras 159–160).

Roxburghshire elected to take early retirement and pursue a career as a planning consultant. George Ovens, RCC's Depute County Planning Officer, was appointed Depute Director of Physical Planning but other members of RCC's planning staff moved to jobs elsewhere in Scotland. The number of planning staff transferring from the existing county councils amounted to less than twenty people. The new regional planning department was split down the middle and Paul Gregory, Regional Planning Co-ordinator with the RPU, and the author were appointed Assistant Directors of Physical Planning with responsibilities for strategic planning policy and development, and local planning and development control, respectively.[34]

Within three months of local government reorganisation, the staffing of the physical planning department was augmented by the appointment of a number of qualified planners to bolster the development control section and widen the skills of the strategic planning and development section, which also had responsibility for implementing projects and the countryside, and by the end of 1975 the Department of Physical Planning had a complement of thirty-three persons (see Figure 5.2).[35] Many of the staff present in the department at the end of 1975 would remain for the duration of the life of the BRC: the author, Paul Gregory, Trevor Burrows, John Gray, Ian Borthwick, Colin Smith, Alistair Lorimer, Alasdair MacLean, Frank Bennett, Hamish Crawford, George Inglis and John Young. George Ovens would retire in 1985; David Douglas would leave the department in 1986 to pursue a career as a planning consultant, becoming the first Chief Executive of Scottish Borders Enterprise (SBE), the local enterprise company established under the umbrella organisation Scottish Enterprise, in 1990. Paul Gregory would rise to become Director of Planning and Development in 1987 and the author would become Depute Director.

Figure 5.2 shows that, apart from the departmental secretary and secretarial staff, there were only two other female members of staff in 1975 out of a complement of twenty-eight professional and technical staff; the landscape architect and the assistant development officer. Ten years later, the situation would be unchanged. It is fair to say that planning, like other similar professions, was very much a male preserve. For instance, only 7 per cent of RTPI members were female

---

[34] Staffing information is based on the Borders Regional Council's staff directory for May 1975.

[35] Staffing information is based on the Borders Regional Council's staff directory for December 1975.

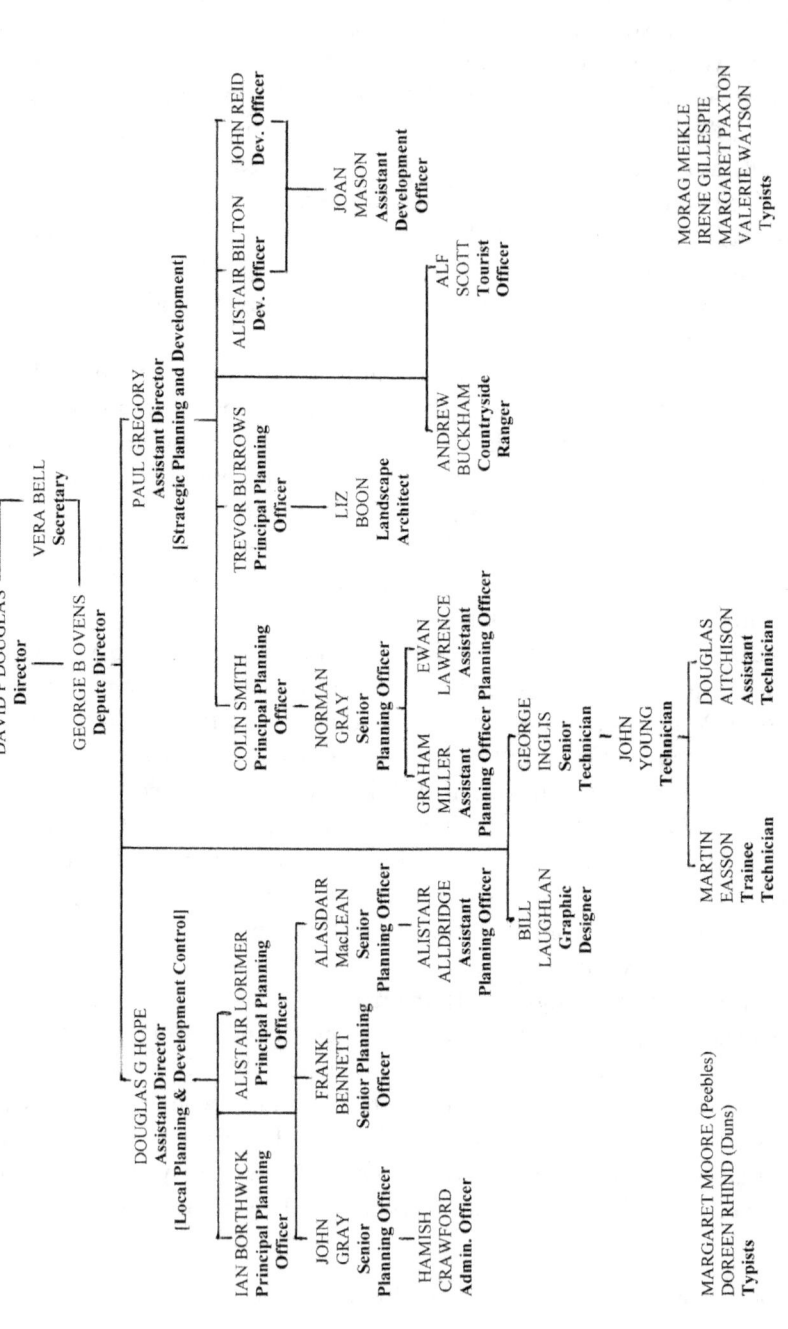

Figure 5.2 Department of Physical Planning, December 1975

in 1971. According to a research study of the time, the social status of membership was described as 'undifferentiated middle class' with nearly half coming from professional or executive backgrounds; two thirds had fathers who had attended public or grammar schools. Forty-five per cent of the membership had qualified in another profession, such as architecture or engineering before entering planning; 34 per cent held a degree in planning or another discipline such as geography; and the remaining 21 per cent were direct entry planners who had taken a diploma in planning or the RTPI's own professional exams.[36]

In order to deal with the range of functions delegated to it, the Planning and Development Committee established four sub-committees, covering development control, building control, industrial development and tourism. These sub-committees met monthly with the full Planning and Development Committee meeting six times a year. The Director of Physical Planning (Physical Planning and Development from 1978) had responsibility for structure and local planning, development control, industrial development and promotion, public transport, tourism promotion and the countryside. Building control was the responsibility of the Property Services Department but there was close liaison between the development control section of the Department of Physical Planning and the building control section of the Property Services Department. Indeed, the two sections shared area offices in Peebles and Duns. The immediate task for the Director of Physical Planning was to prepare a Regional Report for submission to the SoS by May 1976, as required by the 1973 Act, and establish a competent system for dealing with planning applications (development control). It was also imperative that the planning policies of the constituent county councils, embodied in the existing county development plans, should be co-ordinated across the region.[37] In relation to industrial development and promotion, the immediate challenge for the regional council was to continue the momentum built up by the previous local authorities in association with the Development Commission in Berwickshire and Kelso, and the SIEC in Peeblesshire, Roxburghshire and Selkirkshire, in promoting the economic development of the area and co-ordinating the servicing of industrial sites and the provision of new factory space in the form of advance and nursery factories.

---

[36] Cherry, G. E., *The Evolution of British Town Planning*, p. 255.
[37] Borders Regional Council, Development Control Policies, Report by Director of Physical Planning, September 1975.

The co-ordination of public transport within the Scottish Borders was a responsibility of the Department of Physical Planning until 1982, at which point responsibility was transferred to the Department of Roads and Transportation. There was no local authority involvement in public transport prior to the Transport Act 1968, which introduced rural bus subsidies on a fifty/fifty basis between central and local government. By 1974, passenger use of buses in the Borders had declined by 45 per cent since 1956, whereas bus mileage had only decreased by 8 per cent. The decline in the patronage of public transport was made even worse by the closure of several railway lines in the Borders after 1956, including the Waverley Line in 1969.[38] Bus subsidisation was seen as an essential element in maintaining rural population. After 1975, the regional council pursued a number of innovative projects in order to increase the use of bus transport within the region, including a co-ordinated public transport timetable and bus stop information boards, concessionary fares for the elderly, a half-fare card (the first scheme in Scotland) and the introduction of rover tickets during the summer months, which were especially useful for outdoor enthusiasts. In 1979, the council, in association with the health board, introduced the Border Courier Service, unique in Scotland, which combined minibus passenger transport with the transport of medical supplies, samples, files and so on between health board offices and hospitals. The council also experimented with other services, such as the Border Harrier, which accessed the remoter parts of the Ettrick and Yarrow Valleys.[39]

To further encourage outdoor activities, an annual guided walks programme commenced in 1976, combined with the publication of a series of Countryside Walk Cards, which described a selection of the most interesting walks in the Borders. In association with the emerging community councils, a survey of rights of way was instigated and the first register of rights of way in the Borders was established. Rights of way maintenance became an increasing responsibility of the ranger service, which also had to cope with the consequences of Dutch elm disease, which arrived in the Borders in the mid-1970s, and the spread of giant hogweed along the banks of the River Tweed and its tributaries.[40]

---

[38] *Regional Report 1976*, pp. 16–17.
[39] See *Report on Principal Activities and Achievements 1975–1983*, Department of Physical Planning and Development, 1983.
[40] See *Southern Reporter*, 27 March 1980.

THE REGIONAL REPORT 1976

The new Department of Physical Planning was required by the SoS to prepare, by May 1976, a Regional Report which reviewed the plans and policies inherited by the regional council, set down the main issues affecting life in the region and the objectives and priorities of the regional council for the future.[41] Anticipating the requirement to prepare Regional Reports, the SDD published its first Planning Advice Notes (PAN) on a range of subjects, in July 1975, to provide specific advice on the preparation of Regional Reports. Thirteen PAN were published in the period July–December 1975. Over the next twenty years some fifty PAN would be published, which laid down specific guidance and advice on policies which planning authorities must have regard to, otherwise they risked the SoS making changes to structure and local plans or overturning development control decisions on appeal.[42]

The Regional Report was submitted in June 1976. It set out the main issues affecting life in the Borders Region and focussed on the problems and opportunities for the next five years, 1976–1981. The Report points out that the Borders had the smallest population of the nine Scottish mainland regions and, unlike most other regions, no single town acted as a focus for industry and commerce. Only two settlements exceeded 10,000 persons (Hawick and Galashiels) and 40,000 persons lived in settlements of less than 1,500 persons. However, the Borders Region offered an environment and a way of life that many people were seeking.[43]

There was conclusive evidence that the Borders Region's population had grown slightly over the past four years (from 98,474 in 1971 to 99,105 in 1974). Public investment in housing, factories and roads had been a principal component of the drive to create employment and halt depopulation. However, the prospect of public expenditure cuts gave cause for concern. The capital expenditure programme for the five years 1976/77–1980/81 showed a reducing spending by both the regional council and the district councils as a result of the government's restrictive borrowing policy. It was imperative, therefore, that both the

---

[41] SBA/1210/10/4, Borders Regional Council, *Regional Report 1976*, BRC, June 1976.
[42] See Appendix 4 for a list of Government Circulars, National Planning Guidelines, National Planning Policy Guidelines and Planning Advice Notes.
[43] *Regional Report 1976*, pp. 1–2.

regional council and the SDA should continue to seek maximum grant aid from the EEC.[44]

The report re-affirmed the principal objective of the regional council to resist any reversion to depopulation.[45] It also set out a wide range of issues to be tackled, the most important of which were: the lower than average proportion of persons in the economically active age groups and the high proportion of retired people, which was placing an increasing burden on health and social services; the narrow base of the economy and the lack of career opportunities for the most talented school leavers; the continuing need for a pool of rented housing for incoming workers and the shortage of modern reasonably priced private houses; the lack of a major shopping centre; and the need to improve the road network, particularly the trunk roads through the region, including improvements to the road system in the centres of Hawick and Galashiels. There was no mention in the Regional Report of any intention to seek the reinstatement of the Waverley railway line through the region, it being generally accepted in the 1970s that its permanent closure was a fait accompli.[46]

In relation to the countryside, the report identified the need to continue supporting jobs based on the development of the region's natural resources (agriculture and forestry); for the region-wide co-ordination of conservation area policy; a review of landscape policy; the promotion of hardwood tree and hedge planting; clarification of forestry consultation procedures; an examination of the potential of the region's forests, coast, lochs and reservoirs for recreation; and a region-wide tourist development plan.[47]

The Director of Physical Planning was reluctant to embark on a major region-wide structure plan until the rate of development warranted such a substantial commitment of scarce staff resources. Consequently, the Regional Report indicated that the regional council proposed to produce a settlement strategy rather than a structure plan. It was considered that a settlement strategy would provide the necessary guidance for the regional and district councils, private developers and the public as to the future role of each of the main settlements.[48] It would also provide the framework for the preparation of local plans. In view of the procedural requirements involved in preparing local plans and the

[44] *Regional Report 1976*, pp. 18–21.
[45] *Regional Report 1976*, pp. 3–5.
[46] *Regional Report 1976*, pp. 31–34.
[47] *Regional Report 1976*, pp. 35–36.
[48] *Regional Report 1976*, pp. 23–24.

limited staff resources available, however, it would be some time before the whole of the region would be covered by local plans; the priorities being Galashiels/Tweedbank and Hawick.[49] It was hoped that the SoS would accept this approach. However, in responding to the Regional Report, Scottish Office officials pointed out that the 1972 Act required the regional council to prepare a structure plan for the Borders Region and work commenced on a structure plan in 1977 (see Chapter Six).

A NEW DEVELOPMENT CONTROL SYSTEM

The amalgamation of four existing systems of development control presented a significant challenge to the Department of Physical Planning. Some work had been done, however, by the working group of planning officers prior to reorganisation on the new procedures to be adopted in relation to the recording of applications, their assessment and decision-making. It was decided that the development control system would be based on the four new districts and the records of previous applications to the former county councils had to be re-assembled to fit the new district boundaries. Files and methods of recording varied from county to county; for instance, the 4,000 Peeblesshire applications, with associated correspondence and decision notice, were kept in individual brown envelopes stored in Midlothian County Council headquarters in Edinburgh, along with those for the Gala Water area of Midlothian. In total, some 25,000 application files were transferred to the new planning department, including several hundred undecided applications, for applications were being received by the out-going authorities right up until 4.30pm on 15 May 1975. In addition, new applications were deposited with the new regional council immediately the office opened on 16 May. Whilst some developers rushed to submit applications before the changeover date, others delayed submission until after the date and these all had to be dealt with within the statutory period (there was no relaxation because of the changeover).

At the outset, the operation of development control rested largely on the shoulders of two members of staff, Alistair Lorimer based in the area office in Duns and John Gray with assistance from Hamish Crawford based at headquarters in Newtown St Boswells, who dealt with the other three district areas, until Ian Borthwick took up his post in the area office in Peebles and took over responsibilities for Tweeddale District. It would be two years before Frank Bennett, who had been appointed to

---

[49] *Regional Report 1976*, pp. 24–27.

assist with the preparation of local plans, was transferred to the development control section and took over Roxburgh District. The arrangement of a Planning Officer for each of the four districts would continue for the next ten years.

In the first calendar year, 1976, 1,352 planning applications were received and 1,310 were determined, 91 per cent of which were approved. Eighty-four per cent of the planning applications determined were decided within the statutory period of two months, compared with 71 per cent nationally, and almost half were dealt with within one month; a significant achievement given the early staffing difficulties.[50] The determination of the vast majority of planning applications (almost 90 per cent) was delegated to the Director of Physical Planning and his Depute. Where objections to an application were received or the Director considered that the application should be refused, it was referred to the Development Control Sub-committee of the Planning and Development Committee. In the first few years, rarely more than a dozen applications were considered at the monthly meeting of the Development Control Sub-committee. The Assistant Director responsible for development control presented the details of each application, the results of consultations and any objections received, and the Director's recommendation with conditions as required, usually with the aid of photographs (slides) of the site and surrounding area. Every site was visited by the Assistant Director but site visits by the Sub-committee were rare. The Sub-committee agreed with the Director's recommendation in the vast majority of cases.

The number of applications received gradually increased during the 1970s and reached a high point of 1,430 in 1979 before declining to an average of 1,200 applications in the 1980s. The proportion of approvals remained fairly consistent over this period at around the 90 per cent mark. Two-thirds of applications concerned the erection, alteration or extension of residential property or the erection of ancillary buildings such as garages within the curtilage of residential property.[51] Almost 60 per cent of the refusals of planning permission related to residential development. Of the twenty-two appeals to the SoS submitted before the end of 1976, all those decided were in favour of the regional council, indicating that the SoS endorsed the council's policies, particularly that relating to housing in the countryside. The *Border Telegraph* noted in a report dated 19 April 1977, that 'Over 25% of the 64 residential

[50] BRC/5/60, Minute of Development Control Sub-committee, 19 April 1977.
[51] See Department of Planning and Development Annual Report, 1987, p. 41.

refusals were for sporadic housing in the countryside, an issue that would be a constant source of friction both within the development control sub-committee and between landowners, prospective developers and planning officers'.[52]

Prior to the 1972 Act, decision-making on planning applications was based on the principle that a planning application concerned only the applicant and the planning authority; consultations were minimal, largely restricted to statutory undertakers and selected statutory bodies. Indeed, in the 1950s, the DHS expected applications to be decided within fourteen days. Although applications required to be recorded in a register of planning applications, and were therefore a matter of public knowledge, there was no obligation to give any public notice or notify neighbours. In 1975, only a range of proposals which may have a significant and possibly adverse effect on amenities such as refuse tips, sewage works, hot food shops, bingo halls and cat or dog boarding kennels, described as 'bad neighbour' developments under Section 23 of the 1972 Act, required to be advertised by the applicant in the local press and on the site. Applications for alterations to listed buildings required to be advertised by the planning authority in the local press, the *Edinburgh Gazette* and on site. Applications for proposals that might adversely affect the character of a conservation area might also be advertised by the planning authority in the local press and on site. However, neighbour awareness of building alterations to adjoining property was limited. In the majority of cases, such alterations only came to the attention of neighbours when a building warrant was applied for (which required neighbour notification), by which time planning permission would most likely have been granted. Often objections were made on the grounds of amenity, which was not a building control matter, leading to frustration and neighbour conflict.

In a bid to widen the public's knowledge of planning proposals, in February 1978, the Planning and Development Committee agreed that a weekly list of applications received should be displayed in libraries throughout the region.[53] Copies of the application plans were also made available for display in libraries in the larger towns: Duns, Eyemouth, Selkirk, Galashiels, Hawick, Jedburgh, Kelso and Peebles. The public were encouraged to contact and/or visit the respective planning officers at headquarters in Newtown St Boswells or at the area offices in Duns

---

[52] Extract from *Border Telegraph*, Galashiels, 19 April 1977.
[53] BRC/5/60, Minute of Development Control Sub-committee, 21 February 1978, Report on Public Involvement in Development Control.

and Peebles where joint planning and building control offices had been established, in order to view plans and discuss proposals.

With the establishment of community councils in the Borders (there were about sixty in the region by 1978), although there was no statutory requirement to consult community councils, many had become active in the development control process. Accordingly, it was agreed to consult community councils on all applications required to be advertised under Section 23 of the 1972 Act, all listed building and conservation area applications and applications for major developments that were likely to be of interest to the community within which it was located. Community councils could request any other application that they wished to see. It was recognised that a balance had to be struck between administrative efficiency and the involvement of the public in planning and it was hoped that increasing the participation of the public in the development control process would not lead to delays in decision-making.

In order to co-ordinate development control policy on key issues across the region, in advance of the preparation of local plans, detailed development control policies were agreed by the Planning and Development Committee in September 1975.[54] These related to housing in the countryside; development in residential areas; conservation areas and listed buildings; the preservation of trees and woodlands; display of advertisements; caravan and chalet sites; and other development in the countryside.

Housing in the countryside had been strictly controlled by each of the former county planning authorities since the publication in 1961 by the then DHS of its policy guidance on 'New Houses in the Country'.[55] The policy of the regional council continued the policy of the former county councils in restricting housing in the open countryside to development which could be shown to be necessary and essential to the specific needs of the area, that is for agriculture and forestry or some other rural land use. In villages, the rehabilitation and conversion of existing buildings was encouraged and well sited and well-designed new houses were permitted but additions to existing ribbon development and scattered houses were not permitted. In existing towns, new residential development should have diversity in the layout, design and form of development and in the size and type of

---

[54] Borders Regional Council, Development Control Policies, Report by Director of Physical Planning, September 1975.
[55] Department of Health for Scotland, *New Houses in the Country* (Edinburgh: HMSO, 1961).

dwellings. All designs of new development should respect the existing quality and appearance of the surrounding area. Development briefs should be prepared for larger sites.

In conservation areas, applications required to be accompanied by detailed plans or sketches including the elevations of new development, its setting and particulars of colour and materials. New building and additions to existing buildings were assessed against the character and appearance of the area. The demolition and replacement of buildings might be permitted if it was shown that existing buildings were of an inappropriate character or wholly beyond repair. However, the alteration or demolition of statutory listed buildings was only permitted after full consultation with the Civic Trust, Georgian Society and local conservation groups. Existing trees should be retained in any new development in conservation areas. A high standard of design was expected for any proposed signs or advertisements.

In addition to housing in the countryside, roof extensions in the main towns of Hawick and Galashiels were an equally challenging feature of the Scottish Borders. In the 1950s, large flat-roofed dormers came into fashion as a means of providing additional living space in the top floor flats of Victorian terraced properties across Scotland. In the 1960s, roof extensions as high as, or even higher than, the ridge of the roof, in order to comply with building regulations, and flush with the front wall of the property, became common features of towns throughout Scotland and in Hawick and Galashiels in the Borders. Planning authorities adopted different attitudes to these roof extensions. Some, but not all, authorities required planning permission for roof extensions on the grounds that the extension materially affected the external appearance of the building. In the Borders, a survey in 1977 of properties in the Victorian terrace areas of Hawick and Galashiels revealed that almost 80 per cent of some 1,500 dwellinghouses surveyed possessed dormers, 50 per cent of which dated from the 1960s onwards; half of these modern dormers covered greater than 50 per cent of the roof area.[56]

After 1975 and the introduction of the Town and Country Planning (General Development) (Scotland) Order 1975, planning permission was required if the roof area of the extension exceeded 10 per cent of the original roof area. The BRC consistently refused planning permission for roof extensions that touched or rose above the ridge level, rose flush with the front wall, extended the full length of the building or otherwise

---

[56] BRC/5/60, Minute of Development Control Sub-committee, 19 December 1977, Report on Dormers and other Roof Extensions.

were considered too large. In conservation areas, only dormers of traditional design were encouraged although modest dormers of a more modern design were accepted to allow property improvement. This policy was an early source of tension between the regional council and the four district councils, particularly Roxburgh and Ettrick and Lauderdale District Councils, who were the housing authority. They argued that restricting such extensions was inconsistent with the policy of seeking to improve sub-standard housing, assisted by grants from the housing authorities, and would lead to a greater demand for new housing. The district councils considered that roof extensions should only be refused where they were seriously detrimental to the character and amenity of the area. However, the regional council continued with its policy, supported on appeal by the SoS. Nevertheless, the large number of 'box' dormers and roof extensions already prevalent in the 1970s would continue to be a feature of the Victorian terrace areas of Hawick and Galashiels.

The development control policies, agreed in 1977, expanded and modified would be subsequently incorporated into the local plans. They would become the mainstay of development control policy for the next ten years. In particular, the housing in the countryside policy would be strictly enforced; it would be the 1990s before this policy was gradually relaxed as pressure grew for additional housing in the countryside attached to existing building groups.

THE ACTION PLAN FOR DEVELOPMENT

Unemployment in the Borders Region in November 1975 stood at a lowly 3.3 per cent, compared with 6.0 per cent in Scotland as a whole and 4.5 per cent in the UK, a reflection of the success of the local authorities in the Borders in attracting industry to the area and full employment in the textile industry.[57] During the five years preceding reorganisation, some fifty manufacturing firms had established themselves in the region, creating some 3,000 new jobs, nearly half in industries new to the Borders. Nevertheless, whilst efforts had been made by the local authorities and the development organisations to diversify the economy, textiles and agriculture remained dominant. The textile industry was vulnerable to economic recession and competition from abroad and job losses continued. In agriculture, although the heavy losses of the 1960s, averaging around 180 jobs annually, had slowed to

[57] Borders Regional Council, *Borders Region in Figures*, 1984 edition.

sixty jobs per annum in the early 1970s, concerns remained about the ageing structure of agricultural employment.[58]

The Scottish Development Agency (SDA) was established by the Labour government in 1975 to further economic development, promote industrial efficiency and improve the environment of industrial areas.[59] The SDA took over the activities of the SIEC, which had for many years built government factories in Scotland, and the Small Industries Council for the Rural Areas of Scotland (SICRAS), which had fostered the development of small businesses in rural areas, villages and small towns. It also took over the administering of grants for derelict land clearance, which had been the responsibility of the SDD. In order to continue the work of the previous local authorities in promoting the area and co-ordinating the provision of new factory space in the form of advance and nursery factories, Alistair Bilton and John Reid, the Development Officers attached to the JPAC and EBDA respectively, were transferred to the Department of Physical Planning. Their first task was to draw up an 'Action Plan for Development' for submission to the newly established SDA. This was approved by the regional council in December 1975.[60]

The Action Plan, submitted to the Development Commission and the SDA in January 1976, set out the council's proposals for industrial promotion and development in the region over the next five years in order to secure a co-ordinated approach to the provision of industrial sites, the building of advance factories and financial assistance for industrial expansion. The promotion of the region's assets as a location for industrial development was an integral part of the 'Action Plan', involving attendance at exhibitions and conferences at home and abroad, including trips to London and Aberdeen, the nerve centre of the new offshore oil industry, and to European destinations such as Basle and Brussels. During the next five years, new industrial development was concentrated in Galashiels/Tweedbank, Hawick and Selkirk. In Galashiels, the former station yard was cleared and serviced to provide some 7.7 ha of land for industry, a site for a new health centre and car parking for some 130 cars. At Tweedbank, the former Tweedbank Farm was converted into a craft centre and new factories constructed

---

[58] *Regional Report 1976*, p. 41–44.
[59] Wannop, Urlan A., 'The Evolution and Roles of the Scottish Development Agency', *Town Planning Review*, July 1984, Vol. 55, No. 3, pp. 313–321.
[60] Borders Regional Council, *Action Plan for Development*, Report by Director of Physical Planning, December 1975.

by the SDA on the industrial estate. The former railway line from Wood Street at the western end of Galashiels to Tweedbank was landscaped to form a combined footpath/cycle track, the 'Galashiels Walkway'.[61] The advance factory programme by the SDA also continued in Peebles, Eyemouth, Duns and Coldstream.

On the tourism front, a future strategy for tourist information centres throughout the region was drawn up; the principal centres being in Jedburgh and Melrose, with local centres in Coldstream, Kelso, Lauder, Hawick and Peebles.[62] The Jedburgh TIC was housed in a new building funded by the Scottish Tourist Board as one of its national centres on one of the main road entrances to Scotland. A wide range of publications were proposed, including 'Where to Stay in the Borders', which would become an annual publication, and publications advertising towns and villages, castles, abbeys, houses and gardens, battlefields, museums and monuments throughout the region as well as activities such as walking, horse riding and trekking. Town trails were waymarked and promoted in many of the Border towns and the attractions of the Scottish Borders marketed through attendance at shows and exhibitions such as the Royal Highland Show in Edinburgh and holiday fairs in London, Holland and Germany.

CONCLUSIONS

The date 16 May 1975 marked a watershed in the history of local government and town and country planning in Scotland. The pattern of local government, comprising counties of cities, counties and, within them, large and small burghs and landward districts, was replaced by a more uniform arrangement of regions and districts, plus three island councils. The town and country planning function fell rather uneasily into this structure.[63] However, in the Scottish Borders, the regional council had responsibility for all planning functions, and for industrial development and promotion, public transport, tourism promotion and the countryside. The new Department of Physical Planning (which quickly became the Department of Physical Planning and Development) took on the responsibilities for industrial development and promotion, public transport, tourism promotion and the countryside, and relied in

---

[61] Cairns, W. J. and Partners, *Galashiels Walkway: Project Review*, SDA & Borders Regional Council, February 1980.

[62] BRC/5/67, Minute of Tourism Development Sub-committee, 27 May 1975.

[63] Cmnd. 4150 (Edinburgh: HMSO, 1969), paras 188–219.

the first instance on the staff transferred from the previous county councils. Since PCC had no planning staff of its own, SCC had only one, and a number of staff from RCC's planning department departed for other planning authorities, staffing was a major issue. However, within three months, the department had augmented its staff complement through the appointment of some twelve additional staff.

The most immediate tasks for the new department were to prepare a Regional Report and establish a competent system for dealing with planning applications whilst, at the same time, continuing the momentum built up by the previous local authorities through the activities of the JPAC and EBDA in promoting the area and co-ordinating the provision of factories across the region in order to diversify the economy and retain population. By the late 1970s, BRC was firmly established as the general planning authority covering an area of 1,820 sq miles with a population of almost 100,000 people. The regional council had taken up the planning reigns and set out its objectives for the future of the region in its Regional Report. An 'Action Plan for Development' had been approved and agreed by the SDA and good progress had been made in implementing the proposals for economic development in the region. There was conclusive evidence that the decline in the region's population had been arrested and optimism for the future. A new development control system had been established and development control policies on key issues adopted; the most challenging being the control of housing in the countryside.

Across the planning spectrum, a number of recurring themes had emerged, the most significant being: the need to aim for population growth based on the promotion and development of industry and tourism; the need to improve road communications with the Central Belt of Scotland and northern England; the need to continue to resist rural depopulation by retaining services and facilities in the smaller settlements; the need to place more emphasis on town centre improvement; the need to develop the region's natural resources, its land and landscape; the increasing involvement of planning in forestry and rural land use; and the need to provide for an expansion in countryside recreation, whilst conserving its amenity, wildlife and historical heritage.

6

Development Planning Takes Shape

INTRODUCTION

FOLLOWING THE REORGANISATION OF local government in 1975, the development planning system was composed of National Planning Guidelines, regional reports and structure and local plans.[1] The impetus for the establishment of guidance from central government came from the environmental problems emerging as a result of the demand for sites for oil-platform construction yards in the north and west of Scotland. The *Coastal Planning Guidelines*, published in 1974, were followed by National Planning Guidelines (NPG) on a diverse range of development circumstances and types, including agricultural land, housing land, nature conservation, rural planning priorities and forestry, guidelines of much more relevance to the Scottish Borders (see Appendix 4). NPGs were widely acknowledged as an innovative and helpful mechanism to planning authorities in defining national interests in selected topics. However, according to Begg and Pollock, 'they tended to be rather bland and fall far short of representing a comprehensive compendium of government policy interests or in providing a national framework for land-use planning'.[2]

The requirement for regional reports stemmed from the government's desire to establish a regional framework for policymaking and for determining resource priorities as quickly as possible following reorganisation. The foresight of the constituent counties of the Borders Region meant that a regional report for the Borders Region was prepared within the stipulated time of one year. Although regional reports had the potential

---

[1] Hayton, K., 'Planning Policy in Scotland', in M. Tewdwr-Jones, *British Planning Policy in Transition* (London: UCL Press, 1996), pp. 78–97.
[2] Begg, H. M. and S. H. A. Pollock, 'Development Plans in Scotland since 1975', *Scottish Geographical Magazine*, Vol. 107, No. 1, 1991, pp. 4–11.

to be a vehicle for corporate planning, they were intended primarily as a physical planning document. The SoS only offered observations on the submitted regional report; formal approval was not required. The production of regional reports was the subject of debate and controversy and there followed considerable speculation on their future.[3] In 1982, the SDD informed all regional and island councils that there would be no requirement to review regional reports in view of the progress on structure plans; the range of other policy documents that had been developed, such as Housing Plans and Transport Policies and Programmes; and because of the increasing financial and manpower constraints under which central and local government was operating. According to many, an opportunity had been lost to continue the co-ordinated working within authorities that the process of preparing regional reports had encouraged.

The preparation of sub-regional plans in Scotland during the 1960s, such as those for the Falkirk/Grangemouth growth area, the Moray Firth growth area and for the Scottish Borders, aimed at integrating land use planning with economic development. According to Wannop, this combination was the impetus for the Wheatley recommendations for the creation of regional councils and the expectation that the planning undertaken by them would include economic as well as land use considerations.[4] However, structure plans emerged as essentially land use documents with three main functions: to state and justify the authority's policies and general proposals for strategic development and the other use of land and provide guidance on development and issues of major importance; express national and regional policies in relation to the land use planning of the area; and provide a framework for local plans, which in turn would provide further guidance on the control of development at local level.[5]

Detailed provisions as to the form and content of structure and local plans and the procedure for their preparation and approval were contained within the Town and Country Planning (Structure and Local Plans) (Scotland) Regulations 1976 – amended by the Town and Country

---

[3] Wilkinson, M. and B. Howat, *Regional Reports and Structure Plans in Scotland*, Occasional Paper No. 3, 1977, Glasgow: Planning Exchange; McDonald, S.T., 'The regional report in Scotland', *The Town Planning Review*, Vol. 48, No. 3 (July 1977), Liverpool University Press, pp. 215–232.

[4] Wannop, Urlan A., *The Regional Imperative: Regional Planning and Governance in Britain, Europe and the United States* (London: Regional Studies Association, 1995), pp. 13–14.

[5] SDD Circular 28/1976, Structure and Local Plans (Edinburgh: HMSO, 1976).

Planning (Structure and Local Plans) (Scotland) Regulations 1983 – and SDD Circular 28/1976 (amended by Circular 32/1983).[6] PAN 27: Structure Planning, published in 1981, and PAN 30: Local Planning, published in 1983, gave comprehensive advice on best practice for the preparation of structure and local plans.[7] Structure plans were intended to provide a vision for the future, a framework for co-ordinating private and public sector investment, and the basis for decision-making on proposals that raised issues of regional significance. They provided a context for local plans, which should form the basis for sound development control decisions and give clear guidance to potential developers, particularly those engaged in industrial development and housebuilding. Both structure and local plans should clearly inform the public about proposals for development, redevelopment or improvements in the area.

The 1972 Act required planning authorities to involve the public at specific stages in the production of structure and local plans. The procedure for the preparation of structure plans required advertisement of the intention to prepare the structure plan, the publication of a survey report and report on the major issues to stimulate public interest in the plan, followed by the publication of a draft plan, which should be the subject of public consultation and consultation with representative organisations. The finalised structure plan should take account of all representations received. There was a further opportunity to submit formal objections to the finalised plan prior to submission to the SoS for approval. Should objections be submitted that could not be resolved, the SoS could hold an Examination in Public (EIP) prior to approving the plan with or without objections.

Similarly, the planning authority was required to publicise the intention to prepare a local plan and the key issues to be addressed in order to stimulate public discussion. The public had a second opportunity to be involved through consultation on the draft proposals and policies to be included in the plan. The finalised local plan, produced after considering the responses to the consultative draft local plan, was also subject to a period of public consultation, at which time formal representations could be made in relation to the proposals and policies in the local plan.

---

[6] The procedure for the preparation of structure plans is described in E. Young and J. Rowan-Robinson, *Scottish Planning Law and Procedure*, pp. 80–94 and N. A. Collar, *Planning*, pp. 43–51. The procedure for the preparation of local plans is described in E. Young and J. Rowan-Robinson, *Scottish Planning Law and Procedure*, pp. 100–106 and N. A. Collar, *Planning*, pp. 54–65.

[7] SDD PAN 27, 'Structure Planning', November 1981 and SDD PAN 30, 'Local Planning', September 1984.

Any unresolved objections required the holding of a local plan inquiry chaired by a reporter from the Scottish Office Inquiry Reporters Unit (SOIRU) (now the Directorate for Planning and Environmental Appeals (DPEA)). Thus, objectors had an opportunity to convince a planning expert, independent of the planning authority, that a policy or proposal in the local plan was not appropriate or soundly based. On receipt of the report of the local plan inquiry, the planning authority must consider the reporter's recommendations and give clear reasons if it wished to deviate from them. Prior to adoption, the local plan must be submitted to the SoS. The SoS did not approve the local plan but had the power to 'call-in' the local plan for decision if there was clear evidence that statutory requirements had not been fulfilled or issues of national importance were involved. However, this power was little used.[8]

THE FIRST STRUCTURE AND LOCAL PLANS

The section of the Department of Physical Planning responsible for strategic planning and economic development commenced work on the structure plan in 1977 with the updating and revising of the factual information in the regional report. This proved to be time-consuming; the implementation of the council's 'Action Plan for Development' and the projects inherited from the previous county councils took priority. As a result, in 1978, the structure of the department was changed and sub-divided into three sections: a Development Section, with responsibility for economic development, project implementation, public transport, tourism promotion and the countryside; a Structure and Local Plans Section responsible for both the structure plan and subsequent local plans; and a separate Development Control section (see Appendix 1b). The name of the department was changed to Department of Physical Planning and Development to properly reflect the extent of its responsibilities.

The structure plan Report of Survey was published in September 1978 along with a Consultative Report, which examined the scope for change in the region and the major issues to be tackled in the structure plan.[9] This report set out three alternative strategies for future growth and suggested draft policies and proposals for future development. Reflecting

---

[8] Bruton, M. J., Crispin, G., Fidler, P. M. and Hill, E. A., 'Local Plan P.L.I.s in Practice', *The Planner*, January/February 1982, p. 16.

[9] SBA/1210/11/3, Borders Region Structure Plan: Report of Survey, September 1978.

the new attitude to public participation, the Consultative Report was the subject of a wide-ranging programme of public consultation during October, November and December 1978.[10] Broadsheets and leaflets were distributed throughout the Borders Region to libraries, council offices, post offices and village shops. A manned exhibition toured the region over a six-week period, stationed in each of the main towns for a number of days. Well-attended public meetings were held in Duns, Eyemouth, Kelso, Jedburgh, Hawick, Selkirk, Galashiels and Peebles, and meetings held with each district council, several community councils and voluntary groups. In total, some 190 organisations were formally consulted and almost 2,000 people visited the touring exhibition. Over 450 people attended the eight public meetings.[11] This level of public involvement had never been seen before and reflected the increasing public interest in the future of the Borders Region, when much was expected of the new regional council.

The finalised structure plan was approved by the regional council on 13 November 1979, taking full account of the representations received during the consultation process.[12] It was approved, with minor modifications, by the SoS on 3 December 1980, after a short EIP in May 1980[13]. Concerned as it was with broad policy, rather than the detailed use of specific parcels of land, the structure plan was different in form from the 'old style' county development plans. It comprised a written statement and a key diagram (not on a map base), which showed at a glance the principal locations for future development and the strategic road network and identified major policy areas such as Areas of Great Landscape Value (AGLV) (Figure 6.1).

The aim of the structure plan strategy, simply put, was to maintain and improve the quality of life of the people in the Borders. In 1980, the regional council saw the salvation of the Borders as being linked to job retention and creation and the construction of housing to meet the needs of the existing population and incoming workers; encouraging

[10] SBA/1210/11/1, Borders Region Structure Plan: Consultative Report, September 1978. Advice on the publicity and consultation measures to be taken was outlined in SDD PAN19: Publicity & Consultation in Structure and Local Plans, 1978.

[11] SBA/1210/11/5, Borders Region Structure Plan: Report on Public Involvement and Consultation, January 1979.

[12] SBA/1210/11/6, Borders Region Structure Plan: Written Statement, November 1979.

[13] SBA/1210/11/9, Borders Region Structure Plan: Report of Examination, May 1980 & SBA/1210/11/10, Borders Region Structure Plan: Written Statement (Approved with Modifications), December 1980.

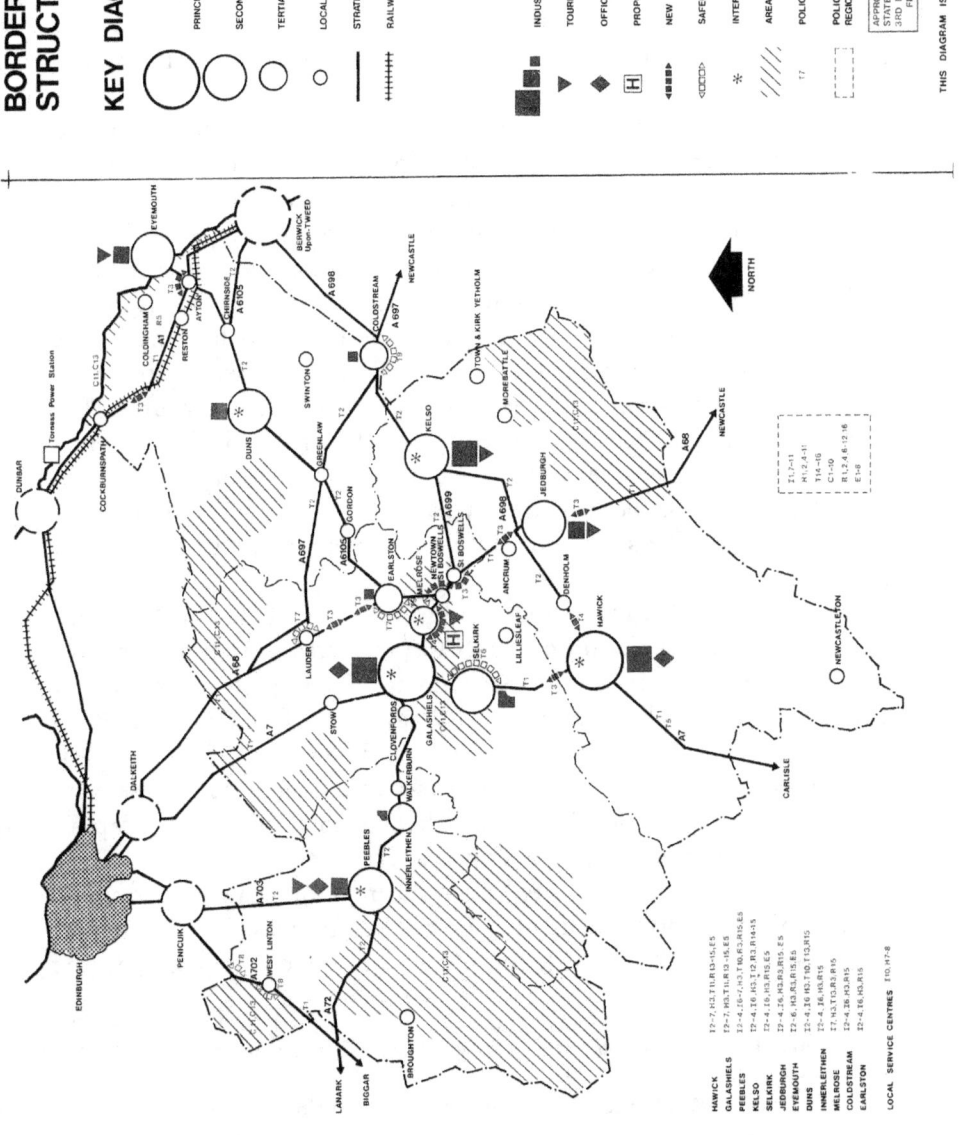

Figure 6.1 Borders Region Structure Plan 1980: Key Diagram

housebuilding for commuters to Edinburgh and the Lothians, or elsewhere, was not on the agenda. Indeed, the idea of constructing houses in the Borders, in Tweeddale for instance, for such purposes was strongly resisted. Most houses were built either by the four district councils and the SSHA, or by a handful of local private housebuilders. Improving road communications to the north and south was for the purpose of improving access to markets, not for the purpose of improving access to employment opportunities outwith the region. BRC policy was very much aimed at improving job opportunities, particularly for young people, within the region, to arrest the out-migration of the young and able.

The structure plan made it clear that, in an area with a dispersed settlement pattern and scattered population where the cost of providing basic services was high, and at a time when limited public spending made positive action difficult, it was necessary to identify priorities and concentrate investment where it was most needed and would benefit the region as a whole. The strategy was therefore based on priority being given to the development of large-scale industry and housing in the main centres of population with small-scale development in the local service centres and villages where basic services were available. The structure plan identified a settlement hierarchy of Principal, Secondary and Tertiary Centres where large-scale developments would be encouraged and Local Service Centres, which would act as rural holding points where smaller scale and infill development would be encouraged (see Figure 6.2).[14]

The structure plan was based on the 1976-based Registrar General's estimated 1991 population of 108,230 (an increase of approximately 9,000 people on the 1974 mid-year estimate). The structure plan set out guideline figures for likely population change in the four districts and the twelve main towns in the region over the period to 1991 (Table 6.1). It was stressed that because of the uncertain economic future, these were for guidance only and local plans should be flexible enough to adapt to a lower or higher rate of population change.[15]

The structure plan indicated that future large-scale development would be concentrated in the Galashiels–Hawick–Kelso triangle, which included Selkirk and Jedburgh. Within the central corridor, the

[14] SBA/1210/11/10, Borders Region Structure Plan: Written Statement, December 1980, pp. 21–23.
[15] SBA/1210/11/10, Borders Region Structure Plan: Written Statement, December 1980, pp. 25–27.

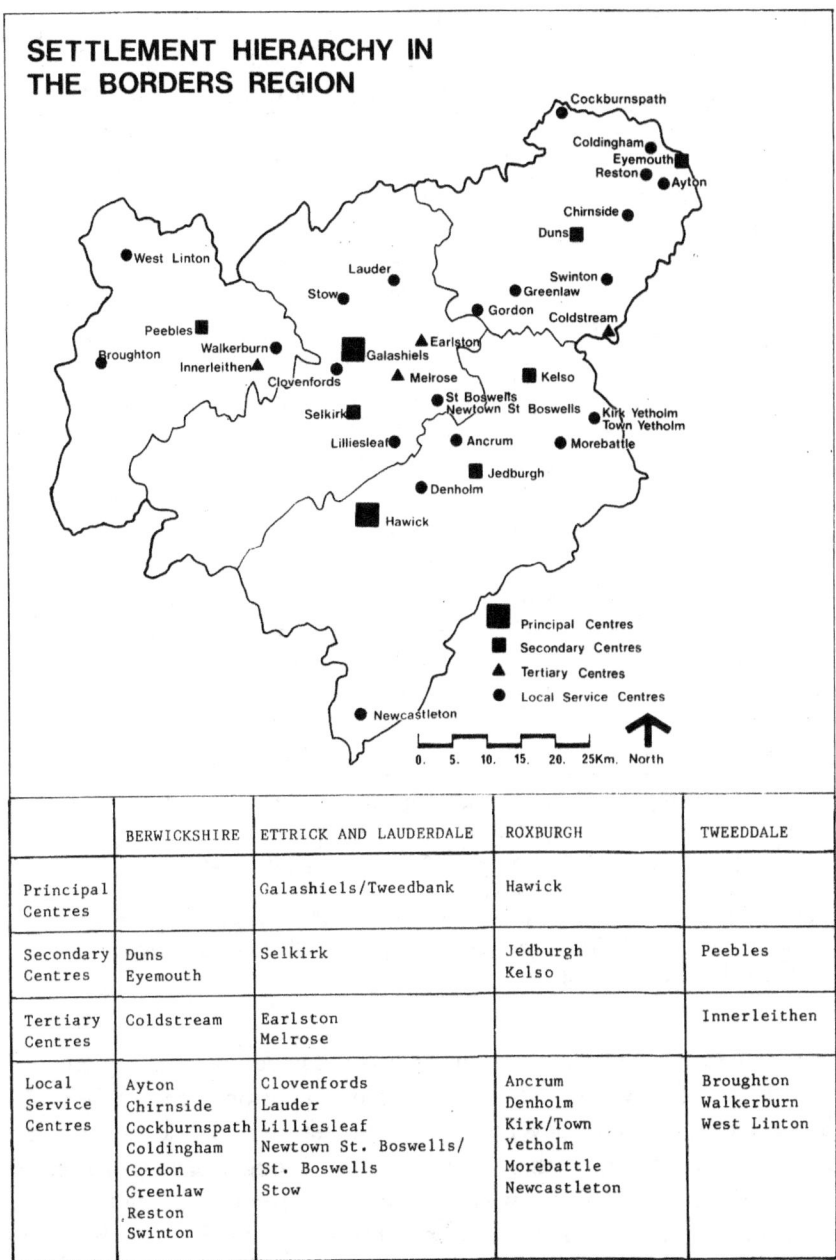

Figure 6.2 Borders Region Structure Plan 1980: Settlement Hierarchy

Table 6.1 Borders Region Structure Plan 1980: Population Guidelines

	1974 Pop.	1991 Proj. Pop.	Population Increase	1991 Act. Pop.
Duns	2002	2500	498	2450 (+448)
Eyemouth	2797	3700	903	3477 (+680)
Coldstream	1429	1700	271	1677 (+248)
Landward	11172	11300	128	11570 (+398)
Berwickshire	17400	19200	1800	19174 (+1774)
Galashiels/Tweedbank	12788	16300	3512	13766 (+978)
Selkirk	5628	5850	222	5952 (+324)
Melrose	2181	2200	19	2276 (+95)
Earlston	1520	1700	180	1641 (+121)
Landward	10183	10250	67	10403 (+220)
Ettrick & Lauderdale	32300	36300	4000	34038 (+1738)
Hawick	16520	17550	1030	15719 (-801)
Jedburgh	3990	4500	510	4088 (+98)
Kelso	5140	6150	1010	6045 (+905)
Landward	10150	10130	-20	9494 (-656)
Roxburgh	35800	38330	2530	35346 (-454)
Peebles	6064	6600	536	7080 (+1016)
Innerleithen	2351	2500	149	2581 (+230)
Landward	5185	5300	115	5662 (+477)
Tweeddale	13600	14400	800	15323 (+1723)
Borders Region	99100	108230	9130	103881 (+4781)

(Note: The actual population increase during the period 1974–1991 would be 4,781 persons, compared with the projected 9,130 persons; 4,342 of which would be within the twelve main towns. The landward area would see an increase of only 439 persons. Most noticeably, the population of Hawick would continue to decline and there would be slower than projected growth in the population of Galashiels/Tweedbank. The largest proportional population increases would be in Peebles, Kelso and Eyemouth.)

development of housing and industry was focussed on the completion of Tweedbank. Elsewhere, it was considered that priority should be given to the promotion and development of industry in Hawick in the first five years with the growth of Kelso seen as a longer term prospect. In Berwickshire, development was centred on Duns and Eyemouth, which had experienced exceptional growth in the 1970s. There was a balanced approach to the development of tourism, service industries and office accommodation in Peebles.[16]

---

[16] SBA/1210/11/10, Borders Region Structure Plan: Written Statement, December 1980, pp. 26–30.

Most population growth was, therefore, proposed for Galashiels/ Tweedbank, Hawick and Kelso, followed by Eyemouth, Jedburgh and Peebles. The development of Tweedbank accounted for much of the growth in Galashiels/Tweedbank.[17] However, following the election of the Conservative government in 1979, deep cuts were made to the SSHA's capital spending allocation from 1980–1981 onwards and the SSHA's housebuilding programme at Tweedbank came to a halt with only some 250 dwellings constructed.[18] The population of Galashiels/ Tweedbank would only grow slowly and the actual population in 1991 would be 13,760 persons, not much above the 1981 population of 13,300 and considerably less than the projected 1991 population of 16,300 persons.[19] The population of Hawick was projected to increase by some 1,000 people to 17,550 by 1991.[20] In the event, the population of the town would continue its downward spiral to a figure of 15,700 in 1991. The population of Kelso increased considerably during the 1980s, as projected, largely as a result of the attraction of industry to the town and associated private housing development. The population of Selkirk increased above the modest increase projected in the structure plan, again largely as a result of the development of new industries, whilst the population of Jedburgh remained fairly stable.

In Berwickshire, Eyemouth's population continued to rise as a result of the development of fish- and food-related industries but not quite at the rate envisaged. The populations of Duns and Coldstream increased as envisaged in the structure plan as a result of the continued development of their respective industrial estates. In Tweeddale, Peebles stands out as the growth area, indeed the population of Peebles grew faster than any other town in the Borders during the period 1974–1991, largely as a result of its attraction as a dormitory for Edinburgh and the Lothians and as a retirement community. Interestingly, the population statistics also show that the structure plan's aim of stabilising the population of the landward areas was not over-optimistic. The landward

---

[17] For a list of preferred housing sites, see SBA/1210/12, Galashiels-Tweedbank Local Plan: Written Statement, p. 16.

[18] For a history of the SSHA, see Hogan, J. J. and H. M. Alqaddo, *Policy Succession in a Scottish Quango: The Scottish Special Housing Association 1937–1984*, Scottish Government Yearbook, 1985, pp. 171–186.

[19] See 1991 Resident Population figures for settlements over 500 residents in BRC/PD/1: 1992 Annual Report by Department of Planning and Development, Borders Regional Council, 1993, p. 16.

[20] SBA/1210/14, Hawick Local Plan Written Statement (adopted November 1981), p. 21.

populations of Berwickshire, Ettrick and Lauderdale and Tweeddale districts all increased above that projected. However, the landward population of Roxburgh District, particularly the south-western part, like that of Hawick, continued to decline. The decline in Newcastleton, remote from the main centres of population, made worse by the closure of the Waverley Line, was of particular concern.

In determining the local plan programme, two approaches were available to planning authorities; a 'mosaic' approach, with a number of local plans covering parts of the authority's area or a district-wide approach, which was adopted by some of the smaller district councils. Most authorities opted for the 'mosaic' approach, encouraged by SDD, with priority given to those areas under greatest development pressure. The structure plan proposed a programme of fifteen local plans. This was eventually reduced to twelve, comprising individual local plans for seven of the main settlements and five rural local plans. The Galashiels/Tweedbank, Hawick and Eyemouth Local Plans were adopted in 1981, quickly followed by the Kelso Local Plan in 1982, the Selkirk and Peebles Local Plans in 1983 and the Jedburgh Local Plan in 1984.[21] The rural areas of the region were covered by five local plans; the Ettrick and Lauderdale North Local Plan, adopted in 1985, which covered the Gala Water Valley, Lauderdale and the Melrose/St Boswells area; the Tweeddale (Part) and Berwickshire (Part) Local Plans, adopted in 1986, which excluded Peebles and Eyemouth; the Ettrick Forest Local Plan, adopted in 1987, which covered the Ettrick, Yarrow and Ale Valleys including Ashkirk; and the Roxburgh (Part) Local Plan, adopted in 1989, which covered Roxburgh District outwith the Hawick, Kelso and Jedburgh Local Plan areas (Figure 6.3).[22]

Local plans comprised a written statement incorporating a proposals map for the local plan area, individual inset maps for the main settlements and more detailed proposals maps for the central areas of the main settlements. The proposals map showed at a glance the policies and proposals applicable to all the land within the local plan area. Government guidance indicated that proposals in structure and local plans must be realistic and capable of implementation, which required the co-operation of a wide range of organisations. Consequently, in framing proposals and the timescale for their implementation, cognisance was required of the plans

---

[21] Copies of the adopted local plans for Galashiels/Tweedbank, Eyemouth, Hawick, Kelso, Selkirk, Peebles and Jedburgh can be viewed at Scottish Borders Council's Heritage Hub in Hawick, ref: SBA/1210/12-18.

[22] Copies of the five rural local plans can be found at SBA/1210/19-23.

Figure 6.3 Borders Regional Council 1980s Structure and Local Plans

and programmes of not only regional council departments responsible for economic development, tourism, traffic and transport, social services, education and water and drainage infrastructure, but also those of district councils, responsible for housing, and many other organisations, such as the Trunks Roads Authority, SDA, SSHA and CCS.

The structure of the local plan written statements followed similar lines with policies and proposals relating to housing, economic development, traffic and transportation, built environment, community services, public utilities, tourism, recreation and leisure, and landscape, Written statements also provided comprehensive details of the reasoning behind the policies and proposals set out in the local plan and the means of implementation of the plan. A proposals map showed the policies and proposals applicable to the land within the local plan area. The local plans for the seven settlements included a more detailed proposals map for the central area of the settlement. The five rural local plans included inset maps for each of the main town and villages.

The procedure for the preparation of the twelve local plans followed a similar path, with the publication of an Issues Report (or Project Report), which summarised the survey findings and set out the main issues for discussion; a Consultative Draft Local Plan prepared in response to the comments received on the Issues Report; and a Finalised Local Plan, which took account of the responses to the Consultative Draft Local Plan. Eight of the twelve Finalised Local Plans generated unresolved objections which required the holding of a local plan inquiry, all eight of which were subsequently adopted subject to minor modifications in accordance with the recommendations of the inquiry reporter.

By way of example, work on the Galashiels/Tweedbank Local Plan commenced in August 1975. A Project Report, approved in October 1975, formed the basis for the first stage of consultation on the main problems and issues affecting the area.[23] The public participation process included a public exhibition in Galashiels over a four-week period in November 1975, attended by 1,000 people, and a public meeting in the Volunteer Hall attended by 100 people. The Draft Galashiels/Tweedbank Local Plan was approved in December 1976 and was the subject of a second public exhibition and public meeting in February 1977. Again, the exhibition attracted some 1,000 people and the public meeting was attended by approximately 100 people. Consultation on the draft local plan continued throughout the summer and autumn of 1977.[24] Final approval of the local plan was delayed, pending the finalisation of the structure plan, and it was April 1980 before the finalised local plan was approved by the regional council

---

[23] SBA/1210/12, Galashiels-Tweedbank Local Plan: Project Report, October 1975.

[24] SBA/1210/12, Galashiels-Tweedbank Local Plan: Public Participation Report, August 1980.

for submission to the SoS.[25] The local plan was adopted in June 1981, without the need for a public inquiry, following the approval of the structure plan in December 1980.

DEVELOPMENT PLAN POLICIES AND PROPOSALS

Housing policy

An adequate supply and range of housing was seen as a vital factor in the regional council's efforts to expand the economy. The assessment of housing land requirements in the 1970s was relatively crude when compared with the techniques adopted today. Housing land requirements were based on a simple methodology based on household projections, local authority house waiting lists, past private housebuilding rates and an assessment of land availability (land with planning permission or zoned for housing purposes in existing development plans). Discussions with the housing authorities, the four district councils in the Borders, on their housing plans informed the planning authority on their requirements for rented and special needs housing.

In the region as a whole, land with planning permission or zoned in development plans amounted to some 250 ha in 1976, capable of accommodating over 4,000 dwellings in addition to the 1,250 dwellings under construction or programmed over the next five years.[26] The anticipated population growth could be accommodated on this land although there might be minor shortages in some settlements. Consequently, local plans carried forward the existing allocations, with some deletions, and only a few new sites were allocated for housing development. The availability of a pool of housing for general needs and for incoming workers was seen as essential. Accordingly, district councils and the SSHA were encouraged to ensure that housing for incoming workers was available in the main centres of population; in the Central Borders the full development of Tweedbank was considered particularly important. In Galashiels and Selkirk there were sufficient sites for rented housing. In Hawick, existing sites for rented housing, principally at Stirches, were sufficient to meet the district council's requirements. Previous amendments to the Roxburgh County Development Plan had made

---

[25] SBA/1210/12, Galashiels-Tweedbank Local Plan: Written Statement (adopted June 1981), p. 7.

[26] SBA/1210/11/10, Borders Region Structure Plan: Written Statement, December 1980, p. 35.

large-scale allocations of land for housing in Kelso and Jedburgh but in order to accommodate the projected population growth in Kelso, and provide choice, additional sites were allocated for rented housing. In Berwickshire, almost 90 per cent of the houses constructed in Eyemouth in the previous ten years had been built by the town council and SSHA and sufficient land was available to accommodate the projected growth of population. In Peebles, land for local authority housing was concentrated at Kingsmeadows and on the site of former mill premises at Damcroft and Damdale close to the town centre.

Only a handful of private houses were built each year in the Borders; for instance, private housebuilding in Galashiels and Hawick averaged ten houses per annum in the 1970s. However, the low level of private housebuilding did not reflect the large amount of land across the region with planning permission or zoned for private housing in the county development plans. Peebles was the exception due to its attraction as a retirement community and with commuters to the Edinburgh area. The population of the town in 1981, at 6,700 persons, exceeded the projected 1991 population of 6,600 persons. Consequently, the local plan, adopted in December 1983, after full consultation with the local community, increased the population guideline figure to 7,100–7,200 persons and additional land for private housing was allocated south of the river Tweed; there was little concern at this time over the capacity of the Tweed Bridge to accommodate the additional traffic generated by housing development to the south of the river.

Housing for the elderly was a particular issue across the Borders; in 1976 the population of the Borders over retiral age amounted to over 21 per cent of the population, compared with 16 per cent for Scotland as a whole. From the 1950s onward, local authorities were involved in the provision of specific housing for the elderly, the handicapped and single people. In the late 1960s and 1970s, charitable organisations became more involved and in the Scottish Borders, housing associations such as Hanover, Bield, Kirk Care (Church of Scotland) and the Royal British Legion provided sheltered housing. Discussions with these organisations provided an indication of the likely scale of future land requirements.[27]

There was also a marked shortage of modern, low-cost homes for younger people and 'starter' families. Consequently, district councils were urged to make surplus land available for private development by

---

[27] SBA/1210/11/3, Borders Region Structure Plan: Report of Survey, September 1978.

servicing sites for individual housing plots. Private developers were also encouraged to provide more 'low-cost' housing and development briefs and design guides were proposed for the larger sites, which encouraged developers to provide a range of housing. The aim of such guides was not to foster stereotyped solutions through rigid control but to allow flexibility in design and layout, whilst respecting the character and identity of the existing community (now called 'place-making'). Unfortunately, in the Borders, a lack of resources (and perhaps expertise) meant that such guidance tended to set out minimum requirements, which resulted in minimum standards of design and layout and stifled innovation. Consequently, many private housing developments in the 1970s and 1980s comprised stereotyped estates of three-bedroomed bungalows with a white roughcast finish at a standard housing density.

Outwith the main settlements, housing policy encouraged infill housing in villages but prohibited 'ribbon development'. Encouragement was given to the improvement of empty and semi-derelict properties. At the time of approval of the structure plan in 1980, housing in the countryside continued to be prohibited, a policy stemming from government policy of the early 1960s. Only housing for essential rural workers, in agriculture or forestry, was allowed with stringent occupancy conditions. Additions to existing groups of houses, such as agricultural workers cottages, or to building groups centred on farms (the 'ferm toun'), was not allowed. However, the rebuilding and conversion of redundant farm buildings was encouraged.

The council's strict housing in the countryside policy was loosened in 1985 following the publication of SDD Circular 24/1985, which recognised that the changing rural economy required a more flexible approach to housing in the countryside. All the local plans adopted after 1985, whilst endorsing the general policy set out in the structure plan that housing development in the open countryside would not normally be permitted unless shown to be necessary, allowed sympathetically designed and sited new housing within and adjacent to existing building groups in the countryside, subject to a number of criteria. In the remote Ettrick and Yarrow Valleys, where stabilisation of the population was a major issue, the local plan also indicated that, owing to the sporadic nature of housing in the valleys, isolated housing development in the countryside would be possible, again subject to certain criteria. Local plan policy also encouraged the conversion of agricultural buildings and other non-residential buildings to residential use, as well as the re-use of such buildings for craft workshop/tourist related activities.

Economic development

The promotion and development of industry was the key to regenerating the economy and increasing the population of the region. The principal policies of the structure plan were, therefore, to continue with the acquisition and servicing of sites for industry in the main towns in association with the SDA, to attract new industries to the region, and continue to encourage existing firms to develop and expand. Additional land was allocated for industrial development in Hawick (10 ha), Galashiels (10 ha) and Eyemouth (4 ha); 6 ha was zoned for industry in Kelso in the existing county development plan and remained undeveloped.[28]

In Hawick, it was estimated that an additional 1,660 jobs would be required to achieve the projected 1991 population of 17,550 persons. There was little land readily available for development within the existing industrial areas of the town apart from the Burnfoot Industrial Estate and the finalised Hawick Local Plan allocated a 10 ha greenfield site for industry on the northern edge of the town at Burnhead Farm. This decision would prove most contentious. The allocation of the site was the subject of objections but following a local plan inquiry in July 1981, the allocation was supported, in principle, by the inquiry reporter and a reduced area of 8 ha was retained in the adopted local plan. However, with an unwilling owner, compulsory purchase of the land was necessary to ensure its development. This long-running saga, involving extensive discussions and negotiations, terminated in the decision of the SoS not to endorse the compulsory purchase of the site, following another public inquiry in 1988 (Figure 6.4). Consequently, there was little new industrial development in Hawick in the 1980s, much to the annoyance of the district council and the Hawick members on the regional council, reinforcing the commonly held view that Hawick did not obtain its fair share of development promotion and investment.[29]

There were no such objections to the allocation of additional land for industry in Galashiels/Tweedbank. An additional area of 6 ha was allocated for industrial development at Tweedbank (Tweedside Park) and an area of 4.5 ha was allocated at Easter Langlee, Galashiels. In Eyemouth, an additional 4 ha of land was allocated for industry on

---

[28] SBA/1210/11/10, Borders Region Structure Plan: Written Statement, December 1980, pp. 31–33.

[29] For further information on the issue of Burnhead Farm, see articles by Bill Chisholm in *The Scotsman*, dated 30/05/75, 22/07/75, 26/05/81, 02/07/81, 04/09/81, 21/03/86, 23/04/86, 31/3/88; and 10/01/89.

DEVELOPMENT PLANNING TAKES SHAPE

Figure 6.4 Press coverage of Burnhead, Hawick Saga, 1975–1988

the north side of Acredale Road. In Kelso, there were large allocations for industry at Pinnaclehill in the existing county development plan. A lack of public drainage had prohibited the full development of this site but a planned new sewage works at Crown Point would enable the development of this area and the allocation was retained in the local plan.[30] Elsewhere, in Jedburgh, the county development plan had, likewise, made large allocations for industry at Annfield/Hartrigge on Oxnam Road. This land was held for future expansion by two major companies: L. S. Starrett, specialising in precision tools and Mainetti (UK) Ltd specialising in plastics. Little land was available for other industries other than a small area at the former station yard. The local plan, therefore, allocated an additional 5 ha of land adjacent to the Mainetti site for industrial development. In Selkirk, the emphasis was on the environmental improvement of the Riverside Industrial Area, including the redevelopment of vacant industrial sites and premises in conjunction with the SDA, and the provision of a new access from the A7 to provide access to a greenfield site at North Riverside identified for long-term industrial development. In Peebles, industrial development was concentrated on the former March Street railway depot and a site at South Park, zoned in the county development plan.

Outwith the above main settlements, local plans allocated small sites for industry in Duns, Coldstream, Earlston and Innerleithen and in selected villages such as Stow and Newcastleton, where the council supported small-scale industrial developments and provided small business units and workshops. In fact, in the smaller settlements throughout the region, craft-based industries, such as wood turning, pottery, jewellery, stoneware, clock making and cheese making, were supported by the regional council with support from SDA schemes such as PRIDE (Programme for Rural Initiatives and Developments) and DRAW (Development of Rural Area Workshops).

Traffic and transport

The region was solely dependent on road transport. There was a general acceptance that the Waverley Line rail link had been lost and, in fact, various lengths of the route were identified for alternative developments such as road improvements, industrial developments and walkways. Efforts were therefore directed at improving the road network and

---

[30] SBA/1210/15, Kelso Local Plan Written Statement (adopted July 1982), pp. 12–13.

public (bus) transport. The structure plan identified the strategic road network and the SDD was encouraged to continue improving all four trunk roads through the region: the A1, A68, A7 and A702.

Local plans identified in more detail the road proposals set out in the structure plan. On the A1, the priority was by-passes for Ayton and Cockburnspath. On the A68, a proposed Newtown St Boswells/ St Boswells by-pass along the former railway line, proposed in the structure plan, was withdrawn following the receipt of objections but a Newtown St Boswells by-pass to the east of the village would be resurrected in the late 1980s. By-pass lines for Earlston and Lauder continued to be safeguarded. On the A7, the council continued to press for improvements to the A7 within Dumfries and Galloway Region and Cumbria to the M6. No firm proposals were made for road improvements to the A7 in Hawick and Galashiels but discussions continued with SDD on ways to reduce problems of vehicular/pedestrian conflict in these town centres. A by-pass for Selkirk continued to be safeguarded, as were by-pass routes for West Linton and Carlops on the A702 but with little prospect of being constructed.

The regional council concentrated its efforts on improvements to the A68–A7 link, the A6091 between Galashiels and the A68.[31] Phase I, which provided access to the new Borders General Hospital was constructed in 1985, and Phase II, the Melrose by-pass, was programmed for 1985/1986. The line of Phase III, the final link with the A68 at Leaderfoot would prove somewhat contentious, passing through the site of the Trimontium Roman Camp, and would not be resolved until 1993, following a public inquiry into objections to the route. Elsewhere, the idea of creating a single east–west route from Berwick-upon-Tweed to the Central Borders and then to Peebles and Lanarkshire, first referred to in the Mears Report of 1948, was no longer council policy, with emphasis placed on improvements to the existing strategic road network as and when possible within the regional council's capital budget.[32] As a consequence, the safeguarding of by-passes for Innerleithen and Walkerburn was removed from the structure plan. The continued improvement of the A703, a busy commuter route between Peebles and Edinburgh, became a higher priority. In Kelso, a relief road and new bridge over

---

[31] SBA/1210/11/10, Borders Region Structure Plan: Written Statement, December 1980, pp. 39–40.

[32] Mears, F. C. *A Regional Survey and Plan for Central and South-East Scotland*, pp. 50–51.

the Tweed was proposed in the longer term.[33] In Berwickshire, whilst a Coldstream by-pass on the A697 was still considered desirable, no agreement could be reached with Northumberland County Council and no route for the by-pass was identified in the Berwickshire (Part) Local Plan, simply a reference that discussions would continue. The increase in heavy forestry traffic on relatively minor roads was an issue in the south-west of the region, and the need for road improvements on local roads between Newcastleton and Jedburgh and between Newcastleton and the English border at Kielder would be identified as a high priority. Over the succeeding years, this would become a much wider issue across the Borders Region and neighbouring Dumfries and Galloway.

Following local government reorganisation in 1975, BRC became increasingly involved in the provision and integration of public transport. The council saw the solution to the rural transport problem as requiring an amalgam of conventional bus services and other modes. The council, therefore, pursued a policy of encouraging, and supporting financially, the extension of the basic public transport service into areas without services through the licensing of school buses to carry passengers (which was an innovation in 1980), the introduction of postbuses (there were fourteen in operation in 1980) and the establishment of the Border Courier Service, introduced in conjunction with the Borders Health Board, comprising four multi-purpose vehicles providing a mixed passenger and goods service between all the health centres in the region and the main hospital, Peel Hospital, which served all the main towns and rural areas with little or no public bus service.[34]

Built environment

The town centres of the main Border towns consisted of a mixture of land uses and activities, including not only retail and office premises and other non-retail uses such as cafés, pubs and hotels, but also housing, small service industries and business premises. This variety of uses formed an essential part of their character. In order to protect the retail character of the main shopping streets in the largest towns, local plans identified the prime retail frontages where the loss of retail units to other uses such as building societies, financial and legal services, travel

---

[33] SBA/1210/11/10, Borders Region Structure Plan: Written Statement, December 1980, p. 41.

[34] SBA/1210/11/10, Borders Region Structure Plan: Written Statement, December 1980, pp. 42–43.

agencies and other non-retail uses was prohibited. However, neither of the two principal centres in the Borders, Galashiels and Hawick, had the population to attract the larger chain stores and it was not considered, in 1980, that the situation was likely to change in the foreseeable future. The Borders Co-operative and Woolworths were the mainstay of retailing, supported by an array of local shops, ranging from butchers and bakers to clothing and footwear shops. Structure plan policy encouraged the more effective use of existing town centres and resisted shopping developments outwith town centres, in accordance with government policy expressed in Circular 43/71.[35,36]

A tightly packed urban fabric had developed over many years, with a range of building styles and materials, and a substantial number of buildings were listed as buildings of special architectural or historic interest. As a consequence, the centres of all the main towns in the region, apart from Galashiels, were designated as conservation areas. As of 1980, three of these – Hawick, Jedburgh and Kelso – were designated as 'outstanding' by the Historic Buildings Council for Scotland. Local plan policy sought to protect town centres from development that would damage their character and visual amenity, and rehabilitation and the infilling of gap sites was preferred to redevelopment. Local plan policy was supplemented by guidance on a range of matters, including materials to be used in rehabilitation projects, the external painting of buildings, the control of advertisements and the design of shop fronts.[37]

Local plans set out proposals for the centres of the main towns in more detail and identified proposed redevelopment/rehabilitation projects, such as the rehabilitation of the Howegate/Drumlanrig Square area in Hawick, the former station yard in Galashiels and the run-down Meeks and Dicksons Yards area in Eyemouth. BRC inherited a number of un-implemented road proposals, which affected the amenity and character of the main town centres. These were re-assessed against the changing attitude towards the conservation of the historic centres of Border towns, characterised by narrow streets and problems of restricted road access, traffic congestion and lack of parking and loading facilities. In Galashiels, the long-standing proposal for a re-aligned A7 trunk road through the town centre was scrapped and a one-way trunk

---

[35] Scottish Development Department Circular 43/71: Shopping Location Policy: Out-of-Town Shopping Centres, December 1971, Edinburgh: SDD.

[36] SBA/1210/11/10, Borders Region Structure Plan: Written Statement, December 1980, p. 59.

[37] SBA/1210/11/10, Borders Region Structure Plan: Written Statement, December 1980, p. 57.

road system proposed utilising Bank Street/High Street and an improved Ladhope Vale, thus removing through traffic from the main shopping street, Channel Street, which would become a pedestrian priority area. In Hawick, the local plan proposed that A7 trunk road traffic should be diverted from the High Street along Commercial Road. A new bridge over the River Teviot was proposed to replace North Bridge with a new road along the former railway line (Mart Street) providing a new connection between the A7 and the A698 to Jedburgh and Kelso. In Kelso, the proposal in the county development plan for a major outer distributor road around the town, incorporating a new bridge over the Tweed, was incorporated into the local plan. However, a proposal for an inner relief road, which required the demolition of a number of town centre properties was deleted. In Peebles, the previous proposal for the widening of Old Town, which required the demolition of thirty-seven properties, was removed due to the adverse effect on the character of the conservation area. The road-widening proposal for the Cuddy Bridge was scaled down in response to the large number of objections.

There were twenty-seven conservation areas distributed throughout the region from Skirling and Carlops in the west to St Abbs in the east. All the local plans emphasised the need to protect and enhance the character of conservation areas and the listed buildings contained within them. Local plan policies emphasised that the design of new buildings and alterations to existing buildings within conservation areas, and the materials used, would be subject to tight control; encouragement was given to the restoration of derelict buildings and the infilling of gap sites. In certain conservation areas, schemes for the undergrounding of overhead electricity and telephone cables, and the replacement of lighting columns by lighting on buildings, were proposed along similar lines to that undertaken in Lauder, the first conservation area to be the subject of an undergrounding scheme. A scheme for the upgrading of dilapidated buildings in Lauder, entitled 'The Little Houses Scheme', implemented by the NTS, with 50 per cent grants from the Historic Buildings Council, was the basis for similar schemes proposed for a number of other small communities.[38] Local plans also incorporated policies on the control of the display of advertisements, with a higher standard of design required for non-illuminated signs and a prohibition on illuminated signs. The upgrading of landscaped areas, open spaces and greens within villages was encouraged and the regional council supported tree planting through its tree planting scheme. The increasing

[38] See Built Environment chapters in each adopted local plan.

awareness of the archaeological heritage of the region, accompanied by the appointment of an archaeologist, was recognised with a safeguarding policy for the 130 scheduled and 500 unscheduled sites and monuments scattered throughout the region.

Countryside policy

In accordance with government advice expressed in NPGs, the structure plan included a policy protecting prime agricultural land (classified by DAFS as A+, A or B+ land) from development unless there was an over-riding need for the land.[39] The structure plan and local plans gave expression to the council's support for agriculture as a major land user and employer in the region. The structure plan also recognised that both the upland and the lowland landscapes of the Borders Region were largely the result of the efforts, over several centuries, of a number of major landowning families. The lowland estates of the Tweed Valley were recognised as a valuable resource in landscape and wildlife terms, and local plan policies re-iterated the need to balance efficient land management with the conservation of the essential elements of the Border's landscape, the mixed woodlands and hedgerows that were a particular asset for landscape and wildlife conservation.[40] Landowners and farmers were also encouraged to build on the growing interest in countryside pursuits through the development of holiday accommodation, farm trails and farm visits.

Over 14 per cent of the region was afforested in 1980. Commercial forestry provided much needed employment in the west and south-west of the region, and the structure plan encouraged commercial afforestation subject to new planting being integrated with farming and the landscape. An agreed consultation procedure with the Forestry Commission ensured that the regional council had some influence over large-scale planting of more than 500 ha anywhere in the Borders Region. Within the designated AGLVs, all planting proposals were submitted to the regional council for comments.[41] Structure and local plan policy on afforestation would be sorely tested during the 1980s when large private forestry schemes were encouraged by the huge

[39] See NPG3: Priorities for Development Planning, SDD, 1975 and PAN1: Agriculture in Scotland, SDD, July 1975.

[40] SBA/1210/11/10, Borders Region Structure Plan: Written Statement, December 1980, pp. 43–44.

[41] SBA/1210/11/10, Borders Region Structure Plan: Written Statement, December 1980, pp. 44–45.

import deficit in timber and the investment opportunities provided by the government's grants and tax incentives.

The area of broad-leaved woodlands in the Borders had halved since the Second World War and covered less than one per cent of the region. The disappearance of hedgerow trees was particularly noticeable in the lowland landscape of Berwickshire where the intensification of agriculture had led to increased field sizes and the consequent loss of hedges, hedgerow trees and copses. Broadleaved woodlands were concentrated on the larger estates, stretching from those of Wemyss & March Estates in Tweeddale to Roxburghe Estates round Kelso. These estates were recognised as a valuable resource in landscape and wildlife terms and structure plan policy encouraged hardwood planting, with financial assistance where appropriate, in consultation with the CCS.[42]

The designated AGLVs were revised and the area reduced from 65 per cent of the region to six areas covering 27 per cent of the region. In AGLVs, where conflict arose between development and conservation, precedence was generally given to the protection of the landscape and wildlife. Large-scale developments such as mineral working, overhead power lines and industrial buildings were not generally permitted within AGLVs.[43] Although most of the natural vegetation of the Borders had long since disappeared, numerous semi-natural areas were valued as wildlife habitats of national importance, for instance, the heathland areas of the Tweedsmuir Hills, Newcastleton Hills and the Moorfoot Plateau. The region possessed over sixty Sites of Special Scientific Interest (SSSI) and over 200 local wildlife sites and the structure plan indicated that, in conjunction with the Nature Conservancy Council for Scotland (NCCS), these would be protected, and the designation of further sites encouraged.[44]

Local plans detailed the boundaries of the areas to which particular countryside policies applied, such as AGLVs, SSSIs and listed wildlife sites, and reinforced the policies set out in the approved structure plan. Local plans set out clear policies to protect these areas from inappropriate development, with stringent controls on tourist-related developments that might be allowed. Some areas of the region were subjected to excessive pressure during the summer season, particularly the Berwickshire

---

[42] SBA/1210/11/10, Borders Region Structure Plan: Written Statement, December 1980, p. 45.

[43] SBA/1210/11/10, Borders Region Structure Plan: Written Statement, December 1980, pp. 47–49.

[44] SBA/1210/11/10, Borders Region Structure Plan: Written Statement, December 1980, pp. 45–46.

coast, the St Mary's Loch area and the Meldons/Manor Valley area of Peeblesshire. Local plans signposted the council's intention, in conjunction with landowners and managers, the CCS and other countryside and wildlife organisations, to produce management plans for the most vulnerable areas, such as the Eildon Hills and St.Mary's Loch/Tweedsmuir Hills AGLVs, the St Abbs National Nature Reserve (NNR) and the Voluntary Marine Reserve between Eyemouth and St Abbs, in order to manage visitor pressure.[45]

Tourism and recreation

The structure plan sought to increase the general level of tourism in the region through promotion and marketing, by encouraging the provision of more tourist accommodation, particularly self-catering, and through the provision of countryside recreational facilities. Eyemouth, Jedburgh, Kelso, Melrose and Peebles were seen as the main tourist centres. The structure plan therefore encouraged new tourist accommodation and the provision of major tourist facilities in these tourist centres and along the major tourist routes; the A1, A68 and A7.[46] Camping and caravanning were important elements of holiday accommodation in the region. Almost 60 per cent of the static caravan stances were concentrated along the Berwickshire coast and the structure plan discouraged the development of further caravan/chalet sites east of the A1. Elsewhere, caravan/chalet sites were directed to areas where the impact on the countryside could be minimised, such as the forested areas of the west and south-west, and stringent controls were placed on camping/caravan/chalet sites, if permitted, in AGLVs.[47]

Across the Borders countryside there were a range of tourist attractions – towers, castles, historic houses and gardens – where tourist facilities had been expanded, such as at Traquair House, Bowhill, Floors Castle and the Hirsel, and recent developments such as the Woodland Visitor Centre at Monteviot House, developed by Lothian Estates. Structure and local plan policy reflected the council's support for the continued development of these attractions and for other appropriate tourism-related developments in the countryside, such as the expansion

---

[45] Ibid.
[46] SBA/1210/11/10, Borders Region Structure Plan: Written Statement, December 1980, pp. 50–53.
[47] SBA/1210/11/10, Borders Region Structure Plan: Written Statement, December 1980, p. 54.

of the Forestry Commission's facilities at Glentress, near Peebles and at Craik Forest, south of Hawick, the development of recreational facilities at the new Megget Reservoir in the upper Yarrow Valley and at Cove and Coldingham Bay on the Berwickshire coast.[48] Through the provision of interpretation facilities at viewpoints and car parks, the council sought to improve the public's awareness of the countryside and help to reduce potential conflicts between tourism and recreation and land management. Many visitors sought out the quieter and remoter areas of the region and planning policy encouraged the expansion of fishing, shooting, golf, horse riding and sailing activities. There were some 2,400 km of pedestrian rights of way in the Borders in 1980 and the waymarking and maintenance of footpaths and riding routes and the negotiation of access agreements was a priority for the regional council.

Implementation

The PAG described the development plan as the 'key feature' of the planning system.[49] However, although the development plan set out the framework for the future use of land and its development, it cannot dictate when development will take place. Although the planning acts enable planning authorities to assist and undertake development, as well as encourage it, as pointed out by Young and Rowan-Robinson, the choice whether to develop land lies, largely, with the private sector, short of undertaking a programme of compulsory land acquisition and development.[50] The power to acquire land in the public interest has long been the subject of ideological differences between the Conservative and Labour parties. As Young and Rowan-Robinson commented in 1985, the Conservative Party saw the public acquisition of land as a means to an end; the Labour Party viewed public ownership as an end in itself.[51] The 1947 Act sought to transfer the development value of land to the state by providing that where land was acquired compulsorily, compensation was to be restricted to 'existing use' value. This enabled planning authorities to decide on the suitability of land for a particular purpose irrespective of the value that the land might be able to command on the open market. However, following the change in government in 1951 the

---

[48] SBA/1210/11/10, Borders Region Structure Plan: Written Statement, December 1980, p. 55.

[49] *The Future of Development Plans* (London: HMSO, 1965).

[50] Young, E. and J. Rowan-Robinson, *Scottish Planning Law and Procedure*, pp. 72–73.

[51] Ibid., pp. 394–403.

Town and Country Planning (Scotland) Act 1954 made limited provisions for the payment of compensation to landowners and the Town and Country Planning (Scotland) Act 1959 enacted a return to market value as the basis for compensation for land acquired by public bodies.

The Labour government attempted to reintroduce a betterment levy with the Land Commission Act 1967, but this was repealed with the change in government in 1970. It tried again in 1974 with the publication of the White Paper *Land*, which declared that 'the key to positive planning was acquisition by the community of development land at the value of its current use rather than at a value based on speculation as to its possible development'.[52] The Community Land Act 1975 implemented most of the White Paper's proposals and gave local authorities the power, indeed the duty, to acquire all land needed for private development. The cost of buying land would be borne by central government and any surplus arising from disposals would be shared between central government and the authority collecting the surplus. The Community Land Act was not well received and there were questions over whether there was adequate funding available.[53] It was intended that the community land scheme be introduced in stages and before it came into full effect it was repealed by the Conservative government in 1980.[54]

Thus, whilst Section 102 (1) of the 1972 Act as amended by Section 92 (4) of the Local Government, Planning and Land Act 1980 enabled regional, island and district councils to acquire land compulsorily for planning purposes where a landowner refused to negotiate or where a large number of land interests required to be acquired, this was subject to confirmation by the SoS and the onus was on the planning authority to make the case for acquisition. This has been shown to be fraught with difficulties in the Scottish Borders; the acquisition of the land to enable the development of Tweedbank and the lack of the development of an industrial site in Hawick are just two examples. The difficulty of assembling land for town centre rehabilitation schemes is a common reason for local authority inaction.

Nevertheless, government guidance indicated that policies and proposals in structure plans and local plans must be realistic and capable of implementation. Whilst the regional council had responsibility for

---

[52] White Paper, *Land* (Cmnd. No. 5730) (London: HMSO, 1974).

[53] Wilkinson, H. W., 'The Community Land Act 1975', *The Modern Law Review*, Vol. 39, No. 3 (May 1976), pp. 311–317.

[54] See Local Government, Planning and Land Act 1980 and the Community Land Act 1975 (Appointed Day for Repeal) Order 1983.

Planning and Development, Roads and Transportation, Education, Social Work, and Water and Drainage, the four district councils were responsible for Housing, Environmental Health and Parks and Recreation. Plans and programmes of the region and district councils contributed to the aims and objectives of the structure plan, for instance, the regional council's Transport Policy and Programme (TPP), which set out the five-year programme for capital and revenue expenditure on road construction and improvement, and transport provision; the Action Plan for Development, which outlined the council's proposals for capital and revenue expenditure on industrial development and promotion; and the Housing Plans produced by the four district councils, which set out the five-year programme for rented housing provision in the region.[55]

In the Scottish Borders, the SSHA was the principal provider of rented housing until abolished in 1989 by the Conservative government. Eildon Housing Association, established in 1973 to provide special needs housing, would play an increasing role in housing provision throughout the 1980s. The SDA, until replaced by Scottish Enterprise in 1991, would be the main provider of new factories and would also finance environmental improvements and the rehabilitation of derelict land and gap sites throughout the region. The Scottish Tourist Board, the Scottish Borders Tourist Board (SBTB) and the CCS would play a vital role in tourism and recreation provision. Many aspects of the countryside involved a range of organisations responsible for agriculture, forestry and landscape and wildlife conservation. The implementation of the policies and proposals in local plans, therefore, required partnerships with a variety of agencies and the co-operation of many businesses, not least private housebuilders and private industry. Much of the council's efforts would be directed at working with the private sector to achieve the aims of the structure plan and local plans.

CONCLUSIONS

When the new development plan system of structure and local plans was introduced with the reorganisation of local government in 1975, it was envisaged that development planning would change in a number of ways. It was intended to become a continuous process with plans being more speedily produced and kept up to date through monitoring and review. In this way, it was hoped that plans would better reflect

---

[55] SBA/1210/11/10, Borders Region Structure Plan: Written Statement, December 1980, pp. 76–77.

changing circumstances. Also, by involving the public more widely in plan-making, structure plans and local plans would be more responsive to their interests. It was hoped that the new system of structure and local plans would avoid the delays of the previous county development plans. However, it would be 1980 before the Borders Region had an approved structure plan, one of the first in Scotland; it would be 1989 before there was fully approved structure plan coverage of Scotland.[56] It would also be 1989 before there was total local plan coverage of the Scottish Borders and, thus, a complete development plan covering the whole region. It was envisaged that some 300 local plans would be required to achieve complete local plan coverage of Scotland. By 1990, 210 local plans (70 per cent) had been adopted.[57] Continuous monitoring of the structure plan was difficult with the staffing resources available when efforts were directed towards producing total coverage by local plans. It is no surprise that the SoS had reservations about the ability of the procedures introduced in 1976 to produce speedily prepared structure and local plans which could be kept up to date, and a number of changes were made to the procedures by way of legislation and guidance to speed up the process.[58]

The process of structure and local plan preparation would be a subject of detailed scrutiny by a number of academics. Coon, in his *Assessment of Scottish Development Planning* in 1989, went so far as to describe the development plan output, somewhat provocatively, as 'ambiguous, illogical, contradictory, unsubstantiated, inapposite, tendentious, obscure and poorly presented'. He suggests that there was some support for his view and quotes both Derek Lyddon, former Chief Planner at SDD and Urlan Wannop, former Chief Planner at Strathclyde Regional Council.[59] Derek Lyddon, in an address to the Scottish Society of Directors of Planning (SSDP) in 1985, suggested that planners had 'forgotten the craft of synthesis, putting things together, making a coherent whole'.[60] Begg and Pollock, in their review of development plans in Scotland between 1975

---

[56] Coon, A. G., 'An Assessment of Scottish Development Planning', *Planning Outlook*, Vol. 32, Issue 2 (1989), p. 79.

[57] SDD, *Planning Bulletin No.1*, February 1990.

[58] Town and Country Planning (Structure and Local Plans) (Scotland) Regulations 1983 [which superseded the 1976 Regulations] and Circular 32/1983: Structure and Local Plans [which amended SDD Circular 28/1976]. See also E. Young and J. Rowan-Robinson, *Scottish Planning Law and Procedure*, pp. 107–108.

[59] Coon, A. G., 'An Assessment of Scottish Development Planning', *Planning Outlook*, Vol. 32, Issue 2 (1989), pp. 81–83.

[60] Lyddon, D., *Performance of the Planning Process 1975–1985*, SSDP AGM, 31 May 1985.

and 1990, were more conciliatory, suggesting that, whilst the structure plans prepared in England were cumbersome and inflexible documents and had attracted widespread criticism over a prolonged period, Scottish structure plans were more concise and had, in general, confined themselves to genuine strategic planning matters.[61] They had also been prepared more quickly than those in England, taking an average of three years and six months compared to eight years in England. Begg and Pollock also observed that whilst the land-use planning system had a reputation as a negative process, local plans in Scotland were increasingly being used to promote development opportunities as a means of facilitating the implementation of proposals.[62] PAN 32 entitled Development Opportunities: Local Plans, published in 1988, utilising the Roxburgh (Part) Local Plan as an example, illustrated how local plans could act as a promotional vehicle for marketing proposals to the private sector.

In tandem with the new approach to development planning, there was an increasing awareness of the need for more openness and public involvement in planning. Emphasis was placed on the benefits to be gained from early consultation with a wide range of interests in order to sort out problems that might arise from proposals and those who are directly affected. Perhaps, inevitably, the plan preparation process tended to focus on the concerns of those who had the inclination, skills and resources to participate, and certain sectors of society were neglected. The success of the consultation and public involvement process is difficult to determine. Evidence from elsewhere in Scotland suggested that the somewhat abstract form of structure plan policies did little to stimulate public interest and that it may be that consultation through representative groups, such as community councils, was the best way forward. It was considered that public participation may have most to contribute to local plans.[63] In the Scottish Borders, the planning authority employed a wide variety of ways to involve the public, including the production of leaflets, posters and newsletters, exhibitions with audio-visual displays, models etc. and public meetings in order to attract the widest section of the community possible. The vast majority of proposals and policies incorporated in local plans were found to be acceptable and would form the basis for development in the Borders Region into the 1990s.

[61] Begg, H. M. and S. H. A. Pollock, 'Development plans in Scotland since 1975', *Scottish Geographical Magazine*, Vol. 107, No. 1, 1991, pp. 8–9.
[62] Ibid., pp. 9–10.
[63] See *Review of the Management of Planning*, SDD, April 1977.

The structure plan, like the 'old style' county development plans was primarily concerned with land use. As SDD Circular 32/1983 stated, 'The overall purpose of development planning is to set out the planning authority's policies and proposals for the use of land in the best interests of the community . . .' Whilst the intention of the new development plan system was to broaden the focus away from land use, PAN 27: Structure Planning, issued in 1981, advised planning authorities that structure plans should concentrate on land use issues and that economic, social and other policies should only be included in so far as they contributed to the land use aspects of the plan. The preoccupation with land use, therefore, continued and the structure plan focussed on strategic land use issues, such as settlement patterns, the scale and location of industry and employment, and the transport system. Countryside conservation and recreation and tourism were only considered appropriate where there was a strategic planning issue.

The 1980 structure plan set out a strategy for development in the 1980s with the declared aim to maintain and improve the quality of life for people in the Borders, resist rural depopulation and concentrate on providing jobs, housing, facilities and services. It laid the foundations for the preparation of local plans, which, in turn, provided the detailed guidance for the control of development at the local level. Implementation, however, required the co-operation of a range of organisations. The regional council had responsibility for important aspects of infrastructure, such as roads and water and drainage, but structure and local plans required to dovetail with the housing plans of the district councils. The role of the SDA was crucial not only in providing industrial sites and property but also in environmental improvements and economic regeneration. Although not strictly within the formal remit of town and country planning, as expressed in the Planning Acts, the local plans for the landward parts of the Borders Region gave expression to the council's support for agriculture and forestry as a major land user and employer in the region. Local plans were the springboard for dialogue between BRC and landowners and farmers, the larger estates and conservation bodies such as the Royal Society for the Protection of Birds (RSPB) and Scottish Wildlife Trust (SWT), the CCS and NCCS on the management of the countryside. Through the 1980s rural land use and the rural economy would become of increasing interest to the regional council, as planning authority, as radical changes in government and EC agricultural policies threatened the economic and social fabric of rural areas.

7

The 1980s: Challenges and Achievements

INTRODUCTION

THE 1980S WERE A period of economic volatility. The Conservative government, elected in 1979, pursued a host of free-market reforms, including privatisation, reducing the powers of trade unions, deregulation and lower income tax rates.[1] Despite considerable lobbying from the regional and district councils, the government withdrew Assisted Area Status from the Scottish Borders in 1982, which resulted in the region no longer being eligible for government or European Community regional economic development funds.[2] This meant that financial inducements were no longer available to incoming firms and for investment projects by existing companies. Compared to the rest of Scotland, the Borders had a relatively low proportion of overseas manufacturing investment, reflecting its lack of success in attracting inward investment.

Despite continuous lobbying of government, supported by local Members of Parliament, particularly Sir David Steel, the Conservative government would not be persuaded that the Scottish Borders deserved development area status. The government's attitude is amply illustrated in the views expressed by George Younger, former Scottish Secretary on a visit to Hawick in 1987 when he suggested that: 'The Borders is a good example of how an area can fend for itself. With a certain amount of help from the local authorities and the SDA, the Borders people have

---

[1] Harrison, B., *Find a Role?: The United Kingdom 1970–1990* (Oxford: Oxford University Press, 2011).

[2] Borders Regional Council, *The Effect of the Loss of Development Area Status on the Borders Region,* A Joint Report by Borders Regional Council, Berwickshire District Council, Ettrick and Lauderdale District Council, Roxburgh District Council, and Tweeddale District Council, July 1980; Borders Regional Council, *The Borders Region: The Case for Continued Regional Development Assistance,* 1982.

done their own thing successfully'.[3] His comments incensed Galashiels Councillor Drew Tulley, who would subsequently become Chairman of the Planning and Development Committee, who demanded that a further attempt should be made to put forward a case for the reinstatement of development area status.

In April 1985, the Borders lost priority status for European Social Fund (ESF) assistance, which limited the amount available for vocational training. However, the Borders, along with other rural areas in the UK, remained eligible for assistance under the Guidance Section of the European Agricultural Guidance and Guarantee Fund (EAGGF), which was used to provide support for the agricultural industry through initiatives such as the Less Favoured Farming Areas, Farm/Woodland Initiative, Set Aside and Farm Diversification Scheme and direct support for projects involving the processing and marketing of agricultural and fishery products, such as grain drying and storage, potato grading and storage, egg packing, vegetable and fish processing.[4]

Pressures were being imposed on the agricultural sector, however, through reduced EEC support in response to the growing surpluses as a result of the EEC's drive for self-sufficiency. Quotas were imposed on the dairy sector and on cereals. Capital grant schemes were severely cut back in the mid-1980s with EEC grants on buildings and infrastructure improvements reduced from 32.5 per cent to 15 per cent (from 37.5 per cent to 30 per cent in Less Favoured Areas). The UK-funded Agricultural Improvement Scheme offered no grants for buildings; support being switched to environmentally positive and energy saving projects. Support for co-operative enterprises had also been cut and grant aid for marketing and processing had been reduced to 15 per cent from 25 per cent. UK grants for grain drying and storage had ceased. Even the advisory services, previously free, had to be paid for.[5] Increasingly, the public were viewing rural areas as a national asset, to be husbanded in a way that served a broad range of interests, of which farming was only one. The concerns at the impact of agricultural change resulting from a combination of new farm technology and the subsidies provided in the 1970s

---

[3] See *Southern Reporter*, 19 March 1987.

[4] SBA/1210/24, Scottish Borders Structure Plan 1991; Report of Survey, Part 4 Rural Development, pp. 2–3; for a list of FEOGA grants 1981–1986, see Lilwall, N. B. and J. M. Winning, *Agricultural Development Opportunities in the Scottish Borders*, Edinburgh School of Agriculture, December 1986, Appendix 9, p. 78.

[5] Lilwall, N. B. and J. M. Winning, *Agricultural Development Opportunities in the Scottish Borders*, pp. 11–12.

were perfectly illustrated in Marion Shoard's book *The Theft of the Countryside*, published in 1980.[6] In the book, Shoard called for a radical programme of action that included extending the planning system to the farmed countryside and the designation of new national parks in lowland England. Few of Shoard's suggestions would be acted upon by government but the book certainly drew the government's attention to the public's increasing concerns and would eventually lead to changing attitudes to sustainable farming that we see today.

Despite the council's best efforts, the Borders Region in 1990 remained dependent on a relatively narrow range of industries and a small number of companies; employment in the region increased by only about 300 people between 1981 and 1989.[7] Whilst the region was successful in creating jobs to replace those lost in existing industry, the rate required to achieve the population growth envisaged in the 1980 structure plan was not achieved. Although the population of the region continued to grow, from an estimated 100,370 in 1977 to an estimated 103,500 in 1990, the increase of 3,000 people was well below the projected figure of 8,000 people; a reflection of the over-optimistic national forecasts of the late 1970s, which were not realised largely as a result of changing economic circumstances. The development of Tweedbank came to a halt in 1980 and did not recommence until 1990; there was little growth in Hawick, with no progress on the acquisition and development of the industrial site at Burnhead. Only in Tweeddale did population growth outstrip that projected, largely as a result of pressure for retirement homes and from Edinburgh commuters rather than as a result of job creation. Depopulation remained an issue, particularly in the remoter rural areas of south-west Roxburghshire, the Ettrick and Yarrow Valleys in Selkirkshire and the southern parts of Tweeddale District. The population of the region continued to be imbalanced with almost 22 per cent of the population over retirement age in 1990 (compared with 17.7 per cent in Scotland as a whole).[8]

The number of houses built by the public sector dropped dramatically after the election of the Conservative government in 1979. Local authority expenditure was capped and councils were not allowed to use the funds raised from council house sales under the 'Right to Buy'

---

[6] Shoard, M., *The Theft of the Countryside* (London: Temple Smith, 1980).

[7] SBA/1210/24, Scottish Borders Structure Plan 1991; Report of Survey, Part 1 Introduction, p. 26.

[8] SBA/1210/24, Scottish Borders Structure Plan 1991; Report of Survey, Part 1 Introduction, pp 9–10.

scheme introduced in 1980 to fund housebuilding.[9] The emphasis of public sector housing policy moved away from housebuilding to the improvement and modernisation of the existing housing stock. The involvement of the SSHA virtually ceased in 1980 and various housing associations – Hanover, Bield, Link, Royal British Legion and Kirk Care, for example – concentrated on housing for special needs rather than incoming workers. Eildon Housing Association constructed a number of sheltered housing schemes, single person flats, hostels for the mentally handicapped and houses for the elderly and disabled, at various locations across the Borders. In the Borders as a whole, throughout the 1980s, private house completions were relatively small in number, ranging from 100 to 250 units per annum. Development was patchy; whilst most of the land allocated in Peebles was developed by 1990, in the Central Borders many sites zoned for development prior to 1975 remained undeveloped.[10]

Nevertheless, during the 1980s, much was achieved in resolving the issues identified in the structure plan and implementing its policies and proposals. Industrial sites were serviced and factories provided; land renewal projects were implemented; and a wider choice of private housing and housing for special needs was provided. Central area redevelopment and rehabilitation schemes, conservation and facelift schemes, and a wide range of countryside recreation projects were completed. The strategic road network continued to be improved and stability was achieved in the public transport network; a number of unconventional schemes were initiated to support rural areas. However, some issues were not tackled or were overtaken by events and new issues arose as a result of changing national policies and priorities and changing attitudes to new development and land use change.

CHANGES IN DEPARTMENTAL STRUCTURE

Responsibility for public transport was transferred from the Planning and Development Department to the Roads and Transportation Department in 1982. Also, in 1982, tourism marketing and promotion became solely a district council function, with the subsequent establishment in 1983 of the SBTB, funded jointly by the four district councils. The completion

---

[9] Parkinson, M., 'The Thatcher Government's urban policy 1979–1989', *The Town Planning Review*, Vol. 60, No. 4 (October 1989), pp. 421–440.

[10] SBA/1210/24, Scottish Borders Structure Plan 1991; Report of Survey, Part 1 Introduction, pp. 10–11.

of the Borders Region Structure Plan, approved in December 1980, expansion of the department's economic development role, and the loss of responsibility for public transport and tourism marketing and promotion led to a re-appraisal of the structure of the Department of Planning and Development. Additional staff was employed on development promotion and additional members of staff were engaged as the department became more involved in implementing projects and on other matters such as the countryside and ranger service. Consequently, from January 1983, the department comprised three sections with a revised complement of thirty-seven staff compared to thirty-three at the end of 1975 (Figure 7.1) (see Appendix 1c), comprising:

1. A Planning Policy and Development Control section responsible for the local plan programme and for the administration of development control.
2. A Design and Implementation section responsible for implementing projects, providing design guidance and advice, and for the council's countryside remit.
3. An Economic Development section responsible for the promotion of the Borders Region, industrial property management and business development.

As the 1980s progressed, the department's role in economic development and project implementation continued to increase. In development control, although the number of planning applications received reduced in the early 1980s, there was an expansion of related activities, such as enforcement. The introduction of fees for applications in 1981 and a requirement for neighbour notification placed additional burdens on the department.[11] On David Douglas's departure in 1986 the responsibilities of the three sections was reviewed and, in April 1987, a new departmental structure was implemented comprising a Development Section, responsible for the council's industrial land and buildings, industrial promotion, town centre rehabilitation and the countryside, including the ranger service; a Planning and Policy section, responsible for the review of the structure and local plans, and for all other planning policy matters; and a Development Control section, incorporating posts dealing with enforcement, conservation areas, listed buildings and design guidance (see Appendix 1d). The early 1980s saw the introduction of

---

[11] The Town and Country Planning (Fees for applications and Deemed Applications) (Scotland) Regulations 1981 and The Town and Country Planning (General Development) (Scotland) Order 1981, Article 7.

Staff Photo 1986

Back Row: Douglas Hope, Colin Smith, Charles Strang, Quentin McLaren, John Gray, George Inglis, John Young, Peter Tench, Paul Gregory, Trevor Burrows

Middle Row: Charles Johnston, Alister McDonald, Douglas Scott, Alasdair Maclean, Joan Mason, Jane Williamson, Gillian Maxwell, Brian Frater, Ian Borthwick, Keith Robeson, (unknown)

Front Row: Tom Mackie, Alistair Lorimer, Morag Cavers, David Douglas, George Ovens, Vera Bell, Charlotte Cottingham, Craig Miller

Figure 7.1 Planning and Development Department staff photograph, 1986

the first word processors to the department in the form of the IBM Displaywriter. This microcomputer-based word processor enabled reports to be written, stored, amended and printed without repetitive re-typing, considerably reducing the workload of the department's typists.

Prior to local government reorganisation in 1975, the activities of the planning authorities attracted little attention in the press. As Bill Chisholm, who arrived in the Borders in 1969 and was *The Scotsman*'s staff reporter for thirty-six years, comments 'In the early years of my stint, the planning function across the four Borders county councils was practically invisible'.[12] The profile of the Planning and Development Department, and the Planning and Development Committee, in the local press expanded considerably during the 1980s. At the time there were eight local papers dealing with different areas of the Borders: *Berwickshire News, Kelso Chronicle & Jedburgh Gazette, Hawick Express, Hawick News, Selkirk Saturday Advertiser, Border Telegraph,*

---

[12] In conversation with Bill Chisholm, 25 August 2021.

Southern Reporter and *Peeblesshire News*, plus *The Scotsman*. Through the 1980s, the local press increasingly paid attention to the proceedings of the Planning and Development Committee across the whole range of its activities.[13] Not all decisions had the unanimous support of all members of the committee or, indeed, of the full council and the local press would report these differences of view.[14] In relation to planning applications, reporters wrote articles based on the committee reports produced by officers and recorded the details of planning applications submitted to the committee, the objections, if any, received and the deliberations and decisions of the committee (Figure 7.2).

Whilst reporters might highlight criticisms of the planning process by disgruntled applicants or objectors, there was little expression of opinion on the decisions made. Expressions of criticism would, however, be expressed in the 'Letters' columns of the local papers. The press also recorded the successes and disappointments on the economic development front and strongly supported the council's efforts to attract industry to the region.

ECONOMIC DEVELOPMENT

In 1980, the Borders economy remained heavily orientated towards manufacturing, especially textiles, and the primary sector dominated by agriculture. The best known and largest of the textile and knitwear firms were in Hawick: Lyle & Scott (employing 1,700 people), Braemar Knitwear (1,500 employees) and Pringle of Scotland (1,500 employees). These firms also had branch factories elsewhere in the Borders. There were other important textile and knitwear firms: Barrie Knitwear, Hawick (350 employees); D. Ballantyne Bros. & Co, Peebles (410 employees); Henry Ballantyne, Walkerburn (300 employees); Laidlaw & Fairgreave, Galashiels (820 employees); Gardiner of Selkirk (300 employees); and Andrew Stewart (Woollens) Ltd, Galashiels (130 employees). Reflecting the more recent diversification of industry, BEPI Electronics employed 240 people in Galashiels and Exacta Circuits employed 190 people in Selkirk; Kenmellion, manufacturing scientific and precision instruments in Galashiels, employed 250 people; L. S. Starrett, manufacturing

---

[13] See, for example, *Southern Reporter*, 23 October 1975 & 6 November 1975, 10 January 1980 & 27 March 1980.

[14] See for example, coverage of debates on a management plan for the St Mary's Loch area and the maintenance of the Southern Upland Way, *Southern Reporter*, 27 March 1980.

Figure 7.2 Sample press coverage from 1988

precision tools and Mainetti, manufacturing coat hangers in Jedburgh, both employed 400 people. In Berwickshire, Homac Foods, processing shellfish in Duns, employed 170 people and the Dexter Corporation in Chirnside, manufacturers of non-woven materials, employed over 200 workers. Other firms, such as Broughton Brewery, played a crucial role in providing employment, sometimes in the more rural and remote locations of the Borders.[15]

Despite substantial job losses during the early 1980s, the textile industry remained the major manufacturing sector employing about 6,000 people. However, the Borders textile industry experienced a severe slump in 1989 when a number of firms closed or laid off workers.[16] The electronics sector, on the other hand, developed into a significant industry in the Borders during the 1980s, and employment in electronics grew substantially to over 1,600 persons in 1989; STC Exacta in Selkirk was the largest Printed Circuit Board (PCB) company in the UK. Many of the electronics companies in the region could trace their origins to Currie & Mill, established in 1961, and the two companies that emanated from that partnership: Exacta Circuits and BEPI (Figure 7.3).

In Galashiels, McQueen Ltd, originally a printing and office supplies business, expanded into a desktop publishing and software manufacturing business with a worldwide reputation, at premises firstly at Langlee and then at Netherdale in a former electronics factory occupied by Sprague Electrics. This development was a prime example of the close working relationship that developed between the development officers in the Planning and Development Department and private business after 1975, as described by Mike Gray, the Chair and Chief Executive of McQueen Ltd:

> The Gray family acquired the printing and office supplies business of John McQueen and Son Ltd in 1976. The new company was re-named McQueen Ltd. and the former Buckholm Mill was acquired and expanded, with support from BRC. McQueen entered an era of rapid expansion in the 1980s as a key player in the emerging market of Desk Top Publishing and, in 1984, acquired a greenfield site at Langlee. Speedy support from BRC was essential as timing was critical to keep pace with client demands in a fast-expanding market. A site was acquired and an initial production unit of 12,000 sq. ft completed and then enlarged to 20,000 sq. ft within a couple of years.
>
> With the Buckholm Mill site literally creaking at the seams, McQueen acquired a former electronics factory (50,000 sq ft) at Netherdale in 1988, which was extended by a further 25,000 sq. ft. and provided pan-European solutions for technology clients such as Aldus, Adobe, Apple, Intel, Microsoft and Motorola. McQueen continued to expand with its multi-lingual Call Centre in Edinburgh and operations in the Netherlands, France, Sweden,

---

[15] See Survey of Major Manufacturing and Construction Firms, JPAC and EBDA, 1973.

[16] BRC/PD/1, Department of Planning and Development, *Annual Report, 1989*, Borders Regional Council, February 1990, p. 20.

ELECTRONICS IN THE SCOTTISH BORDERS – FAMILY TREE 1989

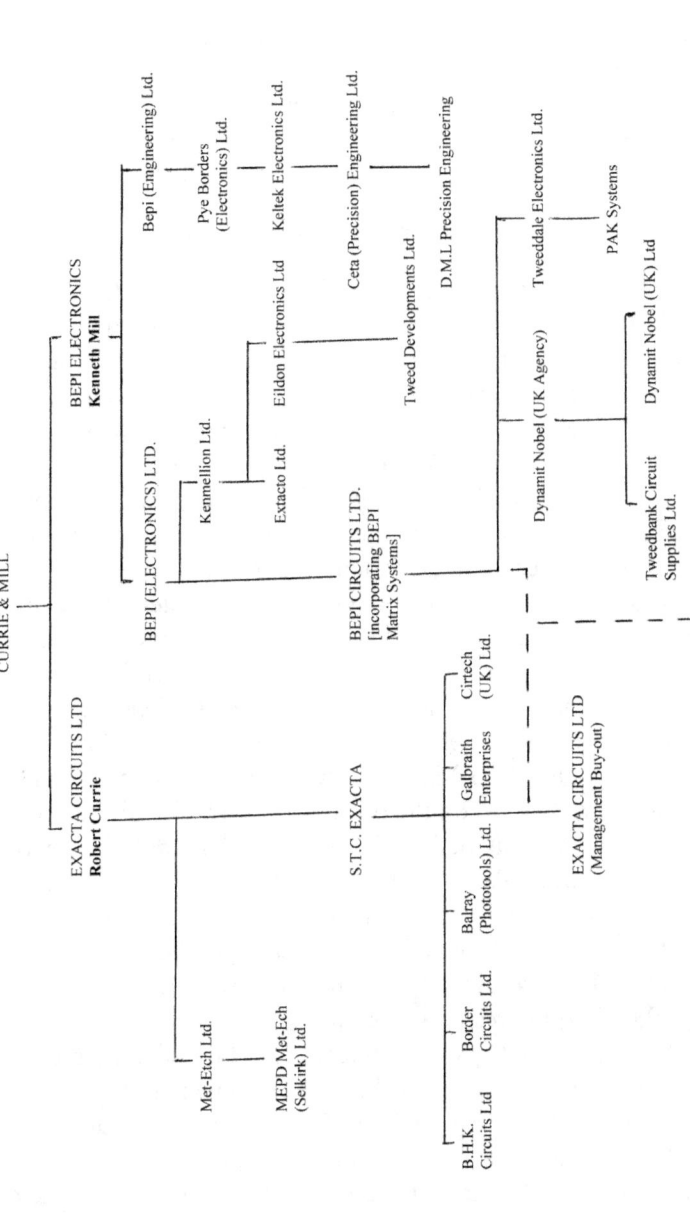

Figure 7.3 Electronics in the Scottish Borders

USA (California and Tennessee), Singapore and the Philippines but with its head office remaining in Galashiels. Borders Regional council support was instrumental in McQueen's success because:

- There was an understanding of the enterprise opportunity for a local company;
- The importance of supporting enterprise was recognised;
- There was an awareness of the need to make quick decisions to deliver results at the pace expected by clients in the computer technology market; and
- There was a positive relationship between McQueen and BRC.

In the 1980s, the servicing of land for industrial development and factory building was seen as a pre-requisite for the continued growth of the Borders economy and its population. As in most rural areas, the involvement of the private sector in the provision of industrial land and premises was relatively limited. Consequently, the Regional Council, in partnership with the SDA was the principal development body. The Regional Council bought and serviced industrial sites in most Border towns, often in association with the SDA: the industrial estates at Langlee in Galashiels, Tweedbank, Oxnam Road in Jedburgh, Pinnaclehill in Kelso, and Acredale in Eyemouth, are examples of the success of this joint programme. The philosophy of the council was to provide small and medium-sized factories and workshops and encourage start-up businesses and employment in the smaller settlements. Workshops were provided in Galashiels at Currie Road in the station yard and at Langlee; at Burnfoot, on Mansfield Road and at Lochpark in Hawick; at Edenside in Kelso and on the old station yard in Jedburgh. In Selkirk, Linglie Mill was sub-divided into workshops, and in Peebles, workshops were built at South Parks and Newby Court, off the High Street in Peebles, was developed for shops/workshops. As a result, the number of industrial properties owned by the Regional Council increased from sixty-nine in 1979 to almost 200 in 1988, with a gross floorspace of almost 30,000 sq metres (see Appendix 5).[17]

The SDA provided several factories at Tweedbank, most notably those occupied by Dynamit (Nobel) UK, producing glass and laminate blanks for PCBs, Tweedbank Circuit Supplies, manufacturing PCBs, and Hill Robinson Thread Company, manufacturing thread for the textile industry. In Hawick, the SDA built factory units at Eastfield Mills.

---

[17] SBA/1210/24, Scottish Borders Structure Plan 1991; Report of Survey, Part 1 Introduction, p. 12; Department of Planning and Development, *Annual Report, 1989*, Borders Regional Council, February 1990, pp. 22–23.

In Selkirk, St Mary's Mill was sub-divided into industrial units. The largest single let, 2,500 sq metres of factory space at Queen Street, Galashiels in 1983, was to F.M.I. Composites, a subsidiary of Fibre Materials Inc of Biddeford, Maine in the USA, which manufactured carbon felt insulation and advanced fibre reinforced materials. Unfortunately, the planned employment of 120 never fully materialised when the US government declined to grant the company export licences.[18]

The contribution of the SDA to the strengthening of the economic base of the Scottish Borders in the 1980s and the provision of increased job opportunities cannot be over-emphasised. By 1988, the SDA had some sixty-two industrial units, mounting to some 27,000 sq metres, located around the region (see Appendix 6).[19] However, following a policy change in 1986, new factories were only built on demand and, in March 1990, the SDA announced that it was to sell off substantial parts of its property portfolio, including all SDA land and buildings at Eastfield Mill, Hawick, Pinnaclehill, Kelso and Tweedbank. This decision, emanating from a severe reduction in the SDA's capital and revenue budgets by the Conservative government, resulted in the SDA's property portfolio in the Borders being reduced from sixty-two units to eleven units.[20]

The SDA also played an active role in land renewal. The redevelopment of the Station Yard in Galashiels, Rodono Mill in Hawick and the Station Yard in Newtown St Boswells are good examples.[21] In Galashiels, SDA funded the clearance and servicing of the former station yard with the construction of a new road through the site to provide improved access to the Langhaugh Industrial Area and to new factory sites, a health centre and car parking for some 135 vehicles. In addition, a footpath, cycle-track and bridle path (the 'Gala Walkway') was constructed along 6.2 km of the former Waverley line from Balnakiel, in the north-west, to Tweedbank in the east. In Hawick, Rodono Mill was demolished and the site prepared for the construction of a new health centre. In Newtown St Boswells the station yard was re-graded and landscaped and a car park constructed together with a site for a

---

[18] SBA/1210/24, Scottish Borders Structure Plan 1991; Report of Survey, Part 3 Economic Development, pp. 17–18.

[19] BRC/PD/1, Department of Planning and Development, *Annual Report, 1989*, Borders Regional Council, February 1990, pp. 23–24.

[20] BRC/PD/1, Department of Planning and Development, *Annual Report, 1990*, Borders Regional Council, February 1991, pp. 23–24.

[21] SBA/1210/24, Scottish Borders Structure Plan 1991; Report of Survey, Part 1 Introduction, p. 12.

new Co-op supermarket. In Eyemouth, the redevelopment of Meeks & Dickson's Yard, a joint BRC and SDA venture, provided twenty-four fisherman's stores, industrial units for marine engineering and workshops for fishing related businesses. At Newcastleton, the former station yard was developed as a caravan site and adjoining land was identified for craft homes and workshop units.[22] One of the last projects undertaken by the SDA was the purchase of Laidlaw & Fairgreave's mill at Walkerburn (formerly Ballantyne's Tweedvale Mills), which closed in 1989 with disastrous consequences for the village, and its conversion into eight workshop units and office space. Part of the mill would be developed as the Scottish Museum of Woollen Textiles and Mill Shop.[23]

To address a gap in the financial provision available for small manufacturing businesses in the region, the Council introduced its Finance for Small Business (FSB) Scheme in 1984. The scheme provided grants up to a maximum of £1,500 and loans up to a maximum of £5,000. The annual report for 1989 records that during the five-year period 1984–1989 more than 100 grants were awarded and it was estimated that some 150 full-time and 40 part-time jobs had been created or protected.[24] The Regional Council also developed a strong promotional expertise, stimulating interest in the Borders as an area for business development, and marketing its products and services. The Planning and Development Department mounted exhibitions and undertook a wide variety of promotional trips to Europe and the United States, often in association with 'Locate in Scotland', established in 1981 jointly by the SDA and the Industry Department for Scotland to provide a 'one door' approach for investment to Scotland.[25]

In order to market the region's products and services, the department produced a number of publications: a business directory, the Scottish Borders Business Directory, which listed some 1,500 firms in the region, and individual guides such as the prestigious 'Scottish Borders Knitwear Buyers Guide' and the 'Electronics in the Scottish Borders Guide', published in five and six languages, respectively (English, Swedish, French,

---

[22] BRC/PD/1, Department of Planning and Development, *Annual Report, 1987*, Borders Regional Council, February 1988, pp. 27–28.

[23] BRC/PD/1, Department of Planning and Development, *Annual Report, 1990*, Borders Regional Council, February 1991, p. 24.

[24] BRC/PD/1, Department of Planning and Development, *Annual Report, 1989*, Borders Regional Council, February 1990, pp. 31–32.

[25] See *Locate in Scotland*, Report by the Comptroller and Auditor General, National Audit Office (London: HMSO, April 1989).

German, Italian and Japanese). A buyer's guide to food and drink, 'A taste of the Scottish Borders' promoted the region as a producer of high-quality foodstuffs and beverages and the Borders Craft Guide provided details of more than thirty craft workshops and studios in the Borders.[26]

ENVIRONMENTAL IMPROVEMENTS AND PROJECTS

The regional council undertook a number of initiatives, many of them jointly with the SDA, to improve the environment of Border towns and villages. Some, such as the Castlegate and Canongate schemes in Jedburgh, and the Woodmarket/Horsemarket scheme in Kelso, were linked to housing association developments. Others, such as the Howegate/Drumlanrig Square scheme in Hawick and the Cuddyside development in Peebles were district council-led rehabilitation or redevelopment projects. Perhaps the most significant project in Hawick was the rehabilitation and redevelopment of the Tower Hotel/Backdamgate area. The historic Tower Hotel, closed in 1981, was acquired by Roxburgh District Council in 1985. The remainder of the site was acquired by the regional council in 1988 to facilitate a co-ordinated redevelopment. Assisted by funding from the SDA, the rear part of the site was cleared for development by Eildon Housing Association with the former hotel partially cleared to reveal the historic Drumlanrig Tower. The Scottish Historic Buildings Trust funded the restoration of Drumlanrig Tower and adjoining property to provide a heritage/visitor centre, textile museum, shops, offices and flats. Complementing this project, the High Street Facelift Scheme, and Town Scheme operating over an extended conservation area, resulted in significant environmental improvements to the town centre.[27]

In Galashiels, the widening of Ladhope Vale in 1989 paved the way for a reorganisation of the A7 traffic system in the town centre utilising Bank Street/High Street and an improved Ladhope Vale, thus removing through traffic from the main shopping street, Channel Street, which

---

[26] See, respectively, BRC/PD/9, Borders Regional Council, *Scottish Borders Business Directory*, 1986; BRC/PD/5, Borders Regional Council, *Scottish Borders Knitwear Buyers Guide*, 1987; BRC/PD/4, Borders Regional Council, *Electronics in the Scottish Borders*, 1988; BRC/PD/6, *A Taste of the Scottish Borders-Buyers Guide to Food and Drink*, 1989.

[27] BRC/PD/1, Department of Planning and Development, *Annual Report, 1989*, Borders Regional Council, February 1990, pp. 40–43.

became a pedestrian priority area, the first in the Borders.[28] At the time, it was hoped that this would unlock the commercial potential of a number of sites within the town centre. The site of the former Valley Mill in Paton Street, on the edge of the town centre, was the site of a 20,000 sq ft Co-op Supermarket, which would become the Co-op Pricefighter Store in 1983, the largest supermarket in the Borders (later Tesco). The Stirling Street/Stirling Place area, an area of mixed uses next to the bus station, was also identified for commercial redevelopment, and would be the location of a Gateway, later Somerfield, supermarket (then B & M Store and more recently, Home Bargains).

A whole raft of studies was carried out in the 1980s, some in-house, and some by consultants on behalf of the Planning and Development Department. In Hawick, the Teviot Study examined the future development potential of the Teviot and Slitrig river corridors, including the Commercial Road area, which would in due course become a major part of the commercial area of Hawick.[29] In Selkirk, an in-depth study of the Riverside Industrial Area, where there was considerable potential for development, examined the opportunities to improve the appearance of this area, improve road access and capitalise on the parcels of unused land.[30] However, although the development of world-famous Selkirk Glass established in 1977, which manufactured paper weights, was a success story, the lack of progress with the overall environmental improvement plan was a disappointment, and the Selkirk Riverside Area remains an area with untapped potential. In Kelso, the Spylaw Road area, a mix of uses and buildings, was the subject of an environmental improvement scheme to upgrade access, provide parking areas, provide the screening of external storage and work areas and landscape screening between the industrial area and adjoining residential areas.[31]

Unemployment in the region soared from a low of 3.7 per cent in 1980 (compared with 8.9 per cent in Scotland as a whole) to a peak of 10.0 per cent in 1983 (compared to 15.1 per cent in Scotland as a whole). Under the government's special employment measures, administered by the Manpower Services Commission (MSC), to create jobs

[28] BRC/PD/1, Department of Planning and Development, *Annual Report, 1990*, Borders Regional Council, February 1991, pp. 37–38.

[29] BRC/PD/1, Department of Planning and Development, *Annual Report, 1988*, Borders Regional Council, February 1989, p. 25.

[30] BRC/PD/1, Department of Planning and Development, *Annual Report, 1989*, Borders Regional Council, February 1990, p. 37.

[31] BRC/PD/1, Department of Planning and Development, *Annual Report, 1988*, Borders Regional Council, February 1989, p. 23.

and training opportunities for school leavers aged sixteen and seventeen years old and the long-term unemployed, the Planning and Development Department sponsored environmental improvement projects. The Community Programme, Planning and Environmental Projects scheme (PEP) grew from two teams of four men in 1983 to over fifty employees working on up to 200 projects each year by 1989. Funding was largely borne by the MSC with contributions from the SDA or the CCS.[32]

The schemes undertaken were designed to be of community benefit, but also enabled the participants in the projects to gain work experience combined with training in appropriate skills. The Department's annual report for 1987 lists the wide range of projects undertaken during the past five years.[33] The environmental projects included environmental improvements in villages throughout the region such as tree planting and the provision of play areas, the provision of picnic tables and seats at various rural locations, the waymarking of the Southern Upland Way and the construction of stiles and bridges on the route, and the removal of derelict beach huts and dune stabilisation at Coldingham Sands.[34] It was estimated that work to the value of £250,000 per annum was carried out throughout the latter years of the 1980s.[35] The success of the scheme was down to teamwork but mention should be made of John Denholm, the Community Programme Manager from 1983 to 1987, and his successor, Tom Mackie, who with Ron Wright, Administration Officer, ensured the smooth running of the scheme.

In April 1988, the government changed the PEP Scheme to Training for Rural Improvement Projects (TRIP) to be administered under the auspices of the Border Training Services Agency (BTS), part of the Regional Council's Education Department. The PEP scheme came to an end in September 1989 and thus ended eleven years of Planning and Development Department involvement in the sponsorship and administration of various temporary employment schemes. In this time, virtually all communities in the region benefited.[36] The Planning and

[32] BRC/PD/1, Department of Planning and Development, *Annual Report, 1987*, Borders Regional Council, February 1988, p. 28.
[33] BRC/PD/1, Department of Planning and Development, *Annual Report, 1987*, Borders Regional Council, February 1988, Appendix 2, pp. 50–51.
[34] BRC/PD/1, Department of Planning and Development, *Annual Report, 1987*, Borders Regional Council, February 1988, Appendix 10, pp. 67–69.
[35] BRC/PD/1, Department of Planning and Development, *Annual Report, 1988*, Borders Regional Council, February 1989, p. 24.
[36] BRC/PD/1, Department of Planning and Development, *Annual Report, 1989*, Borders Regional Council, February 1990, p. 45.

Development Department continued to sponsor countryside projects and in 1990 some forty-two projects were undertaken by the BTS teams funded by the Planning and Development Department. However, with the advent of Scottish Enterprise in 1991, the BTS projects teams were 'wound up' and the Planning and Development Department's involvement in employment training ceased.[37]

From 1983, with landscape design advice available in the Planning and Development Department, greater environmental consideration was given to road projects such as the Melrose by-pass and the Kelso relief road. Landscape advice was also provided on the environmental impact of major developments submitted as planning applications, such as mineral working, caravan sites and golf course developments. The regional council continued the previous local authorities' programmes for the enhancement of conservation areas and had an ongoing programme of development briefs and design guidance for a number of development sites.[38] Until the mid-1980s, records of Tree Preservation Orders (TPOs) and trees in conservation areas, inherited from the previous authorities, were somewhat lacking in content and detail, limiting the council's ability to safeguard protected trees. Following the loss of a prosecution in 1990 in relation to the felling of trees protected by a TPO, which highlighted the inadequacies in the drafting of the original TPO and the absence of monitoring, the thirty-five areas covered by TPOs and protected trees within the region's forty conservation areas were resurveyed in 1991.[39]

There was a growing interest in the historic environment throughout the 1980s but it would be September 1989 before the regional council appointed a Regional Archaeologist, one of nine such officers in Scotland. To provide basic information on the number and location of archaeological sites, a list, known as the Sites and Monuments Record (SMR), was compiled from published sources as a MSC project. More than 10,000 sites were listed, including artefact find spots and features varying in size from standing stones to abbeys and castles, hillforts and field systems, boundaries and road systems. Knowledge of archaeological sites in the Borders also stemmed from the work of local archaeological societies, inspired individuals and university departments.

---

[37] BRC/PD/1, Department of Planning and Development, *Annual Report, 1990*, Borders Regional Council, February 1991, p. 44.

[38] BRC/PD/1, Department of Planning and Development, *Annual Report, 1989*, Borders Regional Council, February 1990, pp. 51–53.

[39] BRC/PD/1, Department of Planning and Development, *Annual Report, 1990*, Borders Regional Council, February 1991, p. 48.

The University of Bradford's work at Trimontium, near Newstead and the Soutra Hospital Research Project were two examples. Although most planning applications had no archaeological implications, where development in the historic burghs was proposed, the archaeologist had a role in carrying out archaeological fieldwork in advance of any proposed development.[40]

THE COUNTRYSIDE

Approximately 10 per cent of the economically active Borders population was engaged directly in agriculture and another 10 per cent employed in jobs dependant on agriculture in 1986. However, there was a continuing loss of agricultural employment; from almost 4,000 persons in 1981 to a little over 2,200 persons in 1989.[41] During the 1980s, the emphasis of EC and government policy switched from the support of production to the encouragement of diversification into non-surplus products, less intensive farming and farm woodlands. The regional council was concerned that changes in agriculture could threaten the rural economy and the social fabric of rural areas and, in order to understand the problems further, commissioned the Edinburgh School of Agriculture to produce a report on agricultural development opportunities. The report, published in 1986, suggested that the outlook for the Borders was for more afforestation, more redundant traditional farm steadings and cottages, and more opportunities for diversification into tourism and recreation.[42] As a consequence, the council re-appraised its policies on afforestation, housing in the countryside and tourism development.

A study funded jointly with the SDA, also published in 1986, examined the prospects for rural development in two pilot areas: south-west Roxburghshire and eastern Berwickshire. It looked at the opportunities for agricultural diversification, including deer farming, goat farming, farm forestry and farm tourism; forestry-related opportunities, including the use of forestry waste for community energy purposes (a novel idea in 1986); opportunities for rural employment; and tourism and

---

[40] BRC/PD/1, Department of Planning and Development, *Annual Report, 1989*, Borders Regional Council, February 1990, pp. 54–56.

[41] For a summary of the agricultural position in 1989, see SBA/1210/24, Scottish Borders Structure Plan 1991; Report of Survey, Part 4 Rural Development, pp. 15–16.

[42] Lilwall, N. B. and J. M. Winning, *Agricultural Development Opportunities in the Scottish Borders*, Edinburgh School of Agriculture, December 1986.

recreation.[43] Another study jointly with the SDA examined the problems and opportunities of a 2,400 ha upland estate in the Lammermuirs, the Whitchester Estate, near Cranshaws. This study focussed on game management, forestry and horticulture but also considered the potential for visitor attractions, rural crafts and holiday accommodation.[44]

In 1982, the first Farming, Forestry and Wildlife Advisory Group (FFWAG) in Scotland was established in the Borders with support from the regional council (FFWAG was originally established in 1969 to promote the conservation of wildlife and the environment amongst the farming community). The first full-time FFWAG Adviser in Scotland was appointed in 1985 with the regional council contributing 25 per cent of the cost.[45] In pursuance of its policy of encouraging amenity hardwood tree planting, BRC introduced a Borders Tree Grant Scheme in 1988, jointly administered with the FFWAG Adviser. Grants were mainly for hedge and hedgerow tree planting and small copses in field corners and headlands and there was an encouraging response from farmers, who wished to plant up small areas of unwanted land and hedgerows.[46] Applications were also received from community councils and this initiative would be expanded in 1990, with funding from the CCS.[47]

The influence of planning on afforestation in Scotland was almost non-existent prior to 1974. Consultation took place between the Forestry Commission (FC) and the Department of Agriculture and Fisheries for Scotland (DAFS) over afforestation in the state sector but there was no comparable arrangement over private sector planting. Planning authorities were not consulted over afforestation in either sector. A review of forestry policy in 1972 considered that 'the responsibilities and functions of the Forestry Commission and of planning authorities in regard to the environmental aspects of private forestry need to be examined'.[48] As a result, it was subsequently decided that 'In considering planting grant applications, the Commission will consult the Agricultural Departments,

---

[43] *Pilot Rural Development Areas Study*, Joint Report by Borders Regional Council and Scottish Development Agency, October 1986.

[44] ASH Environmental Design Partnership, *Economic Development Potential of a Rural Estate: A Study of Whitchester Estate, Berwickshire*, July 1987.

[45] BRC/PD/1, Department of Planning and Development, *Annual Report, 1987*, Borders Regional Council, February 1988, p. 37.

[46] BRC/PD/1, Department of Planning and Development, *Annual Report, 1989*, Borders Regional Council, February 1990, p. 54.

[47] BRC/PD/1, Department of Planning and Development, *Annual Report, 1990*, Borders Regional Council, February 1991, p. 48.

[48] MAFF et al., *Forestry Policy* (London: HMSO, 1972).

planning authorities, and other interests concerned ... with the object of ensuring that agriculture, amenity, recreation and nature conservation requirements are satisfied'. In Scotland, the new arrangements were described in SDD Circular 71/1974 and PAN 2.[49] The agreed consultation process required the regional council to be consulted on all applications within AGLVs and water catchment areas, which together covered 25 per cent of the region; outwith these areas the regional council was consulted only on applications where the planting area was over 500 ha, which is a considerable area. This process worked well until the mid-1980s when the number of applications, approximately ten per annum, doubled.[50]

In 1987, the government announced a package of measures to expand the forestry programme in response to EC concerns over agricultural surpluses and the requirement to find alternative uses for agricultural land. The Forestry Grant Scheme (FGS), introduced in 1981 to promote the involvement of the private sector in forestry planting and the Broadleaved Woodland Grant Scheme (BGS), introduced in 1985 to encourage the establishment of new broadleaved woodlands and the replanting of existing woodlands, were replaced by the Woodland Grant Scheme (WGS), which offered substantially increased grants for both conifer and broadleaved planting and regeneration; the number of WGS applications jumped to over thirty.[51] It was the usual practice for the regional council to consult the local community council on such applications, and in the majority of cases few objections were received. However, a small number generated considerable objections, the most notable being proposals at Gorrenberry (940 ha) near Newcastleton and Philogar (400 ha) astride Dere Street in the Cheviot Foothills. In some cases, amendments to proposals were agreed, usually in relation to the reduction of the area planted or an increase in broadleaved planting. Where objections remained, the proposal was referred to the Commission's Regional Advisory Group, which comprised members from forestry and agriculture, environmental and business and community interests, for decision. In the Gorrenberry case, agreement was reached on an amended scheme for a substantially reduced area.[52]

---

[49] SDD Circular 71/1974: Forest Policy – consultation with planning authorities, SDD: Edinburgh & SDD Planning Advice Note (PAN) 2, 1975, SDD: Edinburgh.

[50] SBA/1210/24, Scottish Borders Structure Plan 1991; Report of Survey, Part 4 Rural Development, pp. 20–21.

[51] BRC/PD/1, Department of Planning and Development, *Annual Report, 1988*, Borders Regional Council, February 1989, p .41.

[52] See coverage in *The Scotsman*, 15/09/87, 01/02/88, 10/03/88 & 09/04/88.

The Philogar scheme was eventually turned down by the Regional Advisory Group.[53]

Increasing controversy over FGS and WGS applications prompted the regional council to undertake a detailed examination of forestry and woodlands in the Scottish Borders in 1987.[54] This showed that half of the Borders' coniferous forest had been planted in the period 1971–1980 and over half of this planting had been undertaken by the private sector. Large-scale planting during this time gained prominence in the press through the large taxation allowances obtained by a number of celebrities. The rapid acceleration of 'blanket' afforestation was the result of tax incentives open to investors paying tax at the highest rates. Investment in woodland could be written off against personal income tax and private forestry companies bought large tracts of land and planted them with single species coniferous woodland, usually sitka spruce, on behalf of high earners in sport and entertainment whose only interest was the financial yield. Much of the timber extracted was transported outwith the region for processing into pulp, paper, chipboard or fibreboard. There were a number of local sawmills but only one large sawmill, at Earlston; a proposal for a major new sawmill on a site near Denholm did not proceed due to the lack of any government assistance. The damage caused by timber extraction traffic to Borders roads, particularly the local roads around Newcastleton and in the Ettrick and Yarrow Valleys was an increasing concern. It was estimated that outstanding work on roads and bridges as a result of timber extraction amounted to £6.2m, far beyond the resources of the regional council. Pleas to the Industry Department for Scotland for financial assistance in 1983 and 1986 came to nothing.[55]

Two areas of the Borders were identified by the CCS in 1981 as National Scenic Areas (NSA), areas of outstanding scenic significance and of national importance: Upper Tweeddale and the Eildon/Leaderfoot area (out of a total of forty areas in Scotland).[56] NSAs were intended to be the subject of strict development control. The regional council continued to develop, and implement, its policies on the countryside throughout the 1980s, taking account of the revision of AGLV coverage in the structure plan, the designation of NSAs and the designation by

---

[53] See coverage in *The Scotsman*, 09/03/89, 12/08/89, 15/08/89 & 10/02/90.

[54] *Forestry and Woodlands in the Scottish Borders*, Planning and Development Department, Borders Regional Council, March 1987.

[55] *Forestry and Woodlands in the Scottish Borders*, pp. 10–13.

[56] Countryside Commission for Scotland, *Scotland's Scenic Heritage* (Perth: CCS, 1978).

DAFS of the Eildon/Whitlaw area, which overlapped with the Eildon/Leaderfoot NSA, as an Environmentally Sensitive Area (ESA). The ESA scheme was introduced in 1987 to help conserve specially designated areas where the landscape, wildlife or historic interest was of particular importance by promoting good agricultural practices.[57] A review of the effectiveness of landscape designations in Scotland was carried out by consultants on behalf of CCS in 1988 and recommended that the definition of NSA objectives should be more explicitly defined but NSA designation, which continues today, has remained weak.[58] In 1990, the CCS published proposals for the management and conservation of the popular mountain areas of Scotland.[59] In its response, the regional council suggested that a wider examination of countryside designations would provide the opportunity for substantial rationalisation and reduction in the number of designations, which, as far as the public was concerned, led to confusion and frustration. However, there was little progress on any review of designations pending the merger of the CCS and NCCS in 1992.

The report on popular mountain areas suggested that for areas of high-quality landscape, wildlife and historic interest and cultural importance, termed 'Heritage Areas', Land Management Forums should be established drawing together the interests of government agencies, local authorities, land managers and communities. The regional council supported this idea and the replacement structure plan approved in 1991 proposed such arrangements for four areas: the Tweedsmuir Hills, the Cheviot Foothills, the Eildon Hills/Bowhill area and the Berwickshire coast.[60] An advisory group was established as part of the process of preparing a management plan for the St Mary's Loch/Tweedsmuir Hills area but no similar formal group was established for other areas.[61]

The Countryside Service of the Planning and Development Department was involved in the management of a number of key sensitive areas, and management plans for a number of these areas were produced,

[57] SBA/1210/24, Scottish Borders Structure Plan 1991; Report of Survey, Part 4 Rural Development, pp. 16–17.
[58] Countryside Commission for Scotland, *A Review of the Effectiveness of Landscape Designations in Scotland*, CSS/SDD, 1988.
[59] Countryside Commission for Scotland, *The Mountain Areas of Scotland: Conservation and Management*, CCS, 1990.
[60] SBA/1210/24, Scottish Borders Structure Plan 1991; Report of Survey, Part 4 Rural Development, pp. 17–18.
[61] Borders Regional Council, *St Mary's Loch/Tweedsmuir Hills Management Plan*, Department of Planning and Development, 1980.

in association with interest groups and landowners and farmers. A Recreational Management Strategy for the Eildon Hills, prepared by the Eildon Hills Advisory Group, in consultation with Buccleuch Estates, was designed to allow increased public access and enjoyment, whilst safeguarding the interests of the landowner. It included a number of proposals, including footpath restoration and the provision of boardwalks, gorse clearance and the re-seeding of worn areas.[62] Lindean Loch, a former reservoir until 1972 and designated an SSSI in 1977, was an important local recreational, educational and conservation resource close to Galashiels and Selkirk. A management plan for the thirty-three acres surrounding the loch, prepared by a management group comprising the regional council, Selkirk Angling Association, Scottish Wildlife Trust (SWT) and the CCS, reconciled the conservation of the wildlife of the area with fishing and public access.[63] Similar advisory groups were established for Alemoor Reservoir, near Roberton and Selkirk Hill.[64] On the Berwickshire coast, the St Abbs/Eyemouth Voluntary Marine Reserve Committee endeavoured to reconcile the often conflicting interests of local fishermen and the growing diving fraternity attracted to this part of the Berwickshire coast.[65] St Abbs Head was designated an SSSI in 1961 for its botanical interest and was managed as a nature reserve by the SWT from 1977 until the land was purchased by the NTS in 1980. Popular for its seabirds, wildflowers and butterflies, it was designated as a NNR in 1984. The St Abbs Head Management Committee comprising representatives from the NTS, BRC, SWT and NCCS oversaw the management of this NNR.[66]

Cove Harbour, purchased in 1971 by BCC, would be a constant source of concern for the regional council. Removal of the over-hanging cliff and repairs to the fisherman's stores and pier were carried out by the county council but recurring landslips endangered the use of the

---

[62] Borders Regional Council, *Eildon Hills Recreational Management Strategy*, Department of Planning and Development, 1987.

[63] Borders Regional Council, *Lindean Reservoir Management Plan*, Department of Planning and Development, 1979 [Revised 1990].

[64] Borders Regional Council, *Alemoor and Watch Water Reservoirs Recreational Management Plan*, Department of Planning and Development, 1986; and Borders Regional Council, *Selkirk Hill Management Plan*, Department of Planning and Development, 1986.

[65] BRC/PD/1, Department of Planning and Development, *Annual Report, 1990*, Borders Regional Council, February 1991, p. 42.

[66] BRC/PD/1, Department of Planning and Development, *Annual Report, 1988*, Borders Regional Council, February 1989, p. 32.

access road to the harbour. In 1987, the decision was taken to close the road access, other than for the two fishermen who used the harbour, and a new footpath and steps were constructed. However, recurring management problems led the council to decide to sell the harbour and it was eventually sold in 1990.[67] Coldingham Sands, acquired by BCC in 1972, was also a constant source of concern. Dune restoration had been carried out successfully in the 1970s but management of the beach huts was an ongoing issue. Although many huts were removed in the 1970s, particularly those on the prominent headland south of the beach, many of the remaining huts were in a dilapidated or dangerous condition. A renewed effort was made in 1989 to contact every hut owner and management practices were tightened in relation to the transfer of ownership of huts and their replacement.[68]

COUNTRYSIDE RECREATION FACILITIES

Outdoor recreation continued to grow at a spectacular rate during the 1970s.[69] Surveys carried out by the Countryside Commission and CCS illustrated the popularity of visiting the countryside as a means of relaxation and freedom from the constraints of urban living. These surveys showed that casual activities, such as simply driving through the countryside and picnicking, visiting the coast or historic buildings such as stately homes, were more popular than more active purposes such as walking, cycling or fishing. Membership of the Camping Club and the Caravan Club increased rapidly during the 1970s, as did membership of the NTS and the Ramblers Association.[70] Countryside management was seen as an imperative to aid the reduction of conflict between visitors and landowners and farmers. Initially, the countryside ranger, funded at a rate of 75 per cent by the CCS, was responsible for the maintenance of the countryside recreational facilities inherited by the Regional Council. These amounted to a number of picnic sites and viewpoint car parks, including toilets, in locations stretching from the

---

[67] BRC/PD/1, Department of Planning and Development, *Annual Report, 1987*, Borders Regional Council, February 1988, p. 32.
[68] BRC/PD/1, Department of Planning and Development, *Annual Report, 1989*, Borders Regional Council, February 1990, p. 48.
[69] Harrison, C., *Countryside Recreation in a Changing Society* (London: TMS Partnership, 1991), pp. 40–44.
[70] For a comprehensive overview of the surveys carried out by the Countryside Commission, see Fitton, M., 'Countryside Recreation – The Problems of Opportunity', *Local Government Studies*, Vol. 5, No. 4, July/August 1979, pp. 57–90.

Meldon Hills in Tweeddale to Renton Barns on the A1 in Berwickshire. The ranger was also responsible for the maintenance of rights of way with assistance from teams funded under the Community Programme. Following the review of section responsibilities in 1983, a Countryside Officer was appointed to supervise the department's countryside activities and the Ranger Service was expanded in 1986 with the appointment of a second ranger.[71]

After 1987, the grant-aid from the CCS decreased by 5 per cent per annum to 60 per cent in 1990, putting pressure on the regional council's finances. Nevertheless, the two countryside rangers, supported by a PEP Team of five manual staff, accomplished a wide range of duties on sites owned or managed by the regional council, including fencing, tree protection, footpath management and waymarking. With some twenty-seven countryside sites, the rangers travelled an average of 30,000 miles per annum. They also provided a guided walks programme and talks to a wide range of groups. The annual programme of approximately thirty walks included farm walks organised through the Borders branch of the National Farmers Union and walks by other specialists, such as local historians and archaeologists. Regular talks were given to schools, community councils and clubs to inform and educate the varied audiences on rights of way and access to the countryside.[72]

The provision of toilets was seen as a vital facility at locations where car-borne visitors were attracted in large numbers, such as the Meldon Hills, St Mary's Loch and Renton Barns on the A1, but they brought with them their own management problems. Toilet blocks were vandalised and problems of litter were all too frequent despite constant monitoring by the rangers.[73] At St Mary's Loch for instance, during the 1980s some 400 cars parked on a summer Sunday, putting pressure on the loch side and the toilets. As a result, measures were taken to restrict vehicular access to the loch side and a 'litter bin free zone' was initiated in an attempt to persuade visitors to take their litter home; this met with mixed results.

The maintenance of rights of way and the promotion of signposted walks was an ongoing task for the Countryside Officer and the rangers. Responding to enquiries and complaints from individual members of

---

[71] BRC/PD/1, Department of Planning and Development, *Annual Report, 1987*, Borders Regional Council, February 1988, p. 35.

[72] BRC/PD/1, Department of Planning and Development, *Annual Report, 1989*, Borders Regional Council, February 1990, pp. 50–51.

[73] BRC/PD/1, Department of Planning and Development, *Annual Report, 1988*, Borders Regional Council, February 1989, p. 30.

the public, walking groups and community councils required action to establish and maintain the rights of way network. In some cases where disputes arose, the council had recourse to formal procedures to establish the use of rights of way and, in a very small number of cases, to legal determination. With the absence of any Direct Labour squad, use was made of contractors, Scottish Conservation Volunteers, the PEP Teams and community councils to clear obstructions and maintain rights of way.[74]

A Rights of Way booklet, produced by the regional council, was continuously updated and revised. A series of 'Walk Cards' was first introduced in 1976 and subsequently updated and expanded as a series of 'Countryside Walks' leaflets. Promoted walks such as the Eildon Walk, the Lyne Walk along the Tweed from Peebles and the Tweed Walk from Newtown St Boswells to Maxton were popular with locals and visitors alike. Leaflets were produced for the Eildon Hills (in association with the SWT) and for the Tweed Walk, and for other outdoor activities, such as the 'Hawick Circular' horse riding route, which caused few problems to the twenty-five landowners and tenants of the land over which the route passed.[75]

Following the Secretary of State's approval in 1979 of the CCS's proposals for a Southern Upland Way, running some 212 miles from Portpatrick in Galloway to Cockburnspath on the Berwickshire coast, the regional council commenced access negotiations, the provision of waymarks, stiles, bridges and information boards along the eighty-five mile stretch between the border with Dumfries and Galloway at Ettrick Head and Cockburnspath. Much of the work on the ground was undertaken by Scottish Conservation Projects volunteers, Job Creation Project teams funded by the MSC and local contractors, with major bridge construction by the Royal Engineers Unit of the Army. It was officially opened in April 1984.[76] Use of the Southern Upland Way remained at a relatively low level but maintenance and upgrading of the route within the Borders Region posed a variety of management issues for the Ranger Service and, in 1990, Mike Baker was appointed Scotland's second Long

---

[74] BRC/PD/1, Department of Planning and Development, *Annual Report, 1987*, Borders Regional Council, February 1988, pp. 33–34; See Department of Planning and Development, *Annual Report, 1988*, Borders Regional Council, February 1989, pp. 30–31.

[75] See Borders Regional Council list of countryside publications (Appendix 3).

[76] For details of the background to the designation of the Southern Upland Way as a long-distance footpath and its route and construction, see the Official Guide by Ken Andrew, published in two parts in 1984, pp. 11–13.

Distance Route Maintenance Warden, the first priority being to improve the waymarking of the route.[77]

In relation to the Pennine Way, there was regular contact with Northumberland County Council's National Park Officer regarding maintenance of this long-distance footpath. Negotiations with landowners for the development of a walk along the Roman Road, Dere Street, from Chew Green on the Pennine Way to St Boswells progressed slowly throughout the 1980s. Nevertheless, with the aid of the Roxburgh PEP Team, the groundwork along the route from Chew Green to south of the River Teviot at Monteviot House was completed in 1989 and the reconstruction by the Army, through its Military Aid to the Civilian Community Scheme, of the 70-metre suspension bridge across the Teviot in 1990 marked the official opening of Dere Street as a long-distance walk.[78]

DEVELOPMENT CONTROL

Until the mid-1980s development control (development management as it is now called) was administered by four planning officers, one for each district area. The planning officers responsible for Ettrick and Lauderdale and Roxburgh Districts were located at council headquarters in Newtown St Boswells but the planning officers responsible for Berwickshire and Tweeddale operated from area offices in Duns and Peebles, respectively, which were shared with building control. The area offices served a vital role in providing access to the planning service for prospective applicants, developers and the public in the far-flung areas of the region. In 1987 the number of planning officers was increased to five and their area responsibilities amended; the combined Ettrick and Lauderdale and Roxburgh Districts was sub-divided into three areas: Galashiels & the Central Borders, Selkirk & Hawick, and the Kelso/Jedburgh area. The development control section was further augmented by the appointment of an enforcement officer and an architect planner to provide advice on design and on listed buildings applications and applications in conservation areas.

The number of planning applications reached a high point of 1,430 in 1979 after which numbers declined throughout the 1980s until 1987

---

[77] BRC/PD/1, Department of Planning and Development, *Annual Report, 1990*, Borders Regional Council, February 1991, pp. 41–42.

[78] BRC/PD/1, Department of Planning and Development, *Annual Report, 1989*, Borders Regional Council, February 1990, p. 49.

when 1,265 applications were received.⁷⁹ Thereafter, the number of applications recovered to 1,500 in 1988, 1,687 in 1989 and 1,734 in 1990; Tweeddale (275), Berwickshire (411), Roxburgh (474) and Ettrick and Lauderdale (574).⁸⁰ Planning authorities had two months in which to decide a planning application, three months for a listed building application. In 1984, 80 per cent of the applications received were dealt with within the statutory period and the proportion dealt with within the statutory period remained above 70 per cent until 1988 when 68 per cent of the applications received were dealt with within the statutory period. The proportion dealt with within the statutory period continued to decrease, to 57 per cent in 1989 and 45 per cent in 1990.⁸¹ This deterioration in performance was put down to a number of factors. The administration of the fee regulations and oversight of the neighbour notification process added considerably to the workload. Whilst the system of neighbour notification was based upon self-certification by the applicant, where issues arose development control officers became involved in ensuring that the statutory requirements had been met. There were other issues: the introduction in August 1989 of a new computer handling system for planning applications, the Ludhouse 'Development Control Manager'; the policy of attempting to secure improvements to proposals, which was time-consuming, rather than simply refuse inappropriate applications; delays in responses from consultees; the increasing number of applications referred to the Planning and Development Committee because of objections received (in the mid-1980s, an average of twenty-three applications were considered at monthly committee meetings but by 1990, the average number of applications referred to the committee had increased to forty-four); and the increasing number of approved applications requiring a Section 50 Agreement prior to the issuing of decision notices.⁸² The proportion of approvals remained fairly constant, however, dropping below 90 per cent only once in 1985, with the average refusal rate over the decade 1977–1989 being 7 per cent. The number of appeals to the Secretary of State also remained steady at between twenty and twenty-five per annum. The appeal success rate

---

⁷⁹ BRC/PD/1, Department of Planning and Development, *Annual Report, 1987*, Borders Regional Council, February 1988, pp. 39–40.

⁸⁰ BRC/PD/1, Department of Planning and Development Annual Reports for 1987,1988 & 1989.

⁸¹ BRC/PD/1, Department of Planning and Development, *Annual Report, 1990*, Borders Regional Council, February 1991, pp. 53–54.

⁸² BRC/PD/1, Department of Planning and Development, *Annual Report, 1990*, Borders Regional Council, February 1991, pp. 55–56.

of approximately 25 per cent (five to six appeals per annum) reflected the strength of the council's planning policies as expressed in its structure and local plans and the consistency in which the Planning and Development Committee interpreted these policies.

Until 1987, enforcement action was taken on an ad hoc basis, primarily in response to complaints from the public; enforcement action played a relatively minor role in development control. However, the appointment of an enforcement officer and the establishment of a formal process led to an increase in enforcement activity in respect of 'breaches of planning control' in relation to non-compliance with planning conditions and unauthorised developments concerning, in particular, development in conservation areas, tree preservation orders and the control of advertisements. Many cases were resolved without the need to take formal enforcement action but required many hours of investigative work before the matter was resolved. At the same time, the monitoring of applications subject to planning conditions was introduced and the enforcement officer was charged with checking compliance with these conditions, which required at least one site visit and, in some cases, a follow-up meeting.[83]

An important element of development control was the provision of guidance and design advice. Advice notes were prepared on replacement windows, shop fronts and tourist signposting. Until the mid-1980s, applications for replacement windows in both listed and unlisted buildings were rare. From 1987 there were an increasing number of cases of replacement windows, particularly uPVC windows, being installed without consent, which prompted the council to produce an advice note on the subject in 1988.[84] In a bid to reduce the impact of the proliferation of tourist signs in the main towns, most of which were conservation areas, and in the countryside, a Guide to Tourist Signposting was produced in consultation with the SBTB, which provided guidance on all forms of signposting relevant to hotels, guest houses, bed and breakfast establishments and other tourist and recreational services.[85]

There were a number of major policy issues in development control during the 1980s. The council's strict housing in the countryside policy, agreed in 1975 and reiterated in the structure plan approved in December

[83] BRC/PD/1, Department of Planning and Development, *Annual Report, 1987*, Borders Regional Council, February 1988, pp. 44–45.

[84] Borders Regional Council, *Replacement Windows Advice Note*, Department of Planning and Development, 1987.

[85] Borders Regional Council, *Guidance on Tourist Signposting in the Scottish Borders*, Department of Planning and Development, 1987.

1980, was relaxed in 1986 following the publication of SDD Circular 24/1985, which endorsed the general principle that new housing in the countryside should be directed towards existing settlements but also recognised that the changing rural economy required a more flexible approach.[86] In response to Circular 24/1985, and to the concerns of some elected members that existing council policy was unduly restrictive, the regional council amended its housing in the countryside policy in October 1986. The presumption against sporadic single houses in the countryside, unless an economic need could be clearly shown, was retained but, with the exception of Tweeddale District where the pressure was greatest, the revised policy encouraged new housing within and adjacent to existing building groups in the countryside, subject to certain criteria.[87] The introduction of the more relaxed housing in the countryside policy was not without its problems. Relaxation led to issues of interpretation of what constituted a building group and whether a particular proposal was well related to that building group. Elected members had their own views on this matter, not necessarily shared by planning officials, leading to tension between members and officials, and inconsistent decision-making. In addition, the more restrictive policy in operation in Tweeddale District contributed to the increased pressure for housing development in the area's villages. Housing in the countryside policy would therefore be re-assessed again in the review of the structure plan produced in 1991.

As a consequence of changes in the nature and structure of agriculture, there was a significant increase towards the end of the 1980s in the number of applications to remove agriculture occupancy conditions previously imposed on new houses on farms. The imposition of such a condition potentially limited the owner/occupier's ability to obtain borrowing from a building society or bank. It also prohibited the sale of the property on the open market should it no longer be required for a farm worker. In considering whether to waive such an occupancy condition, the council wished to avoid any subsequent pressure for further housing on the farm and hence any attempt to circumvent the strict housing in the countryside policy. From October 1986, it was the council's policy to require a Section 50 Agreement, which restricted

---

[86] SDD Circular 24/1985, *Development in the Countryside and Green Belts* (Edinburgh: HMSO, 1985).
[87] Borders Regional Council, *New Housing in the Borders Countryside*, Policy and Guidance Note, December 1993, Planning and Development Department, pp. 5–6.

any further housing on the farm, as an alternative to an agricultural occupancy condition.[88] From July 1988, the erection of certain agricultural buildings, which could previously be erected without planning permission, came within planning control.[89] Thus, any building exceeding 465 sq metres (5,000 sq ft) in area for housing pigs, poultry, rabbits and animals bred for their skin or fur required planning permission. Two poultry farms, the first of seven planned for the Borders Region by Hamish Morison Ltd of Earlston, were subsequently approved prompting the decision to carry out a full analysis of the potential for similar future developments in the Eastern Borders.[90]

Changing government policies on agriculture also encouraged landowners and prospective developers to examine alternative uses both for agricultural land and buildings. At Cardrona, near Peebles, a development comprising 220 houses, a 150-bedroomed hotel and golf course was granted planning approval in 1989 even though the proposal breached structure plan and local plan policies. Members wholeheartedly welcomed the proposal as a boost for tourism in Tweeddale and also as a means of taking some of the pressure for housing development away from Peebles itself, where there were increasing objections to further development on the edge of the town. Planning permission was also granted in 1989 for a similar development near Gordon in Berwickshire.[91] However, not all proposals came to fruition and whilst Cardrona has been developed as envisaged, the Gordon proposal fell by the wayside.

The pressure for housing land on the edges of settlements intensified in the late 1980s where demand exceeded the supply of housing land provided in local plans or where there was no prospect of allocated sites being developed. In most cases, planning permission was refused as development was regarded as premature pending the review of the structure plan. In 1987, almost half the twenty-four appeals to the Secretary of State related to the refusal of planning permission for housing development in Tweeddale. The vast majority of these appeals were dismissed and it was a relief to the council that the SoS continued to support the

[88] BRC/PD/1, Department of Planning and Development, *Annual Report, 1987*, Borders Regional Council, February 1988, pp. 45–46.
[89] See *The Town and Country Planning (General Development) Scotland Amendment Order 1988*.
[90] BRC/PD/1, Department of Planning and Development, *Annual Report, 1987*, Borders Regional Council, February 1988, p. 46.
[91] BRC/PD/1, Department of Planning and Development, *Annual Report, 1989*, Borders Regional Council, February 1990, p. 60.

council's policy of restricting development in rural Tweeddale, particularly around West Linton.[92] However, following the refusal of planning permission for thirty houses at Deanfoot Road, West Linton in 1989, planning permission was granted, on appeal, by the Secretary of State. The Chief Executive of BRC considered this to be one of the worst decisions made by the Scottish Office in the regional council's fourteen-year history; a decision which would open the door for further development at West Linton over the next ten years in response to the growing pressure for housing from the Lothian Housing Market Area.[93]

By 1988, there were only nine supermarkets in the Region larger than 950 sq metres (10,000 sq ft) in floorspace; three in Hawick, two in Galashiels, two in Kelso and one in Peebles and Jedburgh. A retailing study in 1989 revealed the substantial amount of retail expenditure leaking from the Borders; a third of the food expenditure and even more of the non-food expenditure in Tweeddale District was lost to Lothian Region. In Ettrick and Lauderdale District, 15 per cent of the food expenditure and 25 per cent of the non-food expenditure was lost to Lothian Region. This study highlighted the need to improve the range and convenience of shopping facilities.[94] The first result was the approval of a DIY store (B&Q) on the site of the disused skinworks and tannery on Wilderhaugh in Galashiels.[95] The 1990s would see further pressure for large supermarkets and out-of-town retail development easily accessible from a large catchment area and where adequate car parking could be provided.

CONCLUSIONS

At the end of the 1980s, the Planning and Development Department could be well pleased with its achievements; structure and local plan coverage was complete and, notwithstanding the changes brought about by the Conservative government in 1979, economic recovery had continued with the creation of a wide range of employment opportunities on newly created industrial sites spread across the region, developed jointly

---

[92] BRC/PD/1, Department of Planning and Development, *Annual Report, 1987*, Borders Regional Council, February 1988, p. 45.

[93] BRC/PD/1, Department of Planning and Development, *Annual Report, 1989*, Borders Regional Council, February 1990, p. 62.

[94] SBA/1210/24, Scottish Borders Structure Plan 1991; Report of Survey, Part 3 Economic Development, pp. 45–50.

[95] BRC/PD/1, Department of Planning and Development, *Annual Report, 1989*, Borders Regional Council, February 1990, pp. 12–13.

by the regional council and the SDA. However, the loss of Assisted Area status in August 1982, combined with a policy emphasis by the government and the EEC on areas of high unemployment, resulted in a low priority being given to the Scottish Borders in terms of additional assistance. Consequently, employment increased by only 300 people between 1981 and 1989 and the Borders economy remained reliant on a relatively narrow range of industries and a small number of companies. There was disappointment at the lack of progress on the development of industrial land in Hawick. With assistance from the SDA, progress was made on various land renewal projects; derelict areas were cleared and potential development sites created. The regional council and the SDA continued their active partnership in stimulating and undertaking a wide range of redevelopment/rehabilitation projects in many Border towns. Throughout the 1980s, a wide range of environmental improvement projects were undertaken sponsored by the government's special employment measures administered by the MSC.

The population of the Scottish Borders continued to increase, to an estimated 103,500 people in 1990, lower than forecast in 1977 but a considerable achievement bearing in mind the changing economic circumstances of the 1980s. However, there was little growth in the population of Hawick and rural depopulation remained an issue, particularly in south-west Roxburghshire and the Ettrick and Yarrow Valleys. The Scottish Borders remained one of the most sparsely populated areas in Scotland, the UK and Europe. Due to government restraints, the new district housing authorities concentrated on the maintenance and rehabilitation of the existing housing stock rather than new build. The development of Tweedbank came to a halt in 1980 and the involvement of the SSHA in housing provision virtually ceased. After 1985, all Housing Corporation funded schemes were channelled through Eildon Housing Association. The number of private house completions fluctuated with many allocated housing sites lying undeveloped for a number of years. Only in Peebles was the take up of housing land substantial.

During the 1980s, far more attention was paid to countryside issues. To understand the rural economy better, the council commissioned reports on agricultural development opportunities and forestry. It undertook, in conjunction with the SDA, a study of the problems and opportunities in two contrasting rural parts of the Region and developed policies for the countryside with the aim of balancing efficient management with the conservation of the landscape and wildlife. With the expansion of commercial afforestation, there was an increasing awareness of the impact of mono-culture tree planting on the landscape. The Borders Region was one of the first authorities in Scotland to prepare indicative forestry guidelines and design guidance. The regional council also produced, in collaboration with landowners and farmers, a number of management plans for countryside areas and, with grant aid from the CCS, expanded its role in providing parking/picnic facilities in the countryside, maintaining rights of way and promoting countryside pursuits.

From the late 1980s, the number of planning applications grew substantially and the development control section expanded in order to provide comprehensive landscape and design advice on a number of major developments. There was a growing interest in the environment and the word 'heritage' entered the vocabulary of the countryside, recognising the inter-relationships between geology, landscape and scenery, land use and the natural, historical and cultural environment. The Planning and Development Department's staff structure was substantially enlarged during the 1980s to tackle the changing priorities for economic development, town centres, the environment and countryside recreation. During the 1980s, planning staff were easily accessible to the public; the planning desk was always open to the public and no appointment was necessary for a general enquiry. The annual report for 1990 illustrates the scale of the interaction between the department and the public, recording that in that year, each week saw 400 letters being received. Staff attended over 5,000 site meetings in 1990, dealt with 65,000 telephone calls and travelled over 135,000 miles to meetings, many in the evening. There was an extremely good relationship between the press and planning officers with direct communication between the two; there was no constraint on dialogue between officers and the press, within reason. As commented by Bill Chisholm, there was a much better direct link between the department and the press then than the present day 'where the press is fed sanitised statements from communication officers and, in the main, officers are precluded from talking to the press'.

With a relatively small, devoted staff led by its driven Director of Planning and Development, David Douglas, and strongly supported by the Convener, Tom Hunter, the Planning and Development Department punched well above its weight in promoting the region and attracting new firms to the area, facilitating environmental improvements in town and country, encouraging rural development and diversification, and countryside recreation. The regional council, in partnership with the SDA, played a major role in the economic revival of the Borders Region in the 1980s. However, by the end of the decade, the majority of the SDA's properties in the Region had been sold off and the shrinkage of the SDA's role in providing industrial property was placing additional strains on BRC's efforts in this field. There were real concerns about the future of the Borders as the economic recession continued to bite.

8

The 1990s: A Time of Uncertainty

INTRODUCTION

THE START OF THE final decade of the twentieth century saw a number of significant organisational and operational changes amongst Scotland's principal agencies. The establishment of Scottish Homes in 1989 in place of the SSHA and the Housing Corporation, the emergence of Scottish Enterprise (SE) in 1991 and the amalgamation of the CCS with the NCCS in 1992 to form Scottish Natural Heritage (SNH) are just three examples. Scottish Homes was empowered to assist all sectors of the housing market, particularly in areas of 'tenure deficiencies'.[1] With the abolition of the SSHA in 1989 and the transfer of its functions to Scottish Homes, a strategic development plan was drawn up for the phased development of housing for rent and low-cost home ownership at Tweedbank with the intention of completing development by 1996, and sites for owner-occupied housing were identified. Scottish Homes embarked on an expansion of housing at Tweedbank with a further 400 houses of varying tenure over a six-year programme. Its Rural Policy, published in September 1990, identified four key challenges: increasing the supply of housing in rural areas; tackling poor housing conditions; ensuring affordability and tenant and community involvement.[2] However, Scottish Homes seemed determined to by-pass local authorities despite such bodies having an established organisational infrastructure and local accountability. Instead, emphasis was placed on low-cost home ownership rather than social renting, and local

---

[1] See Yanetta, A., *Scottish Homes – The Key to the Future?*, Scottish Government Yearbook 1990, pp. 118–132.
[2] Scottish Homes, *Scottish Homes Rural Policy*, September 1990, Edinburgh.

housing agencies with grants for rent or ownership.³ In the Borders, new housing was provided by Eildon Housing Association and organisations such as Waverley Housing and the Berwickshire Housing Association took over local authority housing responsibilities in the Central Borders and Berwickshire respectively.

Scottish Enterprise (SE) was established in April 1991, an amalgamation of the SDA and the Training Agency, under the Enterprise and New Towns Act 1990. SE thus became responsible for the economic development functions of the SDA; industrial development and job creation and environmental regeneration, and the employment training programmes previously administered by the MSC. There was a marked change in economic development strategy, reflecting the government's view that there had not been sufficient involvement of private business in managing the SDA.[4] Thirteen local enterprise companies (LEC) were established across Scotland to continue the work of the SDA at the local level. The Borders LEC, Scottish Borders Enterprise (SBE), comprised representatives from the local business and industry community with Mike Gray, the Managing Director of McQueen Ltd in Galashiels as Chairman. Other members represented a range of business, tourist and retail interests; the Scottish College of Textiles in Galashiels and the Transport and General Workers Union were both represented. Ken Clark, the Chief Executive of BRC was the only local authority representative.[5] David Douglas, former Director of Planning and Development with BRC was appointed Chief Executive and tasked with continuing the work of the SDA in generating economic growth through the expansion of existing industries and the establishment of new businesses, and facilitating and undertaking environmental regeneration projects. Over the next five years, in partnership with the regional and district councils and the SBTB, SBE would invest over £40 million and lever £60 million for a range of projects across the Region, including the refurbishment of industrial premises and land renewal projects, youth and adult training, and business grants and loans.[6]

---

[3] See Shucksmith, M., *Scotland's Rural Housing: A Forgotten Problem*, Rural Housing Scotland Conference 2019 Paper (Edinburgh: Rural Forum, 2019).

[4] See Fairley, J. and M. G. Lloyd, 'Economic Development and Training: the Roles of Scottish Enterprise, Highlands and Islands Enterprise and the Local Enterprise Companies', *Scottish Affairs*, Vol. 12, No. 1 (Edinburgh: Edinburgh University Press, August 1995), pp. 52–72.

[5] See Borders Regional Council, *Borders Business Post*, No. 18, 1991.

[6] See Scottish Borders Enterprise, *Enterprise Leader*, Issue 10, Spring 1996.

According to Mike Gray, two factors contributed to creating optimum impact in what was one of the smallest local authorities and LECs: the positive effect of contiguous boundaries, which did not always exist elsewhere, with SBE, BRC and SBTB all able to constructively engage in economic development across the Region; and, to a lesser extent but nevertheless important, the fact that the LEC was named 'Scottish Borders Enterprise' and not 'Scottish Enterprise Borders'. Mike Gray also emphasises the support given to SBE by BRC's Convener, Lord Minto, and its Chief Executive, Kenneth Clark. According to Mike Gray, 'Ken Clark's vast experience was of great help to the new private sector led LEC, operating within a governmental environment, and the linkage between the LEC and BRC was also strengthened when David Douglas was recruited to be Chief Executive'. As a result: 'The combination of talented individuals within the LEC and BRC, all willing to work on pragmatic and joint approaches, optimised the funding available across the different organisations and delivered more impact for the Scottish Borders'.[7]

SNH was created under the Natural Heritage (Scotland) Act 1991, which integrated nature conservation with landscape conservation and access, with the purpose of improving the understanding and management of the natural heritage; the flora and fauna, its geological and physiographic features, its natural beauty and amenity. However, issues around landscape designations remained unresolved and SNH put considerable effort into assessing the value of landscapes. The problem, as pointed out by Warren, 'given that beauty is in the eye of the beholder, was finding dispassionate, repeatable and defensible ways of assessing the value of landscapes'.[8] This would be addressed through the development of Landscape Character Assessment techniques, which would prove to be a useful tool for managing change, particularly with the growth of onshore wind farms and with the defining of Natural Heritage Zones.[9] Nevertheless, a Scottish Office review of natural heritage designations in 1996 skirted around the issue and, although SNH recommended to government that NSAs should be made more effective, few substantive changes resulted from this consultation. It would be the year 2000, after considerable pressure from SNH, before the Scottish Executive

---

[7] In conversation with Mike Gray, former Chairman of Scottish Borders Enterprise, 15 July 2022.

[8] Warren, C., *Managing Scotland's Environment* (Edinburgh: Edinburgh University Press, 2002), pp. 185–187.

[9] SNH, *Natural Heritage Zones: A National Assessment of Scotland's Landscapes*, Scottish Natural Heritage: Battleby.

consulted on enabling legislation for national parks. Of more relevance to BRC was the fact that the grant from SNH towards staffing, training and equipping the Countryside Ranger Service and for the operation of a variety of countryside facilities continued to be reduced down to 50 per cent in 1992 (it had been 75 per cent throughout most of the 1980s) putting additional pressure on the council's budget.

The 1990s saw other pieces of legislation and policy statements that had particular relevance to the work of the Planning and Development Department. The White Paper, *This Common Inheritance*, published in 1990, was the UK's first comprehensive survey of all aspects of environmental concern and suggested that local authorities should manage environmental issues more corporately, monitor the state of the local environment and prepare environmental strategies and programmes.[10] The Environment Protection Act 1990 introduced a number of provisions concerning pollution control, waste management, litter and contaminated land, including the establishment of public registers to meet the UK's obligations under EC directives on freedom of access to environmental information. The Planning and Compensation Act 1991 introduced new enforcement powers; new controls over mineral working, work to trees and advertisements; and placed a greater emphasis on development plans in the development control process.[11] The Scottish Office introduced a series of National Planning Policy Guidelines (NPPGs) in 1993 'to provide statements of government policy on nationally important land use and other planning matters', augmented by the continued issue of PANs and Circulars. NPPGs superseded the NPGs issued from the 1970s in response to specific issues such as North Sea oil, aggregate working, skiing developments and major retail developments. NPPGs were broader in scope than the previous seven NPGs and provided more comprehensive coverage of topics of national concern. NPPG1, entitled 'The Planning System', provided an introduction to the planning system and a further seventeen NPPGs were issued during the 1990s covering a wide range of issues from land for housing to the provision of roadside facilities on motorways and included mineral working, opencast coal

---

[10] Department of the Environment, *This Common Inheritance: Britain's Environmental Strategy* (London: HMSO, 1990).

[11] See SDD Circular 8/1992, Planning and Compensation Act 1981: Enforcing Planning Control; Circular 8/1992, Planning and Compensation Act 1981: Enforcement of Tree Preservation Orders, Circular 9/1992, Planning and Compensation Act 1981: Control of 'Fly Posting'; and Circular 10/1992, Planning and Compensation Act 1981: Control over Advertisements and Fish Farming.

working, renewable energy, flooding, rural development, natural heritage and the historic environment.[12]

The enabling pieces of legislation, followed by a number of Regulations and Orders, and the introduction of policy guidance and advice had ramifications for the workload of the Planning and Development Department. In response, staffing continued to grow and the Department saw its accommodation at the Newtown St Boswells headquarters expand and improve. In 1991, a fifth of the staff changed, new technology was installed and there was an entire change in the administrative and clerical staff. A new desktop word processing system and the Ludhouse Development Control Management Information System became operational in 1990.[13] The staffing structure of the Department was reviewed in 1993 to improve the service and value for money (Figure 8.1). There was a greater emphasis on training and improving staff performance and the introduction of additional new technology such as digital mapping, graphics and data handling. Significant administrative changes were made in the development control section with increased delegation to officials to approve non-controversial applications.[14]

THE REGIONAL ECONOMY

A review of the services provided by the regional council was carried out in 1988 against the background of the significant changes in government legislation and the establishment of Scottish Homes and SE. In relation to economic development, the review identified the continuing dependence of the region on a narrow range of industries and the limited access to government and EEC assistance as the prime reasons for the comparatively modest growth in the region's population during the 1980s. Furthermore, the development of a highly export-orientated manufacturing base had resulted in a local economy that was extremely susceptible to changes in world markets. The designation of the Borders Region as a Rural Development Area was considered a priority in order to exploit the potential opportunities for agricultural diversification, afforestation and countryside recreation and tourism.[15]

---

[12] See Appendix 3 for a list of Government Circulars, National Planning Guidelines, National Planning Policy Guidelines and Planning Advice Notes.
[13] See *Department of Planning and Development: Annual Report 1991*, Borders Regional Council, February 1992, p. 1, p. 67.
[14] See *Department of Planning and Development: Annual Report 1993–94*, Borders Regional Council, April 1994, p. 19.
[15] Borders Regional Council, *Regional Review*, June 1989.

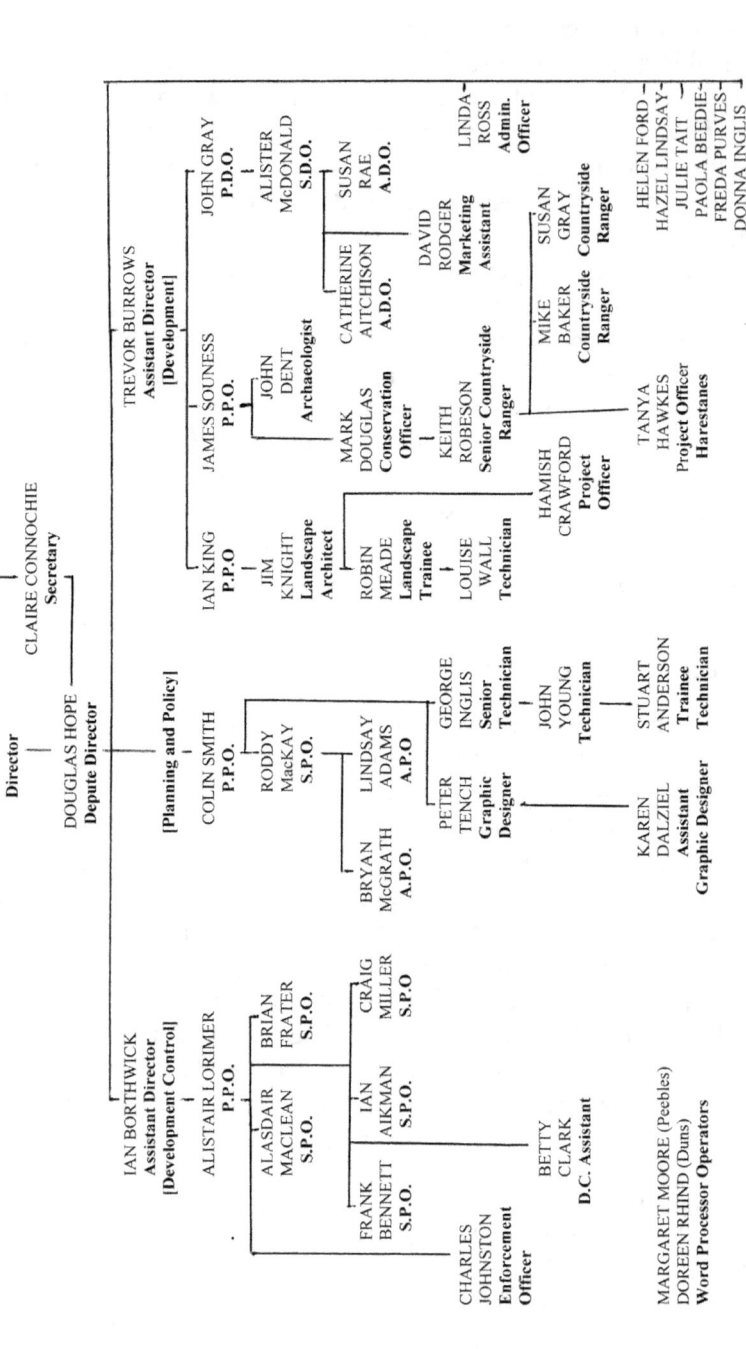

Figure 8.1 Department of Planning and Development, December 1993

The late 1980s economic boom was followed in 1991–1992 by a deep recession as a result of rising inflation and excessive borrowing. Unemployment in Scotland, which had been reducing since 1984 to a low of 8 per cent in 1990, increased dramatically to almost 11 per cent in 1992. In the Borders, which had always had a level of unemployment below the national and Scottish averages, unemployment rose from just over 5 per cent in 1989 to 8 per cent in 1992. The Borders textile industry experienced a severe slump with job losses, redundancies and short time working. Over 700 jobs were lost in Hawick.[16] Nevertheless, Pringle of Scotland, part of the Dawson Group, announced expansion proposals. Throughout the 1980s and early 1990s, leisure and sportswear played a key role in the success of this company with world-renowned golfers such as Nick Faldo and Colin Montgomerie being sponsored by the Group. For the fishing industry 1992 was also a difficult year, through pressure from the government and the EC to reduce fishing catches in an attempt to conserve stocks. The EC introduced restrictions on mesh sizes for white fish and proposals were made to tie up the Scottish cod and haddock fleet for 190 days of the year. The Berwickshire coast's dependence on the fishing industry put it in an economically vulnerable position. Proposals by Eyemouth Harbour Trust for the redevelopment of the harbour and the development of the Gunsgreen area, incorporating proposals for housing, industry, sport and leisure facilities and tourist facilities accessed by a new road, aimed at ensuring the continued survival of the local economy.

During 1989, the EEC proceeded with the reform of the Structural Funds to coincide with the proposals for a Single European Market in 1992.[17] The European Regional Development Fund (ERDF), the European Social Fund (ESF) and the Guidance Section of the European Agricultural Guidance and Guarantee Fund (EAGGF) were to be distributed under five Objectives. The Scottish Borders was eligible for EC support under Objectives 3, 4 and 5(a). Under Objectives 3 and 4, support from the ESF was available for vocational training schemes for the long-term unemployed over twenty-five years old and for young people under twenty-five years old, respectively. However, the Borders eligibility for ESF assistance under these Objectives was severely limited because of its relatively low levels of long term and youth unemployment.

---

[16] See *Department of Planning and Development: Annual Report 1991*, Borders Regional Council, February 1992, pp. 22–23.

[17] See *Department of Planning and Development: Annual Report 1989*, Borders Regional Council, February 1990, pp. 14–15.

Objective 5(a) provided assistance to fund agricultural processing and marketing projects, and indirect support for farmers through the Less Favoured Farming Areas Scheme, the farm/woodland scheme, set aside and farm diversification scheme. However, to the BRC's dismay, the Scottish Borders was not included in the EC's list of rural areas eligible for Objective 5(b) assistance, which provided substantial funding for a range of development projects. The only rural areas of Scotland that qualified were the Highlands and Islands Development Board area and the western parts of Dumfries and Galloway Region, along with Rural Mid-Wales and Devon and Cornwall. In response, the BRC lobbied the European Commission (EC) through the Convention of Scottish Local Authorities (COSLA) as part of its campaign for greater financial assistance for rural areas in Scotland.[18]

As part of this lobbying, a major conference entitled 'Rural Development: Future Strategies' was held in Galashiels in November 1990, with support from COSLA, to bring to the attention of the government and the EC the problems of rural areas like the Borders.[19] The conference, attended by over 150 delegates, brought together leading figures in rural development from across the UK. It focussed on the different approaches to rural development in the Highlands and Islands, in Wales and rural England. The main point coming out of the conference was that rural needs cannot be measured by the rate of unemployment, which drove government and EC policy on assisted areas and resulted in a low priority being given to areas like the Scottish Borders. Whilst it was recognised that local authorities in Scotland had shown innovation in rural development, more could be done with government support. It was concluded that a strategy for rural areas was required and that areas like the Borders Region should have a status similar to that of an Assisted Area in terms of UK and EC assistance.

In May 1991, BRC appointed an EC consultant in Brussels and continued to lobby for designation as an Objective 5(b) area, which would provide access to the ERDF and support for industrial infrastructure. However, whilst considerable sympathy was shown to the Scottish Border's case, it was indicated that the region was unlikely to qualify for support under Objective 5(b) without the wholehearted support

---

[18] See *Department of Planning and Development: Annual Report 1990*, Borders Regional Council, February 1991, p. 11.

[19] See *Conference on Rural Development Future Strategies: Summary of Speeches and Workshops*, Borders Regional Council, April 1991.

of the UK Government.[20] In June 1992, the Department of Trade and Industry, the Scottish Office and Welsh Office jointly issued a consultation paper on a review of Assisted Areas in Great Britain. In response, the regional council prepared a strong case for the Borders Region being designated as an Assisted Area.[21] This study concluded that the region was significantly disadvantaged relative to other areas of the UK because: the levels of investment in manufacturing were the lowest of any region or county in Great Britain; the Borders Region had one of the lowest GDPs per head of population in the UK; the Borders Region was characterised by the lowest wages in Scotland, high prices and a severe lack of affordable housing.[22] However, the Borders Region was not included in the re-drawn Assisted Areas in August 1993.

Nevertheless, after years of campaigning, in December 1994, the EC announced that the Borders Region had qualified for Objective 5(b) status, which opened the way for grant assistance towards a number of community initiatives, including RETEX, which helped areas dependent on the textiles industry; PESCA, which aided areas dependent on fishing; and LEADER, which supported rural regeneration projects.[23] Against this uncertain background, the first structure plan, approved in 1981, was replaced in 1991, signalling new directions for planning in the Borders Region.

THE BORDERS REGION STRUCTURE PLAN 1991

The procedure for the preparation of the replacement structure plan followed a similar path to that adopted for the first structure plan.[24] The structure plan process was initiated with the issue of a Notice of Intention to commence preparation of the replacement structure plan in October 1989, followed by consultation with a wide range of national, regional

---

[20] See *Department of Planning and Development: Annual Report 1991*, Borders Regional Council, February 1992, p. 13.

[21] See *Review of Assisted Areas of Great Britain: The Case for Borders Region*, Borders Regional Council, September 1992.

[22] See *Department of Planning and Development: Annual Report 1992*, Borders Regional Council, February 1993, pp. 10–11.

[23] See *Department of Planning and Development: Annual Report 1994/5*, Borders Regional Council, July 1995, p. 15.

[24] As set out in the Town and Country Planning (Structure and Local Plans) (Scotland) Regulations 1983 (S.I. 1983, No. 1590) and SDD Circular 32/1983, Structure and Local Plans (Edinburgh: HMSO, 1983); see also Collar, N. A. *Planning*, pp. 45–46.

and local organisations, including community councils, interest groups and businesses, on the matters to be included in the structure plan. The draft structure plan was approved in January 1991 and was the subject of a series of exhibitions and public meetings held throughout the region in May and June 1991. The finalised structure plan, the Border Region Structure Plan, *The Scottish Borders 2001: The Way Forward*, was approved in November 1991 (Figure 8.2) and submitted to the SoS on 6 February 1992. It was approved with modifications on 19 November 1993 and became operative on 22 November 1993.[25]

The structure plan emphasised that the Borders Region continued to have a vulnerable economy despite the efforts of the regional and district councils, aided by the SDA (SE after 1991), to attract new industry and encourage existing industry to expand and prosper. The Borders Region remained a rural community, characterised by small towns and villages and a scattered population. A settlement hierarchy of Principal, Secondary and Local Centres, together with Key Villages, was identified, which together had a combined population of 78,000 persons (77 per cent of the Borders population) (see Table 8.1).[26]

Retaining essential services stood a better chance of success if services and facilities were accessible from the maximum support population. Therefore, the bulk of future development would be concentrated in the Principal Centres: Hawick, Galashiels, Peebles, Selkirk, Kelso and Jedburgh. Housing and industrial development was also proposed in the Secondary and Local Centres. The development strategy assumed the full development of Tweedbank over the next decade but the priority was the revitalisation of the Selkirk Riverside Industrial Area and the promotion of industry in Hawick. Several areas of derelict industrial land and out-dated factory premises had been tackled in the 1980s and the structure plan optimistically proposed that the remaining areas of derelict land and empty mills should be cleared or rehabilitated by the end of the century. The regeneration of former industrial areas and the continuation of development on existing sites, rather than the development of new greenfield sites, was the major priority for the 1990s. Hawick was the exception, where a greenfield site was considered essential for the future prosperity of the town. The implementation of land allocations and infrastructure decisions by the regional council required

---

[25] See SBA/1210/24, Borders Region Structure Plan: Report of Survey 1991; Draft Structure Plan 1991; Consultation Report 1991; Written Statement, approved 1993.

[26] See SBA/1210/24, Scottish Borders Structure Plan 1991; Written Statement, pp. 7–9.

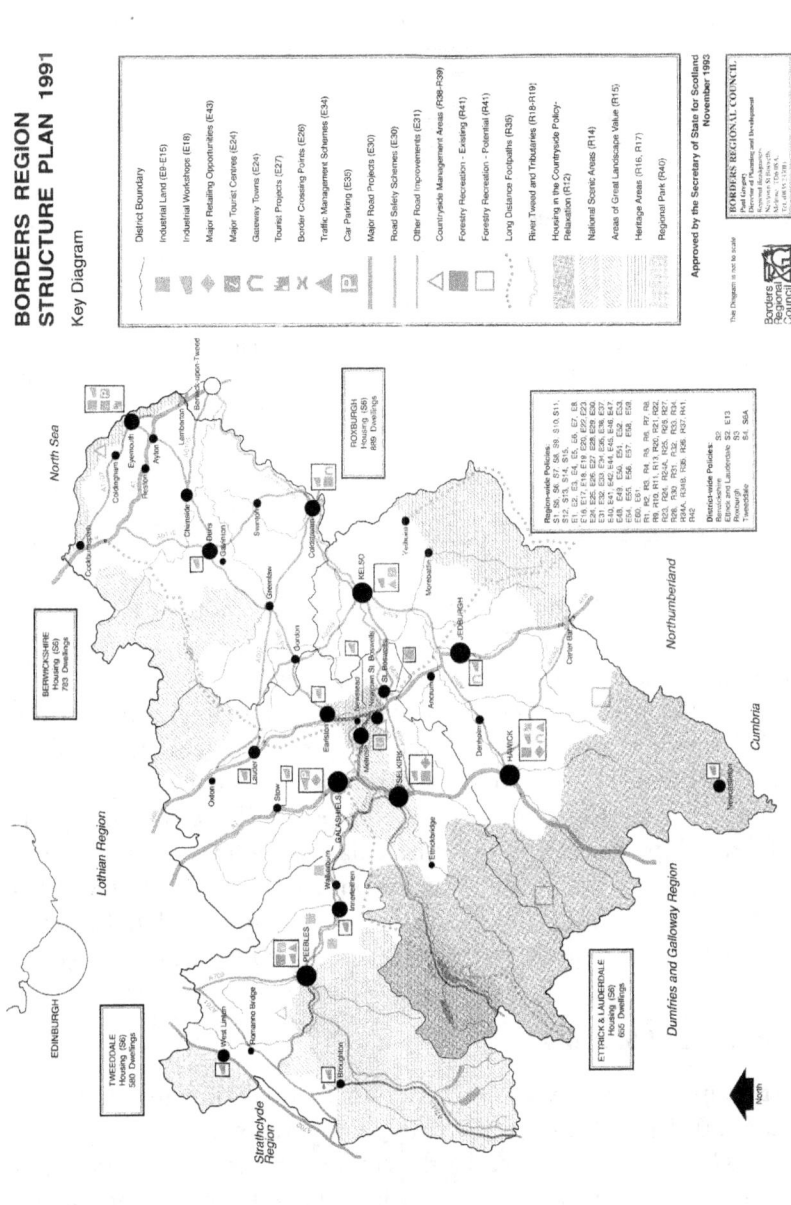

Figure 8.2 Borders Region Structure Plan 1991: Key Diagram

Table 8.1 Borders Region Structure Plan 1991: Settlement Hierarchy

	Berwickshire	Ettrick and Lauderdale	Roxburgh	Tweeddale
Principal Centres		Galashiels Selkirk	Hawick Kelso Jedburgh	Peebles
Secondary Centres	Duns Eyemouth Coldstream	Melrose Earlston		Innerleithen
Local Centres	Chirnside	St Boswells Newtown St Boswells Lauder	Newcastleton	West Linton
Key Villages	Greenlaw Ayton Coldingham Gordon Reston Cockburnspath Swinton	Stow	Denholm Yetholm Ancrum Morebattle	Walkerburn Broughton

the co-operation of a range of agencies, such as Scottish Homes, the Borders Health Board and SBE, and the private sector, and there would continue to be close liaison with these organisations.

To meet the needs of the rural areas, fourteen Key Villages were identified where it was considered vital to retain services and facilities. In many of these, housing and industrial development was proposed, with land set aside for workshop developments. There was also scope for infill development in other smaller villages and, in a departure from previous policy, new housing was encouraged in the countryside in association with existing building groups. Well-sited isolated housing was allowed in the remoter parts of the south and west of the region.

Population and housing

The structure plan was based on a continued population growth up to a projected 2001 population of 105,700, compared with a 1989 population of 102,700 persons.[27] Whilst the creation of large numbers of jobs was considered unrealistic, it was anticipated that the rate of population

---

[27] See SBA/1210/24, Scottish Borders Structure Plan 1991; Written Statement, pp. 9–10.

growth over the previous ten years or so, 3,000 persons, could be sustained. It was accepted that the Region would continue to suffer from net natural decrease, an excess of deaths over births, and that any population increase must stem from net in-migration being greater than the natural decrease, either by reducing out-migration or increasing in-migration. The projected increase was not distributed evenly across the Region, with larger proportional increases in Berwickshire and Tweeddale and a continuing decrease in population in Roxburgh. This raised issues of housing land requirements, particularly in Tweeddale, and the measures to be taken in Roxburgh District to stabilise the population.

The implications for housing demand and supply were assessed utilising a methodology produced by the Convention of Scottish Local Authorities (COSLA) in 1985 because of the lack of positive advice from central government.[28] It would be 1993 before the Scottish Office published guidance and advice on housing land requirements.[29] This assessment indicated a requirement for an additional 3,488 houses in the Region: 783 in Berwickshire; 655 in Ettrick and Lauderdale; 889 in Roxburgh and 1,161 in Tweeddale, requiring a considerable amount of land.[30]

In Berwickshire, there was a lack of allocated sites in the main towns, Duns and Eyemouth, and perceived pressure on Coldingham, Cockburnspath and Reston. In Ettrick and Lauderdale, the completion of Tweedbank was seen as a priority. Housing choice was an issue in the Central Borders with a shortage of quality sites. Melrose/Darnick, Lauder, Newtown St Boswells/St Boswells, Earlston and Stow were seen as suitable locations for widening housing choice. In Roxburgh, Kelso had potential for further expansion but the availability of sites in Jedburgh was a problem. Existing allocations in Hawick were adequate to meet projected need. In Tweeddale, the issue was whether to continue to resist the pressure for housing for commuters from the volume housebuilders, who saw Tweeddale as being within the Edinburgh/Lothians Housing Market Area (HMA). The Regional Council saw Tweeddale as a separate HMA, which should only accommodate the projected housing demand from within its area. In response to objections received from local communities to the scale of the additional

---

[28] *Forecasting Housing Requirements: A Methodology for Structure Planning Authorities*, COSLA, 1985. This methodology was largely reconfirmed in the Draft Planning Advice Note [PAN38] published by SDD in 1991.

[29] SDD National Planning Policy Guideline, NPPG3: Land for Housing (1993); PAN38: Structure Plans: Housing Land Requirements (1993).

[30] See SBA/1210/24, Scottish Borders Structure Plan 1991; Written Statement, pp. 10–12.

housing projected (1,161 units), the structure plan proposed that land for only half the projected requirement, 580 houses, should be allocated in the proposed local plan for Tweeddale District.[31] Even so, there were considerable objections to the allocation of housing land to accommodate this level of housing provision. In approving the structure plan, the Secretary of State agreed to the deferral of the full allocation of 1,160 houses required in Tweeddale until such time as a review of HMAs had been carried out. The results of this review would form the basis for the calculation of housing land requirements up to 2011 in the next structure plan prepared in 1997/98; the thorny problem of future housing in Tweeddale was therefore put on hold and it would be for the new authority, the Scottish Borders Council, to decide the way forward.

Economic development

It was considered that existing industrial sites such as those at Tweedbank, Kelso, Jedburgh and Duns, provided by BRC in association with the SDA, were adequate to meet demand throughout the structure plan period. In Eyemouth, the principal project related to the comprehensive development of the east side of Eyemouth Harbour and the proposals for Gunsgreen. In Ettrick and Lauderdale, the revitalisation of Selkirk Riverside was the main priority. In Roxburgh, the structure plan continued with the allocation of 10.5 ha of land for industry in Hawick. However, in view of the lack of progress with the proposed site at Burnhead, the feasibility of an alternative site at Galalaw Farm, which had been purchased by the district council, was investigated by SBE. This study highlighted the suitability of some 10.5 ha of land at Galalaw for industrial development, which was substituted for the Burnhead allocation in the local plan. Reflecting the accessibility of Peebles to Edinburgh with its universities and research institutes, land at Cavalry Park was identified as a high amenity site for technological office and business use. Eshiels was identified as a potential focus for general industrial development.[32]

The emphasis of the regional council's efforts, in conjunction with the four district councils and the new local enterprise company, SBE, was to

---

[31] See SBA/1210/24, Scottish Borders Structure Plan 1991; Written Statement, pp. 20–21.

[32] See SBA/1210/24, Scottish Borders Structure Plan 1991; Written Statement, pp. 28–29.

continue to provide serviced industrial sites, property conversions and new workshop units in the smaller settlements, and continue with the programme of environmental improvements and land renewal schemes.[33] Tourism was recognised as an important sector of the Borders economy and the structure plan highlighted the proposed Tower Hotel redevelopment in Hawick, a proposed Marine Interpretation Centre in Eyemouth and proposed improvements at the border crossing points of Carter Bar (on the A68), Lamberton (on the A1) and Coldstream (A696).[34]

Roads and transportation

Particular attention was drawn in the structure plan to the potential impact of the Single European Market in 1992 and the opening of the Channel Tunnel in 1994 on the economy of the Scottish Borders, with its reliance on agriculture and export-orientated industries. Road transport links were, therefore, considered important and the structure plan placed emphasis on the dualling of the A1 through the Borders and improvements to the A7, particularly south of Hawick, and to a Selkirk by-pass. The structure plan made no mention of the re-opening of the closed Waverley Line, simply that it was important to retain and improve the public transport links with Edinburgh, Berwick-upon-Tweed and Carlisle.[35] Interestingly, the structure plan suggests that the regional council should investigate the feasibility of establishing an airstrip in the Central Borders, a proposal first raised in the 1960s, since there was increasing evidence of the demand for such a facility as an inducement for potential inward investment in the Region.[36]

Continued improvements were also proposed to the strategic road network, without concentrating on any single east to west route, and to a number of town centre schemes in Hawick, Kelso and Galashiels. In Hawick, a traffic management initiative, including the diversion of through traffic along Commercial Road, was urgently required and in Kelso, the construction of the proposed outer distributor road, including a new bridge over the Tweed, was a priority. In Galashiels, the

[33] See SBA/1210/24, Scottish Borders Structure Plan 1991; Written Statement, pp. 29–30.
[34] See SBA/1210/24, Scottish Borders Structure Plan 1991; Written Statement, pp. 30–32.
[35] See SBA/1210/24, Scottish Borders Structure Plan 1991; Written Statement, p. 32.
[36] See SBA/1210/24, Scottish Borders Structure Plan 1991; Written Statement, p. 34.

implementation of the Ladhope Vale improvement scheme had removed through traffic from Channel Street, which had been partially pedestrianised. Further improvements were possible, related to potential commercial developments at Huddersfield Street. In Peebles, consideration would be given to a new bridge over the Tweed in the longer term, particularly if the pressure for housing south of the river persisted.[37]

Urban environment

The structure plan continued to lay emphasis on the policy of conserving and enhancing town centres, including rehabilitation schemes and traffic management. There was also a need to improve the range of shops and the variety and quality of goods sold by encouraging well-designed new developments. Food retail outlets were encouraged within defined town centres, in accordance with government policy, but there was considerable potential for non-food retail developments, particularly in Galashiels and Hawick, at edge of town locations, where adequate car parking could be provided.[38]

The council's policies on conservation areas and listed buildings remained unchanged. Effort would be concentrated on direct action to improve or enhance environmental quality, through the improvement of derelict sites and buildings, face-lift schemes and environmental improvements, and through the preparation of design guides and development briefs. The management of trees and woodlands in built up areas would continue through Tree Preservation Orders and tree planting schemes.[39]

Rural development

The structure plan expressed the regional council's concerns about the fragmentation of government rural policy. The issues of particular concern were the lack of alternative rural employment and rural housing needs. The structure plan continued to support the provision of workshops through the conversion of redundant properties and through new-build within the local centres and key villages. It also supported agricultural diversification and rural tourism projects and indicated the

[37] See SBA/1210/24, Scottish Borders Structure Plan 1991; Written Statement, p. 33.
[38] See SBA/1210/24, Scottish Borders Structure Plan 1991; Written Statement, pp. 34–35.
[39] See SBA/1210/24, Scottish Borders Structure Plan 1991; Written Statement, pp. 35–36.

regional council's desire to establish a rural consultative group, with representatives from statutory bodies and the agricultural community to discuss rural issues.[40]

In relation to housing policy, the shortage of affordable housing for local needs, particularly housing for rent, was a particular concern. The provision of special needs housing and social housing was the responsibility of Scottish Homes, the district councils and social housing providers such as Eildon Housing Association. The structure plan encouraged the rebuilding of existing derelict and semi-derelict residential property and the conversion of agricultural and other non-residential buildings to residential use subject to certain criteria. The revised housing in the countryside policy, adopted in 1986, encouraged new housing associated with existing building groups in Berwickshire, Ettrick and Lauderdale and Roxburgh Districts. In Tweeddale, where this policy did not apply, there was evidence that the more restrictive policy was putting extra pressure on the villages. Accordingly, the council amended the policy in the structure plan to include Tweeddale District. In the remoter south and west of the Region, rural depopulation continued to be a major issue. It was also an area with a dispersed settlement pattern. Accordingly, the council was persuaded to relax its policy further in the Ettrick and Yarrow Valleys, the upper Teviot, Slitrig and Borthwick valleys, and in Liddesdale. Within these areas, the structure plan indicated that there would be a presumption in favour of sensitively designed and well sited isolated housing subject to certain criteria.

In operating the housing in the countryside policy since 1986, there were sometimes difficulties in interpreting what constituted a building group and what constituted an acceptable addition. Noting that the Scottish Office had issued planning advice on the siting and design of new housing in the countryside, the structure plan indicated that the regional council proposed to issue a policy and guidance note on new housing in the countryside, which would provide guidance on the constitution of building groups and acceptable additions.[41] This was issued in 1993.[42]

---

[40] See SBA/1210/24, Scottish Borders Structure Plan 1991; Written Statement, pp. 41–42.

[41] See SDD Planning Advice Note PAN36: Siting and Design of New Housing in the Countryside (1991).

[42] Borders Regional Council, Policy and Guidance Note, *New Housing in the Borders Countryside*, Planning and Development Department, December 1993.

Forestry

The rate of private afforestation accelerated rapidly through the 1980s and there was an increasing awareness of the environmental and social implications of the creation of large-scale afforestation. In 1985, COSLA set up a working party to consider forestry issues and the implications for local authorities. Its report, published in 1987, recommended the preparation of regional forestry strategies.[43] The BRC was one of the first planning authorities to undertake a review of forestry guidance and the production of regional forestry guidelines.[44] Following representations from the CCS and COSLA, the Scottish Office issued Circular 13/1990, which recommended that regional planning authorities should prepare Indicative Forestry Strategies to indicate the sensitivity of different areas of their region to further planting and the potential for further planting. The Borders Region Indicative Forestry Strategy was incorporated into the structure plan. In addition to the area occupied by existing forestry planting (16.0 per cent) and the area deemed unsuitable (7.3 per cent), it identified preferred areas for planting amounting to 12.5 per cent of the region; potential areas amounting to 48.4 per cent of the region and sensitive areas amounting to 15.8 per cent of the region. Ten sensitive areas were identified: the Pentlands, Tweedsmuir Hills, Cheviot Foothills, Lammermuir Hills, Greenlaw Moor, Moorfoot Hills, Eildon Hills/Whitlaw area, Newcastleton Fells, the Border Ridge and the Berwickshire Coast. Many of these areas coincided or overlapped with existing conservation or landscape designations, such as SSSIs, ESAs, NSAs and AGLVs.[45]

The structure plan indicated that within sensitive areas, there were a number and complexity of sensitivities, which would make it extremely unlikely that any large-scale forestry proposal would be acceptable. Within the preferred and potential areas, which amounted to 60 per cent of the Scottish Borders, there was scope for afforestation. Any new planting was required to comply with the standards of design and best practice set out in the Forestry Commission's suite of environmental

---

[43] See Mather, A. S., 'The Changing Role of Planning in Rural Land Use: the Example of Afforestation in Scotland', *Journal of Rural Studies*, Vol. 7, No. 3 (1991), pp. 299–309.

[44] See SBA/1210/24, Scottish Borders Structure Plan 1991; Report of Survey, Part 4 Rural Development, pp. 20–21.

[45] See SBA/1210/24, Scottish Borders Structure Plan 1991; Written Statement, pp. 50–53.

guidelines on landscape design, wildlife and conservation, archaeology and recreation/access.[46]

Mineral working

Mineral working, principally of sand and gravel, was a significant rural land use in Tweeddale. Hard rock quarries were distributed throughout the Borders Region. Mineral extraction emerged as a major planning issue in the early 1990s when a number of planning applications for new quarries were received. Three applications were received for significant sand and gravel quarries at Ingraston, South Slipperfield and Tarfhaugh, near West Linton, as operators looked for new sites to serve the Edinburgh and Lothian market rather than any significant increase in demand from within the Scottish Borders.

In modifying the structure plan, the SoS acknowledged that whilst the Borders Region offered an important source of commercially viable material, well organised campaigns opposed to mineral working developments, particularly in Tweeddale, had served to illustrate the need for more detailed guidance to reconcile the competing needs of the industry and the potential environmental impacts of mineral extraction. Accordingly, a phased review of all workings was proposed, in particular to assess progress on restoration where extraction had ceased.[47] New workings would be subject to a full environmental assessment, in accordance with the Environmental Assessment (Scotland) Regulations introduced in 1989, and would require inclusion of detailed proposals for restoration and after-use of the site. Work commenced in September 1993 on a review of mineral working in the Borders Region with a view to preparing a Minerals Subject Local Plan but it would be 1998 before a draft Minerals Subject Local Plan was produced.[48]

Rural heritage

Pending the review of existing countryside designations by SNH, countryside conservation policy was based on the existing NSA and

---

[46] See Forestry Commission Best Practice Guidelines, *Forestry and Water, Forest Recreation, Forest Landscape Design, Forestry and Archaeology*, Forestry Commission: Edinburgh, 1988 onwards.

[47] See SBA/1210/24, Scottish Borders Structure Plan 1991; Written Statement, p. 48.

[48] See Scottish Borders Council, Minerals Subject Local Plan: Draft 1998, Department of Planning and Development.

AGLV designations. However, anticipating the review of designations, the structure plan recommended four areas of the region for designation as Heritage Areas: the Tweedsmuir Hills, the Cheviot Foothills, the Eildon Hills/Bowhill area and the Berwickshire Coast.[49] Advisory groups or forums were proposed for each area to co-ordinate conservation and management. Support was given to the recently established Tweed Forum, which consisted of twenty bodies, including the regional council, formed to co-ordinate the various interests, reconcile conflicts and provide advice on the sustainable use of the Tweed river system.[50] The structure plan recognised the wide range of nature conservation designations in the region (three NNRs, ninety-six SSSIs, six Special Protection Areas and five RAMSAR sites) and included policies for their protection and conservation. It also recognised the rich heritage of archaeological and historic sites, with policies to protect sites and their settings, maintain an up-to-date record of sites and monuments and improve access to sites and their interpretation.

The structure plan emphasised the continued need to provide and maintain countryside facilities and services, continue with the maintenance of rights of way and the expansion of the Ranger Service. Particular emphasis was placed on the development of cycle routes through the Scottish Borders and the promotion of the region's forestry resource (Forestry Commission and private) for recreation. Emphasis was also placed on the requirement for countryside management plans for particular sensitive areas. The structure plan also proposed the commencement of procedures for extending the Pentland Hills Regional Park, designated in 1986, into the Borders Region in collaboration with Lothian Regional Council. This was a departure from the position of the regional council in the 1980s when the council did not favour inclusion of that portion of the Pentlands in the Borders Region in the proposed Regional Park on the grounds that it would place an excessive burden on council spending.

---

[49] See SBA/1210/24, Scottish Borders Structure Plan 1991; Report of Survey, Part 4 Rural Development, pp. 17–18; See SBA/1210/24, Scottish Borders Structure Plan 1991; Written Statement, pp. 45–47.

[50] See SBA/1210/24, Scottish Borders Structure Plan 1991; Written Statement, p. 47.

CONCLUSIONS

The general objectives of the planning system as set out in the Scottish Government's National Planning Policy Guideline, NPPG1: The Planning System, published in 1993 were to set out the land use framework for promoting economic development; to encourage economic, social and environmental regeneration; and to maintain and enhance the quality of the natural heritage and the built environment. In simple terms, the requirement was to prepare statutory plans, secure their implementation, and ensure that proposed development complied with such plans. The replacement structure plan, *The Scottish Borders 2001: The Way Forward*, approved in November 1993, set out the strategic framework for future development up to 2001 and beyond. It would provide the basis for the preparation of replacement local plans, the council's economic development strategy, the council's responsibilities for maintaining and enhancing the built environment and the rural environment, and the control of development.

Proposals and policies in the structure plan needed to be realistic and capable of implementation, not only in terms of the regional council's financial resources, but also having regard to the financial and manpower resources available to other implementing agencies, such as SBE and Scottish Homes. Accordingly, continued co-operation with such organisations was of paramount importance and liaison with a wide range of public and private sector organisations was integral to the successful implementation of the proposals and policies in the structure plan.

The 1991 structure plan was less optimistic than its predecessor. Population growth in recent years had been comparatively modest and fell short of the effort required to support a healthy, balanced and self-sustaining region. The Borders Region had barely turned the corner from dealing with the effects of sustained outward migration. However, the Scottish Borders had a great deal to offer. The region did not suffer from transport congestion, industrial and environmental pollution, or the loss of community identity, problems experienced elsewhere and more and more people and businesses were turning towards areas like the Scottish Borders. However, sustainable economic growth would only be achieved if more young people could be persuaded to stay in the region and significant numbers of people could be attracted to the area. This was dependent on attracting industry and encouraging the expansion of existing businesses, employment training, the provision of affordable housing, essential infrastructure and community services.

The next chapter describes how the Planning and Development Department sought to implement the proposals and policies of the 1991 structure plan and prepare for the twenty-first century against the background of changing economic circumstances and organisational changes, and the increasing awareness of environmental issues.

9

Preparing for the Twenty-first Century

INTRODUCTION

THIS CHAPTER EXAMINES THE role of the Planning and Development Department leading up to the reorganisation of local government in 1996, when the BRC and its four constituent district councils were replaced by the Scottish Borders Council (SBC). During the early 1990s, four district-wide local plans were produced to replace the twelve local plans adopted in the 1980s. They were prepared in tandem with the new structure plan, *The Scottish Borders 2001: The Way Forward*, approved in November 1993. The replacement local plans applied in detail the policies and proposals incorporated in the approved structure plan, in order to provide a basis for co-ordinating public and private investment and for the control of development up to 2001. The procedure for the preparation of the replacement local plans followed a similar path to that adopted for the first local plans.[1] The Berwickshire Local Plan was adopted, subject to several modifications, in March 1995.[2] The Roxburgh Local Plan was adopted, subject to several modifications, in May 1995.[3] The Ettrick and Lauderdale Local Plan was adopted, subject to several modifications, in July 1995.[4] The Tweeddale Local Plan was adopted, subject to several modifications, in June 1996.[5] A substantial

---

[1] As set out in the Town and Country Planning (Structure and Local Plans) (Scotland) Regulations 1983 (S.I. 1983, No. 1590) and SDD Circular 32/1983, Structure and Local Plans, Edinburgh: HMSO, 1983; see also Collar, N. A. *Planning*, pp. 54–63.

[2] SBA/1210/26, Berwickshire Local Plan Written Statement, Adopted November 1994.

[3] SBA/1210/25, Roxburgh Local Plan Written Statement, Adopted May 1995.

[4] SBA/1210/27, Ettrick and Lauderdale Local Plan Written Statement, Adopted July 1995.

[5] SBA/1210/28, Tweeddale Local Plan Written Statement, Adopted June 1996.

number of policies in the replacement local plans were unchanged from the previous local plans but new policies reflected the economic, social and environmental changes outlined in the approved structure plan. Many of the proposals in the previous local plans had been implemented and new allocations for housing and industry were required to reflect the strategic proposals in the approved structure plan (Figure 9.1).

The BRC was one of the leading local authorities in Scotland campaigning for a stronger voice for rural communities. For more than two decades, perceived to be at a considerable disadvantage compared with the Highlands and Islands, the regional council, strongly supported by its Members of Parliament, particularly Sir David Steel, had sought more recognition by government of the problems of rural areas like the Borders Region. Under the umbrella of COSLA, the regional council brought the problems of rural areas to the attention of government through the gathering of evidence on the extent of rural disadvantage in Scotland.[6] The regional council and other rural local authorities argued that more coherent and integrated policy making was required at government level. However, it would be December 1995 before the government published a White Paper on rural development, which set out in one document the government's policies for rural communities and how they were put into practice.[7] Unfortunately, the White Paper painted a rosy picture of the economy of rural Scotland and there was little discussion of the threats hanging over rural areas, where the economic structure remained heavily skewed towards lower skilled and lower paid employment with many families living on low incomes and facing problems of access to housing, public transport, services and facilities.[8]

Perhaps, the most far-reaching element of the White Paper was the proposed establishment of Local Rural Partnerships to prepare integrated local strategies for rural development, to pursue joint working and promote community-led initiatives. At the same time, COSLA issued guidance on the preparation of regional strategies and the formation of rural partnerships.[9] By the spring of 1997, twenty-two local rural partnerships

---

[6] See, for instance, *Proceedings of Conference on Rural Development Future Strategies*, BRC, April 1991.

[7] See Scottish Office, *Rural Scotland: People, Prosperity and Partnership*, White Paper (Cmnd. 3041) (Edinburgh: HMSO, 1995).

[8] See, for example: Bryden, J. and A. Mather, The Rural White Paper: Rural Scotland: People, Prosperity and Partnership, *Scottish Geographical Magazine*, Volume 112, 1996 Issue 2, pp. 114–116.

[9] COSLA, *Guidance to New Councils on the Preparation of Rural Strategies*, Edinburgh: COSLA, 1996.

Figure 9.1 Borders Regional Council 1990s Structure and Local Plans

had been registered with the Scottish Office and approved by the Scottish National Rural Partnerships, including one for the Borders Region.[10]

[10] Shorthall, S. and M. Shucksmith, 'Integrated rural development: Issues arising from the Scottish experience', *European Planning Studies*, Vol. 6, Issue 1 (1998), pp. 73–88.

Regional policy on particular issues such as forestry, minerals, sustainable development and renewable energy were also tackled in response to a growing awareness of the threat to the environment from inappropriate development and what we now call 'climate change'. With the publication of the White Paper, 'This Common Inheritance', in 1990, and the subsequent Rio Conference on the Environment and Development (Earth Summit) in June 1992, increasing attention was paid to the principle of sustainable development with the establishment of a Local Agenda 21 Working Group. The regional council produced a policy and action plan for sustainable development in the Borders Region and examined ways to develop a renewable energy strategy for the region following the publication by the Scottish Office in June 1993 of a Draft NPPG on Renewable Energy and a draft PAN on Wind Energy Developments (see Figure 9.2).

The move towards sustainable economic development marked a major shift in emphasis of both BRC and SBE in its attitude to future development in the Borders Region. Nevertheless, the regional council, in partnership with SBE, continued to provide good quality industrial sites and factory floor space by servicing new industrial land, upgrading existing sites and providing new buildings. Marketing and promotion, including attendance at exhibitions, advertising and publishing promotional literature, and the offer of loans and grants to support small firms, served to further promote local businesses and the region as a place to locate. Environmental improvements, whether they be to industrial estates or town centres, served to underpin the local economy. Caring for the environment was an important aspect of the Planning and Development Department's work encompassing town centre improvements, building and village conservation and tree preservation, countryside facilities provision and management, including the ranger service and the archaeological service.

The control of development was a continuing responsibility. From a high point of over 1,700 applications in 1990, the number of applications declined to 1,500 in 1992, a reflection of the deep recession, before recovering to over 1,600 in 1994/95. Although the number of applications received in the 1990s was only slightly above the number received in the 1970s, the administration of development control was very different. Growing environmental awareness and the wider range of public consultation and expertise involved in deciding a planning application required far more staff resources and time. In the 1990s, open access to the public was considered a necessity, resulting in many hundreds of site meetings, evening meetings with community councils and other

Figure 9.2 Sustainable development publications

community groups, telephone calls and correspondence. Consequently, the number of staff administering development control in the 1990s was double that involved in the 1970s.

Whereas in the 1970s almost 90 per cent of applications received were dealt with under delegated powers, in the 1990s, this figure had dropped to some 70 per cent. Over 400 applications required to be referred to the Planning and Development Committee which met monthly, making it difficult sometimes to achieve the statutory time period for decision. Some applications prompted site visits by the committee, resulting in further delay, and applications that were considered contentious were referred to community councils, which also led to delays in decision-making. The majority of Listed Building Consent applications took longer to determine than the three-month statutory period for decision, largely as a result of the consultations required and the need to refer such applications to Historic Scotland. Nevertheless, performance improved during the 1990s after the early setbacks following the introduction of the new Ludhouse Computer System. The overcoming of recurring hardware and software problems and training for professional staff, combined with the setting of targets and service monitoring, resulted in the proportion of applications dealt with within the statutory period increasing from a low of 45 per cent in 1990 to over 60 per cent in 1993/94 and 1994/95, albeit still well below the long-term target of 80 per cent set out by government. Consequently, administration changes were made to the Development Control section in 1993 with the objective of improving the standard of service, with the introduction of a delegated decision process for a specified range of applications with the agreement of the chairman, the local member and the Director of Planning and Development. To assist members of the public in submitting minor applications relating to house extensions, the erection of garages and ancillary buildings (which constituted approximately half of the applications submitted), the department pioneered a Householder Application Form, which simplified the procedure.

Against the background of the impending reorganisation of local government resulting from the Local Government etc. (Scotland) Act 1994, this chapter examines how BRC responded to the challenges of the 1990s as a result of the changing economic priorities, the growing awareness of the need to manage the environment, and the need for a more integrated approach to rural planning.

HOUSING POLICY

In allocating land for housing in local plans, the aim of the regional council was to provide for a variety of sites in terms of both size and location, which would be capable of being developed economically for the wide range of house types demanded by the market. The role of the four district councils, Scottish Homes and housing associations was crucial for the provision of special needs housing and affordable housing for local needs, whether to rent or buy. There was no statutory authority which would allow the regional council to allocate land to meet particular housing needs; to zone land for special needs housing, rented housing for local needs or for low-cost home ownership. However, it was the regional council's policy to encourage the provision of a wider choice of housing through the use of development briefs, negotiation and appropriate legal mechanisms.

The population of Berwickshire grew from 18,000 in 1977 to 19,100 in 1991, which was broadly in line with the 1980 structure plan projection.[11] The 1991 structure plan projected a continued population increase to 20,200 persons by 2001, requiring some 800 additional houses in addition to the existing supply of almost 350 house plots. Consequently, a further 39 ha of housing land was allocated in the Berwickshire Local Plan in addition to the undeveloped allocated land in existing local plans. Over half of this additional land was in Eyemouth and Duns, with large allocations in Ayton and Cockburnspath and smaller allocations in Greenlaw and Reston.[12]

In Ettrick and Lauderdale District, the increase in population between 1977 and 1991 was substantially less than that projected in the 1980 structure plan and the actual 1991 population, at 34,000 persons was well below the projected figure of 36,300 persons. The 1991 structure plan set a target population figure for 2001 of 35,000 persons, reflecting the less optimistic assessment of growth in the 1990s.[13] It was projected that land for an additional 655 houses required to be allocated for housing in addition to the land allocated in existing local plans that remained undeveloped. The Ettrick and Lauderdale Local Plan, however, allocated land with a combined capacity of over 1,200 houses, in order to provide a range of sites to meet the need for flexibility and choice. There was a history of land-banking by local builders and it was considered that a number of sites may not be developed within the timescale of the local plan. The newly allocated sites were distributed amongst the larger settlements, Galashiels, Selkirk, Melrose and Earlston but substantial allocations were also made in Lauder, St Boswells and Newtown St Boswells.[14]

In Roxburgh District, the population declined between 1977 and 1991 from 35,760 persons to 35,346 persons (compared with a projected figure of 38,330 persons). Accordingly, the 1991 structure plan simply

---

[11] SBA/1210/26, Berwickshire Local Plan Written Statement, p. 10.
[12] SBA/1210/26, Berwickshire Local Plan Written Statement, pp. 13–14.
[13] SBA/1210/27, Ettrick and Lauderdale Local Plan Written Statement, p. 10.
[14] SBA/1210/27, Ettrick and Lauderdale Local Plan Written Statement, pp. 13–14.

aimed to stabilise the population at around 35,000 persons in 2001.[15] Nevertheless, it was projected that land for a further 889 houses was required in addition to the existing land supply of 709 plots as a result of the reduction in family size and the need to attract incomers and stem outward migration. The Roxburgh Local Plan therefore allocated an additional 34 ha of land for housing with a capacity of some 920 houses, concentrated in Hawick, Jedburgh and Kelso but with smaller allocations in Denholm and Sprouston.[16]

In Tweeddale District, the population increased dramatically from 13,800 persons in 1977 to over 15,300 persons in 1991, well above the projected figure of 14,400 persons. The Registrar General's 1991 population projection projected a continued increase in population to a 2001 figure of 16,500 persons. This resulted in a housing requirement of 1,161 houses, much to the concern of local communities. In response to the concerns raised, the approved structure plan as modified by the Secretary of State stipulated that only half this requirement be provided in the Tweeddale Local Plan with the shortfall to be re-assessed in the review of the structure plan, proposed for 1997/1998.[17] Four options for the distribution of this housing requirement were the subject of public consultation: a West Linton option, which placed emphasis on development in West Linton; a Romannobridge option which identified Romannobridge as a major growth point; a Dispersed Growth option which spread new housing between Peebles, Innerleithen, Broughton, West Linton and Romannobridge; and a Peebles option, which concentrated housing in Peebles.[18] Not surprisingly, there was little public consensus on the options put forward and the regional council had a difficult task in deciding the distribution of future housing. By way of compromise, the favoured option dispersed housing amongst the main settlements: Peebles, Innerleithen, Broughton and West Linton.[19] Even so, land for some 335 houses out of the 580 house requirement was allocated to Peebles, with land for 110 houses in West Linton. In Peebles, 275 of the proposed houses were on three sites south of the River Tweed. It was emphasised in the local plan that it was essential that an additional crossing of the river be investigated before consideration was given to any further development south of the river.[20] In West Linton,

[15] SBA/1210/25, Roxburgh Local Plan Written Statement, p. 10.
[16] SBA/1210/25, Roxburgh Local Plan Written Statement, pp. 13–14.
[17] SBA/1210/28, Tweeddale Local Plan Written Statement, pp. 13–15.
[18] SBA/1210/28, Tweeddale Local Plan Written Statement, pp. 15–17.
[19] SBA/1210/28, Tweeddale Local Plan Written Statement, pp. 17–22.
[20] SBA/1210/28, Tweeddale Local Plan Written Statement, p. 90.

Robinsland Farm was identified as a housing site for approximately 100 houses, half the number originally envisaged, with a new access direct from the A702 east of the village.[21]

Local plans supported developments for special needs housing, for rented housing for local needs and low-cost home ownership in locations where residential development would not normally be permitted. No sites for such housing were identified but local plans provided guidance on the matters to be taken into account on the receipt of a planning application for such developments, including the provision of a detailed agreement (under Section 50 of the Planning Act) that would ensure that the residential units would remain as low-cost housing for successive occupiers. In addition, the local plan required an element of affordable housing in the largest residential developments but did not specify what constituted a large development or the proportion of affordable housing that should be provided.[22] It would be 2005 before the Scottish Executive (the Scottish government after the election of the Scottish Parliament in 1999) issued planning advice on the provision of affordable housing and indicated that sites above a defined size should contribute 25 percent of the housing units to affordable housing[23] It would be 2010 before more comprehensive advice was embodied within PAN 2/2010.[24]

Throughout the region, infill development was encouraged in the Principal, Secondary and Local Centres and the Key Villages specified in the structure plan. Other villages were identified where there were opportunities for infill development or where there was a general policy of restraint either because of the special character of the village or due to lack of services. Local plans emphasised the importance of good layout, design and materials to ensure that all new development was sympathetic and complementary to the character of the surrounding area. Development briefs were to be prepared for larger developments. Reflecting the growing awareness of the need to conserve energy, local plans encouraged the design of energy efficient buildings and layouts, utilising sensible orientation and building materials. All four local plans included a commitment to produce Village Plans for the smaller villages, to provide advice on village boundaries and the areas where

[21] SBA/1210/28, Tweeddale Local Plan Written Statement, pp. 95–97.
[22] SBA/1210/27, Ettrick and Lauderdale Local Plan Written Statement, pp. 18–19.
[23] Scottish Executive, PAN 74: Affordable Housing, 2005.
[24] Scottish Government, PAN 2/2010: Affordable Housing and Housing Land Audits, August 2010.

small-scale and infill housing would be favoured, and supplementary planning guidance on the required form and layout, siting, design and materials required to reflect the local distinctiveness of each village.[25] Village Plans for Berwickshire were approved in September 1995, for Roxburgh in February 1996, for Ettrick and Lauderdale in March 1996 and for Tweeddale in April 1997.[26]

In response to new government policy and guidance on housing, there was a major change in housing in the countryside policy with the development of new housing encouraged within or adjacent to specified 'preferred building groups'; sixteen in Berwickshire District, six in Ettrick and Lauderdale District and seven in Roxburgh District.[27] Limited development was also permitted within or adjacent to other non-specified building groups subject to certain criteria, including no adverse effect on the viability of the farming unit, countryside amenity, landscape or nature conservation. A new policy and guidance note 'New Housing in the Borders Countryside' was published in December 1993, which provided advice on the siting and design of new housing in the countryside. The conversion of existing buildings, including agricultural and other non-residential building, to residential use, the rebuilding of derelict residential buildings and the erection of new residential buildings on derelict residential sites was also encouraged. However, there continued to be a presumption against single houses in the countryside not related to any building group unless there was an economic need.[28]

ECONOMIC DEVELOPMENT

The BRC continued to give a high priority to expanding the regional economy, in co-operation with other agencies, including SBE. The regional council continued to highlight to the government and to the EC the Scottish Borders' need for additional financial assistance and

[25] SBA/1210/27, Ettrick and Lauderdale Local Plan Written Statement, pp.14–15.

[26] See Scottish Borders Council, Berwickshire Village Plans: Supplementary Planning Guidance, September 1965; Roxburgh Village Plans: Supplementary Planning Guidance, February 1996; Ettrick and Lauderdale Village Plans: Supplementary Planning Guidance, March 1996; Tweeddale Village Plans: Supplementary Planning Guidance, April 1997.

[27] National Planning Policy Guideline 3: Land for Housing (NPPG 3), Edinburgh: Scottish Office, 1993 and Planning Advice Note 36: Siting and Design of New Houses in the Countryside (PAN 36), Edinburgh: Scottish Office, 1991.

[28] Borders Regional Council *New Housing in the Borders Countryside*, Policy and Guidance Note, December 1993.

continued to make every effort to attract inward investment, in association with Locate in Scotland. Special emphasis was given to promoting the region's products and services. Nevertheless, the servicing of land for industrial development remained a priority for the continued growth of the Borders Region's economy and its population.

In Berwickshire District, there was sufficient undeveloped allocated industrial land available to meet demand over the local plan period. In Eyemouth, the area allocated at Acredale in the existing local plan was reduced by half and replaced by an area at Gunsgreen, part of the comprehensive development of this area.[29] In Ettrick and Lauderdale District, Selkirk Riverside was the principal focus for action; priority being given to new development and redevelopment in this area. The former munitions factory at Charlesfield, near St Boswells, was identified for industrial development. Elsewhere, additional land was allocated for industry at Tweedbank (Tweedside Park) and in Galashiels, Earlston and Lauder.[30] In Roxburgh District, the acquisition of Galalaw by the district council had alleviated the problem of the lack of industrial land in Hawick. Existing sites in Kelso (Pinnaclehill) and Jedburgh (Oxnam Road) were sufficient to cater for demand in those towns.[31] In Tweeddale District, land at South Parks in Peebles and in Innerleithen and Walkerburn provided opportunities for industrial development. Cavalry Park, in Peebles, was identified for high technology office and business use. Small sites were available in Broughton and West Linton for workshop units.[32]

Local plan policy reflected that of the structure plan to ensure that a range of serviced sites and premises was made available, in association with district councils and SBE. Local plans reinforced the policy of providing small industrial units and workshops on allocated industrial sites. During the period 1981–1991, the number of industrial units owned by BRC increased from 73 to 201. In the 1990s, whilst some additional workshop units were constructed in Galashiels, Peebles, Newcastleton, Newtown St Boswells and Earlston, more emphasis was placed on the conversion of existing redundant properties and improvements to existing premises and industrial estates, including a number of landscaping schemes. Improvements were carried out to industrial estates in Eyemouth, Kelso, Selkirk and Tweedbank. Perhaps the largest

[29] SBA/1210/26, Berwickshire Local Plan Written Statement, pp. 23–24.
[30] SBA/1210/27, Ettrick and Lauderdale Local Plan Written Statement, pp. 23–24.
[31] SBA/1210/25, Roxburgh Local Plan Written Statement, p. 24.
[32] SBA/1210/28, Tweeddale Local Plan Written Statement, pp. 37–38.

single scheme was the comprehensive development at Gunsgreen in Eyemouth involving the regional council in partnership with SBE, BDC, Eyemouth Harbour Trust, SWT and Eyemouth Golf Club to provide a new harbour, marine centre, industrial estate, eighteen-hole golf course, land for new housing and a new sewage treatment plant, with a major new access and distributor road.[33]

Thus, the regional council through its Planning and Development Department was committed to the improvement and diversification of the economy through the creation of sustainable economic development opportunities for the business community by: ensuring an adequate supply of quality industrial and commercial sites and premises; promoting the Scottish Borders as a location for inward investment; marketing local products and services; and providing financial and business development assistance. The department's marketing strategy placed emphasis on publications and the promotion of trade development. Updated versions of the textiles guide, the guide to gifts and crafts and the food and drink producers guide were published and promoted at trade events.[34] Each year, the department organised a full programme of exhibitions, often in association with SBE and trade organisations, throughout the country, including the Highland Show in Edinburgh and events in Birmingham and Harrogate. Overseas, the department participated in events in Europe, the United States and Japan to publicise the region's businesses and products in an effort to revitalise the region's economy.

The FSB Scheme was reviewed in 1992 and expanded to apply to small businesses with up to twenty-five employees. New ventures, existing businesses, manufacturing or business-to-business service firms moving into the region could apply for grants up to a maximum of £3,000 and loans up to a maximum of £8,000.[35] During the period 1992–1995, over 75 per cent of awards were made to manufacturing businesses and 40 per cent of successful applications came from villages or workshops in rural areas. It was estimated that well over 150 full-time jobs were supported/protected each year as a result of the FSB Scheme.[36] Also in 1992, an Exhibitions Grant Scheme was introduced to help small firms

---

[33] SBA/1210/26, Berwickshire Local Plan Written Statement, p. 5.

[34] See *The Borders Collection: a Buyer's Guide to Textiles from the Scottish Borders*, Borders Regional Council, 1992 Update; *A Buyer's Guide to Gifts and Crafts made in the Scottish Borders*, Borders Regional Council, 1991; *A Taste of the Scottish Borders: a Buyer's Guide to Food and Drink*, 1991 Update.

[35] Borders Regional Council, Finance for Small Business leaflet, 1992.

[36] BRC/PD/1, Department of Planning and Development, *Annual Report 1994/95*, Borders Regional Council, p. 12.

with their marketing efforts, with grant assistance to attend trade exhibitions and events; nineteen such awards were made in 1993 and thirty-six awards in 1994. In a further effort to support small businesses in the more rural areas, a Village Shops Scheme was introduced in 1992 to assist the retention or establishment of shops selling convenience items in communities that would otherwise have no local shopping facilities. Although only a handful of awards were made each year, the grants awarded helped some applicants to improve their premises and equipment and stay in business.[37]

Following the announcement by the EC in December 1994 that the Borders Region had qualified for Objective 5(b) status, the Planning and Development Department was given the task of co-ordinating the council's programme of development projects across the whole of the Scottish Borders for the next six years (1994–1999) in liaison with SDD, SBE and other partners. The resultant Single Programme Document (SPD), the Borders 5(b) Plan was approved in April 1995 and included a range of projects, including the development of village workshops at various locations, heritage projects, the publication of buyers' guides for core industrial sectors, trade exhibitions and promotions.[38]

Tourism played an important part in the economy of the Borders Region and local plans encouraged the improvement and expansion of existing tourist accommodation, such as caravan and camping sites, hotels, guest houses, bed and breakfast and self-catering establishments. They also supported new tourism developments subject to there being no adverse impact on countryside amenity, landscape or nature conservation. In Ettrick and Lauderdale there was a chronic lack of hotel accommodation in the Galashiels area and a site at Tweedbank, close to the A7–A68 link road, was considered suitable for a hotel development and efforts would be made to attract a developer, without success.[39] The Ettrick and Lauderdale Local Plan also indicated support for a major tourist information and interpretative facility at Leaderfoot Viaduct, which was close to the A68 and to the Roman Fort, Trimontium, to be developed jointly with the NTS.[40] Although there would be various proposals for the opening up of the former railway viaduct, nothing would come of this proposal.

---

[37] BRC/PD/1, Department of Planning and Development, *Annual Report 1992*, Borders Regional Council, p. 39.
[38] Borders Regional Council, *Borders Business Post*, Autumn Edition, 1995, p. 7.
[39] SBA/1210/27, Ettrick and Lauderdale Local Plan Written Statement, p. 25.
[40] SBA/1210/27, Ettrick and Lauderdale Local Plan Written Statement, pp. 25–26.

In Roxburgh District, emphasis was placed on reinforcing the role of Hawick and Jedburgh, with its Abbey, Mary Queen of Scot's House and Castle Jail, as Gateway Towns, with improvements to town centre tourist facilities and attractions.[41] In Hawick, several projects under the banner 'Hawick 2000' were directed at improving the image of the town centre, increasing its attraction for investors, shoppers and tourists, principal amongst them the Tower Hotel project.[42] The council was also committed to the provision of low-key visitor-related facilities at the English border at Carter Bar on the A68.[43]

In Tweeddale, attractions ranged from historic houses such as Neidpath Castle and Traquair House to the peace and quiet of the Manor Valley. Peebles was extremely attractive to day visitors from both the Edinburgh and Glasgow areas.[44] The local plan encouraged the improvement and expansion of existing facilities such as Rosetta Caravan Park, developed by PCC in the 1970s and sold-off in the 1980s, which BRC saw as a vital tourism facility in Peebles.[45] All four local plans recognised the importance of the River Tweed as a recreational and tourist asset and a major source of income and employment.[46] Full recognition was given to the need to support the Tweed River Commissioners in the exploitation of the tourist potential of the fishery whilst protecting its amenity, conservation and heritage significance through the medium of the recently established Tweed Forum, formed to protect, enhance and restore the rich natural, built and cultural heritage of the Tweed and its tributaries.

BUILT ENVIRONMENT

The 1988 Household Survey into shopping habits in the Borders Region identified a significant retail trade leakage to centres outwith the region; Edinburgh, Berwick-upon-Tweed and Carlisle.[47] Consequently, local plans encouraged a greater range of shopping provision through redevelopment and rehabilitation. Food retail outlets were encouraged in

---

[41] SBA/1210/25, Roxburgh Local Plan Written Statement, pp. 25–26.
[42] SBA/1210/25, Roxburgh Local Plan Written Statement, pp. 77–78.
[43] SBA/1210/25, Roxburgh Local Plan Written Statement, p. 26.
[44] SBA/1210/28, Tweeddale Local Plan Written Statement, p. 39.
[45] SBA/1210/28, Tweeddale Local Plan Written Statement, pp. 91–92.
[46] See, for instance, SBA/1210/28, Tweeddale Local Plan Written Statement, pp. 39–40.
[47] SBA/1210/24, Scottish Borders Structure Plan 1991; Report of Survey, Part 3 Economic Development, pp. 45–49.

existing town centres and in appropriate edge of town centre locations but edge of town locations were resisted in accordance with government advice. There was no such restriction on non-food retail developments, which were allowed within the defined built-up areas of the main towns.

The Ettrick and Lauderdale Local Plan identified a number of town centre development opportunities in Galashiels and Selkirk Riverside was highlighted as a location where non-food retailing would be encouraged.[48] Many sites in Galashiels would remain undeveloped for various reasons, but the site of the former Comelybank Mill and the Hunter's Bridge Road area would be redeveloped as non-retail parks. A large supermarket, ASDA, would be constructed on the former Station Yard. In Selkirk, a large furnishing warehouse would be constructed at Dunsdale Haugh.[49]

The Roxburgh Local Plan identified a number of projects in Hawick, in addition to the Tower Hotel/Backdamgate project, to improve the image of the town centre: a 'Town Scheme' and a 'Facelift Scheme', which provided grant assistance to owners and occupiers within the conservation area to carry out repairs and maintenance work in a traditional fashion.[50] The disused Tower Mill, close to the Tower Hotel, was identified as being suitable for commercial or tourism use and would eventually be redeveloped as an entertainment venue, the 'Heart of Hawick'. The adjoining site of the former Corn Exchange would be the site for the Heritage Hub, the centre for the Scottish Borders Archive and Local History Service. The whole of the Commercial Road area was identified as a Rehabilitation Action Area, in association with the re-routing of the A7 along Commercial Road and the construction of a new bridge over the Teviot and new road (Mart Street) to link the re-routed A7 with the A698. Planning permission was granted in 1992 for a 50,000 sq ft supermarket and petrol filling station on the site of the former auction mart and in due time, the Commercial Road area would be redeveloped for a variety of commercial uses, including food supermarkets. Victoria Mills on Victoria Road also offered potential for development and would be the site of the new Hawick Community Hospital, opened in 2005.

Local plans endorsed the council's policy of promoting Town Schemes and Facelift Schemes to underpin the local economy through

---

[48] SBA/1210/27, Ettrick and Lauderdale Local Plan Written Statement, p. 78.
[49] SBA/1210/27, Ettrick and Lauderdale Local Plan Written Statement, p. 27.
[50] SBA/1210/25, Roxburgh Local Plan Written Statement, pp. 77–78.

regeneration and enhancement. In addition to the Hawick 2000 initiative, principal amongst these were the environment improvements to the Market Square/Channel Street/Overhaugh Street area in Galashiels in association with traffic management improvements. Elsewhere, town centre improvements, including building face-lifts and hard landscaping schemes were carried out in Duns, Coldstream and Eyemouth with plans for further improvements in Hawick (Drumlanrig Square), Kelso and Selkirk.

Shop fronts were recognised as an important element of the townscape within town centres and local plans encouraged attractive, sensitively designed shop fronts, with the use of traditional materials in conservation areas. A design guide on Shop Fronts and Shop Signs was produced in 1991 to assist developers and persuade shop owners away from the standard shop fitter's solutions.[51] Local plans also emphasised the need for a high standard of design for advertisements in conservation areas and indicated that illuminated signs would not normally be permitted in conservation areas, which included most town centres. Following a study of upper floors in several Border towns, which highlighted that under-use was a problem, local plans encouraged the re-use of upper floors in town centres as a positive way of improving the urban fabric and restoring the housing stock. However, this would be an ongoing issue and remains today a problem in many town centres.

Local plan policies on conservation areas, listed buildings, sites of archaeological interest and tree preservation remained unchanged. Forty of the region's towns and villages were designated conservation areas, eleven of which were designated as 'Outstanding', giving access to grants from the Historic Buildings Council for Scotland. All were covered by Article 4 Directions, enabling the council to exert additional controls over minor alterations and extensions to buildings and higher standards of design and materials were expected than elsewhere. Trees were also afforded additional protection within conservation areas. The Ettrick and Lauderdale Local Plan rectified a glaring omission by proposing the designation of the older part of Galashiels, centred on the Mercat Cross, as a conservation area.[52]

Two grant schemes were available to owners of buildings that were designated as listed buildings, of which there were 2,150 in the region, or were within conservation areas: Historic Buildings Grants, which were available for repairs to listed buildings, and the Conservation Area

[51] Borders Regional Council, *Shop Fronts and Shop Signs*, 1991.
[52] SBA/1210/27, Ettrick and Lauderdale Local Plan Written Statement, p. 37.

Enhancement Scheme, which provided funding for enhancement works in conservation areas for public benefit. A Register of 'Buildings at Risk' was maintained in collaboration with the Scottish Civic Trust. One notable example was Dangerfield Mills on Commercial Road in Hawick, unique for the retention of its original machinery, and where the word 'tweed' was coined (see Introduction). In spite of efforts to secure it as a working museum, following its closure in 1991, its future was still undecided in 1996 and although the buildings and machinery continued to be preserved, the building complex and its machinery was destroyed by an arson attack in 2003 and it is now the site of a supermarket.[53] A sad loss!

The archaeological service continued to expand in the 1990s as interest in the rich history of the Scottish Borders grew and the importance of conserving the cultural heritage of the region as part of the planning process was recognised. The issue in 1994 of a NPPG and PAN on Planning and Archaeology provided a clear indication of the important role of archaeology in the preservation of the cultural heritage. This guidance and advice endorsed the approach being taken by the regional council towards the protection of the thousands of archaeological sites in the Borders. The service provided advice to a wide range of groups and individuals, was involved in excavations prior to development proposals and supported private projects ranging from the investigation of the Roman military complex of Trimontium at Newstead run by Bradford University to a documentary survey of the Charlesfield wartime industrial complex.[54]

THE RURAL ENVIRONMENT

A review of agriculture in the Borders Region in 1991 by the Scottish Agricultural College examined the prospects for agriculture against the background of the changing support system, which placed more emphasis on environmental improvements rather than agricultural production. Many grants relating to buildings, drainage and re-seeding had been reduced or removed altogether.[55] The study highlighted the continuing loss of employment in agriculture, the squeeze on farm incomes with

[53] BRC/PD/1, Department of Planning and Development, *Annual Report 1992*, Borders Regional Council, pp. 79–80.
[54] BRC/PD/1, Department of Planning and Development, *Annual Report 1994/95*, Borders Regional Council, p. 24.
[55] Scottish Agricultural College, *The Changing Borders Countryside*, Borders Regional Council, March 1991.

a knock-on effect for businesses supplying farms, and the increasing number of redundant traditional buildings. It was forecast that the cereal production sector would suffer most with increasing pressure to amalgamate holdings. At the same time, there was a requirement for new specialised agricultural buildings for processing and storage. In the uplands, there were constraints on flock sizes from the EC's Common Agriculture Policy (CAP) support limits and the outlook was for more forestry.

Local plans endorsed the policies in the structure plan relating to the protection of prime agricultural land, the encouragement of farm diversification measures and development schemes embracing alternative livestock and crop production, small woodlands, tourist and recreational provision, the creation of wildlife habitats and the conversion of redundant buildings for business purposes. The Borders FWAG (previously FFWAG), funded mainly by the regional council, celebrated its tenth anniversary in 1992.[56] The Senior Farm Conservation Adviser, a former BRC Countryside Ranger, undertook farm visits and provided advice on woodland management, shelterbelt planting for timber, wildlife and game, pond and wetland management, the management of field boundaries, streamside management and the establishment of wildflower meadows. Training courses were run on such subjects as pest control, rehabilitation of farm ponds and best conservation practice. In association with the Borders FWAG, the regional council successfully operated two grant schemes for countryside tree and hedge planting benefiting a wide range of participants, including farmers, landowners and community groups. In the seven years from the start of the scheme in 1988, an estimated 64,000 trees and 22 km of hedging had been planted by 1995.[57]

In relation to commercial forestry, local plans specified the detail boundaries of Preferred, Potential and Sensitive Areas proposed in the Indicative Forestry Strategy, and detailed the policy on commercial forestry where it was considered acceptable; including encouragement for the planting of native species, especially hardwoods, and the treatment of forest edges.[58] From 1992, the regional council was consulted on all WGS applications following the introduction of an extended grant system, and the number of consultations leapt to over 100 schemes

[56] BRC/PD/1, Department of Planning and Development, *Annual Report 1992*, Borders Regional Council, p. 58.
[57] BRC/PD/1, Department of Planning and Development, *Annual Report 1994/5*, Borders Regional Council, July 1995, pp. 19–20.
[58] See, for example, SBA/1210/27, Ettrick and Lauderdale Local Plan Written Statement, pp. 32–33.

per annum.⁵⁹ However, only a handful were referred to the Forestry Advisory Group as a result of objections from the regional council, a testament to the benefits of the consultation procedure and the emerging attitude of foresters towards landscape design, wildlife and conservation considerations.⁶⁰ In many cases, the department's landscape architect was able to influence and improve initial submissions. The re-structuring of existing public forests by the Forestry Commission (Forest Enterprise after 1992) led to an increase in the number of consultations on Forest Design Plans, produced to show how, in the longer term, a more diverse forest resource could be created which maximised economic value but also ensured that forests made a positive contribution to the environment and provide opportunities for public enjoyment. Such an approach was welcomed by BRC.

Major applications for sand and gravel working in the West Linton area of Tweeddale District were received in the 1990s attracting great public interest. The Quarries Action Group, formed in West Linton, won the RTPI's second prize (out of eighty-three entrants) in its Community Planning Award Category, reflecting the community's determination to open up public debate on such a contentious issue.⁶¹ One proposal was approved but two others were refused planning permission.⁶² Local plans set out the detailed criteria against which proposed mineral working would be assessed pending a review of mineral workings in the Border Region with a view to preparing a Minerals Subject Local Plan under section 9(4) of the 1972 Act.⁶³

Local plans defined the detailed boundaries of AGLVs and set out the criteria that applied to any proposed development, the emphasis being on the protection of the heritage significance of the area, whether it be landscape quality, nature conservation or historical, archaeological or cultural interest.⁶⁴ A comprehensive assessment of the landscape in

---

⁵⁹ BRC/PD/1, Department of Planning and Development, *Annual Report 1992*, Borders Regional Council, pp. 63–64.

⁶⁰ BRC/PD/1, Department of Planning and Development, *Annual Report 1993/4*, Borders Regional Council, April 1994, p. 18.

⁶¹ BRC/PD/1, Department of Planning and Development, *Annual Report 1993/4*, Borders Regional Council, April 1994, p. 3.

⁶² BRC/PD/1, Department of Planning and Development, *Annual Report 1993/4*, Borders Regional Council, April 1994, p. 20.

⁶³ Town and Country Planning (Structure and Local Plans) (Scotland) Regulations 1983 (regulation 23).

⁶⁴ See, for example, SBA/1210/27, Ettrick and Lauderdale Local Plan Written Statement, pp. 45–46.

partnership with SNH in 1995 identified thirty basic landscape types falling into six regional landscape character areas: Tweed Lowlands, Lammermuir and Moorfoot hills, Central Southern Uplands, Cheviot Foothills, Midland Valley and Coastal Zone.[65] This assessment would prove invaluable in future dealings with large-scale developments in the countryside, such as wind farms.

COUNTRYSIDE RECREATION

Local Plans set out a number of detailed policies for the encouragement of recreation in the wider countryside, centred on its rivers and lochs, particularly the River Tweed, its hills and forests, the estates and the coast. For the first time, and in response to a growing number of development inquiries, local plan policy supported leisure developments in the countryside such as golf courses accompanied by sensitively laid out and designed housing.[66] Such a proposal by the Duke of Roxburghe was approved in 1994 at Sunlaws, near Kelso, which would become a premier leisure facility; the Roxburghe Hotel and Golf Course, with some thirty luxury houses.[67] For particularly sensitive areas which were subject to recreational pressure, such as the Cheviot Foothills, the St Mary's Loch Area and Coldingham Bay, management plans would be continuously monitored and reviewed.[68] Specific policies limited new static/touring caravan and chalet sites east of the A1 and resisted the expansion of holiday hut sites in Tweeddale. The Tweeddale Local Plan, adopted in June 1996, reiterated the regional council's support for the extension of the Pentland Hills Regional Park to include the area within the Scottish Borders, as circumstances permitted.[69] Nevertheless, SBC would soon renege on this decision and decide to take no action on the grounds that the benefits of such a designation did not merit the costs and administration involved.

The duty, under the Countryside (Scotland) Act 1967, to assert, keep open and free from obstruction all rights of way in the region was the

[65] SBA/1210/39, Scottish Borders Council, *Structure Plan Review 1997: Report of Survey*, Section 7: The Environment.

[66] SBA/1210/25, Roxburgh Local Plan Written Statement, pp. 46–47.

[67] BRC/PD/1, Department of Planning and Development, *Annual Report 1993/4*, Borders Regional Council, April 1994, pp. 20–21.

[68] See, for example, SBA/1210/27, Ettrick and Lauderdale Local Plan Written Statement, pp. 67–68.

[69] SBA/1210/28, Tweeddale Local Plan Written Statement, pp. 81–82.

responsibility of the Ranger Service.[70] This duty was carried out in association with community councils, landowners and a range of voluntary organisations. Long distance routes, such as the Pennine Way, Southern Upland Way and Dere Street, were the subjects of ongoing management supported by SNH. Throughout the 1990s, the workload on rights of way increased although financial restrictions and the reducing grant from SNH meant that less money was available to undertake maintenance and improvements. Rangers also undertook school visits, guided walks and talks to a wide range of clubs and organisations. The first week-long Scottish Borders Walking Festival was held in West Linton in 1992 and has been an annual event ever since, moving from town to town. Cycling enjoyed a resurgence in the 1990s, with a boom in mountain biking. There was a significant increase in recreational cycling at Glentress, near Peebles, and the Tweed Cycleway, a 90-mile route from Biggar to Berwick-upon-Tweed, most of which would be incorporated into the National Cycle Network Route 1 between Edinburgh and Berwick-upon-Tweed, was opened in 1993.

In 1992, the regional council took over Lothian Estates' Visitor Centre at Monteviot and the Harestanes Countryside Visitor Centre was opened by Magnus Magnusson, Chairman of SNH, on 4 April.[71] Harestanes provided a permanent base for the Ranger Service, previously located in Melrose, a countryside visitor centre, shop and café, and adventure playground alongside the steading, which was converted to workshops. Some 30,000 visitors passed through the door in 1992, including school visits, rising to over 40,000 in 1994.[72] By 1994, the regional council managed a wide range of facilities, supported by willing volunteers and voluntary organisations, works being carried out in association with BTS, SBE's Employment Training and SNH. These included landscape work at Coldingham Bay and Lindean Reservoir; viewpoint facilities at Carter Bar, Manor Sware, near Peebles, and St Mary's Loch; picnic sites at the Meldons, Manor Sware, Whiteadder Reservoir, Teviothead, Hexpath and Cambridge Cross Roads on the A697 and Renton Barns on the A1; permanent toilets at St Mary's Loch and Renton Barns, and seasonal toilets at

---

[70] BRC/PD/1, Department of Planning and Development, *Annual Report 1992*, Borders Regional Council, pp. 54–57.

[71] BRC/PD/1, Department of Planning and Development, *Annual Report 1992*, Borders Regional Council, p. 57.

[72] BRC/PD/1, Department of Planning and Development, *Annual Report 1994/5*, Borders Regional Council, July 1995, p. 16.

the Meldons, Cambridge Cross Roads, Whiteadder Reservoir, Teviothead and Legerwood (in association with a farm trail).[73]

SUSTAINABLE DEVELOPMENT

January 1994 saw the publication by the government of *Sustainable Development: The UK Strategy*, the government's response to Agenda 21, the action plan agreed at the Rio Conference in 1992. Agenda 21 was aimed at reversing the effect of environmental degradation and promoted environmentally sound and sustainable development. It also made clear that the planning profession had a vital role to play in promoting and implementing sustainable development. Following an approach by SE, SNH and Rural Forum, BRC, with E&LDC and SBE, undertook a pilot study of sustainable development in Ettrick and Lauderdale District to identify the key issues in the district and the opportunities for sustainable development. It was hoped that the study would provide a robust appraisal of sustainable development opportunities and a framework that could be applied elsewhere in Scotland.[74]

The study reviewed the economic, social and environmental characteristics of the district and assessed the national and international factors affecting the future of the region, such as the EC's CAP, the GATT Agreement, the National Forest Policy, National Energy Policy, National Planning Policy and the policies of bodies such as SE and SNH. It put forward a vision for the future, based on the diversification of agriculture into energy crops; more hardwood planting, including coppicing; ecological diversity through sympathetic land management and wildlife corridors; integrated countryside management and sustainable tourism, skills training, property insulation, wind energy, biofuels, waste recycling, promotion of public transport, improvement of local retail services, a reduction in travel to work and demographic change (redressing the imbalance with in-migration of the young). The study highlighted the need to involve the public and communities fully in any action plan.[75]

The study paved the way for the establishment of a Local Agenda 21 Working Group (chaired by the author) to carry out a full environmental

---

[73] BRC/PD/1, Department of Planning and Development, *Annual Report 1992*, Borders Regional Council, p. 56.

[74] BRC/PD/1, Department of Planning and Development, *Annual Report 1993/4*, Borders Regional Council, April 1994, p. 8.

[75] Scottish Natural Heritage, *Area Sustainability Study of Ettrick and Lauderdale*, Perth: SNH, 1994.

audit of the existing five local authorities in the Borders Region, and the formation of a Borders Forum on Sustainable Development, at a seminar chaired by Magnus Magnusson in March 1995, which had widespread support from industry and public agencies, voluntary and environmental organisations, community councils and the public.[76] This initiative spawned a number of projects, the most important of which was the establishment by SBE of the Tweed Horizons Centre for Sustainable Technology in the former St Columba's College, near Newtown St Boswells, at a cost of £2.7 million. The centre, opened in 1995, provided conference facilities and accommodation for seventeen companies engaged in a range of activities from recycling and energy efficiency to computer software and permaculture.[77]

At the same time, the local authority working group developed an environmental policy for the new SBC, aimed at improving the environmental performance of the new council and integrating sustainable development into the new council's policies and activities. One of the priorities was to produce and implement a regional recycling strategy. Refuse disposal had been an issue for the four district councils since reorganisation in 1975. Prior to 1975, the counties and the burghs had their own local tips but, after 1975, capacity issues arose particularly in Berwickshire and Tweeddale Districts. In Roxburgh and Ettrick and Lauderdale Districts alternatives to the tipping of untreated waste in quarries and holes in the ground were examined without any definitive progress apart from paper and glass collections. There were also issues with leachate at some existing sites, particularly the Ettrick and Lauderdale District tip at Langlee, Galashiels. The regional council supported the establishment of a Waste Management Group to develop and implement a policy for waste disposal throughout the Borders Region but it would be some years before any significant progress was made.[78]

In September 1993, the EC agreed to provide 50 per cent funding towards the cost of a renewable energy study of the Borders Region, a joint BRC and SBE proposal under the ALTENER programme for promoting the use of renewable energy technologies, in particular biofuels. This study examined the potential for wind energy, ranging from single

---

[76] BRC/PD/1, Department of Planning and Development, *Annual Report 1994/5*, Borders Regional Council, July 1995, p. 8.

[77] Scottish Borders Enterprise, *Enterprise Leader*, Summer 1994, p. 4; Spring 1995, p. 2; Summer 1995, p. 1 & p. 4.

[78] Borders Regional Council, *Sustainable Development in the Borders Region*, 1995.

wind turbines to wind farms, short rotation coppicing and the use of forestry residues, anaerobic digestion of livestock slurries, combustion/ gasification of poultry litter, and small hydro schemes. It identified areas where wind energy development could be viable and sites with potential for small hydro schemes.[79] Supported by SBE, a number of projects were submitted to the government under the first Scottish Renewables Obligation (SRO) announced in December 1994 but, much to the consternation of the regional council, none were awarded contracts.[80] BRC was not slow in showing its displeasure since the council felt that the Scottish Borders had considerable potential for renewable energy developments.

In response to the publication of a draft NPPG on renewable energy and a draft PAN on wind energy developments in June 1993, the regional council produced a planning framework for renewable energy, which made positive provision for environmentally acceptable wind energy developments. It identified preferred areas, potential areas and sensitive areas for wind energy developments, which were the subject of wide-ranging consultation in 1995.[81] Unfortunately, this framework did not anticipate the exponential growth in the scale of wind farm developments and turbine size and would require to be modified in the review of the structure plan in 1998. Furthermore, BRC's enthusiasm for wind energy developments to serve the Borders Region waned after the reorganisation of local government in 1996 as proposed schemes increased in size and began to have an impact on the Borders landscape. Nevertheless, the first operational wind farm came on stream at Dun Law, a prominent location near the A68 north of Lauder, with a second, larger development on Bowbeat Hill, north of Glentress Forest. Together it was estimated that these two developments would have the installed capacity to provide over 70 per cent of the domestic electricity requirement in the Borders and that the Scottish Borders would soon become a net exporter of energy from renewable resources.[82]

Recognition of the importance of sustainable development also brought a change in attitude towards the dependence on the motor car

---

[79] Garrad Hassan & Partners, *A Renewable Energy Development Strategy for the Borders Region of Scotland*, BRC, 1995.

[80] Scottish Borders Enterprise, *Enterprise Leader*, Summer 1994, p. 7.

[81] BRC/PD/1, Department of Planning and Development, *Annual Report 1994/5*, Borders Regional Council, July 1995, p. 9.

[82] Borders Regional Council, *Scottish Borders Structure Plan 2001–2018*, pp. 74–75.

PREPARING FOR THE TWENTY-FIRST CENTURY 255

as the form of transport for journey to work and pleasure and, in particular, the re-opening of the Waverley line, closed in 1969. So, twenty-five years after its closure, Lothian and Borders Regional Councils, with Edinburgh and Lothian Enterprise and SBE, jointly funded research into an evaluation of the potential use of a three-phase re-opening of the line; the initial link being between Edinburgh and Galashiels (Tweedbank), followed by Carlisle to Hawick and then Galashiels to Hawick.[83] It would be another twenty years (2015) before the Waverley line was re-opened between Edinburgh and Tweedbank. Pressure continues to have the rest of the line re-opened.

CONCLUSIONS

BRC continued to punch above its weight during the 1990s. The Planning and Development Department, numbering in excess of fifty personnel, embraced new technology, whether it be the new word processors that had replaced electric typewriters, the new computerised development control system, digital mapping or graphic data handling. The graphic design section, responsible for departmental and council publications, brochures and leaflets made use of the latest Apple Mac computers.[84] The multi-disciplinary nature of the department reflected its responsibilities over a wide range of functions and its position at the centre of the regional council's activities.

By 1996, BRC had up-to-date structure and local plans to guide future development up to and beyond the end of the century, and regional policies on a number of key land uses, such as forestry, minerals and renewable energy. Detailed plans had been prepared for almost every community in the Borders, to encourage appropriate small-scale housing and business development across the more rural parts of the region, and the policy on housing in the countryside had been modified, in the light of changing government priorities, in a bid to retain population in the more remote parts of the region. A range of policy guidance and advice had been produced to assist developers and the public on a diverse range of planning matters ranging from redevelopment in conservation areas to advertisements in the countryside.

BRC's bid for Objective 5(b) status had been successful and funding had been agreed for a six-year period from 1994 to 1999; a number of

---

[83] Scottish Borders Enterprise, *Enterprise Leader*, Summer 1995, p. 3
[84] Borders Regional Council, *Department of Planning and Development: Annual Report 1994/5*, July 1995, p. 28.

projects had been awarded grants. Its portfolio of industrial property had continued to expand and new buyers' guides had been published. There had been major achievements with the completion of the Tower Hotel/Backdamgate project in Hawick, the groundwork had been laid for the planned expansion of Eyemouth at Gunsgreen, and the Harestanes Countryside Visitor Centre had been opened. Major roads projects included the completion of the Newtown St Boswells by-pass on the A68 and the A7–A68 link road. The proposed Kelso distributor road and new bridge over the River Tweed (Hunter Bridge) was completed in 1998. However, Hawick continued to be disadvantaged as a result of the lack of a major industrial site and little progress had been made with the revitalisation of the Selkirk Riverside Industrial Area. There was no sign of any movement on the provision of a Selkirk by-pass. Although a great deal had been achieved in a number of town centres with environmental improvements and traffic measures, the continued run-down of the principal centres, Hawick and Galashiels, was a major issue. In the countryside, notwithstanding the continued reduction in grant assistance from SNH, the Countryside Service continued to administer the management and maintenance of a wide range of countryside facilities, and a comprehensive network of footpaths, including Scotland's only recognised coast-to-coast long-distance walk, the Southern Upland Way.

The regional council was committed to the principles of sustainable development through the establishment of the Borders Forum on Sustainable Development. Its vision, amongst other things, was for a more diversified agriculture sector, encompassing biofuels and energy crops, more hardwood planting and ecological diversity, and integrated countryside management and sustainable tourism. In partnership with SBE, BRC investigated a number of sustainable development initiatives, with the Tweed Horizons Centre for Sustainable Development in the vanguard. The regional council also embraced the potential for renewable energy projects, particularly wind energy, in the Scottish Borders.

However, recent regional economic trends did not auger well for the future. At a meeting with local MPs in October 1995, Lord Minto, the Convener of BRC gave a stark warning: job losses in agriculture and textiles had exceeded 7,000 over the past twenty years and, whilst these had been offset by growth in other manufacturing sectors, such as electronics, and the service sector, there was still a continuing need for diversification. The position had been brought into sharp focus by more recent job losses in Hawick where Pringle of Scotland, the region's premier textile firm, had announced 1,000 redundancies. The Borders

Region remained at the bottom of the Scottish league table in terms of both weekly earnings and Gross Domestic Product.[85]

In November 1994 the Local Government etc. (Scotland) Act 1994 abolished the two-tier structure of regions and districts created in 1973 and replaced them with thirty-two unitary authorities. It confirmed that the Borders Region would be retained as a single unitary authority. The initial proposals set out in July 1993 proposed that the Borders Region (renamed Scottish Borders) would comprise only three of its districts; Tweeddale, Ettrick and Lauderdale and Roxburgh Districts, with Berwickshire and East Lothian Districts forming a separate unitary authority. After lobbying on both sides, the Act was amended and proposed that the Scottish Borders should remain unchanged with East Lothian as a separate unitary authority. Local government reorganisation came into effect on 1 April 1996 creating unitary authorities responsible for all planning functions, roads and transportation, social services, education, housing and environmental services. On the face of it, there would be little change in the Borders Region as far as the planning function was concerned. However, there would be a number of challenges. The amalgamation of the five local authorities in the Scottish Borders, with their separate capital programmes and inherited commitments and priorities, provided uncertainty about future departmental budgets. Furthermore, ministerial pronouncements indicated that government cutbacks would be inevitable.

---

[85] Borders Regional Council, *Borders Business Post*, December 1995, p. 5.

Epilogue

COUNTY PLANNING IN THE SCOTTISH BORDERS

The first planning legislation, the 1909 Housing and Town Planning Act arose from the campaign for higher quality living environments, led by the Garden City Movement. Urban sprawl and ribbon development during the inter-war period created new challenges, and the need for large-scale reconstruction after the Second World War led to a number of studies on land utilisation and the future control of development, resulting in the Town and Country Planning (Scotland) Act 1947. This Act, combined with the New Towns Act 1946 and the National Parks and Access to the Countryside Act 1949, created a system designed to fulfil the social, economic and environmental objectives of reconstruction and provide a long-term basis for land management. In Scotland, regional planning was pioneered by Patrick Geddes and taken up by the likes of Robert Matthew and Frank Mears. Mears's *Regional Plan for Central and South-East Scotland*, published in 1948, was the first study to highlight the plight of the Scottish Borders, with its dependence on the textile industry and agriculture and its problems of rural depopulation, which contrasted starkly with the problems of urban sprawl and suburban expansion in the urban areas, which were the driving forces behind the British town planning movement.

The four county planning authorities in the Scottish Borders, established after the Second World War, were under-staffed and under-resourced. Planning committees were advised by the county clerk, assisted by the county surveyor or county architect. The lack of qualified planning staff restricted their ability to produce the development plans required under the 1947 Act and consultants were appointed to undertake this work. It would be 1965 before there was total development plan coverage of the Scottish Borders. Throughout the 1950s, planning activity was centred on development control with emerging issues related to the growth in car ownership and leisure time. The county development plans, updated by formal amendments and augmented by non-statutory studies and reports would provide the framework for development decisions until 1975 and the reorganisation of local government. Development plans were based on the optimistic assumption that the continued loss of population in the landward areas would be offset by growth in the textile industry in the burghs supported by an expanded programme of local authority housing for incoming workers. However, throughout the 1950s and 1960s, the population of the region continued to decline; by over 10,000 people between 1951 and 1971 to below 100,000 people.

The 1960s was a period of great social, cultural, economic and political change and, with the increasing pace of development, the increasingly out-dated county development plans became of diminishing value in determining and controlling the future direction of growth. Prior to the mid-1960s, the challenges being faced by areas such as the Scottish Borders were largely overlooked by government or poorly understood. However, with the re-emergence of regional and sub-regional planning in Scotland in the mid-1960s, the government's attention turned once again to the Scottish Borders. Against the background of the Labour government's plans for expansion of the Scottish economy, the SDD commissioned the Central Borders Plan, which was based on proposals for major growth of 25,000 persons in the Galashiels catchment area. Published in 1968, the Plan included the creation of a settlement of 10,000 people at St Boswells/Newtown St Boswells, and a new village at Tweedbank comprising 1,000 dwellings, an industrial site, a village centre and community and leisure facilities. It is well documented that the proposals for St Boswells/Newtown St Boswells did not win the support of local politicians who preferred to see development take place within the existing burghs, particularly Galashiels and Hawick. The Tweedbank development was considerably delayed due to land ownership difficulties.

Nevertheless, the Central Borders Plan did galvanise the local authorities in the Scottish Borders to adopt a more positive approach to planning and development with the establishment of development associations: the Peebles, Roxburgh and Selkirk JPAC and EBDA. Supported by the SIEC and the Development Commission, these bodies embarked on a wide-ranging programme of industrial site-servicing and factory building, marketing and promotion to diversify the economy and stem depopulation. These efforts would eventually bear fruit and by the early 1970s, out-migration from the region had been reversed and the population increased in 1973–1974 for the first time for over 100 years.

There were fundamental changes in the way town and country planning was administered in the Scottish Borders in the 1960s with the creation of stand-alone planning departments in Roxburghshire and Berwickshire. In addition to involvement in industrial development and promotion, encouraged by SDD, there was a more positive approach to urban development through the establishment of technical working parties for the larger burghs and the production of non-statutory town centre redevelopment plans. Planning in the 1960s was characterised by ambitious proposals for growth in Galashiels, Hawick, Kelso, Peebles and Berwickshire.

Agriculture and forestry operations were largely exempt from planning control but, as the 1960s progressed, there was mounting concern over the effects of the increased mechanisation of agriculture on rural landscapes and the growing pressure for countryside recreation. Rural depopulation attracted more attention and both Roxburghshire and Berwickshire County Councils examined the problems of the landward areas and produced strategies for rural development. Over 60 per cent of the Scottish Borders was designated as an AGLV and increasing pressure on the countryside, particularly around St Mary's Loch and along the Berwickshire coast, required management action by the respective councils but it would not be until the establishment of the CCS in 1968 that positive measures were initiated.

REGIONAL PLANNING IN ACTION

After local government reorganisation in 1975, in partnership with the SDA and subsequently SBE, the BRC continued the momentum built up by the previous local authorities through the activities of the JPAC and EBDA in promoting the area and the provision of serviced industrial land and factories across the region to diversify the economy and retain population. The new system of structure and local plans introduced, for the first time, a regional dimension to the development plan. There was also an increasing awareness of the need for more openness and involvement of the public in planning generally, and the preparation of structure and local plans involved extensive public participation. The involvement of the public in the development control system gradually expanded, eventually incorporating neighbour notification and wide consultation with community councils and other community groups. The press paid increasing attention to the activities of the Planning and Development Department.

Bill Chisholm, Borders District staff reporter for *The Scotsman* from 1969 to 2005, has provided his view of the planning and development service in the Borders:

> Throughout my 36 years as *The Scotsman*'s representative in the Borders, planning disputes and economic development issues would provide me with a vast collection of good and bad news stories. And during the majority of the period the planning service would play an ever-increasing role in shaping the region's fortunes. Frank Constable, from Roxburghshire, a key witness at the Tweedbank proceedings, and Basil Knowles, from Berwickshire, were the pioneers who made sure the important work being tackled by their small teams received the publicity and the credit it merited.
>
> Their expertise was certainly needed in the 1970s as the Borders struggled with the twin issues of depopulation and shrinking traditional industries in the textile and knitwear sectors. The responsibility for attracting inward investment lay exclusively with the Scottish Development Department, which cared little for areas outwith the Central Belt. Once the economic development function found its way into local hands in 1975, the fledgling Borders Regional Council (BRC) was able to come up with a strategy to suit the needs of this unique area. From the sidelines, I watched the planning and development service, with David Douglas at the helm, increase its influence over the communities it served. There is little doubt in my mind that without its presence the Borders would have been a considerably poorer region today.[1]

The Borders Region Structure Plan 1980 was overly optimistic in its projection of the future population; 108,230 by 1991, compared with a 1971 figure of 98,500, based on the development of industrial sites and the diversification of the economic base. By the end of the 1980s, although economic recovery had continued with the creation of a wide range of employment opportunities on industrial sites spread across the region, the population had only increased to an estimated 103,500 in 1991. The loss of Assisted Area status in 1982 resulted in low priority being given to the Scottish Borders in terms of EC funding and the continued decline in the tweed and knitwear sector meant that overall employment in the region increased by only 300 people. The economy of the Scottish Borders still relied on a narrow range of industries and a small number of companies. In partnership with the SDA, considerable effort was put into land renewal, redevelopment and rehabilitation projects in a number of Border towns. However, SSHA housing development at Tweedbank came to a halt in 1980 and would not recommence until the 1990s. There was no progress on the development of industrial

---

[1] In conversation with Bill Chisholm, 25 August 2021.

land in Hawick. Rural depopulation remained an issue, particularly in south-west Roxburghshire and the Ettrick and Yarrow Valleys.

The 1991 Borders Structure Plan was less optimistic than its predecessor. The reform of the EC's Structural Funds put the Scottish Borders at a strong disadvantage compared with neighbouring regions and the Highlands and Islands. The 1990s was a time of uncertainty with a number of operational changes amongst Scotland's principal agencies. The introduction of new legislation and policy statements on the environment raised awareness on climate change and sustainability. However, sustainable economic growth was only possible in the Scottish Borders if more young people could be persuaded to stay and significant numbers of people could be attracted to the area. This was dependent on attracting industry and encouraging the expansion of existing businesses, employment training, the provision of affordable housing and essential infrastructure and community services. After several years of lobbying, the regional council's bid for EC Objective 5(b) status was successful in 1994, opening the way for grant assistance towards a number of community initiatives.

More attention was paid to the rural economy and countryside issues from the 1980s with the switch of EC and government policy from the support of production to diversification, less intensive farming and farm woodlands, which the council considered could threaten the rural economy and the social fabric of rural settlements. Accordingly, the regional council commissioned a number of studies on the impact of the proposed changes and the development opportunities that might result. The first FFWAG in Scotland was established in the Scottish Borders in 1982 with support from the regional council. The Borders Region was one of the first in Scotland to prepare indicative forestry guidelines in response to the increasing awareness of the impact of monoculture tree planting. In collaboration with landowners and farmers, the regional council produced a number of management plans for sensitive countryside areas.

BRC was one of the leading local authorities in Scotland campaigning for a stronger voice for rural communities. Government and EC assistance was very much tied to areas of high unemployment and failed to recognise the problems of rural areas such as the Scottish Borders where the economic structure remained heavily skewed towards lower-skilled and lower-paid jobs, and low-income families facing problems of access to affordable housing, public transport, services and facilities. The region's main industries, textiles and agriculture, remained sensitive to national and international market forces and there were strong indications that job losses in these industries would continue. Recent regional economic trends did not auger well for the future and the regional council continued to argue that the Scottish Borders should be made a Rural Development Area with the same status as the Highlands and Islands where the HIE had a social remit as well as an economic one.

In summary, by 1996, the regional council had up-to-date structure and local plans to guide future development up to the end of the century, with village plans in preparation for almost every settlement in the region, augmented by a range of detailed policy guidance and advice. Regional policies had been prepared on key land uses, such as forestry, mineral working, renewable energy and housing in the countryside. In partnership with SBE, BRC continued to pursue a programme of rural workshop and factory provision, land renewal and rehabilitation projects. With increasing concerns about the effect of development on the environment, the regional council was committed to the principles of sustainable development with the establishment of a Local Agenda 21 Working Group and the Borders Forum on Sustainable Development. Planning policy was very much based on encouraging population growth based on industrial diversification and job creation and the provision of housing for local needs and incoming workers. However, there were emerging concerns over funding with ministerial pronouncements suggesting cutbacks in public spending and projected reductions in spending by SBE and SNH. Furthermore, EC support was on the basis of match funding by the regional council and could be put at risk if matching funds were constrained.[2] There were other concerns: the continuing pressure for housing development in Peeblesshire from the Lothian Housing Market Area; continuing issues of rural depopulation in south-west Roxburghshire and the Ettrick and Yarrow Valleys; the continuing run-down of community facilities in rural areas; the lack of provision of affordable housing; the impact of changes in retailing on the viability and vitality of town centres; and the ability of the council to continue to maintain its range of countryside facilities with increasing tightening of the budget.

---

[2] See Scottish Borders Council, *Report by Director of Planning and Development on provisional Capital Expenditure Programme, 1996/97–2000/01*, Minutes of Meeting of Planning and Development Committee, 8 November 1995.

CHALLENGES TO COME AFTER 1996

Local government reorganisation in 1996, the election of a Labour government in 1997 and the establishment of the Scottish Parliament in 1999 would have far reaching consequences for town and country planning in the Scottish Borders. The Town and Country Planning (Scotland) Act 1997 and the Planning (Listed Buildings and Conservation Areas) (Scotland) Act 1997 served to consolidate legislative changes that had been made since 1972. The Planning etc. (Scotland) Act 2006 would make more drastic changes by introducing the prospect of a spatial plan for Scotland, produced by the Scottish government, to be known as the 'National Planning Framework'. The 2006 Act also introduced Strategic Development Plans (SDP), to be prepared by groups of planning authorities. The establishment of the Edinburgh and South East Scotland Strategic Development Planning Authority, comprising the councils of East Lothian, Edinburgh, Fife (south), Midlothian, West Lothian and the Scottish Borders, would have the effect of removing strategic planning decisions from the new Scottish Borders Council. The 2006 Act also replaced the existing system of structure and local plans by a single local development plan (LDP) for the whole Borders Region.

Further changes to the development plan system were enacted following a review of the Scottish planning system in 2015, when the Scottish government decided that strategic development plans should be replaced by an enhanced National Planning Framework.[3] The subsequent Planning (Scotland) Act 2019 abolished SDPs and replaced them with regional spatial strategies (RSS), which are intended to play a vital role in delivering the national planning strategy at a regional level. However, RSSs will have less status than SDPs for they will not form part of the development plan. Looking ahead, the production of RSSs will provide a number of challenges, not least the need to decide what region the Scottish Borders resides within – Edinburgh and the South East of Scotland or a southern grouping of Dumfries and Galloway and the Scottish Borders. It will also be imperative to engage with stakeholders and, particularly, the public in the process of preparing the future spatial strategy, a major problem with the SES plan prepared by the Edinburgh and South East Scotland Strategic Development Planning Authority in 2013.

---

[3] Purves, G., Strategic Development in Scotland, Submission to UK2070 Commission, April 2019, p. 7.

The 2019 Act also introduced provisions for Local Place Plans (LPPs), produced by local communities, which set out their priorities for the development and use of land in their local area. The LPP will not form part of the development plan but must be taken into account by the planning authority in the preparation of the LDP. Research carried out by RTPI (Scotland) indicates that a considerable amount of funding will be required to facilitate the production of LPPs. Most importantly, support in terms of skills and resources will need to be provided to communities by planning authorities if LPPs are to be effective. According to RTPI (Scotland), in addition to the introduction of RSSs and LPPs, the 2019 Act placed forty-nine new and unfunded additional duties on planning authorities, placing further strain on fragile local authority resources. There is no doubt that additional funding and staff resources are likely to be an issue if the planning service is to continue to function in an effective and efficient manner.

On the economic development front, the role of SBC in economic development continued successfully after 1996, alongside the activities of SBE. There continued to be a strong working relationship between the local authority and SBE which, according to the former Chair of SBE, was somewhat different to experience elsewhere, where local authorities and LECs seemed to be in competition with each other.[4] However, to the consternation of many, the SNP government, elected in 2007, embarked on a restructuring of the enterprise network and abolished LECs, with the majority of their functions transferred to SE, although their remits for local economic development, such as regeneration and small business support, was passed to local authorities. These changes were justified on the grounds of eliminating duplication and unnecessary bureaucracy. However, these reforms reduced the role of SE in economic development at the local level and, according to David Clelland, SE's focus on high growth potential, large firms and national growth sectors led to those firms that do not fit these criteria, which are over-represented in the south of Scotland's business base, being neglected.[5]

In 2016, as part of a review of enterprise and skills, the Scottish government published a report on Regional Partnerships, encouraging regional collaboration. In the same year, the UK government published its Industrial Strategy to boost productivity, create jobs and increase

---

[4] In conversation with Mike Gray, former Chairman of Scottish Borders Enterprise, 22 July 2022.

[5] Clelland, D., *South of Scotland Enterprise – A new approach in the midst of a crisis*, Policy Scotland, 24 April 2020.

earning power with investment in skills, industries and infrastructure. The Edinburgh and South East Scotland City Region Deal was signed by the Prime Minister, First Minister and City Region leaders in August 2018, which amounted to £1.5 billion of investment across the whole area over fifteen years. The development of land at Lowood Estate, acquired by SBC in 2019 to enable the expansion of Tweedbank, would be funded from this budget.

As indicated in earlier chapters, there has been a long-standing perception that the Scottish Borders has lacked the government and EU support given to other areas, such as the Highlands and Islands; indeed, that the whole of the south of Scotland from Stranraer to Eyemouth did not enjoy the same level of national profile and resources as the Highlands despite facing similar challenges of rurality and remoteness. There has been a long campaign for an agency with a broader community development remit like HIE but it would be 2020, following the Scottish government's Enterprise & Skills Review, that South of Scotland Enterprise (SoSE) would be established to drive inclusive growth, increase competitiveness and tackle inequality across the south of Scotland. Many advocates for change have long looked enviously at the wider remit of HIE that encompasses 'social' as well as economic development, and SoSE has been given an overarching aim to sustain and grow communities as well as businesses.

The budget of SoSE is equivalent to HIE on a per capita basis but this must be seen against the reductions in local government funding over past decades when councils have tried to protect essential services such as education and social work (care in the community) and activities such as economic development have been cut back. The budget is also spread across a large geographical area, around 180 miles from east to west, with a large number of relatively small, and sometimes isolated, settlements, which can't really be considered a coherent economic region. Furthermore, linkages between the two local authorities are weak; main roads and rail connections run north–south rather than east–west. There may well be pressure to share funding or projects across the region, and support a more diverse set of interventions, spreading the organisation's resources too thinly. We shall have to see!

To cement the relationship between the two local authorities and the new enterprise company, in October 2019, SBC agreed to support the establishment of the South of Scotland Regional Economic Partnership, in partnership with Dumfries and Galloway Council, SoSE and a range of business interests. According to Clelland, the creation of SoSE represents one of the biggest changes in the economic development landscape in Scotland for many years and, alongside the creation of Regional Economic Partnerships and Growth Deals, signals a shift towards a greater concern with what the Scottish government calls 'regional equity', equivalent to levelling up in England. However, at present, there are too many overlapping and competing initiatives and a mismatch between the objectives of local government and the UK and Scottish governments.

LAST WORDS

The modern British planning system reached its half-century in 1997. During this time, the economic, social and political contexts changed considerably. Whilst the fundamental purpose of planning remained constant, there was a radical change in planning practice. The planning system in 1947 was based on the premise that the majority of proposals in development plans would be implemented by the public sector with the private sector regulated by development control. By the 1980s, the private sector had emerged as a major force in deciding the type and quantity of development that would take place and planning departments were required to work more closely with other partners and the private sector. Government policy in the 1990s placed the emphasis of the planning system on facilitating new development in an expanding and increasingly competitive economy, including the contribution of the planning system to sustainable economic growth. In the 1950s and 1960s public participation did not exist. In 1990, there was a formal requirement for public participation in the preparation of development plans and in development control. There was a more positive attitude to community involvement in planning.

In 1947, although development plans required to be approved by the SoS, planning authorities had a considerable degree of independence over the content of local planning policies. Approval by the SoS was required to ensuring that proper procedures had been followed rather than to impose national planning policy. Over the years, intervention by central government has increased through the preparation of NPGs, NPPGs and PANs, laying down specific guidelines and guidance on a range of policies, which planning authorities must have regard to, otherwise they risked development control decisions being overturned on appeal. Furthermore, the capacity of local authorities to undertake the implementation of their development plans on their own reduced as local authorities came to rely more and more on central government grants and capital expenditure was subject to government approval.

Increasingly, planning authorities had to rely on additional sources of finance to implement proposals, whether from government agencies, such as the SDA (later SE) and SNH, or European funds. Indeed, there was a growing influence of the EC in the stream of directives on regional policy and the environment.

This examination of town and country planning in the Scottish Borders during the period 1946–1996 has reinforced these themes. During this period the Scottish Borders was transformed from a rural backwater to be at the forefront of rural development policy. The practice of town and country planning in the Scottish Borders was transformed from a mainly regulatory system, based on the preparation of county development plans and development control, to a dynamic, proactive activity involved in not only development planning and development control but also economic development and promotion, project design and implementation, urban conservation, rural heritage and countryside management. The Planning and Development Department more than doubled in size and embraced new technology. Its multi-disciplinary nature reflected its responsibilities for a wide range of functions and its position at the centre of the regional council's responsibilities. Partnerships with a wide range of organisations and a co-ordinated approach enabled schemes beyond the capabilities of the planning authority alone to be implemented in both town and country. As the decades progressed, there was an increasing involvement of the public in planning policy and decision-making, in the preparation of development plans and in the process of development control.

Following the reorganisation of local government in 1996, there would be new relationships and new challenges driving the way planning would be practised in the Scottish Borders: amongst them, continuing demographic change, climate change and the requirement for sustainable economic growth. Would town and country planning be able to remain a leading player in meeting these challenges? Perhaps, another book.

Appendices

Appendix 1a: Department of Physical Planning, December 1975   271
Appendix 1b: Department of Physical Planning and
    Development, 1978   272
Appendix 1c: Department of Physical Planning and
    Development, 1983   273
Appendix 1d: Department of Planning and Development, 1988   274
Appendix 1e: Department of Planning and Development, 1993   275
Appendix 2: Scottish Borders Council Archive Sources   276
Appendix 3: BRC (Planning & Development Department)
    Publications   285
Appendix 4: Selected Scottish Office Guidance on Town and
    Country Planning   288
Appendix 5: BRC (P & D Dept) Industrial Properties
    (1 January 1988)   295
Appendix 6: SDA Properties in the Borders Region
    (1 January 1988)   300

Appendix 1a: Department of Physical Planning, December 1975

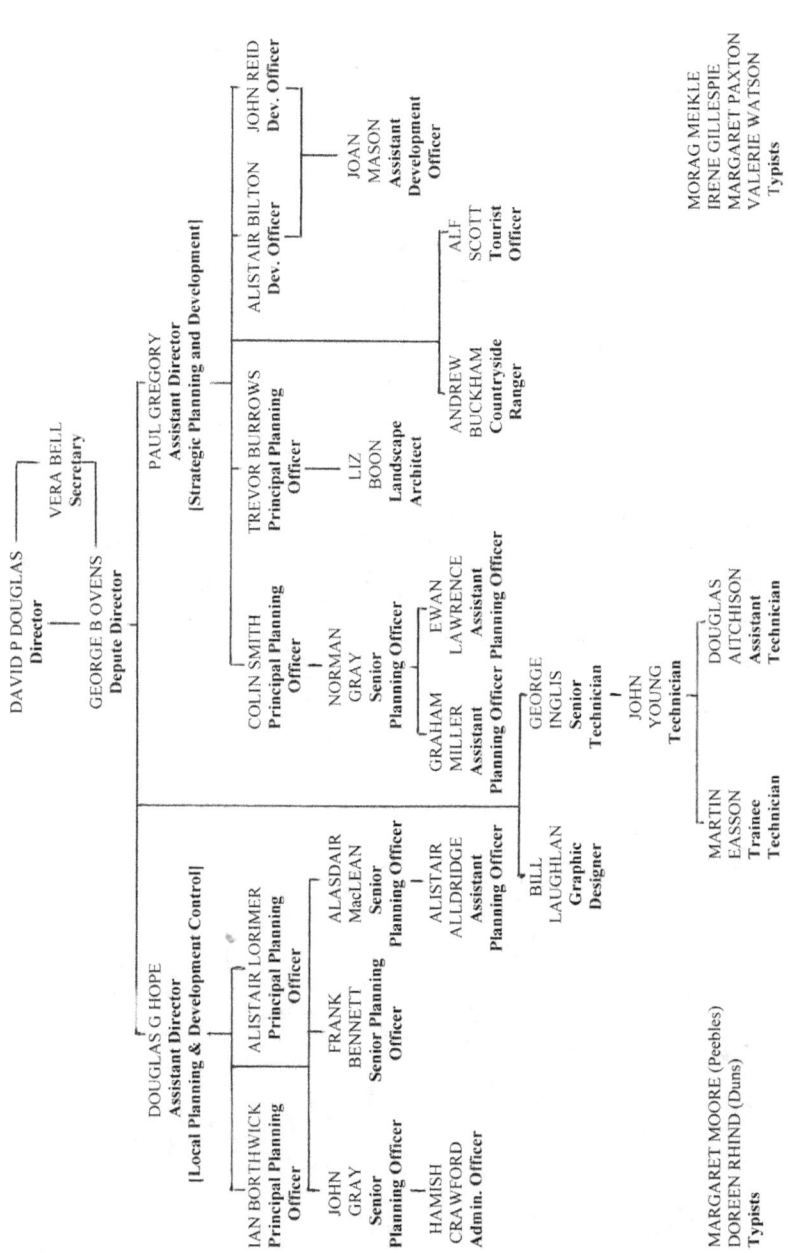

Appendix 1b: Department of Physical Planning and Development, 1978

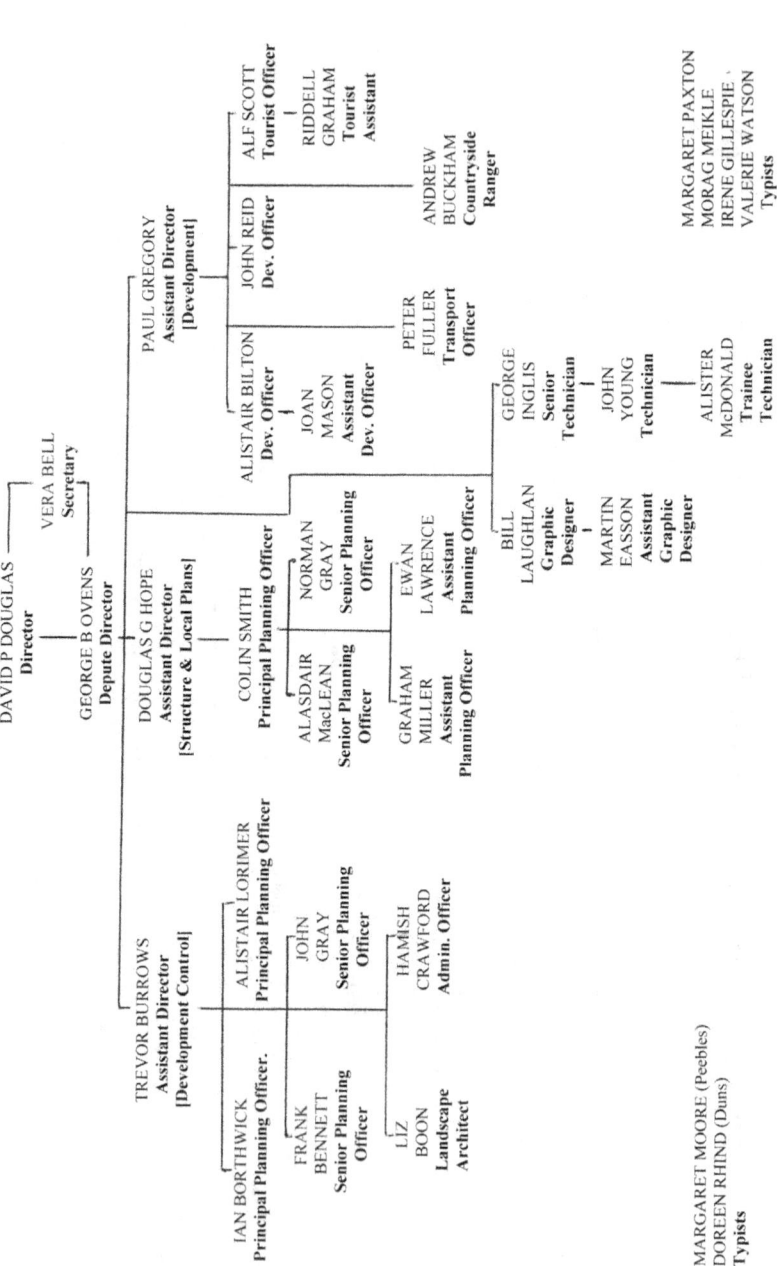

Appendix 1c: Department of Physical Planning and Development, 1983

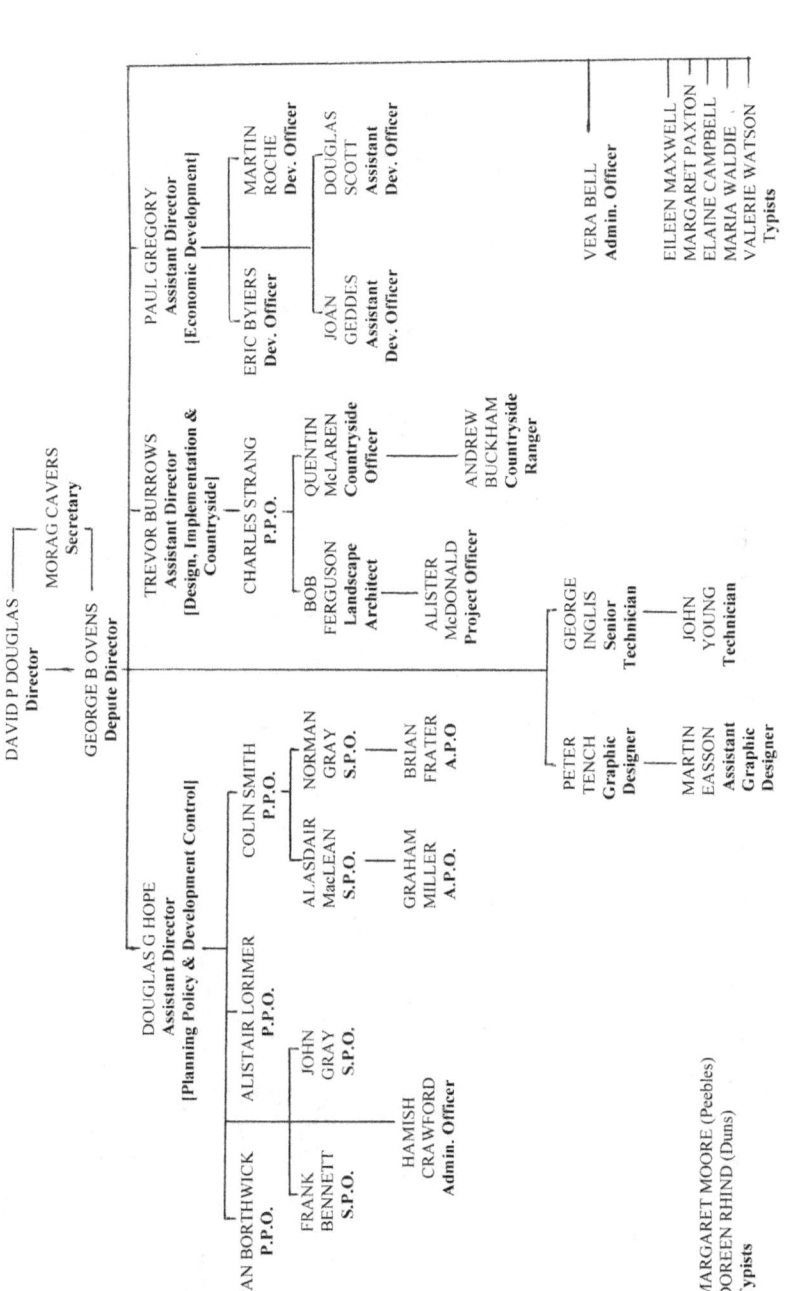

Appendix 1d: Department of Planning and Development, 1988

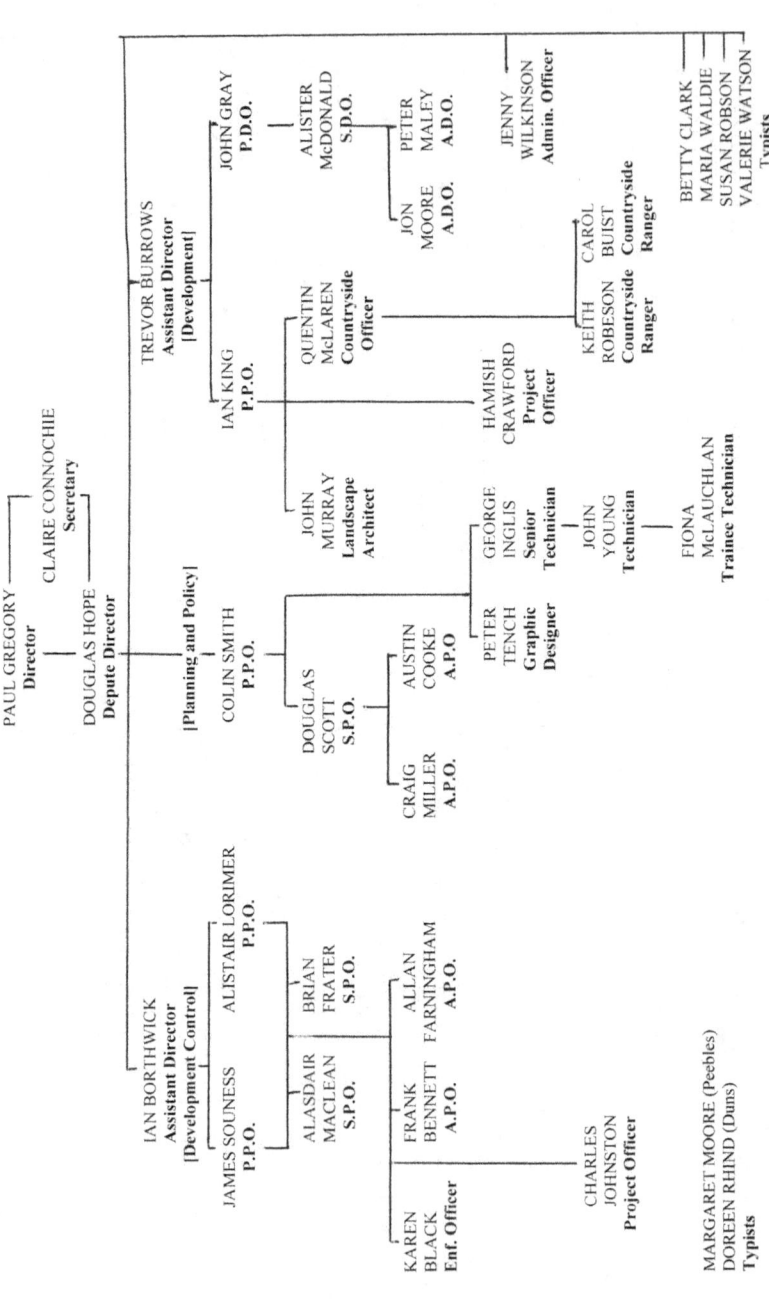

Appendix 1e: Department of Planning and Development, 1993

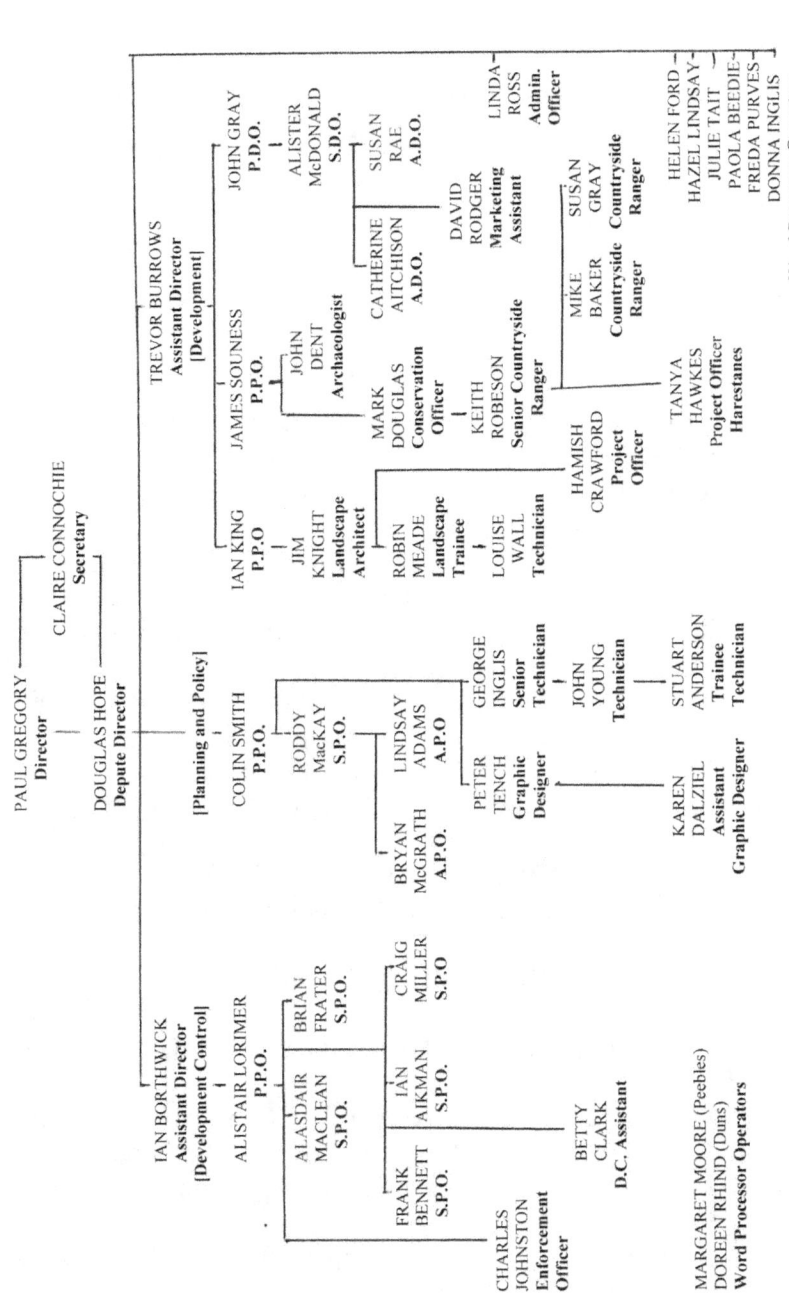

Appendix 2: Scottish Borders Council Archive Sources

COMMITTEE MINUTES AND PAPERS

S/CD/1/16-1/39	Minutes Selkirkshire CC, 1944–1967
S/CD/1/40-1/47	Committee Minutes, Selkirkshire CC, 1967–1975
S/CD/3	Quinquennial Review Selkirkshire Dev. Plan 1964
S/CD/9/1-9/3	Selkirk Clerks Dept Planning appl. and decisions 1944–1975
R/CD/1/72	Minutes of Roxburgh Property & Works Committee, 1953–1967
R/CD/1/76-1/80	Minutes Roxburgh Planning Committee, Feb. 1944–Apr. 1975
R/CD/1/119-1/120	Scottish Border Local Authority Joint Committee, Jan. 1972–Apr. 1974
see also R/CD/38/1	SBLAJC, Jun. 1972–May 1974
R/CD/38/2	SBLAJC Co-ordination Group-1, Jan. 1973–Jun. 1973
R/CD/38/3	SBLAJC Co-ordination Group-2, Jul. 1973–Nov. 1973
R/CD/38/4	SBLAJC Co-ordination Group Circulars
R/CD/1/121	Roxburghshire Countryside Committee
R/CD/37	Minutes of Peebles, Roxburgh and Selkirk Planning Advisory Committee, Dec. 1967–Sept. 1974
R/CD/39/1	Roxburgh CC: Register of planning decisions 1963–1975
R/CD/39/2	Roxburgh CC: File register of planning decisions 1948–1962

R/CD/39/3	Roxburgh CC: Planning applications (56 items)
B/CD/1/134-141	Berwickshire Minutes Planning Committee, Jun. 1944–Apr. 1970
B/CD/1/142	Berwickshire Minutes Planning Committee, Apr. 1970–Apr. 1973
B/CD/1/143	Berwickshire Minutes Planning Committee, Jun. 1973–Apr. 1975
B/CD/9	County of Berwick Development plan 1958–1960
B/CD/12/1	Berwickshire planning applications and decisions 1944–1958
B/CD/12/2	Berwickshire planning applications and decisions 1958–1967
B/CD/12/3	Berwickshire planning applications and decisions 1967–1972
B/CD/12/4	Berwickshire planning applications and decisions 1972–1975
B/CD/12/5	Berwickshire Planning Files 1946–1988
P/CD/1/8-1/38	Peebles County Council minutes, 1948–1949 to 1974–1975
P/CD/29	Peeblesshire County Development Plan 1955
P/CD/30/1	Peeblesshire Register of planning decisions, 1948–1958
P/CD/30/2	Peeblesshire Register of planning decisions, 1958–1976
BRC/5/1-20	BRC P & D Committee minutes, 1974–1996
BRC/5/21-43	BRC, P & D Committee agendas and supporting papers, 1975–1996
BRC/5/60-64	BRC Development Control Sub-committee minutes, 1975–1982
BRC/5/65	BRC Industrial Dev. Sub-committee minutes, 1975–1982
BRC/5/67	BRC Tourism Sub-committee minutes, 1975–1982
BRC/5/83	BRC Industrial Dev. Sub-committee agendas & supporting papers, 1977–1982
BRC/5/85	BRC Tourism sub-committee agendas and supporting papers, 1977–1982
BRC/5/86	BRC Forestry Advisory Group agendas and supporting papers, 1992

BRC/5/87	BRC Forestry Advisory Group agendas and supporting papers, 1993
BRC/5/88	BRC Forestry Advisory Group agendas and supporting papers, 1994

REPORTS

Town and country planning: Scottish Borders pre-1975

SBA/1210/1	Regional Survey & Plan for Central and South-East Scotland, 1946
SBA/1210/2	Selkirk County Development Plan, approved Apr. 1955
SBA/1210/3	Peebles County Development Plan, approved Dec. 1955
SBA/1210/4	Roxburgh County Development Plan, approved Feb. 1965 (4 items)
SBA/1210/5	Berwick County Development Plan, approved Feb. 1965
SBA/1210/6	White Paper; The Scottish Economy 1965–1970: a Plan for Expansion, Jan. 1966
SBA/1210/7	Roxburgh County Development Plan Amendments
SBA/1210/8	Selkirk County Development Plan Quinquennial Review
SBA/1210/9	Central Borders Plan for Expansion by SDD, 1968
SBA/1210/10/1	Central Borders Housing and Industry Survey, Regional Planning Unit, Feb. 1974
SBA/1210/10/2	A Profile of the Borders 1974, Interim Report of Regional Planning Unit
SBA/1210/10/3	The Borders Region 1975, Regional Planning Unit

Town and country planning: Scottish Borders post-1975

SBA/1210/10/4	Regional Report 1976, Borders Regional Council
SBA/1210/11	Borders Region Structure Plan reports (12 items), 1979–1981
SBA/1210/12	Galashiels-Tweedbank Local Plan Written Statement, adopted Jun. 1981

SBA/1210/13	Eyemouth Local Plan Written Statement, adopted Oct. 1981
SBA/1210/14	Hawick Local Plan Written Statement, adopted Nov. 1981
SBA/1210/15	Kelso Local Plan Written Statement, adopted Jul. 1982
SBA/1210/16	Selkirk Local Plan Written Statement, adopted Aug. 1983
SBA/1210/17	Peebles Local Plan Written Statement, adopted Dec. 1983
SBA/1210/18	Jedburgh Local Plan Written Statement, adopted Oct.1984
SBA/1210/19	Ettrick & Lauderdale North Local Plan Written Statement, adopted May 1985
SBA/1210/20	Tweeddale (Part) Local Plan Written Statement, adopted Dec. 1986
SBA/1210/21	Berwickshire (Part) Local Plan Written Statement, adopted Dec. 1986
SBA/1210/22	Roxburgh (Part) Local Plan Written Statement, adopted Dec. 1988
SBA/1210/23	Ettrick Forest Local Plan Written Statement, adopted Dec. 1987
SBA/1210/24	Scottish Borders Structure Plan, approved Nov. 1993
SBA/1210/25	Roxburgh Local Plan Written Statement, adopted May 1995
SBA/1210/26	Berwickshire Local Plan Written Statement, adopted Nov. 1994
SBA/1210/27	Ettrick and Lauderdale Local Plan Written Statement, adopted Jul. 1995
SBA/1210/28	Tweeddale Local Plan Written Statement, adopted Jun. 1996
SBA/1210/29	Ettrick and Lauderdale Village Plans, Mar. 1996
SBA/1210/30	Berwickshire Village Plans, Sept. 1995
SBA/1210/31	Roxburgh Village Plans, Feb. 1996
SBA/1210/32	Tweeddale Village Plans, Apr. 1997

County of Roxburgh, planning reports

SBA/1210/33/1	Report of Technical Working Party, Burgh of Jedburgh, 1964

SBA/1210/33/2	Report on AGLVs and Tourist Development, Roxburgh County Planning Department, Feb. 1965
SBA/1210/33/3	Melrose Technical Working Party Report, 1966
SBA/1210/33/4	Burgh of Kelso Working Party Report, 1968
SBA/1210/33/5	Bowden Village Study, Roxburgh County Planning Department, Mar. 1969
SBA/1210/33/6	Report by SSHA for Tweedbank Working Party, Jun. 1969
SBA/1210/33/7	St Boswells Report by Roxburgh CC, Sept. 1969
SBA/1210/33/8	Town Extension, Jedburgh by Jedburgh Technical Working Party, Feb. 1970
SBA/1210/33/9	Future Development of Gattonside, Roxburgh County Planning Department, Dec. 1971
SBA/1210/33/10	Burgh of Kelso policy statement, Feb. 1972
SBA/1210/33/11	Roxburgh Landward Community Development Strategy, 1972
SBA/1210/33/12	Hawick Technical Working Party report, 1973 (2 volumes)
SBA/1210/33/13	Newcastleton Rural Planning Study, Edinburgh College of Art, 1966
SBA/1210/33/14	Howegate/Drumlanrig Square proposals, Mar. 1975
SBA/1210/33/15	Social Survey of Hawick by A.M. Struthers, Scottish Council of Social Service, Aug. 1944
SBA/1210/33/16	Lilliardsedge Aerodrome, planning report, May 1972

County of Berwick, planning reports

SBA/1210/34/1	Report on Areas of Great Landscape Value and Tourist Development
SBA/1210/34/2	Eyemouth Industrial Estate Report, Aug. 1969
SBA/1210/34/3	Burgh of Duns, Report of Technical Working Party, Aug. 1970
SBA/1210/34/4	Earlston Population and Employment, Sept. 1971
SBA/1210/34/5	Draft Rural Policy for Berwickshire, Mar. 1972
SBA/1210/34/6	Tourism and Recreation in Berwickshire, Oct. 1973
SBA/1210/34/7	Housing and Industry in Berwickshire, Jan. 1974

APPENDICES 281

SBA/1210/34/8   Chirnside Village: an appraisal of its problems
                     and potential, May 1974
SBA/1210/34/9   Agriculture in Berwickshire, Jul. 1974
SBA/1210/34/10   Coldingham Bay Recreation Management Study,
                     Aug. 1974
SBA/1210/34/11   Greenlaw Report, Oct. 1974
SBA/1210/34/12   Conservation Area Policy, Jun. 1973
SBA/1210/34/13   Master plan for urban renewal of Eyemouth
                     Harbour, 1970.

County of Selkirk, planning reports

SBA/1210/35/1   Hollybush, Galashiels, Jan. 1967
SBA/1210/35/2   Galashiels Technical Working Party, Housing
                     Report
SBA/1210/35/3   Galashiels Technical Working Party, Interim
                     Report, 1970
SBA/1210/35/4   Galashiels Technical Working Party, Second
                     Report, Jan. 1973
SBA/1210/35/5   County of Selkirk, Areas of Great Landscape
                     Value and Tourist Development, 1974
SBA/1210/35/6   Yarrow & Ettrick Valleys: A Settlement Study,
                     Mar. 1975
SBA/1210/35/7   Proceedings of working conference; The New
                     Galashiels, 1967

County of Peebles, planning reports

SBA/1210/36/1   Peeblesshire: Mears Report 1946 [LIB/1447]
SBA/1210/36/2   Peeblesshire County Planning: Population,
                     Jan. 1950
SBA/1210/36/3   Peeblesshire County Planning: Employment &
                     Industry, Jan. 1950
SBA/1210/36/4   Royal Burgh of Peebles Growth Plan, 1969
SBA/1210/36/5   Peeblesshire Population, Peeblesshire CC, 1968?
SBA/1210/36/6   Royal Burgh of Peebles Proposed Urban
                     Structure Plan, 1969
SBA/1210/36/7   Eddleston Village Study, 1974
SBA/1210/36/8   Peeblesshire Tourist Development Proposals
                     and AGLVs, Dec. 1966 & Apr. 1967 (approved
                     Jun. 1968)

SBA/1210/36/9   Pentland Hills Conservation and Recreation Report, Sept. 1972

Other reports, pre-1975

SBA/1210/37/1   Interim Report on Population Trends etc., Frank Mears, Mar. 1945
SBA/1210/37/2   Depopulation and rural life in the Tweed Valley, Social Survey by Bertram Hutchinson, Dept of Health for Scotland, Jul. 1949
SBA/1210/37/3   Midlothian County Development Plan Survey Report, Written Statement and Policy & Assumptions, Jul. 1956 (3 reports)
SBA/1210/37/4   The Borders Region, University of Edinburgh, Mar. 1974
SBA/1210/37/5   Eastern Borders Development Agency Constitution, 23 Jun. 1966
SBA/1210/37/6   Eastern Borders Development Association Records, 1966–1977 [D/5]
SBA/1210/37/7   Dev. Plans: Various Coloured & Zoned map and plans for Roxburgh, Berwickshire and Selkirkshire and major towns 1960–1971 [SBA/962]

Other reports, 1975–1996

SBA/1210/38/1   Riding routes in the Hawick area, BRC, Nov. 1977
SBA/1210/38/2   Recreation and Tourism, BRC, Apr. 1978
SBA/1210/38/3   Courier Service Feasibility Study, Interim Report, 1976–1979
SBA/1210/38/4   Galashiels Walkway, Project Review, WJ Cairns & Partners, Feb. 1980
SBA/1210/38/5   St Mary's Loch/Tweedsmuir Hills Management Plan, 1980 [SBA/353/38]
SBA/1210/38/6   Scottish Tourism and Recreation Planning Studies: Borders Region, 1981
SBA/1210/38/7   Scottish Tourism and Recreation Planning Studies: Borders Region, 1980
SBA/1210/38/8   The effect of the loss of development area status on the Borders Region, Jul. 1980
SBA/1210/38/9   The Borders Region: the case for continued regional development assistance, Jan. 1982

SBA/1210/38/10	Pilot Rural Development Areas Study, Oct. 1986
SBA/1210/38/11	Agricultural Development Opportunities in the Scottish Borders, Dec. 1986
SBA/1210/38/12	A Study of Whitchester Estate, Berwickshire, ASH, Jul. 1987
SBA/1210/38/13	A Study of Whitchester Estate, Berwickshire, Exec. Summary, ASH, Jul. 1987
SBA/1210/38/14	Galashiels Development Study 1989 [Roger Tym & Partners]
SBA/1210/38/15	Area Sustainability Study of Ettrick and Lauderdale, SNH, 1994
SBA/1210/38/17	A Renewable Energy Development Strategy for the Borders Region of Scotland, Garrad Hassan and Partners, 1995
SBA/1210/38/18	Qualitative Research on Shopping in the Borders Region, System Three Scotland, September 1989
SBA/1210/38/20	Borders Region Shopping Survey, BRC, May 1989
SBA/1210/38/21	The Changing Borders Countryside, SAC, Mar. 1991
SBA/1210/38/22	Jedburgh Traffic and Environmental Proposals for Central Area, BRC, May 1976
SBA/1210/38/23	Town Centre Management Business Plan 1995–1996 for Hawick and Galashiels, BRC, 1995
SBA/1210/38/25	Sustainable Development in the Borders Region, BRC, 1995
SBA/1210/38/26	Roxburgh for Development Opportunities (Marketing Pack) [SBA/353/33]
SBA/1210/38/27	Forestry and Woodlands in the Scottish Borders, March 1987

Borders Regional Council, Planning and Development Department

BRC/PD/1	Annual reports, 1987–1995 (8 items)
BRC/PD/2	Borders Region in Figures, 1984–1995
BRC/PD/3	Summary of statistics about the Borders, 1975
BRC/PD/4	Electronics in the Scottish Borders, 1988–1993 (2 volumes)
BRC/PD/5	Textile Guides, 1990, 1992 & 1994

BRC/PD/6	Buyers Guide to food and drink 'Taste of the Scottish Borders', 1989–1993
BRC/PD/7	Buyers Guide, gifts and crafts in the Scottish Borders, 1991 & 1994
BRC/PD/8	Arts and Indoor Sports in the Borders Region, 1975
BRC/PD/9	Scottish Borders Business Directory, 1986
BRC/PD/12	Annual Economic Development Reports, 1984–1985
BRC/PD/17	Economic Bulletin, 1991–1995
BRC/PD/18	The Scottish Borders: Our Way of Life, 1986 & 1990
BRC/PD/19	New Housing in the Borders Countryside, Dec. 1993
BRC/PD/20	Report on Organisation and Staffing in the Planning and Development Department, Dec. 1977
BRC/PD/22	Scottish Borders Business Directory, 1992
BRC/PD/23	Leaflet 'Shop Fronts and Shop Signs', 1991
BRC/PD/24	Publications of the Borders Regional Council Planning and Development Department, Jun. 1993

Appendix 3: BRC (Planning & Development Department) Publications

POLICY PLANS

Regional Report 1976
Borders Region Structure Plan: Report of Survey 1978
Borders Region Structure Plan: Written Statement 1980 (reprinted 1982 & 1987)
Eyemouth Local Plan: Written Statement 1981
Galashiels/Tweedbank Local Plan: Written Statement 1981
Hawick Local Plan: Written Statement 1981
Kelso Local Plan: Written Statement 1982
Selkirk Local Plan: Written Statement 1983
Peebles Local Plan: Written Statement 1983
Jedburgh Local Plan: Written Statement 1984
Ettrick & Lauderdale North Local Plan Written Statement 1985
Berwickshire (Part) Local Plan: Written Statement 1985
Tweeddale (Part) Local Plan: Written Statement 1986
Ettrick Forest Local Plan: Written Statement 1987
Roxburgh (Part) Local Plan: Written Statement 1989
The Scottish Borders 2001: The Way Forward: Report of Survey 1991
The Scottish Borders 2001: The Way Forward: Structure Plan Written Statement 1993
Berwickshire Local Plan: Written Statement 1994
Ettrick & Lauderdale Local Plan: Written Statement 1995
Roxburgh Local Plan: Written Statement 1995
Tweeddale Local Plan: Written Statement 1996
Berwickshire Village Plans: Sept. 1995
Roxburgh Village Plans: Feb. 1996
Ettrick and Lauderdale Village Plans: Mar. 1996
Tweeddale Village Plans: Apr. 1997

Renewable Energy Development Strategy for the Borders Region of Scotland, 1995
Sustainable Development in the Borders Region, 1995
Annual Reports 1987–1994/95

ECONOMIC DEVELOPMENT

The Scottish Borders – Our Way of Life, 1986 & 1990
Borders Region in Figures (Annual)
Scottish Borders Business Directory (Annual)
Scottish Borders Business Post (Quarterly)
Borders Economic Bulletins (Monthly)
Tweeddale: where lifestyles prosper with business 1987
Scottish Borders Knitwear Buyers Guide 1987 &1989
Electronics in the Scottish Borders (a guide to products and services) 1988 & 1993
A Taste of the Scottish Borders (a buyers' guide to food and drink) 1989 & 1993
Crafts in the Scottish Borders 1989
Roxburgh for Development Opportunities 1989
A Buyers' Guide to Gifts and Crafts made in the Scottish Borders 1991
The Borders Collection (a buyers' guide to textiles from the Scottish Borders) 1992 & 1994
Tweeddale: Quality in Life and Quality in Business 1992
Finance for Small Business: leaflet on FSB Scheme (1992)
Borders Region Development: The Effect of the Loss of Development Area Status 1980
The Borders Region: The Case for Continued Regional Development Assistance 1982
Review of Assisted Areas of Great Britain: The Case for Borders Region, 1992
Conference on Rural Development Future Strategies, 1991
Forestry and Woodlands in the Borders Region, 1987
Pilot Rural Development Area Study, 1987
Agricultural Development Opportunities in the Scottish Borders, 1987
The Changing Borders Countryside – A Review of Agriculture in the Borders Region of Scotland, 1991
Common Agricultural Policy Reform and its impact on the Borders Region of Scotland, 1992

COUNTRYSIDE

Countryside Leaflets (continually updated) on:

    Ranger-Led Walks
    Cove Harbour
    Lindean Reservoir
    Hawick Circular Horse Riding Route
    Southern Upland Way
    Farming, Forestry & Wildlife Group
    Giant Hogweed
    Rights of Way
    Waymarking Public Paths
    Eildon Hills
    Ranger Service
    Countryside Walks (8)
    Legerwood Farm Trail

Lindean Reservoir Management Plan, 1979
St Mary's Loch/Tweedsmuir Hills Management Plan, 1980
Selkirk Hill Management Plan, 1986
Alemoor and Watch Water Reservoirs Management Plan, 1986
Eildon Hills Recreational Management Plan, 1987
Borders Tree Grant Scheme, 1988
Eildon/Leaderfoot NSA Management Plan, 1989
Archaeology in the Borders – Advice to Developers, 1991
Archaeology in the Borders – Advice to Farmers, 1991
Ranger Led Walks and Countryside Activities, 1994/95
Tweed Cycleway, 1995
Harestanes Countryside Visitor Centre, 1995

DEVELOPMENT CONTROL

Guidance on Tourist Signposting in the Scottish Borders, 1987 & 1993
Building Around Disability in the Scottish Borders, 1987
Replacement Windows Advice Note, 1988
Planning Applications and Community Councils Guidance Note, 1988
Hawick Towerknowe/Backdamgate Redevelopment, 1989
Shop Fronts and Shop Signs, 1991
Minerals Review Report, 1993
New Housing in the Borders Countryside – Policy and Guidance Note, 1993

Appendix 4: Selected Scottish Office Guidance on Town and Country Planning

PLANNING CIRCULARS AND MEMORANDA

<u>Circular No.</u>   <u>Title</u>

[Issued by Department of Health for Scotland]
40/1960   Green Belts and New Houses in the Country

[Issued by Scottish Development Department]
10/1961   Town and Country Planning (Control of Advertisements) (Scotland) Regulations 1961
2/1962   Development Plans: Areas of Great Landscape Value and Tourist Development Proposals
27/1965 and Memorandum   Petrol Filling Stations
36/1970   Town and Country Planning (Scotland) Act 1969
49/1971   Publicity for Planning Proposals (updated 59/1974)
65/1971   Town and Country Planning (Minerals) (Scotland) Regulations 1971
92/1972   Disused Railway Lines in the Countryside
94/1972   Town and Country Planning (Scotland) Act 1972
116/1972   General Information System for Planning
23/1973 and Memorandum   Planning and Noise
68/1973   Town and Country Planning (Use Classes) (Scotland) Order 1973
59/1974   Publicity for Planning Proposals (associated with 49/1971)
61/1974   North Sea Oil and Gas: Coastal Planning Guidelines
71/1974   Forest Policy: Consultation with Planning Authorities

14/1975 and Memorandum	Public Inquiry Procedures
77/1975	Development of Agricultural Land – Consultations with DAFS Land Staff etc.
87/1975	Town and Country Amenities Act 1974: Tree Preservation Orders and Trees in Conservation Areas (amended by circular 7/1984)
126/1975	Town and Country Planning (Listed Buildings and Buildings in Conservation Areas) (Scotland) Regulations 1975
4/1976	Listed Building and Conservation (amended by circular 28/1980)
8/1976	National Land Use Classification
28/1976	Structure and Local Plans
42/1976	Compulsory Purchase Procedures
74/1976	Town and Country Planning (General) (Scotland) Regulations 1976
19/1977	National Planning Guidelines: Petro-chemical Developments; Large Industrial Sites and Rural Conservation (amended by circular 20/1980)
42/1977	Code of Practice for Local Plan Inquiries and Hearings (superseded by circular 7/1985)
43/1977	Code of Practice for Examinations in Public of Structure Plans (superseded by circular 6/1985)
51/1977	National Planning Guidelines: Aggregates
56/1977	Nature Conservation and Planning
38/1978	Consultation with the Royal Fine Art Commission for Scotland (superseded by circular 24/1986)
65/1978	National Planning Guidelines: Location of Major Shopping Developments
20/1980	Development Control in National Scenic Areas (superseded by circular 9/1987)
46/1980	Local Government, Planning and Land Act 1980
47/1980	Town and Country Planning (Determination of Appeals by Appointed Persons) (Prescribed Classes) (Scotland) Regulations 1980; Town and Country Planning (Inquiries Procedure) (Scotland) Rules 1980; Town and Country Planning Appeals (Determination by Appointed Person) (Inquiries Procedure) (Scotland) Rules 1980

24/1981	Development Control (partially replaced by circular 6/1984)
31/1981	Town and Country Planning (Tree Preservation Order and Trees in Conservation Areas) (Scotland) Amendment Regulations 1981
5/1982	Town and Country Planning (Minerals) Act 1981
29/1982	Local Government and Planning (Scotland) Act 1982: Planning Provisions
1/1983	Code of Guidance on Sites of Special Scientific Interest
32/1983	Structure and Local Plans (amended by circular 7/1985)
33/1983	Town and Country Planning (Fees for Applications and Deemed Applications) (Scotland) Regulations 1983
6/1984	Local Government and Planning (Scotland) Act 1982
7/1984	Forestry: A-Consultation with Local Authorities; B-Town and Country Planning (Tree Preservation Order and Trees in Conservation Areas) (Scotland) Amendment Regulations 1984
10/1984	Town and Country Planning (Control of Advertisements) (Scotland) Regulations 1984
22/1984	Town and Country Planning (Scotland) Act 1972: Section 50 Agreements
26/1984	Town and Country Planning (Scotland) Act 1972: Planning Appeals
6/1985	Code of Practice for Examinations in Public of Structure Plans
7/1985	Code of Practice for Local Plan Inquiries and Hearings
17/1985	Development Control: Priorities and Procedures
24/1985	Development in the Countryside and Green Belts
25/1985	Telecommunications Development
18/1986	The Use of Conditions in Planning Permissions
22/1986	Directional Advertising Signs for Tourist Attractions and Facilities
24/1986	Consultation with the Royal Fine Art Commission for Scotland
37/1986	Housing and Planning Act 1986
38/1986	The Location of Major Retail Developments (amended by circular 29/1988)

9/1987	Development Control in National Scenic Areas
16/1987	Housing and Planning Act 1986: Simplified Planning Zones
17/1987	Listed Buildings and Conservation Areas (new provisions and revised guidance); Memorandum of Guidance on Listed Buildings and Conservation Areas 1987
18/1987	Development involving Agricultural Land (amended by circular 29/1988)
13/1988	Environmental Assessment: Implementation of EC Directive. The Environmental Assessment (Scotland) Regulations 1988
26/1988	Environmental Assessment of Projects in Simplified Planning Zones and Enterprise Zones
29/1988	Notification of Applications
6/1989	The Town and Country Planning (Use Classes) (Scotland) Order 1989
7/1990	The Town and Country Planning Appeals (Written Submissions Procedure) (Scotland) Regulations 1990
13/1990	Indicative Forestry Strategies
17/1990	Caravan sites and Control of Development Act 1960: Model Standards
5/1992	The Town and Country Planning (General Permitted Development) (Scotland) Order 1992
6/1992	The Town and Country Planning (General Development Procedue) (Scotland) Order 1992
8/1992	Planning and Compensation Act 1991: Enforcing Planning Control
9/1992	Planning and Compensation Act 1991: Enforcement of Tree Preservation Orders
10/1992	Planning and Compensation Act 1991: Control of 'Fly Posting'
31/1992	Planning and Compensation Act 1991: Control over Advertisements and Fish Farming
18/1995	Simplified Planning Zones
10/1996	Town and Country Planning (Development contrary to Development Plans) (Scotland) Direction 1996
16/1996	National Planning Policy Guideline (NPPG) 8: Retailing
32/1996	Code of Practice for Local Plan Inquiries

NATIONAL PLANNING GUIDELINES (NPG)

NPG1:	North Sea Oil and Gas: Coastal Planning Guidelines, 1974
NPG2:	Aggregate Working, 1977
NPG3:	Priorities for Development Planning (covering agricultural land; land for housing; land for large industry and petrochemical developments; rural planning priorities; National Scenic Areas; nature conservation; the coast; aggregate working; and forestry), 1981
NPG4:	Skiing developments, 1984
NPG5:	High Technology: Individual High Amenity Sites, 1985
NPG6:	Location of Major Retail Developments, 1986
NPG7:	Agricultural Land, 1987

NATIONAL PLANNING POLICY GUIDELINES (NPPG)

NPPG1:	The Planning System, 1993
NPPG2:	Business and Industry, 1993
NPPG3:	Land for Housing, 1993; revised 1996
NPPG4:	Land for Mineral Working, 1994
NPPG5:	Archaeology and Planning, 1994
NPPG6:	Renewable Energy, 1994
NPPG7:	Planning and Flooding, 1995
NPPG8:	Town Centres and Retailing, 1996
NPPG9:	The Provision of Roadside Facilities on Motorways and Other Trunk Roads in Scotland, 1996
NPPG10:	Planning and Waste Management, 1996
NPPG11:	Sport, Physical Recreation and Open Space, 1996
NPPG12:	Skiing Developments, 1997
NPPG13:	Coastal Planning, 1997
NPPG14:	Natural Heritage, 1999
NPPG15:	Rural Development, 1999
NPPG16:	Opencast Coal and Related Matters, 1999
NPPG17:	Transport and Planning, 1999
NPPG18:	Planning and the Historic Environment, 1999

PLANNING ADVICE NOTES (PAN)

PAN1*	Agriculture in Scotland (July 1975)
PAN2*	Forestry Guidelines (July 1975)
PAN3*	The Countryside (July 1975)

PAN4*	Forecasting Employment for Regional Reports and Structure Plans (July 1975)
PAN5*	Planning for Sports, Outdoor Recreation and Tourism (September 1975)
PAN6*	National Coal Board Scottish Areas (August 1975)
PAN7*	Planning and Electricity (August 1975)
PAN8*	Demographic Analysis for Planning Purposes (July 1975)
PAN9*	Nature Conservation guidelines (August 1975)
PAN10*	British Rail (August 1975)
PAN12*	The Scottish Fishing Industry (October 1975)
PAN13*	Planning and Geology (December 1975)
PAN17	High Pressure Methane Gas Pipelines (June 1977)
PAN19	Publicity & Consultations in Structure & Local Plans (1978)
PAN22	Social Surveys (June 1978)
PAN23	Scottish Economic Monograph 1978 (December 1978)
PAN24	Design Guidance (April 1980)
PAN25	Commercial Pipelines (November 1980)
PAN26	Disposal of Land and the Use of the Developer's Brief (February 1981)
PAN27	Structure Planning (November 1981)
PAN29	Planning and Small Businesses (November 1982) and addendum (January 1985)
PAN30	Local Planning (September 1984)
PAN31	Simplified Planning Zones (1987)
PAN32	Development Opportunities, Local Plans (1988)
PAN33	Contaminated Land (1988)
PAN34	Local Plan Presentation (1989)
PAN35	Town Centre Improvement (1989)
PAN36	Siting and Design of New Housing in the Countryside (1991)
PAN37	Structure Planning (1992)
PAN38	Structure Plans: Housing Land Requirements (1993, revised 1996)
PAN39	Farm and Forestry Buildings (1993)
PAN40	Development Control (1993), addendum (1997)
PAN41	Development Plan Departures (1994, revised 1997)
PAN42	Archaeology: The Planning Process and Scheduled Monuments Procedure (1994)
PAN43	Golf Courses and Associated Developments (1994)

PAN44   Fitting New Housing Developments into the Landscape (1994)
PAN45   Renewable Energy Technologies (1994)
PAN46   Planning for Crime Prevention (1994)
PAN47   Community Councils and Planning (1996)
PAN48   Planning Application Forms (1996)
PAN49   Local Planning (1996)
PAN50   Controlling the Environmental Effects of Surface Mineral Workings (1996)
PAN50A   The Control of Noise at Surface Mineral Workings (1996)

* Regional Reports Advice

Appendix 5: BRC (P & D Dept) Industrial Properties (1 January 1988)

COLDSTREAM

Coldstream Workshops (Units 1–9)	885m²	Various tenants

EYEMOUTH

Acredale Workshops (Unit 1)	107.05m²	Aquamart
Acredale Workshops (Unit 2)	210.46m²	Vacant
Meeks Yard (Stores 1–25)	698.05m²	Various tenants
Dicksons Yard (Unit 1)	293.90m²	Eyemouth Marine Engineering Co.
Dicksons Yard (Unit 2)	306.80m²	Coastal Marine Diesel Co.
Dicksons Yard (Unit 3)	71.40m²	Coastal Marine Diesel Co.

EARLSTON

Industrial Estate (Unit 1)	82.00m²	Brian Falconer
Industrial Estate (Unit 2)	102.82m²	W.B. Prints
Industrial Estate	264.10m²	Pringle of Scotland

GALASHIELS

Currie Road (Unit 1)	109.50m²	Roxburgh Textiles (Scotland) Ltd
Currie Road (Unit 2)	105.00m²	Graham Barker Ltd
Currie Road (Unit 3)	109.50m²	Vacant
Currie Road (Unit 4 & 5)	235.95m²	City Electrical Factors Ltd

Currie Road (Unit 6)	115.50m²	W.D.M. Plant Hire
Currie Road (Unit 7)	115.50m²	Scottish Traffic Light Hire
Currie Road (Unit 8)	115.50m²	Extacto Ltd
Currie Road (Unit 9)	115.50m²	Calzeat & Co. Ltd
Currie Road (Unit 10)	115.50m²	Calzeat & Co. Ltd
Currie Road (Unit 11)	120.45m²	Calzeat & Co. Ltd
Currie Road (Unit 12)	109.50m²	Cirtech (UK) Ltd
Currie Road (Unit 12A)	105.00m²	Cirtech (UK) Ltd
Currie Road (Unit 14)	109.50m²	Cirtech (UK) Ltd
Langhaugh (Unit 1)	131.00m²	Borders (Wholesale) Bakery
Langhaugh (Unit 2)	125.25m²	Borders (Wholesale) Bakery
Langhaugh (Unit 3)	125.25m²	B.E.M.C.O. Ltd
Langhaugh (Unit 4)	143.52m²	First in Seconds
Langlee Workshops (Unit 1)	90.34m²	MSC – Community Programme
Langlee Workshops (Unit 2)	91.54m²	MSC – Community Programme
Langlee Workshops (Unit 3)	64.22m²	MSC – Community Programme
Langlee Workshops (Unit 4)	55.05m²	Integrated Microsystems
Langlee Workshops (Unit 5)	79.70m²	Scottish College of Textiles
Langlee Workshops (Unit 6)	91.46m²	Scottish College of Textiles
Langlee Workshops (Unit 7)	90.41m²	Vacant
Langlee Workshops (Unit 8)	142.30m²	George Milne
Netherdale (Bakery Garage)	404.96m²	Robertsons (Bakers) Ltd
Netherdale (Office & Store)	417.60m²	Robertsons (Bakers) Ltd
Netherdale Workshop	225.00m²	N. Bihel
Netherdale Workshop	290.00m²	A. Bunyan & Co.

TWEEDBANK

Craft Centre (Units 1–11)	480.03m²	Various tenants
Industrial Estate (Unit A)	483.20m²	Tweedbank Medical Ltd

Industrial Estate (Unit B)	483.20m²	Ceta (Precision) Engineering Ltd
Industrial Estate (Eildon Mill)	728.00m²	Vacant [previously Jeremy Ballantyne]

SELKIRK

Dunsdale Workshops (Units 1–7)	1080.52m²	Various tenants
Linglie Mill (Units 1–10)	3085.51m²	Various tenants, incl. Selkirk Glass
St Mary's Mill (Unit 1)	825.00m²	Claridge Mills Ltd
St Mary's Mill (Unit 2)	300.00m²	Cademuir Toolmaking Ltd
St Mary's Mill (Unit 3)	1685.55m²	Met-Etch (Selkirk) Ltd
Venture Centre (Units 1–10)	294.00m²	Various tenants

HAWICK

Burnfoot Workshops (Unit 1)	77.00m²	Teviotdale Design Co. Ltd
Burnfoot Workshops (Unit 2A)	107.85m²	Teviotdale Design Co. Ltd
Burnfoot Workshops (Unit 2B)	107.85m²	Teviotdale Design Co. Ltd
Burnfoot Workshops (Unit 3A)	109.00m²	H.K. Knitwear Ltd
Burnfoot Workshops (Unit 3B)	109.00m²	H.K. Knitwear Ltd
Burnfoot Workshops (Unit 4)	128.00m²	Hawick Community Workshop
Burnfoot Workshops (Unit 5)	26.00m²	Criffel Micro Business Systems Ltd
Burnfoot Workshops (Unit 6)	14.00m²	Kathleen McLellan
18/20 Commercial Road Workshop	1564.00m²	Turnbull & Scott (Engineers) Ltd
31 Commercial Road Workshop	94.00m²	Blacklock & Douglas
Lochpark Workshops (Units 2–3)	503.76m²	Sold to James Burgon & Sons

Lochpark Workshops (Unit 4)	79.45m²	Sold to Drysdale & Gray
Lochpark Workshops (Unit 5)	233.69m²	John McAllan
Lochpark Workshops (Unit 7)	261.35m²	McNairn Printers
Lochpark Workshops (Unit 8)	227.65m²	Hunters Bakers
Lochpark Workshops (Units 9 & 9A)	46.00m²	Scott & Thomson
Lochpark Workshops (Unit 12)	98.90m²	John W. Hay
Lochpark Factory	285.30m²	Simon Marcus (Hawick) Ltd
Mansfield Workshops (Unit A)	202.39m²	Robb Bros. Ltd
Mansfield Workshops (Unit B)	104.51m²	Coco Chimney Linings (Borders)
Mansfield Workshops (Unit C)	102.36m²	Ross Gordon Engineering
Mansfield Workshops (Unit D)	210.85m²	Scottish Express International
Mansfield Workshops (Unit E)	300.00m²	McInerney of Scotland Ltd
Mansfield Workshops (Unit F)	537.00m²	McInerney of Scotland Ltd
Mansfield Workshops (Unit G)	548.00m²	George Woodcock & Sons Ltd
Mansfield Workshops (Unit H)	300.56m²	Vacant
Teviot Crescent (Annfield Mill)	645.90m²	Waverley of Hawick Ltd

KELSO

Edenside Workshops (Units 1–10)	648.86m²	Various tenants
The Knowes (Workshop)	306.86m²	Peter Redpath Tyres
The Knowes (Workshop)	171.83m²	L.C.S. Joinery
Rosewood Estate (Units 1–4)	357.24m²	Various tenants
Pinnaclehill Factory	990.00m²	Lyle & Scott Ltd

JEDBURGH

Friars Workshops (Unit 1)	87.00m²	Morrison Plumbing Services
Friars Workshops (Unit 2)	70.50m²	John C Scott
Riverside Workshops (Units 1–7)	866.53m²	Various tenants, incl. Tom Young Knitwear

INNERLEITHEN

Morningside Works	410.00m²	Glentress Cashmere Ltd
Leithen Workshops (Units 1–4)	585.30m²	Various tenants, incl. Devra King Ltd

PEEBLES

Biggiesknowe shops/workshops (2)	71.60m²	Two tenants
Newby Court shops/workshops (4)	245.60m²	Four tenants
Southpark Workshops (Units 1–6)	646.52m²	Various tenants, incl. P.A.K. Systems

Appendix 6: SDA Properties in the Borders Region (1 January 1988)

COLDSTREAM

Guards Road Block 1	498m²	Scott Converting Ltd
Guards Road Block 2 (Units 1 & 2)	432m²	Thame Engineering (Oxon) Ltd t/a Alexander Technology
Guards Road Block 3	465m²	do. do.

DUNS

Station Road Block 1	1313m²	Homac Seafoods Ltd
Station Road Block 2	418m²	Fleming Homes
Station Road Block 3	432m²	Farne Salmon & Trout Ltd
Station Road Block 4	390m²	do. do.
Station Road Block 5 (Units 1 & 2)	403m²	do. do.

EYEMOUTH

Acredale Estate Block 3	951m²	Border Lairds (Quality Foods) Ltd
Acredale Estate Block 4 (Unit 1)	216m²	Hogarth Motors
Acredale Estate Block 4 (Unit 2)	216m²	Border Lairds (Quality Foods) Ltd
Coldingham Road Estate Block 2	1179m²	Scot Supreme Seafoods Ltd

GALASHIELS

Netherdale Block 1 (Units 1 & 2)	432m²	George Thomson (Auto Electricians) Ltd

NEWTOWN ST BOSWELLS

Station Yard Unit 1	100m²	J. Scott (Seeds)
Station Yard Unit 2	100m²	Reform Kitchens & Bathrooms
Station Yard Unit 3	100m²	do. do.
Station Yard Unit 4	100m²	A.J. Borthwick (Chemists)
Station Yard Unit 5	100m²	Border Potatoes
Station Yard Unit 6	100m²	Craig Chapman t/a Wings & Things

SELKIRK

Shawburn	2748m²	Exacta Circuits Ltd

TWEEDBANK

Tweedbank Block 1	1415m²	Hill Robinson Thread Co. Ltd
Tweedbank Block 2	1061m²	Tweedbank Circuit Supplies
Tweedbank Block 3 (Unit 1)	426m²	Hill Robinson Thread Co. Ltd
Tweedbank Block 3 (Unit 2)	426m²	do. do.
Tweedbank Block 4	951m²	Dynamit Nobel (UK) Ltd
Tweedbank Block 5 (Unit 1)	525m²	Fastran Engineering Ltd
Tweedbank Block 5 (Unit 2)	525m²	Quicksilver (C.E.M.C.O.)
Tweedbank Block 7	124m²	Hill Robinson Thread Co. Ltd
Tweedbank Block 8 (Unit 1)	352m²	Sprague Electric (UK) Ltd
Tweedbank Block 8 (Unit 2)	164m²	Tweedbank Circuit Supplies
Tweedbank Block 8 (Unit 3)	172m²	Bronze Age
Tweedbank Block 8 (Unit 4)	354m²	Barbour (Footwear) Ltd
Tweedbank Block 9 (Unit 1)	363m²	Peri-dent Ltd
Tweedbank Block 9 (Unit 2)	184m²	Holders Technology Ltd

Tweedbank Block 9 (Unit 3)	184m²	do. do.
Tweedbank Block 9 (Unit 4)	363m²	Sprague Electric (UK) Ltd

HAWICK

Eastfield Mill Block 1 (Units 1 & 2)	1546m²	James Johnston & Co. of Elgin Ltd
Eastfield Mill Block 2 (Unit 1)	248m²	Brunton & Bell Ltd
Eastfield Mill Block 2 (Unit 2)	248m²	do. do.
Eastfield Mill Block 3 (Unit 1)	93m²	James Johnston & Co. of Elgin Ltd
Eastfield Mill Block 3 (Unit 2)	93m²	do. do.
Eastfield Mill Block 3 (Unit 3)	93m²	Scott Bros. & Co. (Hawick)
Eastfield Mill Block 4 (Unit 1)	93m²	Empty
Eastfield Mill Block 4 (Unit 2)	93m²	Empty
Eastfield Mill Block 4 (Unit 3)	93m²	Empty

KELSO

Pinnaclehill Block 1	2388m²	Keltek Electronics Ltd
Pinnaclehill Block 2	961m²	A. Middlemas & Sons. Ltd
Pinnaclehill Block 3	278m²	Keltek Electronics Ltd
Pinnaclehill Block 6 (Unit 1)	235m²	Border Precision Services Ltd
Pinnaclehill Block 6 (Unit 2)	235m²	B.H.K. Circuit Ltd
Pinnaclehill Block 7 (Unit 1)	72m²	B. & W. Express Delivery

PEEBLES

Southpark Block 1	465m²	Empty

Bibliography

BOOKS

Adams, I., *The Making of Urban Scotland* (London: Croom Helm, 1978).

Adamson, P. and R. Lamont-Brown, *The Victorian and Edwardian Borderland* (St Andrews: Alvie Publications, 1981).

Aldous, T., *Battle for the Environment* (Glasgow: William Collins, 1972).

Ashworth, W., *The Genesis of Modern British Town Planning: A Study in Economic and Social History of the Nineteenth and Twentieth Centuries* (London: Routledge & Kegan Paul, 1954).

Brown, J. L. and I. C. Lawson, *History of Peebles 1850–1990* (Edinburgh: Mainstream Publishing, 1990).

Burton, T. L. and G. P. Wibberley, *Outdoor Recreation in the British Countryside* (Ashford: Wye College, 1967).

Cherry, G. E., *The Evolution of British Town Planning* (Leighton Buzzard: Leonard Hill Books, 1974).

Cherry, G. E., *Town Planning in Britain since 1900* (Oxford: Blackwell Publishers, 1996).

Collar, N. A., *Planning: Greens Concise Scots Law* (Edinburgh: W. Green/ Sweet & Maxwell, 1994).

COSLA, *Guidance to New Councils on the Preparation of Rural Strategies* (Edinburgh: COSLA, 1996).

Countryside Commission for Scotland, *A Park System for Scotland* (Perth: CCS, 1974).

Countryside Commission for Scotland, *Scotland's Scenic Heritage* (Perth: CCS, 1978).

Countryside Commission for Scotland, *A Review of the Effectiveness of Landscape Designations in Scotland* (Perth: CCS, 1988).

Countryside Commission for Scotland, *The Mountain Areas of Scotland: Conservation and Management* (Perth: CCS, 1990).

Crowe, S., *Tomorrow's Landscape* (London: Architectural Press, 1956).

Cullingworth, B. and V. Nadin, *Town and Country Planning in the UK*, 13th edn (London: Routledge, 1996).

Dennison, E. P., *The Evolution of Scotland's Towns* (Edinburgh: Edinburgh University Press, 2017).

Department of the Environment, *This Common Inheritance: Britain's Environmental Strategy* (London: HMSO, 1990).

Department of the Environment, Scottish Development Department & Welsh Office, *New Life for Old Buildings* (London: HMSO, 1971).
Department of the Environment, Scottish Development Department & Welsh Office, *New Life for Historic Areas* (London: HMSO, 1972).
Dower, J., *Fourth Wave: The Challenge of Leisure* (London: Civic Trust, 1965).
Galashiels History Committee, *Galashiels: A Modern History* (Galashiels: Ettrick and Lauderdale District Council, 1983).
Hague, C., *The Development of Planning Thought: A Critical Perspective* (London: Hutchinson, 1984).
Hardy, D., *From Garden Cities to New Towns: Campaigning for Town and Country Planning, 1899–1946* (London: Routledge, 1991).
Hardy, D., *From New Towns to Green Politics: Campaigning for Town and Country Planning, 1946–1990* (London: Routledge, 1991).
Harrison, B., *Finding a Role?: The United Kingdom 1970–1990* (Oxford: Oxford University Press, 2011).
Harrison, C., *Countryside Recreation in a Changing Society* (London: TMS Partnership, 1991).
Hein, C., *The Routledge Handbook of Planning History* (London: Routledge, 2019).
Keeble, L. B., *Principles and Practice of Town and Country Planning* (London: Estates Gazette, 1951).
Mears, F. C., *A Regional Survey and Plan for Central and South-East Scotland* (Edinburgh: HMSO, 1948).
McConnell, A., *Scottish Local Government* (Edinburgh: Edinburgh University Press, 2004).
McMaster, R., A. Prior and J. Watchman, *Scottish Planning Law* (London: Bloomsbury Professional, 2013).
Ministry of Housing and Local Government, Ministry of Transport, Scottish Development Department, *The Future of Development Plans: Report of the Planning Advisory Committee* (London: HMSO, 1965).
Moffat, A., *The Borders* (Selkirk: Deer Park Press, 2002).
Mullay, A. J., *Rails across the Borders* (Stroud: Tempus, 1990).
Nairn, I., *Outrage* (London: Architectural Press, 1958).
Omand, D. (ed.), *The Borders Book* (Edinburgh: Birlinn, 1995).
Paterson, A., *Scotland's Landscape: Endangered Icon* (Edinburgh: Edinburgh University Press, 2002).
Sandbrook, D., *White Heat: A History of Britain in the Swinging Sixties* (London: Little Brown, 2006).
Scottish Development Department, *The Central Borders: A Plan for Expansion, Vol. 1, Plan and Physical Study* (Edinburgh: HMSO, 1968a).
Scottish Development Department, *The Central Borders: A Plan for Expansion, Vol. 2, Economic and Geographical Report* (Edinburgh: HMSO, 1968b).

Scottish Office, *The Scottish Economy 1965–1970: a Plan for Expansion* (Edinburgh: HMSO, 1966).
Shoard, M., *The Theft of the Countryside* (London: Temple Smith, 1980).
Shucksmith, M., *Scotland's Rural Housing: A Forgotten Problem*, Rural Housing Scotland Conference 2019 (Edinburgh: Rural Forum, 2019).
Skeffington, A., *People and Planning: Report of the Skeffington Committee on Public Participation in Planning* (London: HMSO, 1969).
Spaven, D., *Waverley Route: The Battle for the Borders Railway* (Edinburgh: Argyll, 2012).
Taylor, Rattray G., *The Domesday Book* (London: Thames & Hudson, 1970).
Tewdwr-Jones, M. (ed.), *British Planning Policy in Transition: Planning in the 1990s* (London: Routledge, 1995).
Tindall, F., *Memoirs and Confessions of a County Planning Officer* (Ford, Midlothian: The Pantile Press, 1998).
Wannop, U. A., *The Regional Imperative: Regional Planning and Governance in Britain, Europe and the United States* (London: Regional Studies Association, 1995).
Warren, C., *Managing Scotland's Environment* (Edinburgh: Edinburgh University Press, 2002).
White, J. T., *The Scottish Border and Northumberland* (London: Eyre Methuen, 1973).
Young, E. and J. Rowan-Robinson, *Scottish Planning Law and Procedure* (Glasgow: William Hodge & Company Ltd, 1985).

JOURNAL ARTICLES

Atkinson, M., 'The Organization of Local Government in Scotland', *Political Science Quarterly*, Vol. 18, No. 1 (March 1903), pp. 59–87.
Begg, H. M. and S. H. A. Pollock, 'Development Plans in Scotland since 1975', *Scottish Geographical Magazine*, Vol. 107, (Issue 1, 1991), pp. 4–11.
Coon, A. G., 'An Assessment of Scottish Development Planning', *Planning Outlook*, Vol. 32 (Issue 2, 1989), pp. 77–85.
Damer, S. and C. Hague, 'Participation in Planning: A Review', *The Town Planning Review*, Vol. 42, No. 3 (July 1971), Liverpool University Press, pp. 217–232.
Davies, H. W. E. 'Continuity and Change: The Evolution of the British Planning System, 1947–1997*', *The Town Planning Review*, Vol. 69, No. 2 (Apr 1998), Liverpool University Press, pp. 135–152.
Diamond, D., W. Solesbury, U. A. Wannop, L. Wijers and H. Leeflang, 'The Uses of Strategic Planning: The Example of the National Planning Guidelines in Scotland', *The Town Planning Review*, Vol. 50, No. 1 (January 1979), Liverpool University Press, pp. 18–35.
Duffield, B. S., 'TheTourism and Recreation Research Unit', *Scottish Geographical Magazine*, Vol. 98 (Issue 3, 1982), pp. 177–179.

Fitton, M., 'Countryside Recreation – The Problems of Opportunity', *Local Government Studies*, Vol. 5 (Issue 4, 1979), pp. 57–90.

Forbes, J., 'Review of Central Borders Study', *Urban Studies*, Vol. 6 (Issue 1, 1969), pp. 101–103.

Forbes, J., 'A View of Planning in Scotland 1974–84', *Scottish Geographical Magazine*, Vol. 100 (Issue 2, 1984), pp. 104–112.

Herring, H., 'The Conservation Society: Harbinger of the 1970s Environment Movement in the UK', *Environment and History*, Vol. 7, No. 4 (November 2001), pp. 381–401.

Hughes, J. T., 'Policy Analysis in the Highlands and Islands Development Board', *The Journal of the Operational Research Society*, Vol. 33, No. 12 (December 1982), Palgrave Macmillan Journals, pp. 1055–1064.

Levitt, I., 'The Origins of the Scottish Development Department, 1943–1962', *Scottish Affairs*, No. 14, winter 1996, pp. 42–63.

Lloyd, M. G., 'Local Government Reorganisation and the Strategic Planning Lottery in Scotland', *The Town Planning Review*, Vol. 67, No. 3 (July 1996), Liverpool University Press, pp. v–viii.

Lloyd, M. G., 'National Planning Guidelines and Development Plans in Scotland', *Local Government Studies*, Vol. 22 (Issue 4, 1996), pp. 262–272.

Lyall, G. 'Review of Regional Survey and Plan for Central and South-East Scotland', *The Town Planning Review*, Vol. 20, No. 2 (July 1949), pp. 175–178.

McDonald, S. T. 'The Regional Report in Scotland: A Study of Change in the Planning Process', *The Town Planning Review*, Vol. 48, No. 3 (July 1977), Liverpool University Press, pp. 215–232.

MacGregor, B. and A. Ross, 'Master or Servant? The Changing Role of the Development Plan in the British Planning System', *The Town Planning Review*, Vol. 66, No. 1 (January 1995), Liverpool University Press, pp. 41–59.

Mather, A. S., 'The Changing Role of Planning in Rural Land Use: The Example of Afforestation in Scotland', *Journal of Rural Studies*, Vol. 7 (Issue 3, 1991), pp. 299–309.

Midwinter, A., 'A Review of Local Government in Scotland: A Critical Perspective', *Local Government Studies*, Vol. 18 (Issue 2, 1992), pp. 44–54.

Shorthall, S. and M. Shucksmith, 'Integrated Rural Development: Issues Arising from the Scottish Experience', *European Planning Studies*, Vol. 6 (Issue 1, 1998), pp. 73–88.

Stevenson, F. R., 'Planning and Development in Scotland', *The Town Planning Review*, Vol. 26, No. 1 (April 1955), Liverpool University Press, pp. 5–18.

Wannup, U., 'The Evolution and Roles of the Scottish Development Agency', *The Town Planning Review*, Vol. 55, No. 3 (July 1984), Liverpool University Press, pp. 313–321.

Index

Note: *f* indicates a figure; *t* indicates a table

Abercrombie, Patrick, 25, 26
Adamson, Peter and Lamont-Brown, R.
  Victorian & Edwardian Borderland, The, 17
advertisements, 42–3, 86, 164, 246
Agenda 21, 252
AGLVs (Areas of Great Landscape Value), 56, 105–7, 112, 146, 147f, 165–6, 249, 260
agriculture, 2–4, 55, 191–2, 247–8, 260
  Berwickshire, 104–5
  Borders Region 1975, The, 124
  BRC, 165, 203–4
  development, 191–2, 204
  employment, 4, 104, 124, 191
  European funding/quotas, 175, 216
  FWAG/FFWAG, 192, 248
  grants, 175
  housing, 203–4
  Kelso, 8
  Selkirkshire, 103–4
  sheep farming, 103–4
  Shoard, Marion, 176
  Glenrath Farms, 82
Aldous, Tony
  Battle for the Environment, 88
Anderson, T. D., 31, 35, 91
archaeology, 190–1, 247
Areas of Great Landscape Value (AGLVs), 56, 105–7, 112, 146, 147f, 165–6, 249, 260
Areas of Special Control for Advertisements, 43
Ashworth, William
  Genesis of Modern British Town Planning, The, 18
Askew, John Marjoribanks Eskdale, 23, 120
Assessment of Scottish Development Planning (Coon, A. G.), 171
Assisted Areas, 217

Baillie, John Somerville (Jack), 21–2, 29, 30, 35, 38, 91
  Royal Borough of Peebles Proposed Urban Structure Plan, 58
Barlow Report (1940), 25, 31, 32
Battle for the Environment (Aldous, Tony), 88
BCC (Berwickshire County Council)
  AGLVs, 56, 107
  AGLVs and Tourist Development report, 107
  agriculture report, 104–5
  conservation, 99–100
  countryside, the, 55
  development plans, 22, 28, 37–8, 43, 45, 52
  DHS, 31
  Draft Rural Policy for Berwickshire, 103
  holiday accommodation, 42, 57
  housing, 53, 54, 60, 96–7
  illegal encampments, 41–2
  industrial development, 55, 60
  members, 22
  planning committees, 23, 31
  population, 52, 103
  roads, 49–50
  staffing, 22, 35, 37, 91–2
  Torness nuclear power station, 102
  tourism, 107, 109
Beeching, R.
  Reshaping of British Railways, The, 71
Begg, H. M. and Pollock, S. H. A., 171–2
Bell, Vera, 179f
Bennett, Frank, 127, 133–4
BEPI Electronics, 80, 182, 183f
Berwick-upon-Tweed
  industrial development, 82
Berwickshire
  AGLVs, 56
  agriculture, 104–5
  burghs, 113–14

Berwickshire (*cont*.)
  conservation, 99–100
  employment, 4
  holiday accommodation, 41–2
  housing, 40, 96, 156, 225
  illegal encampments, 41–2
  industry, 8, 96
  land, 2
  population, 10, 26, 52, 97, 103, 237
  roads, 49
  rural policy, 103
  settlement hierarchy, 220*t*
  Torness nuclear power station, 102
  tourism, 107, 109
  see also BCC
Berwickshire County Council *see* BCC
Berwickshire District, 115, 116*f*, 220*t*, 221, 237, 240, 241
  Berwickshire (Part) Local Plan, 162
Berwickshire Local Plan, 152, 231, 237, 240
refuse disposal, 253
Bilton, Alistair, 80, 139
Border Courier Service, 130, 162
Border Training Services Agency (BTS), 189–90
Borders Book, The (Omand, Donald), 17
Borders Forum on Sustainable Development, 253, 256
Borders General Hospital, 161
Borders Region, 115–16*f*, 257; *see also* BRC
Borders Region 1975, The (RPU), 122–6
Borders Region Structure Plan 1980, 145–52, 153*f*, 261
Borders Region Structure Plan 1991, 217–28, 229–30, 231, 233*f*, 262
Borders Regional Council (BRC) *see* BRC
Borders Tourist Association, 124–5
Borthwick, Ian, 127, 133, 179*f*
Bowden, 98–9
BRC (Borders Regional Council), 1, 28, 115, 119–41, 260–3
  Action Plan for Development, 138–40, 141, 145, 170
  AGLVs, 166
  Assisted Areas study, 217
  Berwickshire (Part) Local Plan, 162
  Berwickshire Local Plan, 231, 237, 240
  Borders Region Structure Plan 1980, 145–52, 153*f*, 261
  Borders Region Structure Plan 1991, 217–28, 229–30, 231, 233*f*, 262
  built environment, 162–5, 244–7
  computerisation, 179, 201, 213, 255

  countryside policy, 136–7, 138, 165–7, 168, 191–7, 202–3, 250–2, 262
  Department of Physical Planning, 126–34, 139–40, 145, 271
  Department of Physical Planning and Development, 140, 145, 272–3
  Department of Planning and Development, 177–80, 182, 186, 189–90, 195, 205–8, 213, 214*f*, 231, 242, 243, 255, 274, 275
  departmental structure changes, 177–80
  development control, 133–8, 178, 200–5, 234–6
  development plan policies and proposals, 155–70, 259
  economic development, 158–60, 178, 182–4, 213–17, 222–3, 240–4, 255–6
  economy, the, 131–2, 205–6, 213–17, 263
  'Electronics in the Scottish Borders', 186–7
  environment, the, 187–91, 234
  Ettrick and Lauderdale Local Plan, 231, 237, 240, 243, 245, 246
  European funding, 215–17
  forestry, 124, 165–6, 192, 226, 262
  FSB scheme, 186
  Galashiels/Tweedbank Local Plan, 154–5
  Hawick Local Plan, 158
  housing, 136–7, 138, 139, 146–8, 155–7, 170, 202–5, 236–40
  implementation, 168–70, 178
  industrial development, 139–40, 158–60, 182–7, 234, 241, 255–6
  industrial properties, 184, 295–9
  local plans, 152–5, 157, 158, 161, 162, 163, 164, 172, 231–2, 233*f*, 244–6, 250
  marketing, 186–7
  members, 119–20
  'New Housing in the Borders Countryside', 240
  offices, 120–1
  PEP scheme, 189
  Planning and Development Committee, 120, 129, 134, 135, 136, 175, 179–80, 201–2, 235
  promotion, 186, 234, 242
  Property Services Department, 129
  publications, 186–7, 199, 242, 285–7
  recreation, 166–8, 196, 197–200, 250–2
  Regional Report 1976, 131–3, 141
  regional reports, 131–3, 141, 142–3

Roads and Transportation Department, 177
Roxburgh (Part) Local Plan, 172
Roxburgh Local Plan, 231, 238, 240, 245
rural issues, 232–3, 247–50, 262
'Scottish Borders Knitwear Buyers Guide', 186–7
Scottish Borders 2001: The Way Forward, 15, 218, 229, 231
settlement hierarchy, 148, 149f
settlement strategy, 132–3
staffing, 121–2, 126–9, 178, 179f, 273, 207, 213, 214f
structure plans, 132–3, 145–52, 153f, 217–28, 229–30, 231, 233f
sustainability, 234, 235f, 252–5, 256
tourism and recreation, 166–8, 196, 197–200
traffic and transport, 160–2, 163–4, 170
Tweeddale Local Plan, 222, 231, 238, 250
Village Plans, 239–40
walking booklets/leaflets, 199
Waste Management Group, 253
BTS (Border Training Services Agency), 189–90
Buccleuch, Duke of, 3; *see also* Buccleuch Estates
Buccleuch Estates, 3
Buchan, John, 98
building firms, 63
built environment, 162–5, 244–7
burghs, 113–14
Burnhead site, 158, 159f
Burrows, Trevor, 127, 179f
buses, 124, 130, 162

C. H. Dexter Corporation, 83
caravans, 40, 41, 42, 44, 167
Cardrona, 204
cars, 254–5
 county development plans, 48
 leisure use of, 40, 42, 44
 see also roads
Cavers, Morag, 179f
CCS (Countryside Commission for Scotland), 88
Central and South-East Scotland Regional Planning Committee, 26
Central Borders: A Plan for Expansion, The (Scottish Development Department), 62, 68–71, 84, 259
 reaction to, 75–7

Central Borders Plan see *Central Borders; A Plan for Expansion, The*
central government, 12, 13, 65–6, 265
 guidance, 142, 288–94
 HIDB, 79
 housing, 221
 NPG, 12, 292, 142
 NPPGs, 212–13, 229, 292
 see also SDD; PAN
Central Scotland: A Programme for Development and Growth (Scottish Development Department), 66, 84
Charles, F. W. B., 33, 37
Charlesfield munitions factory, 27, 69–70, 96
Charlesfield Farm, 96
Cherry, Gordon, 100
 Evolution of British Town Planning, The, 18
Chirnside, 83
Chisholm, Bill, 179, 207, 261
Civic Amenities Act 1967, 12, 87, 97, 111
Clark, Kenneth, 120, 210, 211
Clelland, David, 265, 266–7
Clyde Valley Regional Plan, 25, 26
Coastal Planning Guidelines, 142
coastline, the, 107, 109, 125
Coldingham Sands, 107, 109, 197
Coldstream, 49, 50, 97
 population, 150t, 151
Colvin-Smith, 63
community councils, 15, 117, 136
Community Land Act 1975, 169
Community Programme, Planning and Environmental Projects (PEP) scheme, 189
compulsory purchase, 32, 168–9
conservation, 12, 16–17, 56, 87–8, 111
 AGLVs, 56, 105–7, 112, 146, 147f, 165–6, 249, 260
 areas, 87–8, 97–8, 99–100, 111, 136–7, 163, 164–5
 Borders Region Structure Plan 1991, 224, 227–8
 BRC, 137, 165–6
 built environment, 97–100, 246–7
 ESA scheme, 195
 listed buildings, 98, 135, 136, 137, 236, 246–7, 264
 local plans, 246
 NSA, 194–5
 rural heritage, 227–8
 SNH, 211
 wildlife, 166, 173, 192
Constable, Frank, 90, 121, 126–7, 261

consultations *see* public participation
Convention of Scottish Local Authorities (COSLA), 216, 221, 226, 232
Coon, A. G.
  Assessment of Scottish Development Planning, 171
COSLA (Convention of Scottish Local Authorities), 216, 221, 226, 232
Cottee, David, 90
Cottingham, Charlotte, 179*f*
countryside, the, 48, 55–7, 87–8, 105–10, 260
  Borders Region 1975, The, 125
  BRC, 136–7, 138, 165–7, 168, 191–7, 202–3, 250–2, 262
  BRC Regional Report 1976, 132
  housing, 136–7, 138, 157, 202–3, 225, 240
  mountain areas, 195
  recreation, 196, 197–200, 250–2
  Shoard, Marion, 176
  tourism, 168
  see also rural issues
Countryside (Scotland) Act 1967, 56, 88, 89, 108–10, 112
Countryside Act 1968, 88
Countryside Commission for Scotland (CCS), 88
countryside rangers, 197–9, 251
county development plans, 22, 35–8, 43, 45–64, 117–19, 259
  amendments, 87
  consultations, 47–8
  countryside, the, 48, 55–7
  criticism, 117
  hand-colouring, 47
  housing provision, 53–4
  industrial development, 54–5
  PAG, 117–18
  population stability, 52, 63–4
  programme maps, 47
  proposal maps, 47
  public participation, 12
  roads and transportation, 48–51, 64
  Skeffington Committee Report, 118
  survey reports, 46–7
  updating, 57–63
  written statements, 47
county planning, 258–60
county planning committees, 23
Cove Harbour, 196–7
Crawford, Hamish, 127, 133
Crowe, Sylvia, 88
  Tomorrow's Landscape, 88

Cullingworth, Barry and Nadin, Vincent
  Town and Country Planning in the UK, 17
Currie, Robert, 80
Currie & Mill, 80, 182, 183*f*
cycling, 251

Dangerfield Mills, 247
Davies, H. W. E., 18
'Fifty years of planning achievements – the evolution of the planning system since 1947', 18
demographics, 122, 132, 156, 176; *see also* population
Denholm, John, 188
Department of Health for Scotland (DHS) *see* DHS
Dere Street, 200
development, rate of, 86–7
Development Areas, 78
development control, 38–43, 44
  BRC, 133–8, 178, 200–5, 234–6
Development of Planning Thought, The (Hague, Cliff), 18
development plan policies and proposals (BRC), 155–70, 259
  built environment, 162–5
  countryside policy, 165–7
  economic development, 158–60
  housing policy, 155–7
  implementation, 168–70
  tourism and recreation, 167–8
  traffic and transport, 160–2
  see also county development plans
DHS (Department of Health for Scotland), 31, 66
  'New Houses in the Country', 136
district councils, 115, 116*f*, 119, 138, 170
  planning control, 200
Doomsday Book, The (Taylor, Gordon Rattray), 87
Douglas, David P., 92, 120, 126, 127, 179*f*, 207, 210, 211, 261
Dower, Michael, 88
  Fourth Wave: The Challenge of Leisure, The, 88
Draft Rural Policy for Berwickshire (BCC), 103
Duns
  conservation, 99–100
  industrial development, 82, 83, 97
  population, 150*t*, 151
  redevelopment, 87

INDEX 311

Eastern Borders Development Association (EBDA), 78, 82, 259
EBDA (Eastern Borders Development Association), 78, 82, 259
economic development, 77–84, 265–6
 BRC, 158–60, 178, 182–4, 213–17, 222–3, 240–4, 255–6
 SE, 209, 210, 265
 SoSE, 266–7
 sustainability, 234
economy, the, 131–2, 138, 174, 215
 Assisted Area Status, 174–5
 Borders Region 1975, The, 122–3, 125–6
 Borders Region Structure Plan 1991, 222–3
 BRC, 131–2, 205–6, 213–17, 263
 European funding, 126, 174, 175, 215–17, 253
 forestry, 193, 194
 FSB scheme, 186
 grants, 11–12, 175, 186, 242–3
 influences, 6–7, 13, 32–3, 66
 SDA, 139
 see also economic development
Eddleston, 41, 59
Edinburgh and South East Scotland City Region Deal, 266
Edinburgh and South East Scotland Strategic Development Planning Authority, 264
Edinburgh University, 89
education, 21
EEC (European Economic Community), 126, 174
Eildon Hills, 196
'Electronics in the Scottish Borders' (BRC), 186–7
electronics industry, 80, 182, 183*f*
employment, 4, 66, 79–80, 123, 176, 188–9, 215, 256–7, 261
 agricultural, 4, 104, 124, 191
 BRC, 138, 189–90, 206
 BRC Regional Report 1976, 132
 BTS, 189–90
 environmental improvement projects, 189
 PEP scheme, 189
 TRIP, 189
enforcement action, 202
Entwistle, Frank, 34, 90, 91
environment, the, 16–17, 87–8, 142, 212
 BRC, 187–91, 234
 see also conservation
Environment Protection Act 1990, 211
Environmentally Sensitive Area (ESA) scheme, 195

erosion, 107
ESA (Environmentally Sensitive Area) scheme, 195
estates, 3, 103, 165, 166
Ettrick and Lauderdale District, 115, 116*f*, 200
 economic development, 241
 Ettrick and Lauderdale Local Plan, 231, 237, 240, 243, 245, 246
 housing, 138, 221, 225, 237, 240
 population, 152, 237
 refuse disposal, 253
 retail, 205
 settlement hierarchy, 220*t*
 sustainability, 252, 253
 tourism, 243
 town centres, 245
Ettrick valley, 103–4
European Economic Community (EEC), 126, 174
European funding, 126, 174, 175, 215–17, 253
Evolution of British Town Planning, The (Cherry, Gordon), 18
Exacta Circuits, 80, 81, 182, 183*f*
exports, 6–7
Eyemouth
 conservation, 99
 housing, 96–7
 industrial development, 82–3, 158–60, 184, 186
 industry, 10, 96–7
 population, 10, 150*t*, 151
 redevelopment, 87

Farming, Forestry and Wildlife Advisory Group (FFWAG), 192, 248
Farrell, Julian, 90
FFWAG (Farming, Forestry and Wildlife Advisory Group), 192, 248
'Fifty years of planning achievements – the evolution of the planning system since 1947' (Davies, H. W. E.), 18
Finance for Small Businesses (FSB) scheme, 186, 242
fishing industry, 10, 215
forestry industry, 17, 55 103, 191–4, 248–9, 260
 Borders Region Structure Plan 1991, 226–7
 BRC, 124, 165–6, 192, 226, 262
 FFWAG, 192, 248
Forth Region, 115
Foulden, 54

Fourth Wave: The Challenge of Leisure, The (Dower, Michael), 88
Frater, Brian, 179f
FSB (Finance for Small Businesses) scheme, 186, 242
Future of Development Plans (PAG), 117–18

Galalaw farm, 222
Galashiels, 5, 61–2, 69
  environmental improvement, 187–8
  expansion, 76
  Galashiels Technical Working Party, 62, 76, 94, 95
  housing, 39, 53, 61, 62, 67, 68
  industrial development, 54, 62, 80, 81, 139, 158, 182, 184, 185
  modernity, 86
  population, 9, 62, 75, 76, 77t, 150t, 151
  retail, 245
  roads, 48–9, 61, 163–4, 223–4
  roof extensions, 137, 138
  SDA, 185
  textile industry, 4, 5–6, 77
  town centre, 163–4, 245
Galashiels/Tweedbank Local Plan, 154–5
Garden City movement, 23
Gattonside, 99
Geddes, Patrick, 25, 258
Genesis of Modern British Town Planning, The (Ashworth, William), 18
Glenrath Farms, 82
Gordon, 204
Gorrenberry, 193
government *see* central government; local government
Grangemouth/Falkirk Regional Survey and Plan, 84
Grant, John A. W., 31, 36
Gray, John, 34, 90, 91, 127, 133, 179f
Gray, Mike, 182–4, 210, 211
Gregory, Paul, 121, 127, 179f
guidance and planning advice, 202
Gunsgreen, 242

Hague, Cliff
  Development of Planning Thought, The, 18
Hall, John B., 22, 90
Hall, John C., 22, 30, 33, 34, 90
Hardie, Baillie John, 7
Harestanes Countryside Visitor Centre, 251
Hattonknowe, 41, 106

Hawick, 7, 69, 256
  Burnhead site, 158, 159f
  Drumlanrig Tower, 187
  environmental improvement, 187, 188
  expansion, 76
  Hawick Local Plan 158
  Hawick Technical Working Party, 76, 94–5
  housing, 30–1, 39, 53, 54, 59, 68, 76
  industrial development, 54, 59, 158, 159f, 184–5, 218
  knitwear industry, 7
  as outstanding conservation area, 163
  population, 9, 76, 77t, 150t, 151
  redevelopment, 87
  roads, 49, 164
  roof extensions, 137, 138
  SDA, 185
  Teviot Study, 188
  Tower Hotel/Backdamgate scheme, 187
  town centre, 163, 164, 245
Heap, Desmond, 31–2
  Outline of Planning Law, An, 32
Henderson, Ross, 90
Heritage Areas, 228
HIDB (Highlands and Islands Development Board), 79
Highlands and Islands, 79
Highlands and Islands Development Board (HIDB), 79
holiday accommodation, 40–2, 56–7, 104, 105–7, 167, 243
Hope, Douglas G., 127, 179f
hosiery industry, 7
hospitals, 70–1, 161
housing, 38–9, 53–4, 66, 67, 176–7, 206
  affordable, 239
  agriculture, 203–4
  Borders Region 1975, The, 123, 125
  Borders Region Structure Plan 1991, 221–2, 225
  BRC, 136–7, 138, 139, 146–8, 155–7, 170, 202–5, 236–40
  BRC Regional Report 1976, 132
  Central Borders: A Plan for Expansion, The, 68–9, 75–6
  for the elderly, 156
  holiday accommodation, 40–2, 56–7, 104, 105–7, 167, 243
  industrial development, 83–4, 139
  industry, proximity to, 23, 24, 25
  Peeblesshire, 29, 39–40, 53, 54, 57–9
  prefabricated, 39
  private, 40, 53, 58–9, 61, 63, 156–7, 177

INDEX 313

roof extensions, 137–8
Roxburghshire, 30–1, 47, 53, 59
Scottish Homes, 209–10
Selkirkshire, 30, 61
social, 38, 39, 53, 60, 61, 170, 177, 239
social, SSHA, 38, 29, 74, 151, 170
survey reports, 47
Tweedbank, 68, 73–5, 151, 209, 259
see also housing in the countryside
Housing and Town Development (Scotland) Act 1957, 33
housing in the countryside, 136–7, 138, 157, 202–3, 225, 240
Housing, Town Planning, etc. Act 1909, The, 23–4, 258
Hudson, Harold, 34, 38
Hunter, Tom, 207

illegal encampments, 40–2
Indicative Forestry Strategies, 226
industrial development, 4–8, 54–5, 62, 69–70, 77–84, 158–60
  Borders Region Structure Plan 1991, 218–20, 222–3, 234
  BRC, 139–40, 158–60, 182–7, 234, 241, 255–6
  SDA, 139–40, 184–6, 300–2
  sustainability, 234
Industrial Revolution, the, 23
industry, 1, 2, 176, 180–2
  craft-based, 160
  electronics, 80, 182, 183*f*
  fishing, 10, 215
  hosiery, 7
  housing, proximity to, 23, 24, 25
  knitwear, 7, 180
  manufacturing, 4
  mineral working, 55–6, 101, 227, 249
  paper, 8
  textile, 4–7, 8, 39, 77–8, 80–1, 123, 180, 182, 215
  see also agriculture; forestry industry; industrial development
infill development, 239–40
Inglis, George, 127, 179*f*
Innerleithen
  housing, 53, 54, 58–9
  population, 10
Interim Development Control, 24, 25

J & J Hall, Architects, 22, 90–1
J. S. Crawford, 63
Jedburgh, 7
  expansion, 76

housing, 39, 53, 54
industrial development, 54, 59–60, 80–1, 160, 184
Jedburgh Technical Working Party, 90, 92–3
as outstanding conservation area, 163
population, 9, 76, 150*t*, 151
redevelopment, 87
textile industry, 7
tourist information centre, 140
town centre, 163
Johnson-Marshall, Percy, 68, 89
Johnston, Charles, 179*f*
Johnston, Robert, 91
Johnston, Tom, 26
JPAC (Peebles, Roxburgh and Selkirk Joint Planning Advisory Committee), 78, 80, 259

Keeble, Lewis
  Principles and Practice of Town and Country Planning, 17
Kelso, 7–8
  environmental improvement, 188
  housing, 53, 54
  industrial development, 54–5, 60, 82, 160, 184
  Kelso Technical Working Party, 93
  as outstanding conservation area, 163
  population, 9, 150*t*, 151
  redevelopment, 87
  roads, 50–1, 164
  town centre, 163, 164
Key Villages, 220
Klein, Bernat, 77–8
knitwear industry, 7, 180
Knowles, Basil, 91, 92, 261

Laing, Duncan, 34
land, 79
  Borders Region 1975, The, 124
  estates, 3, 103, 165, 166
  influence of, 2–4
  renewal, 185–6
  SDA, 185–6
Land (White Paper), 169
Land Commission Act 1967, 169
Land Management Forums, 195
Land Utilisation Survey of Britain, 2
landlord–tenant relationships, 3, 22
landscape advice, 190
landscapes, 211, 250
Landward Community Development Strategy (RCC), 102

Lauder, 164
LECs (local enterprises companies), 210–11, 265
leisure *see* recreation; tourism
Lilliardsedge, 108
Lindean Loch, 196
listed buildings, 98, 135, 136, 137, 236, 246–7, 264
Local Agenda 21 Working Group, 252–3
local enterprises companies (LECs), 210–11, 265
local government, 11–12, 13, 23–4, 113–17, 264
   SBLAJC, 121
   see also BRC *and under individual county councils*
Local Government (Scotland) Act 1973, 115, 116, 119
Local Government and Planning (Scotland) Act 1982, 116–17
Local Government etc. (Scotland) Act 1994, 257
Local Government, Planning and Land Act 1980, 169
Local Place Plans (LPPs), 265
local plans, 143–5, 152–5, 171–3, 231–2, 233f
   Berwickshire (Part) Local Plan, 162
   Berwickshire Local Plan, 231, 237, 240
   countryside, 250
   Ettrick and Lauderdale Local Plan, 231, 237, 240, 243, 245, 246
   Galashiels/Tweedbank Local Plan, 154–5
   Hawick Local Plan, 158
   housing, 157
   road proposals, 161
   Roxburgh (Part) Local Plan, 172
   Roxburgh Local Plan, 231, 238, 240, 245
   town centres, 163, 164, 245–6
   Tweeddale Local Plan, 222, 231, 238, 250
local rural partnerships, 232–3
Lorimer, Alistair, 92, 127, 133, 179f
Lothian Estates, 3
Lothian Regional Survey and Plan, 84
LPPs (Local Place Plans), 265
Lyddon, Derek, 171
Lyle, Robert, 26

McDonald, Alister, 179f
McGregor, Peter, 35
Mackenzie, Charles Ross (Charlie), 22, 89
Mackie, Tom, 179f, 188
McLaren, Quentin, 179f

MacLean, Alasdair, 127, 179f
McMaster, Ray, Prior, Alan and Watchman, John
   Scottish Planning Law, 18–19
McQueen Ltd, 182–4
March Estates, 3
Marchmont, Earl of, 3
Mason, Joan, 179f
Matthew, Robert, 25, 258
Maxwell, Gillian, 179f
Maxwellheugh, 7–8
Mears, Frank C., 21, 25, 258
   Peeblesshire survey, 28–9
   Regional Survey and Plan for Central and South-East Scotland, A, 17, 25, 26–8, 33, 258
media, the, 179–80, 181f, 207, 260–1
Melrose
   Melrose Technical Working Party, 90, 93
   redevelopment, 87
   roads, 50–1, 70, 161, 190
Melrose by-pass, 70, 161, 190
Memoirs and Confessions of a County Planning Officer (Tindall, Frank), 18
Midlothian
   development plans, 45
   staffing, 21–2
migration, 8–9, 126; *see also* population
Mill, Kenneth, 80
Miller, Craig, 179f
mills, 4–7, 8, 77, 81, 186
Milne, Alastair M., 36, 89
mineral working industry, 55–6, 101, 227, 249
Ministry of Transport (MoT), 48–9
Minto, Gilbert, 211, 253
model villages, 23
modernity, 86
MoT (Ministry of Transport), 48–9
mountain areas, 195

National Scenic Areas (NSAs), 194–5
national parks, 56, 88
National Parks and Access to the Countryside Act 1949, 56, 88
National Plan (DEA), 66
National Planning, 12
National Planning Framework, 264
National Planning Guidelines (NPG), 12, 292, 142
National Planning Policy Guidelines (NPPGs), 212–13, 229, 292
Natural Heritage (Scotland) Act 1991, 211

'New Houses in the Country' (DHS), 136
'New Housing in the Borders Countryside' (BRC), 240
New Life for Historic Areas (Department of the Environment, SDD & Welsh Office), 97
New Life for Old Buildings (Department of the Environment, SDD & Welsh Office), 97
New Towns, 25, 33, 84; *see also* Newtown St Boswells
Newcastleton, 3, 186
newspapers, 179–80
Newtown St Boswells, 27, 28, 49, 68, 69, 70, 259
   Central Borders: A Plan for Expansion, The, 75, 76
   industrial development, 27, 70, 185–6
   population, 75
   SDA, 185–6
   St Boswells/Newtown St Boswells Working Party, 96
North British Rayon Factory, 92
Northumberland County Council, 50
NPG (National Planning Guidelines), 12, 292, 142
NPPGs (National Planning Policy Guidelines), 212–13, 229, 292
NSAs (National Scenic Areas), 194–5

objections, 144, 145, 118*f*
Omand, Donald
   Borders Book, The, 17
Ordnance Survey (OS) maps, 37, 46
OS (Ordnance Survey) maps, 37, 46
Outline of Planning Law, An (Heap, Desmond), 32
Ovens, George, 34, 35, 90, 127, 179*f*
overcrowding, 23

PAG (Planning Advisory Group), 117–18
   Future of Development Plans, 117–18
PAN (Planning Advice Notes), 12, 131, 292–4
   2: Forestry Guidelines, 193
   2/2010 Affordable Housing and Housing Land Audits, 239
   27: Structure Planning, 144, 173
   30: Local Planning, 144
   32: Development Opportunities: Local Plans, 172
paper industry, 8
parks, 56, 88
Parle, Victor, 120

Payne, Gordon, 26
PCC (Peebles County Council)
   AGLVs, 56
   development plans, 22, 28, 35–6, 43, 45, 52, 56–8
   holiday accommodation, 40–1, 56–7
   housing, 29, 57
   illegal encampments, 40–1
   industrial development, 81–2
   JPAC, 78, 259
   members, 22
   mineral working industry, 55–6, 101
   planning committees, 28–30, 41, 81
   population, 52
   staffing, 22, 33, 89
   tourism, 40–1, 42–3, 105–6, 109
   Tourist Development Proposals and AGLVs, 105–6
Peebles, 6
   conservation, 98, 165
   Growth Plan, 58
   housing, 53, 54, 57–8, 156, 238
   industrial development, 55, 58, 81, 160, 184
   population, 10, 58, 77*t*, 150*t*, 151, 156
   railways, 51
   roads, 51, 58, 164
   textile industry, 6
   tourism, 244
   town centre, 164
   Urban Structure Plan, 58
Peebles Burgh Council, 58
Peebles Civic Society, 98
Peebles County Council *see* PCC
Peebles, Roxburgh and Selkirk Joint Planning Advisory Committee (JPAC), 78, 80, 259
Peeblesshire, 33
   as AGLV, 56
   burghs, 113–14
   conservation, 98
   employment, 4
   holiday accommodation, 40–1
   housing, 39–40, 53, 54, 57–9
   illegal encampments, 40–1
   land, 2
   mineral working industry, 55–6
   population, 9–10, 52
   roads, 49
   tourism, 40–1, 42–3, 105–6, 109
   see also PCC
Pennine Way, 200
Pentland Hills Regional Park, 228, 250
People and Planning (HMSO), 118

PEP (Community Programme, Planning and Environmental Projects) scheme, 189
Philogar, 193–4
planning, 11–12
  complexity, 15
  enforcement action, 202
  environmental impact, 16–17
  proactive, 16
  rural issues, 16
  see also public participation
Planning (Listed Buildings and Conversation Areas) (Scotland) Act 1997, 264
Planning (Scotland) Act 2019, 264–5
planning advice, 202
Planning Advice Notes (PAN) see PAN
Planning Advisory Group (PAG) see PAG
Planning and Compensation Act 1991, 211
'Planning and Development in Scotland' (Stevenson, F. R.), 17
planning applications
  community councils, 136
  conservation areas, 137
  decisions, 134–5
  development control, 38–43, 133–8
  housing in the countryside, 136
  mineral working, 101, 227
  numbers, 86, 134, 178, 200–2, 207, 234–6
  roof extensions, 137–8
  see also consultations
planning committees, 28–31
  joint, 33
Planning etc. (Scotland) Act 2006, 264
Planning Exchange, 118–19
planning staff see staffing
politics, 13, 22–3, 119–20, 174–5
  compulsory purchase, 168–9
  housing, 176–7
population, 1, 2, 63–4, 85, 115, 156, 176, 206, 259, 261
  BCC, 52, 103
  Berwickshire, 10, 26, 52, 97, 103, 237
  Borders Region 1975, The, 122, 126
  Borders Region Structure Plan 1980, 148, 150*t*, 151
  Borders Region Structure Plan 1991, 220–1, 229
  Central Borders: A Plan for Expansion, The, 68, 69*t*, 75–6, 77*t*
  Coldstream, 150*t*, 151
  Duns, 150*t*, 151
  Ettrick and Lauderdale, 152, 237
  Eyemouth, 10, 150*t*, 151
  Galashiels, 9, 62, 75, 76, 77*t*, 150*t*, 151

Hawick, 9, 76, 77*t*, 150*t*, 151
Innerleithen, 10
Jeburgh, 9, 76, 150*t*, 151
Kelso, 9, 150*t*, 151
Newtown St Boswells, 75
PCC, 52
Peebles, 10, 58, 77*t*, 150*t*, 151, 156
Peeblesshire, 9–10, 52
RCC, 52, 76, 102
Regional Survey and Plan for Central and South-East Scotland, A, 26
Regional Report 1976, 131
Roxburgh District Council and area, 152, 221, 237–8
Roxburghshire, 9, 26, 52, 102
rural depopulation, 1, 8–10, 26, 52, 63, 102–4, 176
SCC, 52, 60, 103
Selkirk, 9, 150*t*, 151
Selkirkshire, 9, 52, 60
stability, 52, 63–4
Tweedbank, 75, 150*t*, 151
Tweeddale District Council and area, 152, 176, 221, 238
power industry, 102
press, the, 179–80, 181*f*, 207, 260–1
Principles and Practice of Town and Country Planning (Keeble, Lewis), 17
Pringle of Scotland, 215
private sector, 11
proactive planning, 16
Profile of the Borders, A (RPU), 122
programme maps, 47
proposal maps, 47, 152–3, 154
Public Health (Scotland) Act 1897, 23
public participation, 12, 15–16, 38, 47–8, 135–6, 146, 172, 260
  consultations, 38, 47–8
  Galashiels/Tweedbank Local Plan, 154
  objections, 144, 145, 118*f*
  press, the, 179–80, 181*f*
  Skeffington Committee Report, 118
  TUCC, 72
public sector, 11–12

qualifications, 21–2, 89

railways, 5, 51
  Beeching report, 71
  Waverley line, 71–3, 255
RCC (Roxburgh County Council)
  AGLVs, 56, 107–8
  AGLVs and Tourism Development report, 107–8

Central Borders: A Plan for Expansion, The, 75–6
conservation, 98–9
countryside, 55, 110
development plans, 22, 28, 36–7, 43, 45, 46–7, 50, 52, 59
holiday accommodation, 57
housing, 30–1, 47, 53, 59
JPAC, 78, 259
Landward Community Development Strategy, 102
members, 22
mineral working industry, 56
planning committees, 30–1
population, 52, 76, 102
programme maps, 47
proposal maps, 47
roads, 50
staffing, 22, 34–5, 37, 59, 89–90
survey reports, 46–7
tourism, 107–8, 109–10
Tweedbank Development, 68, 73–5
written statements, 47
recreation, 88, 166–8, 196, 197–200, 250–2
cars, 40, 42, 44
cycling, 251
visitor centres, 251
walks, 130, 198–200, 251
see also tourism
recycling, 253
refuse disposal, 253
regional approaches, 25
regional councils, 115, 116, 119; *see also* BRC
regional planning, 260–3; *see also* BRC
Regional Planning Unit (RPU) *see* RPU
regional reports, 142–3
regional spatial strategies (RSSs), 264
Regional Survey and Plan for Central and South-East Scotland, A (Mears, F. C.), 17, 25, 26–8, 33, 69, 258
Reid, John, 82, 139
renewable energy, 253–4
reservoirs, 101–2, 125
Reshaping of British Railways, The (Beeching, R.), 71
Restriction of Ribbon Development Act 1935, 24–5
retail, 162–3, 205, 224, 244–6
ribbon development, 24–5
rights of way, 130, 198–9, 250–1
roads, 26–7, 35–6, 48–51, 61, 64, 66
Borders Region 1975, The, 123–4
Borders Region Structure Plan 1991, 223–4

BRC, 160–2, 163–4
BRC Regional Report 1976, 132
buses, 124, 130, 162
caravans, 40, 41, 42, 44, 167
cars, 40, 42, 44, 48, 254–5
Central Borders Study: A Plan for Expansion, The, 70
Melrose by-pass, 70, 161, 190
SDA, 185
Robeson, Keith, 179*f*
roof extensions, 137–8
Ross, Willie, 72, 79
Roxburgh County Council (RCC) *see* RCC
Roxburgh District, 115, 116*f*, 200
economic development, 241
housing, 138, 221, 225, 238
population, 152, 221, 237–8
refuse disposal, 253
Roxburgh (Part) Local Plan, 172
Roxburgh Local Plan, 231, 238, 240, 245
settlement hierarchy, 220*t*
sustainability, 253
tourism, 244
Roxburghe, Duke of, 3; *see also* Roxburghe Estates
Roxburghe Estates, 3
Roxburghshire
AGLVs, 56
burghs, 113–14
conservation, 98–9
employment, 4
mineral working industry, 56
population, 9, 26, 52, 102
tourism, 107–8, 109–10
see also RCC
Royal Borough of Peebles Proposed Urban Structure Plan (Baillie, John Somerville [Jack]), 58
RPU (Regional Planning Unit), 121
Borders Region 1975, The, 122–6
Profile of the Borders, A, 122
'Rural Development: Future Strategies' conference, 216
rural issues, 16, 216
land, 11
BRC, 232–3, 247–50, 262
housing, 225
Borders Region Structure Plan 1991, 220, 224–5, 247–50
Key Villages, 220
development, 55–7, 100–5, 191–2
heritage, 227–8

rural issues (*cont.*)
  depopulation, 1, 8–10, 26, 52, 63, 102–4, 176
  see also countryside, the

St Abbs Head, 196
St Boswells, 27, 96, 259
St Mary's Loch, 108
SBC (Scottish Borders Council), 231, 250, 253
SBE (Scottish Borders Enterprise), 210–11, 222, 234, 265
SBLAJC (Scottish Border Local Authorities Joint Committee), 121
SCC (Selkirk County Council), 22
  AGLVs, 56
  Central Borders: A Plan for Expansion, The, 75–6
  development plans, 22, 28, 36, 43, 45, 52, 60
  housing, 30, 61
  JPAC, 78, 259
  members, 22
  planning committees, 30
  population, 52, 60, 103
  Report on AGLVs and Tourist Development, 108
  roads, 48–9, 61
  settlement study, 103–4
  staffing, 22, 33–4, 90–1
Scott, Douglas, 179f
Scott, Walter, 5
Scott Report, 25, 31
Scottish Border Local Authorities Joint Committee (SBLAJC), 121
Scottish Borders, 1, 257; *see also* BRC
Scottish Borders Council (SBC), 231, 250, 253
Scottish Borders Council Archive Sources, 276–84
Scottish Borders Enterprise (SBE), 210–11, 222, 234
'Scottish Borders Knitwear Buyers Guide' (BRC), 186–7
Scottish Borders 2001: The Way Forward (BRC), 15, 218, 229, 231, 233f
Scottish Civic Trust, 87
Scottish Development Agency (SDA) *see* SDA
Scottish Development Department (SDD) *see* SDD
Scottish Economy 1965 to 1970: A Plan for Expansion, The (Scottish Office), 66–8, 73, 78, 85, 93

Scottish Enterprise (SE), 209, 210, 265
Scottish Home and Health Department (SHHD), 66
Scottish Home Department (SHD), 49, 66
Scottish Homes, 209–10
Scottish Industrial Estates Corporation (SIEC), 139
Scottish Natural Heritage (SNH), 16, 209, 211–12
Scottish Office *see* central government
Scottish Planning Law (McMaster, Ray, Prior, Alan and Watchman, John), 18–19
Scottish Planning Law and Procedure (Young, Eric and Rowan-Robinson, Jeremy), 18
Scottish Special Housing Association (SSHA), 38, 39, 74, 151, 170
SDA (Scottish Development Agency), 139–40, 173, 210
  industrial development, 130–40, 184–6, 300–2
  properties, 300–2
SDD (Scottish Development Department), 66, 131
  Circular 13/1990, 226
  Circular 24/1985, 157, 203
  Circular 28/1976, 144
  Circular 32/1983, 144, 173
  Circular 71/1974, 193
SDP (Strategic Development Plans), 264
SE (Scottish Enterprise), 209, 210, 265
Selkirk, 6, 256
  environmental improvement, 188
  housing, 53, 62–3, 68
  industrial development, 54, 80, 81, 160, 184, 185
  population, 9, 150t, 151
  roads, 48, 61
  textile industry, 6, 78
Selkirk County Council (SCC) *see* SCC
Selkirkshire
  AGLVs, 56
  burghs, 113–14
  employment, 4
  holiday accommodation, 104
  land, 2
  population, 9, 52, 60
  settlement study, 103–4
  see also SCC
settlement hierarchy, 148, 149f, 220t
SHD (Scottish Home Department), 49, 66
SHHD (Scottish Home and Health Department), 66

Shoard, Marion, 176
Theft of the Countryside, The, 176
shop fronts, 246
SICRAS (Small Industries Council for the Rural Areas of Scotland), 139
SIEC (Scottish Industrial Estates Corporation), 139
Single Programme Document (SPD), 243
Sites and Monuments Record (SMR), 190
Skeffington Committee Report, 118
Small Industries Council for the Rural Areas of Scotland (SICRAS), 139
Smith, Colin, 127, 179f
SMR (Sites and Monuments Record), 190
SNH (Scottish Natural Heritage), 16, 209, 211–12
social influences, 3, 13
SoSE (South of Scotland Enterprise), 266–7
South of Scotland Enterprise (SoSE), 266–7
South of Scotland Regional Economic Partnership, 266
Southern Upland Way, 199–200
SPD (Single Programme Document), 243
SSHA (Scottish Special Housing Association), 38, 39, 74, 151, 170
staffing, 21–2, 33–5, 43–4, 59, 89–92, 258
  BRC, 121–2, 126–9, 178, 179f, 273, 207, 213, 214f
Stevenson, F. R.
  'Planning and Development in Scotland', 17
Stodart Committee, 117
Strang, Charles, 179f
Strategic Development Plans (SDP), 264
structure plans, 132–3, 143–4, 171–3
  Borders Region Structure Plan 1980, 145–52, 153f, 261
  Borders Region Structure Plan 1991, 217–28, 229–30, 231, 233f, 262
Sturrock, Alistair, 89–90
sub-regional plans, 143
supermarkets, 205
survey reports, 46–7
Sustainable Development: The UK Strategy (Department of the Environment), 252
sustainability, 234, 235f, 252–5, 256

tartan, 5
'Taste of the Scottish Borders, A' (BRC), 187
Tay Valley Plan, 26
Taylor, Gordon Rattray
  Doomsday Book, The, 87
technical working parties, 87, 92–7, 110

Tench, Peter, 179f
Teviot Study, 188
textile industry, 4–7, 8, 39, 77–8, 80–1, 123, 180 182, 215
Theft of the Countryside, The (Shoard, Marion), 176
This Common Inheritance (White Paper), 212, 234
Thompson, Jim, 90
Tindall, Frank, 22
  Memoirs and Confessions of a County Planning Officer, 19
toilets, 198
Tomorrow's Landscape (Crowe, Sylvia), 88
Torness nuclear power station, 102
tourism, 40–3, 44, 105–8, 112, 243–4
  Borders Region 1975, The, 124–5
  Borders Region Structure Plan 1991, 223
  BRC, 140, 166–8
  countryside, 168
  development, 140
  holiday accommodation, 40–2, 56–7, 104, 105–8, 167, 243
  tourist information centres, 124–5, 140
tourist signs, 202
Town and Country Planning (General Development) (Scotland) Order 1948, 57
Town and Country Planning (General Development) (Scotland) Order 1975, 137
Town and Country Planning (Interim Development) (Scotland) Act 1943, 28
Town and Country Planning (Scotland) Act 1932, 24
Town and Country Planning (Scotland) Act 1947, 11, 29, 168, 258
  county development plans, 35–8, 45–6
  development control, 38–43
  implementation, 31–43
  staffing, 33–5
Town and Country Planning (Scotland) Act 1954, 169
Town and Country Planning (Scotland) Act 1959, 169
Town and Country Planning (Scotland) Act 1969, 12, 119
Town and Country Planning (Scotland) Act 1972, 12, 118, 119, 144, 169
Town and Country Planning (Scotland) Act 1997, 264
Town and Country Planning (Structure and Local Plans) (Scotland) Regulations 1976, 143–4

Town and Country Planning (Structure and Local Plans) (Scotland) Regulations 1983, 144
Town and Country Planning in the UK (Cullingworth, Barry and Nadin, Vincent), 17
town centres, 162–3, 244–6
  redevelopment plans, 87, 92, 93, 99–100, 111
town planners, 11, 21–2; *see also* staffing
TPOs (Tree Preservation Orders), 190
trade, 6–7
Training for Rural Improvement Projects (TRIP) scheme, 189
Transport Users Consultative Committee (TUCC), 72
transportation, 130
  Borders Region 1975, The, 123–4
  Borders Region Structure Plan 1991, 223–4
  BRC Regional Report 1976, 132
  railways, 5, 51, 71–3, 255
  SDA, 185
  Waverley line, 71–3, 255
  see also roads
tree planting, 100, 124, 192–4; *see also* forestry industry
Tree Preservation Orders (TPOs), 190
TRIP (Training for Rural Improvement Projects) scheme, 189
TUCC (Transport Users Consultative Committee), 72
Tulley, Drew, 175
Turner, Robert, 35
tweed, 5
Tweed Basin, 26–7
Tweed Horizons Centre for Sustainable Technology, 253
Tweedbank
  Galashiels/Tweedbank Local Plan, 154–5
  housing, 68, 73–5, 76, 151, 209, 259
  industrial development, 139–40, 158, 184
  population, 75, 150*t*, 151
  Tweedbank Development, 68, 73–5, 76, 259

Tweedbank Working Party, 74
Tweeddale District, 115, 116*f*, 200, 238
  economic development, 241
  housing, 203, 204–5, 221–2, 225, 238
  mineral working industry, 227, 249
  population, 152, 176, 221, 238
  retail, 205
  settlement hierarchy, 220*t*
  sustainability, 253
  tourism, 204, 244
Tweeddale Local Plan, 222, 231, 238, 250

urban environment, 58, 224
Uthwatt Report, 25, 31

Victorian & Edwardian Borderland, The (Adamson, Peter and Lamont-Brown, R.), 17
Village Plans, 239–40
village reports, 99
visitor centres, 251

Walkerburn, 186
walks, 130, 198–200
Waste Management Group, 253
Waverley line, 71–3, 255
West Linton, 58–9, 205, 238–9
West Linton Residents Association, 59
Wheatley Commission, 114–15, 117
White Paper of the Scottish Economy, 62
Whyte, Alan, 90
wildlife, 166, 173, 192
Williamson, Jane, 179*f*
windows, 202
Wolfe, James Nathan, 68
Womersley, Peter, 86
Wright, Ron, 189
written statements, 47

Yarrow valley, 103–4
Young, Eric and Rowan-Robinson, Jeremy
  Scottish Planning Law and Procedure, 18
Young, John, 127, 179*f*
Younger, David, 174–5

EU representative:
Easy Access System Europe
Mustamäe tee 50, 10621 Tallinn, Estonia
Gpsr.requests@easproject.com

www.ingramcontent.com/pod-product-compliance
Lightning Source LLC
Chambersburg PA
CBHW050202240426
43671CB00013B/2215